CASTLES

ENGLAND ✛ SCOTLAND ✛ WALES ✛ IRELAND

CASTLES

ENGLAND ✛ SCOTLAND ✛ WALES ✛ IRELAND

The definitive guide to the most impressive buildings and intriguing sites

Based on the classic book by
PLANTAGENET SOMERSET FRY

D&C
David and Charles

A DAVID & CHARLES BOOK
David & Charles is a subsidiary of F+W (UK) Ltd.,
an F+W Publications Inc. company

First published in the UK in 2005
Reprinted 2005
This UK paperback edition published in 2008

This book is based on the research undertaken for *Castles of Britain and Ireland* by Plantagenet Somerset Fry, last paperback edition published in August 2001.

Distributed in North America
by F+W Publications, Inc.
4700 East Galbraith Road
Cincinnati, OH 45236
1-800-289-0963

A catalogue record for this book is available from the British Library.

ISBN-13: 978-0-7153-2212-3 hardback
ISBN-10: 0 7153 2212-5 hardback

ISBN-13: 978-0-7153-2692-3 paperback
ISBN-10: 0-7153-2692-9 paperback

Printed and bound in China by SNP Leefung
for David & Charles
Brunel House   Newton Abbot   Devon

Commissioning Editor Mic Cady
Desk Editor Louise Crathorne
Project Editor Marilynne Lanng
Chief Compiler Pip Leahy
Design Alison Myer
Picture Research Bea Ray
Illustrations Neil Bromley
Map (page 7) Ethan Danielson
Production Controller Ros Napper

Visit our website at www.davidandcharles.co.uk

David & Charles books are available from all good bookshops; alternatively you can contact our Orderline on 0870 9908222 or write to us at FREEPOST EX2 110, D&C Direct, Newton Abbot, TQ12 4ZZ (no stamp required UK mainland).

Pictures:
1 Dunnotter Castle
2–3 Kilchurn Castle
4–5 Corfe Castle
8–9 Alnwick Castle
20–21 Ludlow Castle
118–119 Castle Stalker
172–173 Pembroke Castle
208–209 Cashel Castle

CONTENTS

USING THIS BOOK

DEFINING CASTLES

Castles includes descriptions of hundreds of castles in England, Scotland, Wales and Ireland. The definition of the word 'castle' is generally taken to be a fortified military residence. In this respect they are considered to be different to their British precursors, hill forts, Roman forts and Saxon burghs, for example. All of these were military establishments but they were not usually also places to live in permanently. Some hill forts were undoubtedly lived in, but here the distinction given is that they were communal in their purpose, whereas castles were built and owned for, and by, one individual and his family and retainers, rather than the wider community. However, not all the castles described in this book fit into a neat category; they have been included to provide a fuller picture.

PROVIDING MORE INFORMATION

As well as describing the castles as architecture, wherever practicable some background information is provided. Especially important or interesting castles are given more space and more background information. In order to help provide context, the book has a key dates and events list on pages 8 and 9, and a series of introductory features on pages 10 to 19. There are also ten special features on such subjects as Life in early castles, Weapons, Food and drink, and so forth, throughout the book.

THE CASTLES INCLUDED

We have included as many castles as possible; usually they are excluded only if their history is so obscure that there is little of use to say, or if there is actually very little

(if anything) to be seen on the ground. *Castles* includes more individual castle descriptions than any comparable book, and we would be delighted to hear from readers who wish to provide more information or who think that other castles should be added. Useful addresses are on p253.

OPENING TIMES AND ACCESS INFORMATION

Basic opening times and access details are provided for those castles regularly open to the public; contact information for organizations such as the National Trust and English Heritage and other sources is on p253. Please note that the presence of a castle in this book does not necessarily mean that it is open or accessible to the public. Many castles are on private land or are not accessible, but can be viewed from roads or paths. Where possible this information is provided, but in case of uncertainty permission should always be sought before approaching any castle: in particular this is because many ruins are in potentially unstable or unsafe states.

LOCATIONS AND MAP REFERENCES

If the castle is in the village or town that has its name (Anstey, Laugharne, Totnes) the location information is limited to its county or statutory area (see map opposite). If it is in a very small settlement, or in the countryside, the nearest village or town is named. Every entry is provided with a national grid map reference. All reputable large-scale maps – especially those from the Ordnance Survey organizations of Britain and Ireland – include the grid, and accurate locations can be plotted.

Counties of the Republic of Ireland

1 Carlow
2 Cavan
3 Clare
4 Cork
5 Donegal
6 Dublin;
   Fingal, Dublin City,
   South Dublin,
   Dun Laoghaire-
   Raithdown
7 Galway
8 Kerry
9 Kildare
10 Kilkenny
11 Laois
12 Leitrim
13 Limerick
14 Longford
15 Louth
16 Mayo
17 Meath
18 Monaghan
19 Offaly
20 Roscommon
21 Sligo
22 Tipperary
   north and south
23 Waterford
24 Westmeath
25 Wexford
26 Wicklow

Counties of the United Kingdom and Northern Ireland

1 Aberdeen
2 Aberdeenshire
3 Anglesey
4 Angus
5 Argyll and Bute
6 Bedfordshire
7 Berkshire
8 Blaenau Gwent
9 Bridgend
10 Bristol
11 Buckinghamshire
12 Caerphilly
13 Cambridgeshire
14 Cardiff
15 Carmarthenshire
16 Ceredigion
17 Cheshire
18 Clackmannanshire
19 Conwy
20 Cornwall
21 Cumbria
22 Denbighshire
23 Derbyshire
24 Devon
25 Dorset
26 Dumfries and
   Galloway
27 Dundee
28 Durham
29 East Ayrshire

30 East
   Dunbartonshire
31 East Lothian
32 East
   Renfrewshire
33 East Riding of
   Yorkshire
34 East Sussex

35 Edinburgh
36 Essex
37 Falkirk
38 Fife
39 Flintshire
40 Glasgow
41 Gloucestershire

42 Greater London
43 Greater
   Manchester
44 Gwynedd
45 Hampshire
46 Herefordshire
47 Hertfordshire

48 Highland
49 Inverclyde
50 Isle of Wight
51 Kent
52 Lancashire
53 Leicestershire
54 Lincolnshire
55 Merseyside
56 Merthyr Tydfil
57 Midlothian
58 Monmouthshire
59 Moray
60 Neath Port Talbot

61 Newport
62 Norfolk
63 North Ayrshire
64 North Lanarkshire
65 North Yorkshire
66 Northamptonshire
67 Northumberland
68 Nottinghamshire
69 Orkney Islands
70 Oxfordshire
71 Pembrokeshire
72 Perth and Kinross
73 Powys
74 Renfrewshire
75 Rhondda
   Cynon Taf
76 Rutland
77 Scottish Borders
78 Shetland Islands
79 Shropshire
80 Somerset
81 South Ayrshire
82 South Lanarkshire
83 South Yorkshire
84 Staffordshire

85 Stirling
86 Suffolk
87 Surrey
88 Swansea
89 Torfaen
90 Tyne and Wear
91 Vale of Glamorgan
92 Warwickshire
93 West Dunbartonshire
94 West Lothian
95 West Midlands
96 West Sussex
97 West Yorkshire
98 Western Isles
99 Wiltshire
100 Worcestershire
101 Wrexham

Northern Ireland

102 Antrim
103 Armagh
104 Down
105 Fermanagh
106 Londonderry
107 Tyrone

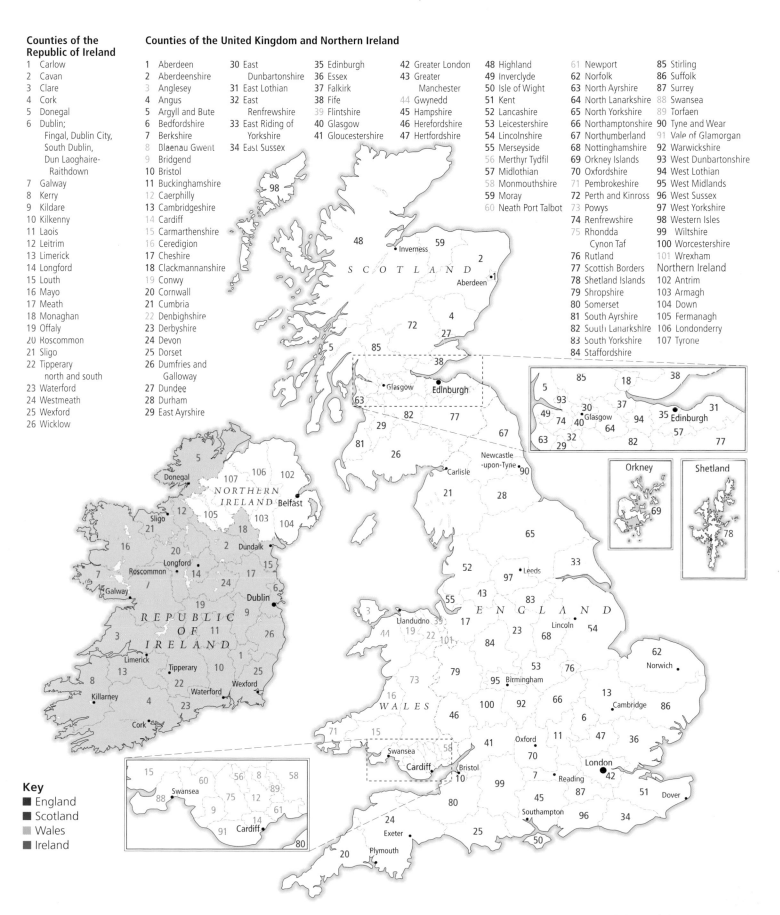

Key

- ■ England
- ■ Scotland
- ■ Wales
- ■ Ireland

COUNTY MAP 7

KEY DATES

Castles are a product of their times, and of the dominant personalities of those times. For much of British and Irish history, it is the monarch who is the most important single influence on events – for good or ill. By their nature, castles date from times of war, insecurity and danger. As peace and security become the norm, castles are either abandoned or adapted for more peaceful times.

The key events set out below are intended to help put castles into their historical context. Included are dates and events from English, Scottish, Welsh and Irish history, but this is not intended to be a full summary of the history of the four countries, and there are fewer events as castles decline in importance. The list includes English, Scottish and some Irish kings, and the early Welsh princes; their years as monarchs are in bold.

Key
- England
- Scotland
- Wales
- Ireland

- **43AD–411** Roman conquest of Britain
- **432** St Patrick arrives in Ireland
- **871–899 Alfred the Great**
- **1002–1014 Brian Bórú**
- **1039–1063 Gruffydd ap Llywelyn ap Seisyll**
- **1042–1066 Edward** (the Confessor)
- **1058–1093 Malcolm III**
- **1063–1075 Bleddyn ap Cynfyn**
- **1066 Harold II**
- **1066 September** Battle of Stamford Bridge
- **1066 September** William the Conqueror lands in Britain
- **1066 October** Battle of Hastings
- **1066–1087 William I**
- **1067** Chepstow Castle
- **1068** Warwick Castle
- **1069–1070** Harrying of the North
- **1075–1081 Trahaern ap Caradog**
- **1076** Colchester Castle begun
- **1078** White Tower, Tower of London completed
- **1080** Cardiff Castle
- **1080** Windsor Castle
- **1080** Domesday Survey ordered
- **1081–1137 Gruffydd ap Cynan ap Iago**
- **1087–1100 William II**
- **1093** Battle of Alnwick – Malcolm III of Scotland and his son Edward killed
- **1093–1097 Donald III**

- **1095** Council of Rockingham
- **1096** Alnwick Castle begun
- **1097–1107 Edgar**
- **1100–1135 Henry I**
- **1107–1124 Alexander I**
- **1124–1153 David I**
- **1127** Rochester Castle keep begun
- **1135–1154 Stephen**
- **1137–1170 Owain Gwynedd**
- **1138–1148** Civil war between Stephen and Matilda
- **1138** Scots invade Northumberland
- **1138 August** Battle of the Standard – Scots are defeated
- **1140** Hedingham Castle
- **1141** Stephen captured by Matilda's forces at Battle of Lincoln. Matilda elected Queen of England. Later in year Stephen released. Matilida leaves England in 1148
- **1146** Giraldis Cambrensis born at Pembroke
- **1148** Matilda leaves England
- **1153–1165 Malcolm IV**
- **1154–1189 Henry II**
- **1165–1214 William I**
- **1165** Orford Castle begun
- **1166–1175 Ruaidhrí Ó Conchubhair**
- **1170–1195 Dafydd ap Owain Gwynedd**
- **1170** Murder of Thomas Becket at Canterbury
- **1170** Normans arrive in Co. Wexford: Richard de Clare, Earl of Pembroke (Strongbow) comes to Ireland.
- **1171** Strongbow becomes King of Leinster. Henry II visits Ireland
- **1173** Trim Castle

- **1173** Henry's son and the barons revolt against Henry II
- **1174** Battle of Alnwick. William I invades northern England in support of barons' rebellion against Henry II. William captured and forced to accept Henry II as superior
- **1185** Prince John (later King John) created Lord of Ireland
- **1189–1199 Richard I** (the Lionheart)
- **1189–1200** Framlingham Castle rebuilt
- **1194–1240 Llywelyn Fawr** (Llywelyn the Great)
- **1199–1216 John**
- **1210** Submission of Irish kings to John
- **1214–1216** Barons' Revolt
- **1214–1249 Alexander II**
- **1215** Magna Carta
- **1216–1272 Henry III**
- **1216** Prince Louis of France invades England
- **1217** Battle of Lincoln between armies of Henry III and Louis. Louis defeated
- **1240–1246 Dafydd ap Llywelyn**
- **1246–1282 Llywelyn ap Gruffydd ap Llywelyn**
- **1249–1286 Alexander III**
- **1264–1267** Barons' War
- **1264** Battle of Lewes
- **1265** Battle of Evesham – Simon de Montfort killed
- **1266** Hebrides and Isle of Man given to Scots by King of Norway
- **1268** Caerphilly Castle begun
- **1272–1307 Edward I**
- **1277** Edward begins his war on Wales. In December Edward defeats Llywelyn ap Gruffydd ap Llywelyn

- **1277** Flint Castle, the first of Edward's iron ring
- **1283** Caernarvon, Conway and Harlech Castles begun
- **1284** Statute of Wales: Wales comes under Direct Rule
- **1286–1290 Margaret**
- **1290–1292** First Interregnum
- **1292–1296 John Balliol**
- **1295** The Auld Alliance
- **1295** Beaumaris Castle
- **1295–1363** Scottish Wars of Independence
- **1296** Battle of Dunbar (between Balliol and Edward I)
- **1297** Battle of Stirling Bridge
- **1298** Battle of Falkirk – Wallace defeated
- **1296–1306** Second Interregnum
- **1306–1329 Robert I (the Bruce)**
- **1307** Battle of Loudoun Hill
- **1307–1327 Edward II**
- **1312** Piers Gaveston executed
- **1314** Battle of Bannockburn
- **1315** Edward Bruce invades Ireland. Edward proclaimed King of Ireland
- **1316–1318 Éadbhard I (Edward)**
- **1326** Execution of Hugh Despenser.
- **1327–1377 Edward III**
- **1329–1371 David II**
- **1337–1453** Hundred Years' War
- **1346** Battle of Neville's Cross
- **1348** Black Death arrives in England
- **1348** Foundation of the Order of the Garter at Windsor
- **1358** Death of Queen Isabella.
- **1371–1390 Robert II**
- **1376** Edward the Black Prince dies
- **1366** Statutes of Kilkenny
- **1377–1399 Richard II**
- **1381** Peasants' Revolt
- **1385** Bodiam Castle
- **1390–1406 Robert III**
- **1399** Richard II goes to Ireland
- **1399** Richard II imprisoned at Pontefract Castle
- **1399–1413 Henry IV**
- **1400–1409** Owain Glyndwr's Revolt
- **1403–1409** Percys' Revolt
- **1403** Battle of Shrewsbury

- **1406–1437 James I**
- **1408** Battle of Bramham Moor
- **1413–1422 Henry V**
- **1422–1461 Henry VI**
- **1437–1460 James II**
- **1441** Herstmonceux – one of first castles built in brick, along with Caister
- **1453–1485** Wars of the Roses
- **1460–1488 James III**
- **1460** Battle of Wakefield
- **1461–1470 Edward IV**
- **1461** Battle of Mortimer's Cross
- **1470–1471 Henry VI**
- **1471 April** Battle of Barnet: death of Richard Neville, Earl of Warwick
- **1471 May** Battle of Tewkesbury: death of Edward, Prince of Wales
- **1471–1483 Edward IV**
- **1483 Edward V** – one of the princes allegedly murdered in the Tower of London
- **1483–1485 Richard III**
- **1485** Battle of Bosworth Field
- **1485–1509 Henry VII**
- **1488** Battle of Sauchieburn
- **1488–1513 James IV**
- **1499** Execution of Perkin Warbeck
- **1509–1547 Henry VIII**
- **1511** Thornbury Castle, England's last important fortified manor built
- **1513–1542 James V**
- **1513** Battle of Flodden Field
- **1534** Act of Supremacy
- **1536–1540** Dissolution of the Monasteries
- **1536** Pilgrimage of Grace
- **1536** Act of Union with Wales
- **1541–1547 Henry VIII King of Ireland**
- **1542–1567 Mary, Queen of Scots**
- **1542** Battle of Solway Moss
- **1543–1548** Rough Wooing
- **1547–1553 Edward VI**
- **1547** Battle of Pinkie
- **1553–1558 Mary I**
- **1554** Mary marries Philip of Spain
- **1558–1603 Elizabeth I**
- **1560** Treaty of Edinburgh
- **1567–1625 James VI**
- **1567–1573** Scottish Civil War
- **1569** Rising of the North

- **1573** Fall of Edinburgh Castle
- **1587** Execution of Mary, Queen of Scots at Fotheringhay Castle
- **1588** Spanish Armada
- **1594–1603** Nine Years' War
- **1603–1625 James I** (Union of the Crowns of Scotland and England; end of the war with Spain)
- **1605** Gunpowder Plot
- **1609–1613** Plantation of Ulster
- **1625–1649 Charles I**
- **1641–1648** Irish Rebellion of 1641 and Confederate Wars
- **1642–1646** English Civil War
- **1648–1651** English Civil War
- **1649–1660** The Commonwealth
- **1649** Start of Cromwell's campaign in Ireland
- **1649–1685 Charles II**
- **1653** Cromwell's Act of Settlement
- **1660** Restoration of the Monarchy
- **1660–1685 Charles II**
- **1666** Great Fire of London
- **1678** Lethendy Tower built, one of last tower houses in Scotland
- **1685–1688 James II (VII of Scotland)**
- **1688** Glorious Revolution
- **1689–1745** Jacobite uprisings
- **1689–1702 William III & Mary**
- **1689–1694 Mary II**
- **1689 – 90** James II flees to Ireland
- **1690** Battle of the Boyne
- **1702–1714 Anne**
- **1707** Act of Union with Scotland
- **1714–1901 Hanoverian monarchs,** including **Queen Victoria**
- **1746** Battle of Culloden Moor – last military battle on British soil
- **1746** Blair Castle besieged – last siege of a castle in Britain
- **1798** Wolfe Tone's Rebellion
- **1800** Ireland Act of Union
- **1803–1815** Napoleonic Wars
- **1914–1918** World War I
- **1917–present House of Windsor,** including **Elizabeth II**
- **1919–1921** Anglo–Irish War
- **1921** Anglo–Irish Treaty
- **1939–1945** World War II – last active use of castles on British soil

EARLY FORTIFICATIONS

Dun Aenghus, Ireland: a promontory fort. Forts like this exist in large numbers along the coast of Ireland, and there are some on the British coast. Typically built of drystone walling, they could easily be defended, but with their backs to the sea, there was no easy escape for the defenders if their attackers broke through. Building and defending such forts, and their counterparts inland, required cooperation and determination.

Castles are defined as buildings with two primary purposes: places of defence and attack, and places in which to live. And they belonged to a particular individual, unlike prehistoric forts, for example, which were communal in their purpose and function.

But the idea of castles grew out of fortifications that men had used for centuries. In England, some of the most conspicuous of these are the great hill forts built in the Iron Age. Outstanding examples of these are Maiden Castle and Hod Hill in Dorset, and Danebury in Hampshire. These monuments consist of enormous earthen ramparts, originally topped by wooden walls and walkways, and surrounded by deep ditches. Some of these were only used at certain times of year, or during periods of war, but at Danebury, for example, excavations have revealed the remains of hundreds of huts, as well as many other features, including thousands of pits used for storing grain. Such forts were at the core of highly organized and sophisticated tribal societies.

It was the Roman invasion that sounded the death-knell for the hill forts. Not only did the Romans overrun them with comparative ease despite their formidable defences, but the kind of society the Romans introduced revolved around towns, often in river valleys. Virtually all the ancient hill forts were abandoned. An exception is Old Sarum, the precursor of Salisbury in Wiltshire. Here the original hill fort was re-used several times, being finally abandoned only in the 13th century.

A typical Norman motte castle as depicted on the Bayeux Tapestry. All the essential features of an early castle are shown here, including the wooden tower on top of the mound. The soldiers in the centre are attempting to burn the castle down – a danger for all wooden structures. But a simple coat of whitewash could provide some measure of fireproofing. Wet hides draped over the walls were another form of fire control.

The motte castle at Sandal. This clearly shows the basic Norman castle plan: a great mound of earth (often originally faced with planking), surrounded by a deep ditch. Thrown up by the thousand across Britain, these mounds enabled the Normans to control great swathes of countryside. The motte would have been topped with a wooden tower, later replaced with stone fortifications, as seen here.

Roman military fortifications were built with typical efficiency. Even temporary marching camps were well built, with many still surviving. Such camps could be built at the end of each day's advance, as a base for future advances, or as a place to fall back to if required.

After the Romans left, some of the old hill forts were re-occupied, including Cadbury in Somerset, which some think may have been the headquarters of King Arthur. A systematic fortification building programme was undertaken in the 9th century by King Alfred to counter attacks and invasions by Vikings. Called burghs, these forts were highly effective when manned by determined troops, but when the Normans invaded they were ineffective, presumably because the necessary infrastructure had collapsed.

It was the Normans who introduced the kinds of fortifications that we all know as castles. They based these on structures in use on the European mainland since at least as early as the 9th century. Within a very short time of the invasion, Norman castles were built all over the British Isles; they were to become the symbol of Norman might and conquest, and were the focus of great historical events for the next 700 years.

The basic plan of most Norman castles is the same, with the motte (mound) at the centre of the defences. Greater variety followed when stone defences and buildings were added. Here at Duffus Castle (Scotland) the stone tower is linked to the outer defences of the bailey by a great curtain wall.

BUILDING CASTLES

Building technology: these masons are using scaffolding in the way we do today. A big castle needed large numbers of skilled workers as well as teams of labourers. The expense could be enormous, and that alone shows how important such buildings were to their owners. Ideas of what was best in castle design changed over time, resulting in some castles being substantially rebuilt.

The Normans built their wooden motte and bailey castles to help conquer in purely military terms, but the stone castles that followed were intended to dominate in psychological ways as well.

London's White Tower is a perfect example. It was begun in 1070 specifically to intimidate the people of the city, who were considered to be dangerously rebellious. Nothing like these immense stone structures had been seen in Britain before.

The idea of castles as physical symbols of feudal power was not new on the European mainland, where they had been used to control and dominate since the 9th century.

Castles were a central element of the feudal system: they belonged to the lords who built them. The king granted the lords land and other benefits; in return the lords paid fealty and service. Within their fiefdoms the lords could do pretty much as they pleased. For example, the Marcher Lords – William FitzOsbern at Hereford, Roger of Montgomery at Shrewsbury and 'Fat' Hugh 'The Wolf' of Avranches based at Chester – held complete sway along the whole Welsh border and made raids deep into Wales itself.

FitzOsbern's castle at Chepstow was the first purpose-built stone castle in Wales and said one thing: control. But this does

Castle ruins at Crom in Ireland: castles were built to withstand attack, and that meant they were very strong and very well built. Even in ruins, this castle's masonry looks substantial, especially at the base of the tower.

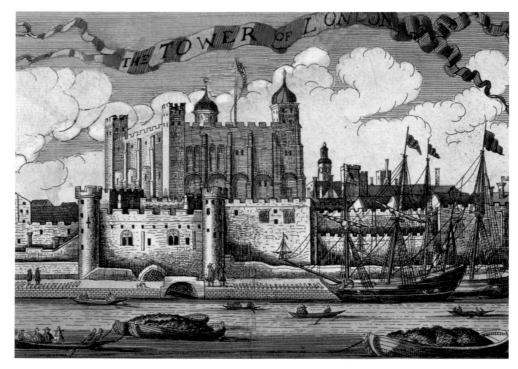

The White Tower of the Tower of London: begun not long after the Conquest, William's huge stone tower dominated the London skyline. Its massive bulk was a constant reminder to Londoners that they had a new, mighty ruler. The Tower has been adapted many times over the centuries, but even romantic pictures such as this one from the 18th century do not hide its massive bulk or strength.

not mean that Wales gave up without a struggle. There had been resistance against the Normans ('the French' as the native Welsh chroniclers called them) since their arrival. In 1094 there was an uprising across the country that amounted to open war.

There were similar uprisings in the North; the reprisals were as fast and equally merciless. The Norman lords made excursions into Scotland, and Richard FitzGilbert de Clare – 'Strongbow' – mounted vicious campaigns in Ireland. Strongbow's actions reverberated down through the centuries of Ireland's history and his name is still reviled in parts of the country.

Wherever the lords came they had to build castles – for defence, to regroup in, to hold provisions in, and to rule from. And castles were also home to the lord's family and close retainers. As the first wooden castles were replaced by more permanent and secure structures of stone, so there were opportunities to introduce some degree of comfort and architectural improvements. Some of these ideas came from the religious wars we know as the Crusades. The Crusader castles – symbols of Christian religious imperialism in the Muslim world – were of stone and had to withstand attacks and the depredations of weather for a long time. They were far from easy support and supply chains, so had to be strong and self-contained. Castle builders applied what they learned during the Crusades and elsewhere to mighty fortresses all over the British Isles.

There are many natural defensive spurs and hills in Wales, natural places to build castles. Castell y Bere is built on such a rocky outcrop. The native Welsh would not surrender to Norman rule, and so castles such as this were at the heart of a bloody struggle, and often changed hands. The Welsh princes built castles of their own, including this one, and they became important centres for their wars. Castell y Bere was abandoned at the end of the 13th century.

LATER CASTLES

Castles played a vital role in medieval history. They were the strong places from which attacks and rebellions were begun, and they were the refuges that offered protection when needed. Castles were built and destroyed often, and many of the castles in this book were already ruins in medieval times. Sometimes they remained in ruins because their strategic value had diminished; sometimes it was because their owners and their families could not afford to repair them, or were dead.

Castles in disputed regions were particularly vulnerable, obviously, and it was in these areas that there were most castles. It is no coincidence that some of the mightiest castles in Britain are in Wales, which fought against 'foreign' rule from the time of the Norman Conquest through to the 15th century. It was not until 1485, when Henry Tudor defeated Richard III at the Battle of Bosworth, that Wales looked for peace with its neighbour, for Henry had Welsh blood, and became the first 'Welsh' king of England.

Scotland and Ireland were also frequently at open war with the English. Like Wales, Scotland's rugged and wild landscapes aided its native warriors. They could behave like guerrilla fighters, disappearing into the mountain fastnesses when they wanted to. But castles played a key role here, as well. They guarded the important towns, ports and passes, and some became the strongholds of the Scottish clans. Scottish leaders sought help from many quarters in their struggles with the English, often bringing soldiers in from elsewhere in Europe, and these fighters brought with them new ideas on castle design from the Continent.

Bolton Castle, Yorkshire. Master-mason John Lewyn built it for Richard le Scrope, 1st Lord Bolton, in 1399. It was adapted and rebuilt many times in succeeding centuries, becoming a document in stone for the history it lived through. It was besieged during the Civil War, holding out for over a year. The Bolton family played a key role in British history, and the castle still belongs to them, an example of historical continuity that makes its story all the more remarkable.

The ruins of Coity Castle, in South Wales: during the course of 500 years it developed from a simple earthwork fortification to a complex set of buildings. It fell into ruins in the 17th century.

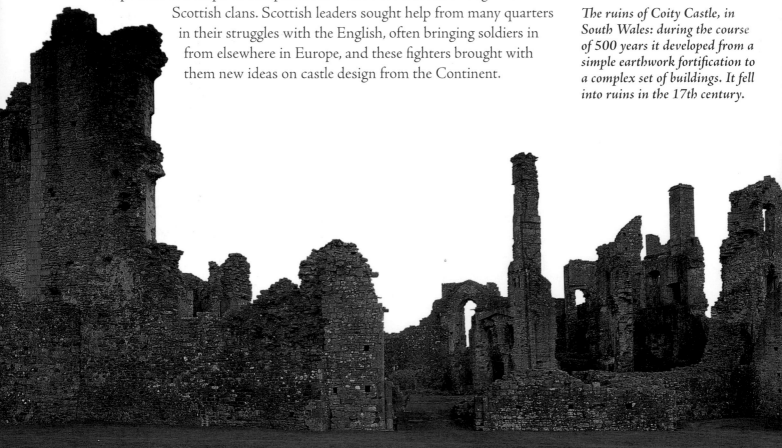

Eilean Donan is the traditional Scottish castle home of the MacRae clan. Originally built in the 13th century, it was left in ruins after bombardment by warships in 1719. It was restored in the first half of the 20th century, and is now well known for its many appearances in films.

The wars in Ireland were among the most bloody and prolonged in the British Isles, and left a legacy of bitterness that could still be detected in the Irish 'troubles' of the 20th century. The visible legacy is hundreds of castles littered across the landscape. Until very recently most of these were half-forgotten ivy-covered ruins, but Ireland's new wealth is helping to restore many of them, often as private homes.

Perhaps the most impressive single group of castles in the British Isles is that in North Wales. The most well known are Caernarfon, Conwy, Beaumaris and Harlech, but a dozen others were also either newly built or rebuilds of existing castles. All were the architectural brainchild of Master James of St Georges, whom Edward I had met in Savoy. The two men worked together to plan a 'ring' of castles that would put an end to resistance in Wales. It was an extraordinary undertaking, involving thousands of workers over a 25-year period and with a total cost of something like £40 million in contemporary terms.

A romanticized view of the legendary Welsh leader Owain Glyndwr. Proclaiming himself Prince of Wales in 1400, he very nearly created a Welsh nation, and for a while kept the English at bay. But after a series of defeats from 1405 onwards he disappeared into obscurity, and no one knows how or where he died.

A VARIETY OF ROLES

Arundel Castle reflected in the waters of the River Arun. It was first built about 20 years after the Norman Conquest. Arundel has been the seat of the Dukes of Norfolk and their ancestors for over 850 years, although it has sometimes reverted to royal ownership.

As guns of various sorts became widespread, castles had to be adapted to make use of them. This gun loop at Balvenie enables the gunner to fire from within the safety of the castle walls. Such holes were often low in castle walls so the gunner had a better chance of hitting his target.

As English society became more settled, so the role of castles as places of defence and offence became less important. In unruly Scotland and Ireland they were still needed, as much as a protection from internecine strife as for anything else. More and more castles became royal property and royal residences. This underlined the fact that the central authority was the monarchy. And they were essential to house the monarch and his huge retinue as he travelled around.

Comfort became much more important, and castles became less forbidding. At the same time, new forms of weaponry meant that castle architecture had to change again and again if it was to keep up with innovative attack methods. Cannons and similar ordnance were a particular challenge in that these increasingly powerful weapons could inflict devastating damage on even the strongest castle if the gunners were skilled enough and determined enough. To counter such threats, castles were adapted to be equipped with platforms for cannons that could fire back at the assaulting ordnance.

Water was one of the best ways of deterring 'sappers', whose job it was to undermine castle walls by tunnelling under them. A breadth of water made any such tunnel longer, and if the water broke through, the sappers would probably be drowned.

Edward I's 'ring' of castles in North Wales inspired much innovation: the emphasis was on the outer walls and gatehouses and on enormous defensive structures such as waterworks that went well beyond the idea of a mere moat.

Soldiers plundering: during times of war and unrest soldiers often killed and plundered in indiscriminate ways, leaving trails of misery and mindless destruction. Many soldiers were mercenaries, taken on for specific campaigns; battle-hardened and ruthless, even the rumour of their approach could throw communities into panic. In this picture the soldiers are drinking, stealing, and destroying anything they don't want or like. Such behaviour was sometimes used as a terror tactic, but wandering bands of lawless soldiers could threaten the structure of society and controls were imposed as society became more settled.

Castles built in the 14th and 15th centuries often looked formidable on the outside, but were essentially domestic in their function inside. Good examples of this are at Bodiam and Herstmonceux. In such castles, the all-important great hall (the setting for virtually all gatherings and meals) could now have large windows, built as it was against the outer walls, with its windows facing into the central courtyard. All the other necessary domestic buildings were protected within the outer walls, including kitchens, ovens, store rooms, cellars and so on. One of the best places to see some of these arrangements is within the shattered ruins of Basing House in Hampshire, where the interior domestic arrangements take on an especial poignancy because large numbers of its defenders were trapped and burned to death here in the Civil War siege that resulted in its eventual total destruction.

Whole towns were often included within defensive structures centred round the castle. Excellent survivals include Edward's Caernarfon and Conwy. In Southampton, the castle has all but disappeared under modern housing, but the formidable town walls, built to protect the city from attack by sea, still stand to their full height in places. They incorporate much of interest, including exciting survivors of Norman domestic architecture. At York, the circuit along the top of the town walls is one of the best ways of exploring the city.

Long after they ceased to have a practical function, castles were often kept by their owners for sentimental or historical reasons. Indeed, there are castles in Britain and Ireland still owned by the families that built them 600 or 700 years ago.

Towers have always been at the heart of castle design, and tower castles and houses were built in very large numbers in Ireland and Scotland. Scotland's Castle Stalker has the added protection of being built on an island, and has always been reached by boat. It originally belonged to the Stewart clan, but passed to the Campbells in the 17th century. Descendants of the original Stewart owners regained it at the beginning of the 20th century.

THE END OF THE CASTLE

The battered walls of Swansea Castle and framed against the shining glass of a modern office block. Whether pristine or ruined, in town or overgrown in the countryside, castles have a powerful attraction and the ability to conjure the past.

Castles gradually ceased to have a defensive role throughout much of the British Isles as society became more settled and secure. But castles came into their own again during the Civil War of the 17th century. As a result, many were destroyed in sieges, and many more were destroyed by both sides so they could not be used again. A prime example is Corfe Castle in Dorset, 'slighted' by the Parliamentarians after a long siege.

The Civil War also brought changes in the nature of what a defensive position was – thick, earth banks with a low profile were actually more effective protection against cannon fire than tall castle walls. Contemporary plans and illustrations show how sophisticated such fortifications could be.

Such ideas were not new, however. Henry VIII had been forced to build new kinds of fortresses along the coast of England as a result of threats of invasion from France and Spain. These were built from scratch with artillery in mind – both from attackers and for defence. Three (Deal, Walmer and Sandown) were built on a 3-mile stretch in Kent to protect a vital safe anchorage between the Goodwin Sands and the coast. Of these Deal is the best preserved, and shows off to perfection the ideas of artillery-based fortifications: low, thick, rounded towers serve as platforms for heavy guns, while lighter guns can be fired from the ports which pierce the towers. Similar 'castles' (they are forts, really) were built to protect many other vulnerable anchorages and ports. These include Pendennis in Cornwall, which was later refortified with the type of angled bastions along its outer walls that were to become the norm for the next 300 years.

Another key example of new thinking in defence is the town walls of Berwick-on-Tweed. Here, triangular bastions deflect enemy fire and enable cross-fire from all angles. At Fort George in Inverness, there are very similar bastions, although these were built nearly 200 years after the walls at Berwick.

A martello tower off the coast of Ireland on the island called Ireland's Eye. Martello towers were all built to a similar pattern. A single cannon was originally placed on a rotating platform on the roof, and the roof was very thick to protect from mortar fire. The body of the tower housed a garrison of men, along with their provisions and ammunition.

The Tower of London has changed dramatically since it was first built by William the Conqueror, but he would still recognize the White Tower today. The Tower and its precincts have had many roles and functions, none more poignant and charming than when the moat (now grassed over as in the picture) was dug up and used for growing vegetables during World War II.

Towers have always been an important part of defensive design. There are hundreds of examples to be seen in Scotland and Ireland, with many still in use today as homes. They were practical structures used for defence until the 16th century and beyond. Later ones were built with guns very much in mind, as the array of gun ports at Dunnottar Castle in Scotland shows.

Towers came back into fashion as defensive structures in the 19th century as a response to the threat of invasion from France in the Napoleonic Wars. More than a hundred were eventually built, but their guns never fired a shot in anger or defence. New developments in artillery technology – rifled barrels firing metal shells – rendered all such defences virtually useless, but in the 1860s new forts were once again built all round the coast of England. These included the last great fortifications ever built in the British Isles. Some were armour plated to withstand artillery attack.

The last threatened invasion of Britain by sea came in World War II. The answer was to refortify many of the coastal fortifications sometimes built hundreds of years before, and included the construction of thousands of pillboxes. These tiny concrete boxes housed machine-gun emplacements, and were often cleverly and effectively disguised as such things as ice-cream kiosks, haystacks and even piles of logs. A far cry from the great castles of the likes of Edward I, they were the correct response to the ever-changing nature of war.

A castle in name only, Castle Drogo in Devon was created in the early years of the 20th century for a multimillionaire by architect Edwin Lutyens. It combines notions of medieval life with modern comfort. Among the most interesting parts of the castle is the kitchen, with its giant pestle and mortar – seen on the left of the picture.

England

Many castles in England now stand in neat lawns and among colourful flowerbeds. On sunny days they are the epitome of romance. But this disguises their often bloody and violent past.

Some of the most important castles in England are still in use — Windsor and the Tower of London are the most famous examples. A number are still lived in by the descendants of those who built them, sometimes 500 or more years ago. Some ruined ones drowse in remote rural settings, perhaps unrecognized even by locals. They are a central part of the story of England, and often of significant architectural importance.

ASHTON KEYNES

An earthwork enclosure near the centre of the village, the fortress at Ashton Keynes was founded in the 12th century and occupied until the 13th. Low mounds and ditches outline the two baileys. The site is accessible.

LOCATION: WILTSHIRE
MAP REF: SU 049943

BAMPTON

Bampton dates from the 12th century – King Stephen captured the castle in 1136 and another castle was licensed on this site exactly two centuries later. There are no remains.

LOCATION: NR TIVERTON, DEVON
MAP REF: SS 959225

BARNSTAPLE

This was one of north Devon's most important castles during medieval times. Judhael de Totnes, who established a Cluniac monastery in Barnstaple, built the castle, probably on the site of an earlier fortification. Similar to the castle at Totnes (see page 35), its fate was very different as by the end of the 14th century it was in ruins.

LOCATION: DEVON
MAP REF: SS 557332

BERRY POMEROY

On a wooded hill close to the River Dart, this evocative ruin of a 16th-century fortified manor house enclosed by medieval defences has an unusual gatehouse with polygonal towers. In 1547 Edward Seymour, Duke of Somerset and Protector of Edward VI, acquired the castle. Despite ambitious building projects by the Seymour family, Berry Pomeroy was abandoned by the beginning of the 18th century in favour of their country house in Somerset. Stripped of any valuable materials, the place was in ruins not long after. The property is managed by English Heritage and events are staged occasionally.

LOCATION: NR TORQUAY, DEVON
MAP REF: SX 839623
OPEN: ENGLISH HERITAGE: APR–OCT DAILY

BICKLEIGH

The chapel at Bickleigh, built in 1090 and the oldest complete building in Devon, would originally have been enclosed inside the bailey of the castle that stood here. A 15th-century fortified moated manor later occupied the site, although much of this was destroyed during the Civil War: only the gatehouse was repaired. The property is privately owned.

LOCATION: NR TIVERTON, DEVON
MAP REF: SS 937068

BRIDGWATER

William de Briwere built the castle at Bridgwater around 1202. A substantial structure in the Middle Ages, the castle was built to a rectangular plan on the west bank of the River Parret. More or less destroyed during the Civil War, only the 13th-century water gate and some of the curtain wall remain and are accessible.

LOCATION: SOMERSET
MAP REF: ST 30237

BRISTOL

Established on the edge of the already prosperous town, Bristol Castle was built by the Bishop of Coutances. It had the third-largest keep in the country (only Colchester and the White Tower in London were bigger). This once impressive fortress was destroyed in 1650 on government orders although interesting fragments remain on Castle Green. The site is freely accessible and there are information panels.

LOCATION: CASTLE GREEN, BRISTOL
MAP REF: ST 594732

CARY

The centre of a large estate, there was a castle with a substantial keep at Castle Cary and this appears to have been enclosed within banks and a moat. Dates are uncertain, but during the civil war in the 12th century the lord here fought against King Stephen. There are no remains.

LOCATION: NR WINCANTON, SOMERSET
MAP REF: ST 641322

CASTLE COMBE

Little remains of the medieval castle that once stood above this famously picturesque Cotswold village. The castle began as a cluster of earthwork and timber enclosures, and ditching; some of the enclosure walling was converted to stone. The site is near a manor house which is now a hotel.

LOCATION: NR BATH, WILTSHIRE
MAP REF: ST 837777

CHRISTCHURCH

Richard de Redvers probably raised a motte castle here in around 1100. There are remains of a late 12th- or early 13th-century keep but the castle was slighted after the Civil War. Close by are the ruins of a constable's house built in 1160 with one of only five Norman chimneys still surviving in England.

LOCATION: DORSET
MAP REF: SZ 160927
OPEN: ENGLISH HERITAGE: DAILY

COMPTON

Compton was fortified against French raids on the south Devon coast. Dating from the 14th century it was built by, and remains, the home of the Gilbert family: Sir Humphrey Gilbert, a half-brother of Sir Walter Raleigh, colonized Newfoundland. The castle was a location in the 1995 film adaptation of Jane Austen's *Sense and Sensibility*.

LOCATION: NR MARLDON, DEVON
MAP REF: SX 865648
OPEN: NATIONAL TRUST: APR–OCT

CORFE

LOCATION: DORSET
MAP REF: SY 958823
OPEN: NATIONAL TRUST: DAILY
SEE PAGE: 24

DARTMOUTH

The distinctive towers of Dartmouth Castle, one cylindrical and one square, command the cliffs at the narrowest part of the entrance to Devon's Dart estuary. A fortress was first built here around 1400 when the town's mayor, John Hawley (said to have been the inspiration for the Shipman of Dartmouth in Chaucer's *Canterbury Tales*) was given a royal order to build a defensive castle to protect the town and river from attack by the French. Further additions were made during the 15th century when Dartmouth Castle received the first purpose-built artillery tower in the country. More gun emplacements were added to this fortress during its long defensive history which included a successful siege by Royalist forces during the English Civil War (they capitulated to the Parliamentarians after holding the fortress for three years). Dartmouth's last gun emplacements were erected, and manned, during World War II. There are displays in the castle depicting its history.

LOCATION: DEVON
MAP REF: SX 887503
OPEN: ENGLISH HERITAGE; DAILY

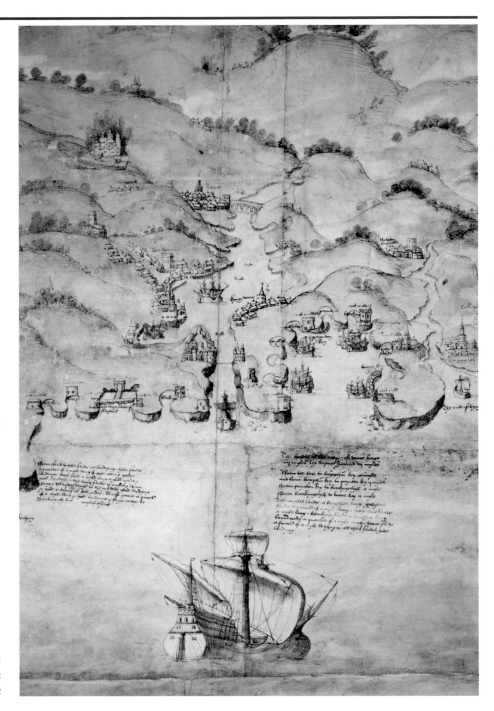

Right: detail of a panoramic map from 1539, showing coastal fortifications around the mouth of the River Dart

DEVIZES

The 12th-century *Acts of Stephen* refer to the 'impregnable fortifications' of Devizes Castle but little remains. The first wooden castle was burned down but rebuilt in stone by Roger, Bishop of Salisbury in around 1120. A Royalist stronghold, it was badly damaged in 1645 during a bombardment by Cromwell's army. The site is privately owned and not accessible.

LOCATION: WILTSHIRE
MAP REF: SU 002613

DORCHESTER

Dorchester Castle was probably a motte and bailey construction. Both King John and Henry III spent money on the castle but by the end of the 13th century it seems to have been abandoned. There are no remains. A 19th-century county prison now occupies the site.

LOCATION: DORSET
MAP REF: SY 692909

Artillery forts

Henry VIII instigated a series of artillery forts along the south and east coasts of England in response to threats of invasion from France and Spain. The forts were usually low, sturdy circular structures that made a difficult target for ships to fire on. Their strength allowed them to accommodate heavy cannons and guns.

Corfe

The jagged ruins of this once-powerful fortress dominate the horizon at the entrance to the Isle of Purbeck. Corfe Castle was a favourite residence of King John, who built remarkable domestic quarters there, creating the best-appointed apartments of any royal castle in England at the time.

Originally a motte castle built in the late 11th century, the outline of Corfe's precincts remained the same for most of its history. The keep probably dates from the reign of Henry I: Henry's brother, Robert, Duke of Normandy, was held at Corfe after his defeat at Tinchebrai in 1106.

The fall of Normandy to the French in 1204 and the castle's location close to the south coast doubtless added momentum to the strengthening of its defences. When King Stephen besieged the castle 60 years earlier, the outer baileys were probably protected only by wooden palisades; a stone curtain and defensive towers (not completed until around 1285) must have been pressing additions. Henry III continued improving the defences at Corfe and spent even more on the castle than King John.

Corfe lost its royal status in the 16th century when Elizabeth I sold it, and was owned by Sir John Bankes by the time the Civil War broke out in 1642. The

The castle ruins from Corfe Castle village. Captured by the Parliamentarians in February 1646, the demolition began almost immediately, but such was Corfe's strength that the destruction took many months.

garrison at Corfe, led by Sir John's widow after his death in 1644, held out against the Parliamentarians during two sieges but an act of treachery forced capitulation in February 1646.

The following month the order came for Corfe to be slighted. This led to the virtual destruction of what must have been one of Britain's most fascinating castles.

Top: Corfe Castle as it looked before it was besieged and subsequently destroyed during the Civil War. The castle fell following an act of treachery. It had been held under the leadership of Lady Bankes, who was allowed to leave with dignity, carrying the castle keys.

Middle: Following the slighting in 1646 the castle remains in much the same condition today.

Bottom: The Bankes family built Kingston Lacy House as their new family home. Corfe's keys are still kept there.

DUNSTER CASTLE

The present imposing fortified manor house known as Dunster is a replacement of an earlier Norman earthwork castle built by the de Mohun family. Stonework was later added although there are no remains except for a mound, scarped out of a natural hill. The Luttrell family bought Dunster in 1376 and lived there for 600 years. Little damage was inflicted on the castle during the Civil War even though it was a Parliamentary stronghold, captured by the Royalists in 1642 and retaken by the Parliamentarians after a long siege. Successive generations of the family have made their mark on the castle (it was supposedly an 18th-century Luttrell who removed the ruins of the Norman fortress) and not a great deal remains of the medieval edifice, only the 13th-century gatehouse. Dunster's last restoration was in the 19th century by the Victorian architect Salvin, who reconstructed parts of the manor in Gothic Revival style.

LOCATION: NR MINEHEAD, SOMERSET
MAP REF: SS 991434
OPEN: NATIONAL TRUST: MID-MAR TO EARLY NOV SAT–WED. GARDENS AND PARK: DAILY

EXETER 'ROUGEMONT'

William I met with considerable resistance at Exeter, which held out against a siege lasting 18 days. Baldwin de Brionne, William's Sheriff of Devon, then raised a castle here. Only parts of the outer walls and the gatehouse, one of the country's earliest examples of Norman building work, still exist. The ruins are now part of Rougemont public gardens.

LOCATION: DEVON
MAP REF: SX 921930

FARLEIGH HUNGERFORD

The manor house at Farleigh, sited with its back to a deep dyke, was built by the Montfort family and sold to the first Speaker of the House of Commons, Sir Thomas Hungerford, in 1369. Following the custom of the time, Sir Thomas fortified the house and built a square enclosure with curtain, cylindrical corner towers and an extensive array of domestic buildings. He failed to obtain a licence to crenellate but received a pardon for this oversight in 1383. Walter, Sir Thomas' son, added an outer bailey and moat to Farleigh Hungerford in the 15th century. The church of St

Leonard, notable for its 14th-century wall paintings and the Hungerford tombs, was within its precincts and used as the castle chapel.

Falling into decay, stone from the castle was eventually used to build nearby Farleigh House. Farleigh Hungerford's extensive remains are still impressive and there is an interesting museum on site. Occasional events take place in the summer.

LOCATION: NORTON ST PHILIP, SOMERSET
MAP REF: ST 801577
OPEN: ENGLISH HERITAGE: APR–SEP DAILY; OCT–MAR SAT–SUN

GIDLEIGH

Gidleigh Castle probably started as a fortified manor house in around 1300. All that now remains is a small tower built of granite rubble. The site is private and not accessible.

LOCATION: NR CHAGFORD, DEVON
MAP REF: SX 670844

HEMYOCK

A compact late 14th-century rectangular enclosure castle built mainly from chert, a local flint stone. Some of the original rendering on the exterior walls has been uncovered.

Hemyock was built as a small working castle by Sir William Asthorpe, who held several high-ranking posts during the reigns of Edward III and Richard II. The castle was partly demolished by Charles II in the 1660s. Privately owned, open on some bank holidays.

LOCATION: DEVON
MAP REF: ST 135133
OPEN: SOME BANK HOLIDAYS

LAUNCESTON

Guarding the main route into Cornwall, the fortress at Launceston was raised very soon after the Conquest. A circular stone keep was erected in the following century and further substantial improvements carried out in the 13th century. The castle's importance then began to decline and by 1650 it was a virtual ruin. It was in such a bad state of repair when the Parliamentarians seized it in the Civil War, they didn't bother to slight it. Nevertheless, the 17th-century cartographer, John Norden, described the castle as 'this triple-crowned mounde' and visitors today can still see exactly what he meant.

LOCATION: CORNWALL
MAP REF: SX 330846
OPEN: ENGLISH HERITAGE: APR–OCT DAILY

LUDGERSHALL

Eventually used as a hunting lodge by Henry III, Ludgershall was first developed as a medieval fortification soon after the Conquest. Excavations have revealed a complex series of buildings from several periods, and a garden feature. There are some remains, which are open to the public at all reasonable times.

LOCATION: WILTSHIRE
MAP REF: SU 264513

LYDFORD

This is an example of a castle whose great tower was raised before the motte, which was subsequently piled up around the tower base. Measuring around 16m (52ft) square, the tower, which dates from late in the 12th century, is now roofless, much as it was in the 18th century when it was repaired and used as a gaol and stannary (tin-mining) court, but fell into decay again. Freely open to the public (English Heritage).

LOCATION: NR OKEHAMPTON, DEVON
MAP REF: SX 510848

MALMESBURY

A castle was founded here early in the 12th century but there are no remains. It was certainly besieged during the troubles in King Stephen's reign. The monks from the nearby abbey were given permission to dismantle the castle around 1216.

LOCATION: WILTSHIRE
MAP REF: ST 935872

MARISCO

Henry III ordered a castle to be built on this island in the mid-13th century. A Royalist supporter, Thomas Bushell, restored the medieval castle during the Civil War and most of the visible remains are from this date or later although some of the original curtain wall still exists. The Landmark Trust maintain the property and the keep provides holiday accommodation.

LOCATION: LUNDY ISLAND, DEVON
MAP REF: SS 141437

MARLBOROUGH

Remains of Marlborough's large motte are in the grounds of Marlborough College. The fortress here certainly existed during King Stephen's time and Henry II added stone buildings. The castle was still garrisoned in the mid-14th century but was in ruins by the early 15th century. It is not open to the public.

LOCATION: WILTSHIRE
MAP REF: SU 183686

Perkin Warbeck

A claimant to the throne of Henry VII, Warbeck may have been an illegitimate son of Edward IV. He first claimed that he was the Earl of Warwick (the real earl was in prison), then said he was one of the princes in the Tower and thus the Duke of York. European monarchs accepted Warbeck's claims and in 1497 he tried to invade England at Cornwall but was captured. Warbeck was executed in 1499.

MARSHWOOD

Some parts of the rectangular great tower that was erected on this motte still exist. It was probably built in the 12th century.

LOCATION: DORSET
MAP REF: SY 404977

MEMBURY

Excavations here during World War II revealed a rectangular earthwork inside which were building foundations of a 12th-century tower replaced by a 13th-century (or later) mansion.

LOCATION: WILTSHIRE
MAP REF: SU 305745

KING ARTHUR AND CAMELOT

THE STORY OF KING ARTHUR AND HIS COURT AT CAMELOT HAS BEEN TOLD FOR CENTURIES. NO ONE KNOWS THE ORIGINS OF THE STORY OR WHETHER IT IS ROOTED IN FACT. WAS ARTHUR A KING IN EARLY BRITAIN, A TRIBAL CHIEF, OR WAS HE THE EMBODIMENT OF THE CHIVALRIC VALUES PEOPLE WANTED IN THEIR KINGS?

STORIES OF KING ARTHUR AND THE KNIGHTS OF THE ROUND TABLE AND THEIR QUEST TO FIND THE HOLY GRAIL RESOUND WITH BRAVERY AND CHIVALRY AS WELL AS ROMANCE, BETRAYAL AND MAGIC. ARTHUR'S CASTLE, CAMELOT, IS VARIOUSLY SAID TO HAVE BEEN IN WALES, CORNWALL, HAMPSHIRE AND SOMERSET. THE MOST RECENT THEORIES POINT TO SOMERSET'S CADBURY CASTLE, A HILL FORT THAT WAS KNOWN LOCALLY AS CAMALAT IN THE 15TH CENTURY.

King Arthur enters Camelot, from a 14th-century drawing

MERE

Set high on a natural ridge, the castle at Mere was built by Richard, Earl of Cornwall in the 13th century. This rectangular structure had six towers, a hall, inner and outer gates and a chapel although there are no remains. It was demolished at the end of the 18th century. The site is open to visitors.

LOCATION: WILTSHIRE
MAP REF: ST 809325

MONTACUTE

A very early castle, which may have had some stonework, was built here. Montacute was a motte castle surrounded by a ditch: it stood inside a bailey that was also enriched by ditching. The site is within National Trust parkland.

LOCATION: SOMERSET
MAP REF: ST 493169

NEROCHE

Begun in the 11th century as an earthwork enclosure, erected on the site of a much earlier earthwork ring, in the 1100s the smaller enclosure was made into a motte and bailey castle and in the 12th century a shell enclosure was built. The site is accessible.

LOCATION: NR BUCKLAND ST MARY, SOMERSET
MAP REF: ST 272158

NETHER STOWEY

An early motte castle with two baileys, Nether Stowey was given a substantial rectangular great tower probably around the mid-12th century.

LOCATION: NR BUCKLAND ST MARY, SOMERSET
MAP REF: ST 187396

Domesday Book
William the Conqueror commissioned a survey of all the lands, villages, people and animals in the whole of England. His aim was to assess the value of the lands so he could determine what taxes could be levied. The report was completed in 1086.

NUNNEY

A distinctive quadrangular castle with closely spaced circular corner towers and surrounded by a deep moat, the compact French-style Nunney Castle was built by John de la Mere who obtained a licence to crenellate in 1373. It would have been roofed like a French château. Besieged by the Parliamentarians in 1645 the north wall of the castle was badly damaged by cannon fire: the wall finally collapsed, but not until 1910 when it blocked the moat (since cleared). After the Civil War the castle was slighted and rendered uninhabitable, but not destroyed. As a consequence this four-storey fortification with its towers, still almost at their original height, is a substantial ruin and makes a dramatic backdrop to the centre of this pretty Somerset village.

LOCATION: NR FROME, SOMERSET
MAP REF: ST 737457
OPEN: ENGLISH HERITAGE: OPEN ACCESS

OKEHAMPTON

Excavations in the late 20th century have shown that the motte castle at Okehampton, built early in the reign of William I, had a great square tower made of granite and shale rubble. Set on top of a naturally fortified ridge, the castle was greatly extended in the 14th century in the form of buildings round an elongated bailey; it has been compared with German hill-top castles such as Staufen and Rothenburg. The later additions consisted of a number of buildings beginning at the bottom of the slope down from the tower, such as kitchen, lodgings, solar, hall, guardrooms and chapel, and then a gatehouse leading to a long barbican causeway that had its own outer two-storey gate block. The castle was abandoned in the first half of the 16th century but this is still the site of one of the largest castle ruins in the South West, and is set in a beautiful riverside location.

LOCATON: NR OKEHAMPTON, DEVON
MAP REF: SX 584942
OPEN: ENGLISH HERITAGE: APR–SEP DAILY

OLD SARUM

Outlines of foundations and extensive earthworks remain at Old Sarum, an important operational base and royal residence during William I's reign, and the site where he chose to pay off his army in 1070, and take the Oath of Allegiance from his lords in 1086. Old Sarum has a history dating back to neolithic times: it was an Iron Age hill fort, the Romans occupied it and it was also a Saxon burgh. The Conqueror put up a motte and bailey castle; then after the Bishopric of Sherborne was transferred to Old Sarum, a cathedral and ecclesiastical buildings were erected inside the bailey. Friction between the inhabitants of the castle and the cathedral led to the move of the episcopal see to a site nearer the river, known as New Sarum, or Salisbury, in the 13th century where a new cathedral was begun in 1220. The castle at Old Sarum received further 12th- and 13th-century additions and remained in use until it was demolished in the early 16th century.

LOCATION: NR SALISBURY, WILTSHIRE
MAP REF: SU 138327
OPEN: ENGLISH HERITAGE: DAILY

OLD WARDOUR

A unique and lavish castle of the type that was driven by design rather than defensive necessity, Old Wardour was built by the 5th Lord Lovel, who obtained a licence to crenellate his home in the 1390s. The unusual structure consists of a hexagonal-plan range of apartments round a hexagonal courtyard with flanking towers to the entrance. Old Wardour was lost by the Lovels after a relatively short time. The Arundell family acquired it and had the castle remodelled in the 1570s by Elizabethan architect Robert Smythson. Captured by Parliamentarian forces in 1643 it was attacked again in 1644, this time by the previous owner and Royalist, Lord Arundell. Unfortunately the damage inflicted on the building was so severe that the Arundells had to abandon it. They later built a grand 18th-century mansion in the grounds, keeping the shell of Old Wardour as a feature of the landscaped parkland. It remains one of the country's most romantic ruins.

LOCATION: WARDOUR PARK, NR TISBURY, WILTSHIRE
MAP REF: ST 939263
OPEN: ENGLISH HERITAGE: APR–OCT DAILY; NOV–MAR SAT–SUN

PENDENNIS

One of Henry VIII's artillery forts, Pendennis, along with St Mawes, was intended to defend the Fal estuary. The original 1540s' buildings are a central round gun tower surrounded by a low platform. Additions to the defences were made during Elizabeth I's reign but the castle was only attacked during the Civil War. A Royalist stronghold, it was besieged from both land and sea: the garrison here held out for six months before finally surrendering.

LOCATION: NR FALMOUTH, CORNWALL
MAP REF: SW 827315
OPEN: ENGLISH HERITAGE: DAILY

PLYMOUTH

Superseded by Charles II's Royal Citadel, Plymouth Castle stood just to the north of it above the old town harbour. It was probably built in the 15th century. There is a very small part of the wall remaining. The site is open and accessible.

LOCATION: DEVON
MAP REF: SX 482539

PLYMPTON

Plympton, now part of Plymouth's suburbs, was an important trading port until the River Plym silted up. A timber castle was rebuilt in stone in 1141. Parts of the cylindrical shell wall survive on top of the motte. The site is accessible.

LOCATION: PLYMOUTH, DEVON
MAP REF: SX 544557

PORTLAND AND SANDSFOOT CASTLES

Portland and Sandsfoot were artillery forts erected by Henry VIII to defend the south coast. Portland Castle is less ruinous than Sandsfoot, which stands on the opposite cliff, although the main gun room is now roofless. With a round central citadel, it was in use (but not continuously) until after World War II.

LOCATION: WEYMOUTH, DORSET
MAP REFS: PORTLAND, SY 684743;
SANDSFOOT, SY 674773
OPEN: ENGLISH HERITAGE (PORTLAND):
APR–OCT DAILY

POWDERHAM

More of a stately home than a castle now, Powderham has been home to the same family, the Courtenays, since the 16th century. Originally a fortified manor house built in the late 14th century the castle was drastically remodelled in the 18th and 19th centuries after being damaged in the Civil War. Today's visitors to the 1,618ha (4,000 acre) estate with a deer park, can enjoy the grounds as well as the castle.

LOCATION: KENTON, NR EXETER, DEVON
MAP REF: SX 968836
OPEN: APR–OCT DAILY

POWERSTOCK

An 11th- or 12th-century motte and bailey castle, set in the ancient forest of Poorstock. It was used as a hunting lodge by King John.

LOCATION: NR BRIDPORT, DORSET
MAP REF: SY 522959

RESTORMEL

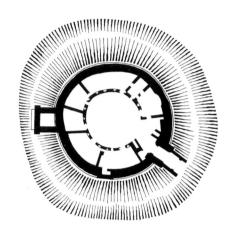

This is a very fine example of a shell enclosure castle raised on an earlier motte. There are substantial remains of the shell enclosure, which was almost completely circular, 2.5m (8ft) thick and erected c.1200. A ring of apartments of stone and wood was raised around the inside of the shell: these included a kitchen, great hall, solar and barrack room for retainers. Edward, the Black Prince lived in the castle for a time. The already abandoned castle was garrisoned by the Parliamentarians during the Civil War but was never occupied again.

LOCATION: LOSTWITHIEL, CORNWALL
MAP REF: SX 104614
OPEN: ENGLISH HERITAGE: APR–OCT DAILY

RUFUS

The present remains of a polygonal tower, built of Portland stone, stand upon the site of an earlier structure, which may have been built as early as c.1100. The tower is from the 15th century. The castle, also known as Bow and Arrow, is accessible.

LOCATION: PORTLAND, DORSET
MAP REF: SY 697711

ST CATHERINE'S POINT

Henry VIII built an artillery fort at the entrance to the River Fowey and to defend the harbour here. There is a 16th-century fort below it.

LOCATION: FOWEY, CORNWALL
MAP REF: SX 118509
OPEN: ENGLISH HERITAGE: OPEN ACCESS

ST MAWES

Built by Henry VIII on the opposite headland from Pendennis Castle, as one of a pair of fortresses defending the Fal estuary against invasion from France and Spain, St Mawes was continuously occupied by military forces until after World War II. However, it has remained remarkably unaltered, undamaged and true to its Tudor origins. More vulnerable than Pendennis, the garrison here capitulated to the Parliamentary forces during the Civil War without a single shot being fired.

LOCATION: CORNWALL
MAP REF: SW 841327
OPEN: ENGLISH HERITAGE: APR–OCT DAILY;
NOV–MAR FRI–MON

ST MICHAEL'S MOUNT

LOCATION: MARAZION, CORNWALL
MAP REF:
OPEN: NATIONAL TRUST: DAILY
SEE PAGE: 32

SALCOMBE

Also known as Fort Charles, the remains of this 16th-century artillery tower stand on an isolated rock next to a stunning Devon estuary beach. Built by Henry VIII to protect the harbour, the fortress was slighted in the Civil War. The site is accessible from the beach but not at high tide.

LOCATION: NORTH SANDS, SALCOMBE, DEVON
MAP REF: SX 733380

The old castle at Sherborne stands in parkland, landscaped in the 18th century by 'Capability' Brown, across the lake from a grand Elizabethan mansion built by Sir Walter Raleigh in 1594. Raleigh, who stopped here en route to Plymouth, was so taken with the castle and its location that he petitioned Elizabeth I for the estate. He tried to convert the 12th-century fortress into a suitable dwelling but eventually built an entirely new home. The now ruinous old castle was designed on a grand scale by the powerful Roger de Caen, Bishop of Salisbury and Chancellor of England during Henry I's reign; he also built the abbey in the town. A Royalist stronghold during the Civil War, it was dismantled after it fell to Parliamentary forces following a 16-day siege which led Cromwell to describe old Sherborne Castle as 'malicious and mischievous'.

LOCATION: SHERBORNE, DORSET
MAP REF: ST 647167
OPEN: ENGLISH HERITAGE (SHERBORNE OLD CASTLE): APR–OCT SAT–THU
SHERBORNE CASTLE (PRIVATELY OWNED): LATE MAR–OCT TUE–THU, SAT–SUN. OPEN BANK HOLIDAY MONDAYS

Above and below: Sherborne Old Castle. Despite petitioning Elizabeth I to grant him the castle, Walter Raleigh abandoned it in favour of a new lodge in the grounds (now incorporated into the new Sherborne Castle).

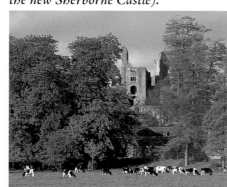

St Michael's Mount

This granite outcrop rising out of the sea in one of the southernmost bays of the Cornish coastline has held a position of strategic importance since early times. St Michael's Mount was known as a safe harbour, a place of pilgrimage and an important trading port, long before any kind of stone fortifications were built (although it may well have been a hilltop fort in neolithic times) and was probably the island known as Ictis to the ancient Greeks, who traded for Cornish tin in the area. It certainly continued as an important port during the Roman occupation of Britain.

Scant documentation shows that at the time of Edward the Confessor (1042–66), the Mount was occupied by a priest but it wasn't until after the Norman Conquest when Robert, Count of Mortain, who owned a large swathe of the West Country and had been made Earl of Cornwall by William the Conqueror, granted the Mount to the French Benedictine abbey at Mont St Michel. In 1135 the Abbot of Mont St Michel had a church built on the Cornish outpost and established a religious community with a prior and a dozen monks: the original church, consecrated in 1144, was destroyed in an earthquake in 1275 but was rebuilt during the next century and is still used as a place of worship.

The St Aubyn family, who acquired the island after the Civil War, still live in the castle and have transformed it into a comfortable mansion. Its terraced gardens are planted with exotic species. The harbour is surrounded by shops and cafés. Access is across a causeway at low tide, otherwise by boat.

In the early part of the 15th century, Henry V declared war on France and the Mount was granted to Syon Abbey, finally severing links with its parent French abbey.

In 1640, two years before Civil War broke out, Sir Francis Bassett, who became a leading Royalist military commander in Cornwall, bought the Mount. He spent considerable sums on gun batteries and other defences and was responsible for constructing the fortified gateway and watchtower on the main approach to the castle. It remains one of the country's most well-preserved Civil War sites.

The Mount eventually fell to the Parliamentarians and in 1647 Colonel John St Aubyn was nominated as military governor. Successive generations of St Aubyns have restored the chapel, which was used as an ammunition store during the Civil War.

SHIPWRECKS

THE RETURN OF THE LIFE BOAT BY MYLES BIRKETT FOSTER RECALLS THE LIVES LOST IN SHIPWRECKS ALONG THE CORNISH COAST. MOUNT'S BAY IS NO EXCEPTION — THERE ARE MORE THAN 50 WRECKS LYING AT THE BOTTOM OF THE SEA. WRECKING — RECOVERING WHAT WAS SALVAGEABLE FROM THE STRICKEN VESSELS — WAS PART OF THE LOCAL ECONOMY.

KNOWLEDGE OF THE COAST AND ITS CURRENTS AND OBSTACLES GAVE CORNISH SMUGGLERS THE EDGE OVER THE EXCISE MEN. PERRANUTHOE, ON THE COAST NEAR ST MICHAEL'S MOUNT, WAS THE CENTRE OF OPERATIONS FOR JOHN CARTER, KNOWN AS THE 'KING OF PRUSSIA'. CARTER NAMED HIS BASE PRUSSIA COVE BECAUSE OF HIS ADMIRATION FOR FREDERICK THE GREAT.

SOMERFORD

This is one of more than 55 castle sites in Wiltshire although little trace of it remains. Excavations here have shown that the original wooden castle was possibly replaced with an unfortified structure.

LOCATION: WILTSHIRE
MAP REF: ST 965831

STOGURSEY

Stogursey, rebuilt by William de Curci in the 12th century, was an enclosure with several baileys. The first known record of the castle is dated 1204 but there was an earlier defensive construction here. The ruins date from the 12th and 13th centuries.

LOCATION: NR BRIDGWATER, SOMERSET
MAP REF: ST 203426
OPEN: LANDMARK TRUST (17TH-CENTURY GATEHOUSE HOLIDAY COTTAGE)

TAUNTON

Dating from the early 12th century, Taunton Castle was an administrative centre of the Bishops of Winchester. The keep once had 4m (13ft) thick walls: now only the foundations remain as it was slighted after the Civil War on Charles II's orders. Taunton supported the Parliamentarian cause and Royalists besieged the castle on several occasions. Although much restored and reconstructed, the great hall has traces of its Norman walls and houses the Somerset County Museum. Judge Jeffreys held his 'Bloody Assizes' here after the Monmouth Rebellion of 1685. The Somerset County Museum is here.

LOCATION: SOMERSET
MAP REF: ST 227248
OPEN: KEEP FOUNDATIONS ARE IN THE GROUNDS OF CASTLE HOTEL

Manpower
It could take more than 2,500 workers to build a new castle. They would have to be garrisoned, provisioned and organized – just like a military campaign.

TINTAGEL

A spectacular sight, the castle at Tintagel sits on a headland silhouetted against the cliffs of the wild north coast of Cornwall. Much of this structure has fallen away into the Channel but the remaining ruins are of the castle built by Richard, Earl of Cornwall in the middle of the 13th century. Standing on the site of an earlier Dark Ages stronghold, this fortress is divided into two parts by an isthmus between the headland and the mainland. Developed after the claim by Geoffrey of Monmouth that Tintagel was the birthplace of King Arthur, and with little economic or military importance, it seems the castle's existence was merely to associate the Earls of Cornwall with King Arthur. There was no keep here but a great hall was erected in the inner ward, on the 'island'; this was rebuilt for the last time in the 14th century. The upper and lower wards are constructed on the 'mainland'. Tintagel was ruinous by the end of the 15th century.

LOCATION: CORNWALL
MAP REF: SX 048891
OPEN: ENGLISH HERITAGE: DAILY

TIVERTON

This quadrangular enclosure castle was built of pink sandstone by the Courtenay family in the 14th century on the site of an earlier 12th-century castle. The quadrangle had towers on the corners (of which a cylindrical south-east and a square south-west remain) and was surrounded by a double moat.

LOCATION: TIVERTON, DEVON
MAP REF: SS 954131
OPEN: PRIVATE: EASTER–OCT SUN, THU, BANK HOLIDAY MONDAYS

Founded by one of the leaders in the Norman Conquest, Judhael de Totnes, the castle here began as a simple example of the most usual type of Norman fortification. However, Totnes is noteworthy for one of the largest mottes and best-preserved shell enclosures in the country. Artificially constructed from pounded earth and rock and covered with a layer of clay, the motte, topped with an almost circular shell keep, dominates the pretty and ancient town beneath. Earthworks are the only remains of the original 11th-century structure which had a square wooden tower on top of stone foundations: the keep was added in the early part of the 13th century and was rebuilt, with crenellations, in the next. As in earlier times, when the local population had capitulated to the Norman invaders, Totnes offered no resistance to the Parliamentary forces in 1646, and the castle remains are substantial.

LOCATION: DEVON
MAP REF: SX 800605
OPEN: ENGLISH HERITAGE: APR–OCT DAILY

TREMATON

An early motte castle, mentioned in Domesday, Trematon received a stone shell enclosure and curtain round the bailey in the 12th century. The gatehouse dates from the 13th century. Richard, Earl of Cornwall bought Trematon in the 1270s. A grand house was built within the bailey walls in the 19th century. The site is privately owned and not open.

LOCATION: SALTASH, CORNWALL
MAP REF: SX 410580

TROWBRIDGE

An earthwork enclosure of the early 12th century was later given stonework of some kind here. The suggestion is that this was a small tower, possibly raised in the time of King Stephen by Henry de Bohun but there are no remains. The moat of the castle is said to be partly defined in the town's curving main street.

LOCATION: WILTSHIRE
MAP REF: ST 854579

WAREHAM

Henry I's brother, Robert, Duke of Normandy was held at Wareham (and other castles); we do not know if the great tower was ready for his arrival in 1106, although it appears to have been completed by 1119. The castle was taken by the Earl of Gloucester, c.1135, and mostly remained in baronial possession until its destruction during the Civil War.

LOCATION: DORSET
MAP REF: SY 920876

ABINGER

The motte castle built here in about 1100 was remodelled in 1140 and destroyed in 1153. Excavations in the 20th century revealed post-holes of a wooden tower and a surrounding palisade. A gap in the circumference of palisade posts might indicate the gateway at the south-west.

LOCATION: NR GUILDFORD, SURREY
MAP REF: TQ 114460

AMBERLEY

The Bishops of Chichester built Amberley in the 14th century, following a licence to crenellate granted in 1377: prior to that the bishops lived in a manor house within the present castle's enclosure. Despite being slighted during the Civil War and the subject of many alterations over the centuries, Amberley retains many of its 14th-century features. It was bought by the Duke of Norfolk in the 19th century but is now currently in use as an hotel.

LOCATION: NR ARUNDEL, WEST SUSSEX
MAP REF: TQ 027132
OPEN: HOTEL AND RESTAURANT GUESTS ONLY

ANSTEY

Anstey had a motte castle, dating from the late 11th, or early 12th century. The surviving low motte, about 9m (30ft) high, was surrounded by a wet moat. The castle was strengthened during the Magna Carta war by one of the opponents of King John.

LOCATION: HERTFORDSHIRE
MAP REF: TL 404330

ALDINGBOURNE

Built in the mid-12th century of locally quarried limestone and flint, the lowest storey of the stone great tower was enclosed inside a mound of earth, which can still be seen. The tower was square in plan, with a small forebuilding at the south-west, a moat and a flat-topped motte.

LOCATION: NR ARUNDEL, SUSSEX
MAP REF: SU 923048

ARDLEY

A sub-rectangular earthwork enclosure with a shallow ditch is all that can be seen here. There are traces of Norman masonry. It may have been an adulterine (unlicensed) castle of Stephen's reign, demolished after 1154 on the orders of Henry II.

LOCATION: ARDLEY WOOD, OXFORDSHIRE
MAP REF: SP 539273

ARUNDEL

LOCATION: WEST SUSSEX
MAP REF: TQ 019074
OPEN: PRIVATE: APR–OCT BUT CHECK FIRST
SEE PAGE: 38

ASCOT D'OILLY

Built in the first half of the 12th century on raised ground surrounded by broad ditching. The tower was demolished, probably late in the 12th century, possibly at the order of Henry II following his suppression of the revolt led by his eldest son, Prince Henry. Only traces of the tower remain.

LOCATION: OXFORDSHIRE
MAP REF: SP 304191

ASHLEY

South of the church are the remnants of earthworks of an enclosure castle. There are foundation traces of domestic stone buildings and a keep, which was rectangular with a cylindrical turret, dating from the 13th century. The castle is also known as Ashley Gains, and is privately owned.

LOCATION: HAMPSHIRE
MAP REF: SU 385308

BAMPTON

In around 1315 Aymer de Valence fortified the site of an earlier motte castle and began a quadrangular enclosure with corner towers and turrets and with a vaulted gatehouse. It was demolished before the end of the 18th century although its remains are now incorporated as part of a farmhouse.

LOCATION: OXFORDSHIRE
MAP REF: SP 310031

BANBURY

Built in the early 12th century by the Bishop of Lincoln, the castle was remodelled late in the 13th century into a concentric plan; both curtains had a corner tower, interval towers and were surrounded by ditches.

LOCATION: OXFORDSHIRE
MAP REF: SP 454404

BASING

Basing House is famous for the role it played in the Civil War. It was built in 1535, on the site of a much earlier castle, for the first Marquis of Winchester, Treasurer to Edward VI, Mary I and Elizabeth I. At the time it was the largest private house in the country. When the Civil War broke out it was the fifth Marquis of Winchester who was defending Basing for the king, living up to his family motto "Aymez Loyaulte" (Love Loyalty), and it is said that the maxim was scratched on every window pane of the house. By 1645, despite being attacked by Parliamentarians on several occasions during a two-year-long seige, Basing was the last major Royalist garrison blocking the route to the west. In August that year around 800 Parliamentary troops launched an assault on the stronghold but the garrison held out. Reinforcements were sent and Cromwell himself joined the attacking force: it wasn't until October that a particularly heavy bombardment finally breached the walls and the ensuing ferocious battle overcame the defenders. Basing was razed to the ground although the earthworks and ruins make fascinating viewing. Civil War re-enactments are usually staged here each year.

LOCATION: NR BASINGSTOKE, HAMPSHIRE
MAP REF: SU 663526
OPEN: HAMPSHIRE COUNTY COUNCIL: APR– SEP; WED–SUN PM

BENINGTON

Raised as a motte castle early in the 12th century, it is encircled by a wide and deep dry moat. In the mid-12th century a small stone tower was erected on the motte, demolished on Henry II's orders in about 1176. The gardens are open for part of the year.

LOCATION: HERTFORDSHIRE
MAP REF: TL 296236

BERKELEY

A motte castle was first built on this rising ground, which overlooks the plains between the Severn and the Cotswolds, by William FitzOsbern, one of William's commanders at Hastings. In the 1100s the castle site became the property of Robert FitzHarding, a supporter of Henry II and Provost of Bristol, and he was granted permission to build a stone castle here. His huge shell keep, unusual in that it surrounds the motte, rather than perching on top, is one of the oldest surviving parts of the castle. Berkeley is famous as the site of the incarceration and murder of Edward II in 1327 as the result of a plot by his wife, Isabella of France, and Roger Mortimer. The castle was remodelled in the 14th century and is still in the possession of direct descendants of the FitzHardings. Only superficially damaged in the Civil War, Berkeley Castle remains intact as a stately family home and retains many of its early features. Visit the website for further information (www.berkeley-castle.com).

LOCATION: GLOUCESTERSHIRE
MAP REF: ST 685989
OPEN: PRIVATE: EASTER; MAY–SEP TUE–SUN; OCT SUN

Arundel

A drawing of Arundel Castle in 1783 by James Lambert. Artefacts and paintings from the magnificent collection amassed by 'the Collector Earl' in the 17th century are displayed inside the castle. Thomas, the 14th Earl of Arundel, was a patron of artists such as Inigo Jones, Rubens and van Dyck. He left England at the outbreak of the Civil War and never returned. Arundel was slighted in 1654 and left more or less a ruin until the 18th century when restoration work began.

At first sight, Arundel is a neo-Gothic Victorian castle, an impression created by the monumental restoration and rebuilding project started here at the end of the 19th century. But much of Arundel's Norman and medieval inheritance still exists in its palatial structure.

This castle's origins go back to the earliest years of the Conquest when Roger de Montgomery was created Earl of Arundel. De Montgomery's only legacy at Arundel now is the motte, which, at over 30m (100ft), dominates the centre of the site and would have first been topped with timber fortifications which were replaced less than a century later with stone. The lowest part of the inner gatehouse and an adjacent stretch of curtain wall (c.1070) are remnants of these early stone defences. The rest of the curtain, built of local flint and enclosing the whole site, was erected in stages between the 12th and 13th centuries. Henry I's widow, Adeliza of Louvain and her new husband, William d'Albini, were responsible for the windowless stone keep built on the motte in 1138 (Matilda stayed here when she came from France to claim the English throne from Stephen). It was under Henry II's aegis that the medieval fortress was further enhanced.

From that time the castle and lands at Arundel descended directly and, more or less, without interruption from the 12th century through a line of d'Albinis, Fitzalans and Howards. Sometimes perilously, the Howard name has been up among the 'movers and shakers' of the day since Tudor times and, as staunch Roman Catholics, the family can boast a saint and two cardinals among their ancestors. The Catholic Fitzalan Chapel, founded in the 14th century, is, unusually, part of a structure that also serves as the Protestant parish church, the two parts divided by a glass wall. Famous for the artistry of the ancient noble tombs, this chapel is still the burial place of the Dukes of Norfolk.

Besieged twice, Arundel was badly damaged during the Civil War and slighted a decade later. Repairs weren't initiated until the 18th century when the 11th Duke, a friend of the Prince Regent and keen amateur architect, began the reconstruction. He created the park and built

Hiorne's Tower, though the main survivor and highlight of his works is the mahogany-lined library, considered one of England's most important interiors from that period. However, it wasn't until the last years of the 19th century that the castle was brought to its current magnificence. The 15th Duke of Norfolk employed the architect and antiquarian, Charles Alban Buckler, to carry out extensive rebuilding and refurbishment. The castle they created remains an affirmation of the finest Victorian craftsmanship incorporated with nearly a thousand years of the history of one of the greatest peerages in the land.

Arundel Castle, standing proud above the River Arun, follows much the same plan as Windsor, with a central motte and two baileys to the north and south. Since Richard III's reign the castle has been the seat of the Dukes of Norfolk, the premier dukedom of England. Along with that title comes the hereditary office of Earl Marshal of England, charging the holder with control of state ceremonial occasions and the headship of the College of Arms.

BERKHAMSTED

A visit to Berkhamsted Castle offers an excellent opportunity to see how a typical 11th-century motte castle looked (without its wooden tower and palisading), and how some motte castles were converted to stone. Both motte and bailey were surrounded by a wet moat, giving the appearance of a castle standing in a lake. Outside the moat is a rampart, almost completely encircled by another moat.

The motte castle belonged to the Conqueror's half-brother Robert of Mortain. By the 12th century it was in the hands of the Crown but was leased and remained in use under various owners until the end of the 15th or early 16th century. Thomas Becket lived here from about 1155–65 and it is thought that he raised the shell enclosure. In 1216 Prince Louis of France besieged and captured Berkhamsted. King John's widow was allowed to live here, and the castle was also used to confine King John of France after his capture at the Battle of Poitiers in 1356.

LOCATION: HERTFORDSHIRE
MAP REF: SP 996083
OPEN: ENGLISH HERITAGE: OPEN ACCESS

BISHOP'S STORTFORD

Sometimes known as Waytemore Castle, Bishop's Stortford began as a motte castle. A rectangular tower was built on the motte top early in the 12th century. The castle was improved in King John's reign, and a licence to crenellate was granted some time in the mid-1300s. The site is acessible.

LOCATION: HERTFORDSHIRE
MAP REF: TK 490215

BLETCHINGLEY

An early enclosure of earthworks, fortified in the 12th century by the addition of a rectangular tower. The castle was associated with Thomas Becket and the powerful de Clare family. It was also besieged and taken by royal forces in the wars between Henry III and his barons in the 1260s.

LOCATION: SURREY
MAP REF: TQ 323506

BOARSTALL TOWER

Boarstall House was demolished in the late 18th century but its medieval gatehouse remains. John De Haudlo built the gatehouse in the very early 14th century, both to impress and as a form of defence. Garrisoned by the Royalists in the Civil War, the castle was surrended after a seige. The gatehouse had been updated for use as a banqueting pavilion or hunting lodge.

LOCATION: NR AYLESBURY, BUCKINGHAMSHIRE
MAP REF: SO 624143
OPEN: NATIONAL TRUST: LIMITED OPENING

BODIAM, SUSSEX

LOCATION: ROBERTSBRIDGE, EAST SUSSEX
MAP REF: TQ 785256
OPEN: NATIONAL TRUST: DAILY
SEE PAGE: 42

BRAMBER

Fragments remain of the buildings here, which began in the 1070s as a motte inside a D-shaped bailey. A stone curtain was added in the 12th century with a square-plan gatehouse, and excavations have revealed the existence of buildings inside the curtain. Rebuilt in the 14th century, subsidence saw its ruination in the 16th century.

LOCATION: NR STEYNING, WEST SUSSEX
MAP REF: TQ 185107
OPEN: ENGLISH HERITAGE: OPEN ACCESS

BRIGHTWELL

The mound of an early 12th-century motte castle can be seen near the village church, and outlines of a moat have been seen from the air.

LOCATION: BERKSHIRE
MAP REF: SI 578908

BRIMPSFIELD

There are some fragments on the site of a 13th-century castle here; it was destroyed by Edward II in the 14th century. It has not been possible to determine the shape.

LOCATION: GLOUCESTERSHIRE
MAP REF: SO 940127

BROUGHTON

Broughton is essentially a 16th-century house surrounded by a broad wet moat with some 14th-century military remains, such as towers and battlements. During the early part of the Civil War, the castle was used for clandestine meetings of the opponents of Charles I.

LOCATION: OXFORDSHIRE
MAP REF: SP 418382

BUCKINGHAM

A church now sits on the levelled site of a mid-12th-century motte on the north side of the Ouse in Buckingham. This may have been a castle held by the Giffard family and was probably demolished at the beginning of the 13th century.

LOCATION: BUCKINGHAMSHIRE
MAP REF: SP 695337

CARISBROOKE

Carisbrooke was a fairly elaborate castle in its time. It started as a very early Norman motte castle built around 1070 by William FitzOsbern. Stonework was probably first added in the 12th century; the castle has a polygonal keep. One of its most notable features today is the gatehouse, dating from the 14th century. Besieged in 1377 by a French commando force, Carisbrooke was also an important artillery fort in the 16th century. Today the castle is most famous as the place where Charles I was held after he escaped from Hampton Court.

LOCATION: NR NEWPORT, ISLE OF WIGHT
MAP REF: SZ 486877
OPEN: ENGLISH HERITAGE: DAILY

CASTLETHORPE

A motte castle with two baileys was raised here in the 12th century but besieged and destroyed in 1215–16. In 1292 William Beauchamp was granted a licence to crenellate a wall round a house and garden, which appears to have stood near the castle site; some of the earthworks still remain.

LOCATION: HANSLOPE, BUCKINGHAMSHIRE
MAP REF: SP 798446

CHICHESTER

A very early motte castle was built here by Roger de Montgomery, one of the Conqueror's commanders c.1066–7. It seems that King John's order to demolish it was ignored by Philip d'Aubigny; the order was repeated by Henry III and carried out in 1217. The Franciscans built a priory on the site of the bailey, and remains of the original castle can be seen in Priory Park.

LOCATION: WEST SUSSEX
MAP REF: SU 863051

DEDDINGTON

Deddington Castle was a 12th-century earthwork double enclosure. Excavations revealed that it had stone buildings inside its structure from various dates. Piers Gaveston, Edward II's favourite, was held briefly at Deddington in 1312 before he was taken to Warwick Castle dungeons and his execution. There is little to see today other than extensive earthworks which conceal the remains.

LOCATION: OXFORDSHIRE
MAP REF: SP 471316
OPEN: ENGLISH HERITAGE: DAILY

BAYEUX TAPESTRY

This isn't a tapestry at all; it is an embroidery created with wool stitched on to linen and it measures more than 70m (230ft) in length and is 51cm (20in) wide. It is a contemporary record of the events leading up to the Battle of Hastings in 1066, and to what happened during and after the Conquest. It is believed that the Tapestry was commissioned by Bishop Odo, a half-brother of William the Conqueror. It is unclear who actually created this beautiful work of art but the style of the needlework indicates that it was made in England, possibly by nuns. The story the Tapestry tells is certainly from a Norman perspective. Apart from its contemporary propaganda role, it give us a insight to everyday life as well as military and Court events. Armour, clothing and artefacts from the period are depicted in vibrant colours.

The Normans in Brittany before the Conquest

Bodiam

Conjure up an image of a storybook castle and it may well resemble Bodiam. This square fortress, totally surrounded by a broad moat, seems to possess qualities that are both ethereal and monumentally solid: it was built towards the end of the 14th century, when castle design was shifting from serious and spartan towards greater comfort and aesthetics. Bodiam's perfect symmetry, created by stout drum towers at each corner and a postern, gatehouse and square interval towers inserted around the sides, was a curious mix of impenetrable fortress and manorial splendour.

The castle's builder, Sir Edward Dalyngrigge, was a wealthy man: his riches were accrued during the Hundred Years War when he crossed the Channel in 1367 to fight alongside key figures in the long-running conflict with France. At one time he fought under Sir Robert Knollys, whose shield of arms is carved on the postern gate at Bodiam. Later, in the 1380s, as Knight of the Shire of Sussex, Dalyngrigge was a major player among

Access to Bodiam Castle is still across the moat, created by an artificial lake. The museum at Bodiam displays some of the objects found during Lord Curzon's excavations in the early 20th century when he dug out the moat.

the county's gentry. Internal unrest coupled with the belief that the south coast was under imminent threat of attack by the French, led Sir Edward to build a well-defended fortress. He obtained the licence to crenellate his existing mansion in October 1385 but instead chose a different, more strategic site to rebuild near a crossing on the River Rother. Bodiam's defences were effective but relatively simple: the ultra-wide moat was built to counteract mining under defensive walls, and further obstructions included a series of three drawbridges, a powerful barbican and a gatehouse fully equipped with all manner of defensive tricks.

Evidence shows that Bodiam was inhabited in some form up until the 17th century but by late in the 1700s the castle had become a celebrated ivy-clad ruin, inspiration for artists and architects. Still enchanting, Bodiam's complete exterior is largely thanks to the restoration work carried out by Lord Curzon early in the last century.

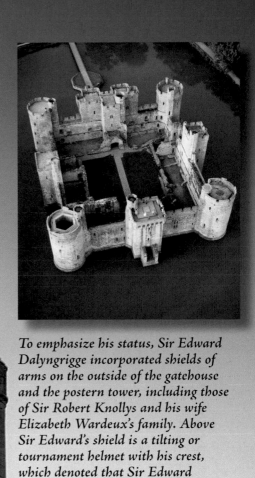

To emphasize his status, Sir Edward Dalyngrigge incorporated shields of arms on the outside of the gatehouse and the postern tower, including those of Sir Robert Knollys and his wife Elizabeth Wardeux's family. Above Sir Edward's shield is a tilting or tournament helmet with his crest, which denoted that Sir Edward could participate in tournaments.

DONNINGTON

This enclosure castle with an added gatehouse tower was built in the 14th century; its greatest days were during the Civil War when the garrison defending it on behalf of Charles I held out for nearly two years against Parliamentary forces. The Civil War earthworks remain.

The castle stood on a high spur over the old London–Bath road and above the River Lambourne. The enclosure was a rectangle with six flanking towers (four cylindrical and two square), inside which were ranges of buildings that used the enclosure walls as their outside walls. The gatehouse is the sole feature of the original castle, for which a licence to crenellate was granted in 1386 to Richard de Abberbury Chamberlain to Richard II's queen, Anne of Bohemia.

LOCATION: NR NEWBURY, BERKSHIRE
MAP REF: SU 461691
OPEN: ENGLISH HERITAGE: OPEN ACCESS

DYMOCK

Traces of a motte castle, probably of the 12th century, have been found in the village. It is known as Castle Tump.

LOCATION: GLOUCESTERSHIRE
MAP REF: SO 711293

FARINGDON

An earthwork enclosure castle was built at Faringdon c.1144, by Robert, Earl of Gloucester, a supporter of Empress Mathilda, but was destroyed by King Stephen a year or two later. There is a mound known locally as the 'Clump', which may be the original earthworks.

LOCATION: OXFORDSHIRE
MAP REF: SU 297957

FARNHAM

On the summit of the mound at Farnham is a stone platform, all that remains above ground of the square, stone great tower that originally stood here, probably built c.1138. It was pulled down on Henry II's orders in 1155. The castle belonged to the Bishop of Winchester, Henry of Blois, but was seized and slighted by Henry II. The bishop rebuilt it a few years later, but in a different form. He encircled the mound with a substantial shell wall up to about 3m (10 ft) thick, with the gatehouse and buttress turrets built in. Garderobe chutes were inserted in the wall and buildings were ranged round the inside. Farnham was attacked during the Civil War and was slighted by the Parliamentarians but it remained a residence of the Bishops of Winchester until the early 20th century. Domestic buildings were added within the castle grounds from the 13th century, and today it is still a mix of the fortified and residential as well as a reminder of the power of the Bishops of Winchester.

LOCATION: SURREY
MAP REF: SU 839474
OPEN: ENGLISH HERITAGE (CASTLE KEEP): APR–SEP SAT–SUN

GLOUCESTER

Although nothing remains of this motte castle of the Conqueror's reign, interesting evidence of its history survives in medieval documents.

A 14th-century sketch
The castle was extended during the reigns of Henry II and III, including a great tower built around 1112. A bridge across the River Severn led to a barbican in the outer wall. Further works were carried out in the 13th, 14th and 15th centuries.

LOCATION: GLOUCESTERSHIRE
MAP REF: SO 828185

GUILDFORD

Guildford Castle keep was probably built by King Stephen and if so, would make it his only known surviving stone building. The original motte and bailey castle was founded just after the Conquest and Guildford became a favoured royal residence and hunting lodge. During Henry III's reign it was one of the most luxurious palaces in England. In 1381 the castle was a clearing house for prisoners taken during the Peasants' Revolt.

Today, the castle consists of a stone keep on top of a motte, surrounded by an outer bailey which has some of its original wall, and a fine 13th-century archway. The keep underwent major conservation work in 2003 when floors and ceilings were restored, and it now houses a museum. The grounds are an added attraction.

LOCATION: SURREY
MAP REF: SU 999495
OPEN: CASTLE: APR–SEP DAILY; OCT, NOV, MAR SAT–SUN; CLOSED DEC–FEB. GROUNDS: ALL YEAR

HASTINGS

Two timber motte and bailey castles were built by the invading Norman army between the time they landed at Pevensey at the end of September 1066 and before the Battle of Hastings: it is thought that they brought pre-fabricated wooden structures from France. The Conqueror quickly moved most of his troops east to Hastings – better for both communication and defence.

Hastings was rebuilt in stone in c.1070, was dismantled by John, rebuilt later by Henry III and dismantled again by Edward II. It was re-erected, but during the 14th century coastal erosion began to claim the buildings. It became completely ruinous after the Dissolution in the 16th century. The remains were repaired in the 19th century. The *1066 Story*, an audiovisual presentation, is open most of the year.

LOCATION: EAST SUSSEX
MAP REF: TQ 822095
OPEN: HASTINGS BOROUGH COUNCIL: DAILY (CLOSED 2 WEEKS IN JAN)

Sir Roger Fiennes, a veteran of the wars in France, was granted a licence to build and crenellate a castle at Herstmonceux in 1441. One of the first to be constructed of brick, it follows a quadrangular plan, with greensand-stone dressings, octagonal towers in each corner and a massive, grand gatehouse, encircled by a wide lake-like moat. Built towards the end of the era of defensive military strongholds, Herstmonceux is more of a great fortified mansion or hall, the onus on style and comfort rather than strength. Fortuitously, the castle never came under attack and suffered little damage in this way, but it was abandoned and its interior gutted in the 18th century. Restored to its former glory in the first half of the 20th century, Herstmonceux became the Royal Greenwich Observatory in 1946. It is now a study centre.

LOCATION: HAILSHAM, EAST SUSSEX
MAP REF: TW 646104
OPEN: PRIVATE. TEL: 01323 834457 FOR TOUR INFORMATION. ELIZABETHAN GARDENS AND GROUNDS: MID-APR TO MID-OCT (CLOSED 30 JUL)

HERTFORD

It is likely that Hertford began as a motte castle quite early in the Norman period as a constable was appointed by the Conqueror, but the earliest documentary evidence of work on Hertford is 1171–74. The grand 15th-century gatehouse and the flint-and-stone curtain wall are the only substantial legacies of this important castle, which became a royal palace in 1304. Elizabeth I spent much of her childhood here.

LOCATION: HERTFORDSHIRE
MAP REF: TL 325125

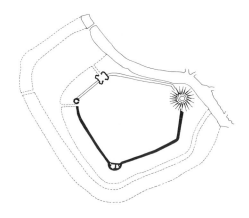

HINTON WALDRIST

A motte castle was erected here late in the 11th century. It was the childhood home of Mary de Bohun, wife of King Henry IV.

LOCATION: BERKSHIRE
MAP REF: SU 376991

KNEPP

This early 12th-century motte castle received a great tower of sandstone, probably in the time of Henry II. The castle is believed to have belonged to the de Braose family.

LOCATION: NR WEST GRIINSTEAD, WEST SUSSEX
MAP REF: TQ 163209

Lewes, one of the very few castles with two mottes associated with one bailey (*see also* Lincoln, page 66), was raised with defensive earthworks and a dry moat in 1069–70, by William de Warenne, the Conqueror's Chief Justiciar and later Earl of Surrey. At the time the River Ouse was navigable, rendering Lewes a useful port as well as an important river crossing, and Warenne made the site his main seat and headquarters (he was buried in Lewes Priory, along with his wife Gundrada). The first wooden castle here was said to have been built on the north-eastern Brack Mount, but defensive priorities shifted so the 12th-century shell keep, with its 13th-century octagonal towers and the magnificent 14th-century barbican are on or near the more westerly mound. Parts of the bailey wall and the

Norman gatehouse still exist. The barbican at Lewes is one of the finest in the country – built of knapped flint, it has corbelled round towers on the corners and a machicolated parapet over the centre pointed arch. From the top there are views over the site of the Battle of Lewes, fought in May 1264, when Simon de Montfort and the barons defeated Henry III and occupied the town. Lewes Castle declined in importance from the 15th century, and over following years became little more than an admirable ruin. In 1846 the London and Brighton South Coast Railway constructed a tunnel, which is still in use, under the bailey. The barbican houses a museum.

LOCATION: HIGH STREET, LEWES, EAST SUSSEX
MAP REF: TQ 415101
OPEN: SUSSEX PAST: DAILY (CLOSED MON IN JAN)

LYDNEY

The remains of a Norman stone castle were excavated in the 1930s in Little Camp, beside Lydney Park. The work showed the castle's plan was pentagonal with uneven sides and had a rectangular tower. Next to the tower was a gateway.

LOCATION: GLOUCESTERSHIRE
MAP REF: SO 617025

MIDDLETON STONEY

A motte castle of about 1140 was erected at Middleton Stoney; the date is authenticated by some pottery discovered in excavations. The earliest documentary evidence is of later date, 1215–16, including an order from John to dismantle the castle.

LOCATION: NR BICESTER, OXFORDSHIRE
MAP REF: SP 534233

MISERDEN

Built in the 12th century near the river, the motte castle here was improved with stonework. There was a shell enclosure of probably the early 13th century. The castle deteriorated, and by the 14th century it seems not to have been worth restoring.

LOCATION: GLOUCESTERSHIRE
MAP REF: SO 945092

MONTFICHET

A castle with a tower on a low motte was raised here in 1066–7 by the Conqueror, soon after he had been crowned in Westminster Abbey. It was demolished in the 13th century.

LOCATION: ADDLE HILL, CITY OF LONDON
MAP REF: CITY OF LONDON

ODIHAM

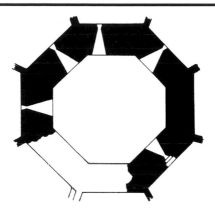

One of King John's favourite castles, all that remains is the shell of the octagonal great tower built between 1207–12. It was from here that John set out to Runnymede to sign the Magna Carta in 1215. The following year, Odiham was besieged and captured by Louis, Dauphin of France. Henry III gave the castle to his sister and it became home to the de Montfort family when Eleanor married Simon de Montfort in 1238. David II, King of Scotland, spent some of his 11 years' exile in England at Odiham.

LOCATION: NORTH WARNBOROUGH, ODIHAM, HAMPSHIRE
MAP REF: SU 726519
OPEN: HAMPSHIRE COUNTY COUNCIL: OPEN AT REASONABLE TIMES – ACCESSIBLE (BY WALKERS ONLY) FROM BASINGTOKE CANAL

OXFORD

Built in 1071 by Robert d'Oilly, the motte at Oxford was later crowned with a decagonal concentric shell wall. The extant square tower is dated before 1100 and known as St George's Tower: it is stepped inwards at several places up its height and has very few openings of any kind.

LOCATION: OXFORD
MAP REF: SP 510061

The Barons' Revolt and Magna Carta

John became king in 1199 and was immediately embroiled in a war to retain his territories in France. He launched several battles that failed and needed to tax his nobles ever more heavily to finance his campaigns. Finally the barons refused to pay taxes to fund overseas battles and they marched to London. John feared that they would attack him and his castles and agreed to accede to their demands to achieve peace. The barons were persuaded to widen their charter to include all citizens and the Church. Magna Carta was signed in June 1215 and was the first time that the rights of the king's subjects were enshrined in law.

PEVENSEY

The Romans constructed one of their coastal forts on the Saxon shore at Pevensey early in the 4th century CE. Called Anderita (or Anderida), it was an elliptical enclosure with flanking D-ended bastions and is one of the largest surviving such examples in Britain, with major parts of its masonry still in relatively good condition.

It was here that William of Normandy landed with his invading force in September 1066. As soon as they landed, William sheltered his forces inside the remains of this fortress. Once the South East of England was under his control, the Conqueror granted Pevensey to Robert, Count of Mortain, who raised a castle in the east end of the fort using a section of the original Roman curtain wall: the remainder of the Roman enclosure became the outer bailey. An unusual Great Tower was constructed in c.1100 but this is in ruins. Undergoing periods of development over the next 300 years, Pevensey fell into disrepair by the beginning of the 16th century. The receding coast meant that the shoreline castle was now inland and much of its importance was lost. It was re-armed during the threat of invasion by the Spanish in the late 16th century and used as an observation and command post in World War II. Events are staged in the summer.

LOCATION: EAST SUSSEX
MAP REF: TQ 645048
OPEN: ENGLISH HERITAGE: APR–SEP DAILY; OCT–MAR SAT–SUN

LIFE IN EARLY CASTLES

THE FIRST NORMAN CASTLES IN BRITAIN WERE OF WOOD, TYPICALLY ON TOP OF AN ARTIFICIAL MOUND SURROUNDED BY A DITCH AND PALISADE. THESE MOTTE (THE MOUND AND ITS BUILDING) AND BAILEY (THE ENCLOSURE) CASTLES WERE BUILT IN THEIR HUNDREDS ALL OVER THE COUNTRY. MANY CAN STILL BE SEEN AS OVERGROWN MOUNDS WITH NO TRACE OF ANY IDENTIFIABLE BUILDINGS. SOME ARE IN THIS BOOK, BUT WE HAVE NOT INCLUDED THOSE WHICH EITHER CANNOT BE EXPLORED FOR VARIOUS REASONS, OR THOSE OF WHICH SO LITTLE IS KNOWN THAT NOTHING USEFUL CAN BE SAID.

These early castles were essential for the invading Normans. They were where they kept their armouries and treasuries, they were where they retreated to at time of need or for rest, and they were the base from where they controlled their surrounding lands.

Essentially offensive and defensive structures, castles were also where the Norman lords and their families lived. It is this dual role of home and fortress that sets castles apart from all other buildings. The lord knew that he had to make his castle as impregnable as possible, but he also had to live there, and he wanted a degree of comfort, not just for its own sake but to show that he

Stories and poetry helped to disguise the often stark reality of life in early castles, and tales of King Arthur and the Knights of the Round Table were hugely popular. This picture shows the first kiss of Lancelot and Guinevere, and is from The Lancelot Romance.

N:PRANDIVM· ET·HIC·EPISCOPVS·CIBV·ET· POTV·BE NE DIC IT·

had wealth, power and status. In other words, most lords did not want to be thought of as violent aggressors lurking behind dark defences only to emerge for conflict.

But the fact is that the earliest castles would have been cheerless by our standards: chill, damp and with few furnishings. The two best places to be were the lord's own chamber, where the best furnishings and fittings would be found, and the hall, where everyone ate and where many would sleep, because here fires were kept for cooking and for warmth.

As the Normans consolidated their conquest, so they became richer and so they could begin to replace their wooden castles with castles of stone. These were more secure (wood was comparitively easy to burn down) and could be more comfortable, with better and bigger ranges of rooms.

The Bayeux Tapestry gives an insight into everyday life in the mid-11th century. Here, a banquet is hosted by the Bishop of Bayeux, Odo, half brother of William the Conqueror. Odo commisssioned the Bayeux Tapestry.

Castle life included much military training, both as essential practice, and to pass the time. Here, five longbowmen are undergoing target training, with their instructor pointing to the butts. One archer has already scored a bullseye.

PORTCHESTER

Another Norman castle (see also Pevensey) was built within the confines of a late 3rd-century Roman Saxon shore fort at Portchester (or Portus Adurni). Much of it is still standing, reputedly having the most complete Roman walls to exist in northern Europe. The Norman castle is a quadrangular enclosure with a great tower, the enclosure's north and west sides provided by the old Roman wall and the tower built into the corner. A moat was cut outside the east and south enclosure walls. The tower, still existing, was built about c. 1100 during the reign of Henry I with 12th- and 14th-century additions: it was used to house prisoners of war during the Napoleonic Wars in the 18th and 19th centuries.

A stragically important site, Portchester was well used: Henry I was a frequent visitor and both Edward III in the 14th century and Henry the V in the next century assembled their armies here before setting out to do battle in France. In the interim, Richard II transformed part of the castle into a small palace in the 14th century. Porchester's importance declined in the 15th century although it was used in the Civil War by the Parliamentarians to billet thousands of troops and to detain prisoners of war when needed. An Augustinian priory was founded in the south-east corner of the Roman fort in the 1130s, and the church remains.

LOCATION: NR FAREHAM, HAMPSHIRE
MAP REF: SU 625046
OPEN: ENGLISH HERITAGE: DAILY

READING

Traces of a motte castle thought to have been built in the grounds of the abbey in the mid-12th century may be the remains of Reading Castle, recorded as destroyed by Henry II in about 1154.

LOCATION: BERKSHIRE
MAP REF: SU 718736

REIGATE

Built by the Earl of Surrey in William II's reign, Reigate was an enclosure castle with a deep surrounding ditch. It must have been enlarged and improved with stone, as the castle was occupied by Royalists in 1648.

LOCATION: SURREY
MAP REF: TQ 252504

ST BRIAVEL'S

An enclosure castle of the 12th century, St Briavel's received a square great tower probably in the time of Henry II, which is recorded as having finally collapsed in ruins in 1752. St Briavel's still has its huge, twin cylindrical-towered gatehouse, built by Edward I, c.1292–3, at a cost of nearly £500. Situated within the Forest of Dean, in the 13th century it served as an arsenal for iron cross-bow bolts which were manufactured at the iron forges operating in the forest. St Briavel's is now a youth hostel.

LOCATION: GLOUCESTERSHIRE
MAP REF: SS 559046
OPEN: ENGLISH HERITAGE: DAILY PM

SHIRBURN

This was a brick-built fortified manor house, begun c.1380. It was quadrangular, with cylindrical towers on the corners and a gate-tower. Surrounded by a moat fed by local springs, the castle was greatly altered in the 18th and 19th centuries.

LOCATION: NR WATLINGTON, OXFORDSHIRE
MAP REF: SU 697960

SOUTHAMPTON

A motte castle was probably built here in the early 12th century. From the accession of Henry II, Southampton Castle, because of the extreme importance of its strategic position on Southampton Water, is continually mentioned in Exchequer records up to the 16th century. Little remains of the castle above ground today, but the town walls are superb.

LOCATION: HAMPSHIRE
MAP REF: SU 420110

SOUTH MYMMS

This was a motte castle built by Geoffrey de Mandeville c.1140–2. He may have had permission from King Stephen or from Stephen's rival, Matilda. It stands on a low spur and consists of a bailey.

LOCATION: SOUTH MIMMS, HERTFORDSHIRE
MAP REF: TL 229026

SWERFORD

Earthworks of an 11th-century motte castle can still be seen here. Excavations revealed pottery of the mid-12th century. The castle was raised by Robert d'Oilly who had been granted leave by William I. This is the same d'Oilly who built castles at Ascot d'Oilly and Oxford.

LOCATION: NR CHIPPING NORTON, OXFORDSHIRE
MAP REF: SP 373312

THERFIELD

A motte castle of the civil war in King Stephen's reign, Therfield was dismantled after the accession of Henry II. Excavations in the 20th century showed that the rampart that ran round the bailey had been first lined with clay and then clad with wooden palisading.

LOCATION: HERTFORDSHIRE
MAP REF: TL 335373

THORNBURY

Said to be the last major fortified manor house to be built in England, Thornbury was raised in the early 1500s by Edward Stafford, Duke of Buckingham. The house was never completed. Henry VIII arrested Stafford on a manufactured treason charge, although in reality he feared Stafford's royal lineage. The duke was executed, and his estates attainted. Thornbury was restored in the 19th century and is now a hotel.

LOCATION: GLOUCESTERSHIRE
MAP REF: ST 633907
OPEN: HOTEL AND RESTAURANT GUESTS ONLY

TOWER OF LONDON

LOCATION: CITY OF LONDON
MAP REF: TQ 336804
OPEN: HISTORIC ROYAL PALACES; DAILY
SEE PAGE: 52

WALLINGFORD

This appears to have been a very early motte castle of c.1071. It was refortified during Stephen's reign, when the king tried and failed to take the castle. An important medieval fortress, John made his formal submission to Pope Innocent III here in 1213, and Edward I (then Prince Edward) was held prisoner by Simon de Montfort in the 1260s. Later, it was a summer residence for Henry VI in the 15th century. Slighted in the Civil War, very little remains of the site.

LOCATION: OXFORDSHIRE
MAP REF: SU 610897

WESTON TURVILLE

There are some remains of a motte castle built here, probably in the 12th century. They are in the grounds of Weston Turville Manor where, in the 14th century, a fortified manor house was erected by the de Moleyns family. That building was later dismantled.

LOCATION: NR AYLESBURY, BUCKINGHAMSHIRE
MAP REF: SP 859104

WHITCHURCH

A 12th-century motte castle here was given stonework later in the century, possibly a great tower. In 1925 sites of drawbridges were discovered, which suggests that this was a castle of some size. It is also called Bolebec Castle and earthworks survive.

LOCATION: BUCKINGHAMSHIRE
MAP REF: SP 799207

WINCHESTER

Winchester Castle developed from 1067 until the beginning of the 14th century when, badly damaged by fire, it was more or less abandoned. Its ruins were finally demolished after the Civil War and only the splendid great hall, started by Henry III in 1222, survives.

As capital of England from Saxon times until the end of the 12th century, Winchester was a favoured royal residence. King John spent a memorable Christmas there in 1206: 1,500 chickens, 5,000 eggs, 20 oxen, 100 sheep and 100 pigs were laid on for the festivities.

The castle was captured by Louis of France in 1216, and Henry III (sometimes known as Henry of Winchester) was born at the castle and baptized in the cathedral; he spent about £10,000 on improvements and restoration. He built the surviving great hall on the site of an earlier structure; it still houses a huge Arthurian Round Table, built for Edward I and painted for Henry VIII.

Nearby was one of the great medieval buildings of Europe, the ecclesiastical castle-palace at Wolvesey, built by Henry of Blois, Bishop of Winchester, c.1129–c.1171. It was a quadrangular castle with a square great tower and a great hall. Mary I and Philip of Spain held their wedding breakfast here after marrying in the cathedral. The 12th-century palace was ruinous after the Civil War but is worth visiting.

LOCATION: WINCHESTER, HAMPSHIRE
MAP REF: GREAT HALL: SU 477294;
WOLVESEY: SU 484291
OPEN: HAMPSHIRE COUNTY COUNCIL (GREAT HALL): DAILY.
ENGLISH HERITAGE (WOLVESEY): APR–SEP DAILY

WINDSOR

LOCATION: WINDSOR AND MAIDENHEAD
MAP REF: SU 970770
OPEN: ROYAL RESIDENCES: DAILY (SHORT CLOSURES TEL 01753 831118 FOR DETAILS)
SEE PAGE: 54

Tower of London

The most famous of England's castles was begun soon after the Conquest and built with one purpose: to overawe the inhabitants of the country's most powerful city. After the Battle of Hastings, the defeated English army had fled to London, and it was imperative for the Conqueror to act quickly to secure the city: he immediately ordered the construction of a castle on a site on the north bank of the River Thames, in the south-east corner of the Roman city walls. By the 1070s the first wooden buildings were being replaced with a huge stone tower. Once finished, its fearsome outline dominated the landscape of London and, as intended, its Anglo-Saxon population. Nothing like this had been seen in Britain before.

The noted castle builder and architect, Gundulf, Bishop of Rochester is thought to have designed the White Tower (as it became known after Henry III had it painted white): he also built the great castles at Rochester and Colchester. This massive, intimidating structure was a model for many other great towers and castles that have played a part in Britain's history.

For nearly a thousand years, the White Tower, William the Conqueror's mighty keep, has remained the focus of England's most famous castle. Within its walls, in 1399, Henry Bolingbroke forced the abdication of Richard II and became King Henry IV; Anne Boleyn was crowned in 1533; Henry VIII's daughter Mary was betrothed by proxy to Philip of Spain in 1554. Today the White Tower houses displays from the Royal Armouries' collection.

ENTRY TO THE TRAITORS GATE

The river entrance was created by Edward I below St Thomas's Tower to replace a watergate inserted by Henry III. A poignant place, it is known as Traitors' Gate because it was often where prisoners accused of treason entered the castle to be incarcerated and put to death. The Archbishop of Canterbury, Thomas Cranmer, Queen Anne Boleyn and Sir Thomas More were unfortunate enough to enter the Tower in this way. In the 14th century Edward III put in another, private, watergate below the Cradle Tower.

By the middle of the 14th century the fortress had taken on the basic concentric plan that still exists today. It was vastly extended during Henry III's reign and again by Edward I, the two monarchs spending the equivalent of millions of pounds on improvements. When Edward died in 1307, the Tower of London was England's most powerful castle and a lavish royal palace.

Roles for the site were expanding: since Henry III's time it was used as a prison, and Edward I set up the Royal Mint here (which remained until early in the 19th century). He also initiated the castle's function as a Treasury (the Crown Jewels were moved from Westminster Abbey in 1303) and as a place for storing records. Perhaps the strangest inhabitants were the exotic animals kept in the Royal Menagerie: as early as 1255 an elephant, presented to Henry III by Louis of France, lived in a purpose-built elephant house at the Tower. At one point, a 'white' bear was kept and taken for regular swims in the Thames.

One of England's greatest castle builders, Edward III, instigated only fairly minor changes although he began to build the Wharf, which was completed by his successor, Richard II: a king who had to take refuge in the Tower when rebels wreaked havoc during the Peasants' Revolt in 1381. The stage for many of the pivotal events of the 15th century, the castle's sinister side was illustrated by the execution of Henry VI in 1471 and the supposed murders of the young Edward V and his brother in 1483.

Then, with the accession of the Tudor monarchs, came the palace's last days as a royal residence. Instead the focus shifted towards its role as prison and place of execution; the turbulence of the Reformation ensured that a large number of political and religious dissenters were interned at the Tower, a situation that continued into the 16th century.

PRISONERS IN THE TOWER

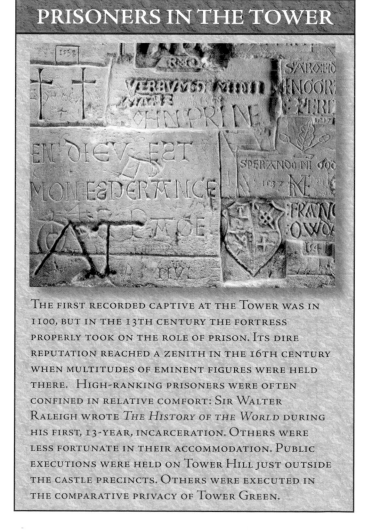

THE FIRST RECORDED CAPTIVE AT THE TOWER WAS IN 1100, BUT IN THE 13TH CENTURY THE FORTRESS PROPERLY TOOK ON THE ROLE OF PRISON. ITS DIRE REPUTATION REACHED A ZENITH IN THE 16TH CENTURY WHEN MULTITUDES OF EMINENT FIGURES WERE HELD THERE. HIGH-RANKING PRISONERS WERE OFTEN CONFINED IN RELATIVE COMFORT: SIR WALTER RALEIGH WROTE *THE HISTORY OF THE WORLD* DURING HIS FIRST, 13-YEAR, INCARCERATION. OTHERS WERE LESS FORTUNATE IN THEIR ACCOMMODATION. PUBLIC EXECUTIONS WERE HELD ON TOWER HILL JUST OUTSIDE THE CASTLE PRECINCTS. OTHERS WERE EXECUTED IN THE COMPARATIVE PRIVACY OF TOWER GREEN.

Windsor

Windsor dates from c.1080 when the Conqueror raised a motte fortress close to a royal hunting forest (now Windsor Great Park) as part of a string of defences around London. The layout of the fortress was a central motte with two flanking baileys; Arundel Castle has a similar plan, developed by the Normans for fortifications which were built on a ridge. Both Henry I and Henry II began to expand the castle and stone was introduced to replace the wooden fortifications: the Round Tower, altered but still extant on top of the Conqueror's motte, dates from 1170.

It was during the reign of the great castle-building monarch, Edward III in the 14th century, that the castle at Windsor began its transformation into one of the world's most iconic royal palaces. Edward's massive Gothic architectural plan included the College of St George in the Lower Ward and a suite of royal apartments in the Upper Ward. He also established the chivalric Order of the Garter, which has always been associated with the castle at Windsor: St George's Chapel, in the Lower Ward, is the Order's spiritual centre. It was Edward IV who began building the Chapel in 1475, and it was completed by Henry VIII in 1528: many British monarchs are buried here including the family of Elizabeth II: her father George VI, the Queen Mother and her sister, Princess Margaret.

Above: The view of the castle from the Thames. Below: The castle from the Great Park, with the Round Tower on the left.

The next major period of development at Windsor was after the Civil War. Charles II and architect Hugh May spent 11 years altering the exterior of the castle and creating a series of splendid baroque state apartments. The Queen's Audience Chamber is perhaps the best preserved of Charles II's interiors although many of the 17th-century baroque features were removed when George III inherited the throne and Windsor became his favourite residence. Work on the castle continued into the 19th century and George IV, with architect Jeffrey Wyatville, continued to transform Windsor in the Gothic Revival style. St George's Hall, used for state banquets, was created by George IV when he joined Edward III's Great Hall and Chapel to make one vast room. Windsor has remained much as it was after George IV carried out his remodelling. Queen Victoria, who used the castle as her principle residence, made few changes although it was during her reign that Windsor entered its heyday. After a severe fire in 1992, damaged rooms were restored to their original designs: rooms that were destroyed have been redesigned in a modern Gothic style. Thus the 20th century also contributed to this royal residence.

King Louis-Philippe of France arriving at Windsor Castle on a state visit on 8 October 1844 (painted by Edouard Pingret). Always an important royal palace, its heyday was during Queen Victoria's reign when the castle was at the centre of the British Empire. Windsor Castle is still a favourite royal residence and a venue for ceremonial state visits.

BACONSTHORPE

A 15th-century fortified manor house built with a flint three-floor gatehouse and quadrangle, Baconsthorpe was partially moated and had a small lake. John Heydon I, who built the inner gatehouse, was a tough and quarrelsome magnate who survived the dangerous sport of backing first one side then the other in the Wars of the Roses. The outer gatehouse was a 16th-century addition. Ruins remain.

LOCATION: NR HOLT, NORFOLK
MAP REF: TG 122383
OPEN: ENGLISH HERITAGE: OPEN ACCESS

BOLINGBROKE

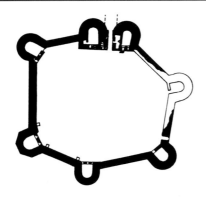

Built in the 1220s by the Earl of Chester, this was the birthplace of Henry IV in 1367. Despite works in the 15th and 16th centuries, the castle was in poor condition before the Civil War. Bolingbroke was held for the king. Excavation revealed low walls and partial towers.

LOCATION: LINCOLNSHIRE
MAP REF: TF 349649
OPEN: HERITAGE LINCOLNSHIRE: DAILY

BOURN

Bourn, an earthwork enclosure with wooden buildings, was erected in the last years of the reign of William the Conqueror and is mentioned in the Domesday Book. The castle was owned by the Picot family. It was demolished in the time of Henry III, and Bourn Hall, now a private clinic, was built across part of the site.

LOCATION: CAMBRIDGESHIRE
MAP REF: TL 322562
OPEN: PRIVATE

BOURNE

An unusual 12th-century motte castle stood here: the mound was inside a bailey surrounded by a ditch and encircled by another ditch, in concentric form. No masonry remains.

LOCATION: LINCOLNSHIRE
MAP REF: TF 0951992

BUCKDEN TOWERS

Buckden was a palace for the bishops of Lincoln in the 13th century. A brick gatehouse, hall, chapel and a great tower, all within a moat and a stone curtain, were added in the 15th century. The buildings remain in use.

LOCATION: NR PETERBOROUGH, CAMBRIDGESHIRE
MAP REF: TL 192677
OPEN: PRIVATE

BUCKENHAM

Extensive earthworks embrace part of today's village. The inner and smaller part is a figure-of-eight site divided by a ditch and with ditching all round. The castle here replaced Old Buckenham Castle, 3km (2 miles) north. In the inner bailey the lower part of a flint rubble cylindrical keep still exists: built c.1140–50, it is the earliest cylindrical great tower in England. Buckenham was demolished in the 1640s.

LOCATION: NEW BUCKENHAM, NORFOLK
MAP REF: TL 084904
OPEN: ACCESSIBLE: CONTACT KEY HOLDER AT LOCAL GARAGE.

BUNGAY

Bungay was built by Hugh Bigod in 1165 on the site of an earlier fortification. Excavations revealed an uncompleted mining gallery under the keep, probably dating from the time that Bigod supported Henry II's son in his unsuccessful 1173–4 revolt. In the 13th century Roger Bigod rebuilt the castle. In the west of the curtain is a pair of twin cylindrical-towered ends flanking an entrance – the remains of his gatehouse.

LOCATION: SUFFOLK
MAP REF: TM 336896
OPEN: BUNGAY CASTLE TRUST: DAILY

BURWELL

This castle, built at the time of Stephen, was excavated in the 1930s. It was raised on the site of a late Roman-British structure. Digging revealed stonework remains of a curtain wall and a gatehouse. The castle was not finished but some fragments remain.

LOCATION: NR CAMBRIDGE, CAMBRIDGESHIRE
MAP REF: TL 587661
OPEN: BURWELL PARISH COUNCIL: OPEN ACCESS

BYTHAM

The mound of a motte castle was built here possibly before 1086 and certainly by 1140. The earthworks contain traces of stonework, but it is not possible to determine the form of the castle.

LOCATION: NR. BOURNE, LINCOLNSHIRE
MAP REF: SK 992186

CAISTER

Caister, built between 1432 and 1446 by a self-made adventurer, Sir John Fastolf, was one of the first major brick buildings in England. Many details of the construction, materials, labour and costs have survived: one of these was a note of an attempt by one mason to overcharge for his work.

The castle has a double enclosure in the form of two quadrangles surrounded entirely by water, but its principal feature was, and still is, the tall, slim, cylindrical great tower: it has five storeys of residential accommodation but is also equipped with machicolated parapet, gun-ports at several levels and constructed of walls more than 1m (4ft) thick. Caister was occupied for a time by the Paston family, whose letters give a remarkable view of country life in the 15th century.

LOCATION: NR GREAT YARMOUTH, NORFOLK
MAP REF: TG 504123
OPEN: SITE: DAILY; MOTOR MUSEUM: MAY–SEP SUN–FRI

CAISTOR LINCOLNSHIRE

A mound near the church is possibly the remnant of a motte castle of the Anarchy (c.1140) – the civil war that followed when Stephen usurped Matilda's throne.

LOCATION: CAISTOR, LINCOLNSHIRE
MAP REF: TA 116012

CAMBRIDGE

A mound and earthworks remain of a medieval castle. The motte was erected c.1068 and houses demolished to make way for it. In the 12th century stonework was added. Edward I extended the buildings, spending £2,630. In the 14th century the castle was 'raided' for stone to build colleges. The castle was slighted in the Civil War.

LOCATION: CAMBRIDGESHIRE
MAP REF: TL 446592
OPEN: LOCAL AUTHORITY: OPEN ACCESS

CASTLE ACRE

CANTERBURY

Raised before 1086, Canterbury was a royal castle for most of its history. Built on the old Roman road between Dover and London, it is likely that this was one of the castles erected by the Conqueror as he headed towards London. It received a substantial great tower of flint rubble with dressings of Caen stone and sandstone and had pilaster buttresses, and two cross-walls inside. Excavations revealed fragments of the great tower. Ruins remain.

LOCATION: KENT
MAP REF: TR 145574
OPEN: LOCAL AUTHORITY: OPEN ACCESS

CARLTON

A motte and some ditching are all that survive from a motte castle, built here possibly in the 12th century by the Bardolph family.

LOCATION: LOUTH, LINCOLNSHIRE
MAP REF: TF 3958352

Castle Acre was raised by William de Warenne soon after the Conquest and was the principal manor among his properties in Norfolk. Extensive excavations at the site show that the first building was a two-storey manor house reinforced in the mid-12th century to construct a keep. The great tower was never finished, though, and a second phase of refortification, where the keep was reduced in size and the outer defences strengthened, was initiated. In later times, the family moved to accommodation in the lower ward. There are visible remains of the west gate: it was probably used by the constable of the castle and seems to have been occupied up to the 14th century although the castle was derelict by 1397. The de Warennes founded a town adjacent to the castle and a Cluniac monastery. The bailey gate is still extant in the village and remains of the monastery are extensive. Substantial earthworks and some stone remain.

LOCATION: SWAFFHAM, NORFOLK
MAP REF: TF 819152
OPEN: ENGLISH HERITAGE: OPEN ACCESS

Castle Rising stands on a large site (5ha/12 acres) with deep Norman man-made ditches and banks. The oval-shaped inner bailey, sandwiched between two smaller outer baileys, contains the foundations of an 11th-century Norman chapel and the extensive remains of the great 'hall' keep which is dated c.1138–40. There are also the ruins of a gatehouse from the same period. Built by William d'Albini II to celebrate his marriage to the widow of Henry I and his consequent acquisition of the Earldom of Sussex, this elegant keep, one of the most important in East Anglia, was one of the most ornate castle/palaces in the country with a noted forebuilding at its east end. For three decades after she was implicated in the murder of Edward II at Berkeley Castle, Castle Rising was the home of Isabella, mother of Edward III. When Isabella died in 1358, the castle passed to her grandson, Edward, the Black Prince. Eventually falling into decline, the site became part of the Howard family estate at the end of the 16th century.

LOCATION: NR KING'S LYNN, NORFOLK
MAP REF: TF 666246
OPEN: ENGLISH HERITAGE: APR–OCT DAILY; NOV–MAR WED–SUN

CHILHAM

This was a great tower castle inside a curtained enclosure surrounded by a ditch built c.1171–5. Henry II took it over as a royal fortress and spent more than £400 on works. The great tower has been partly restored and can be seen from the gardens.

LOCATION: CANTERBURY, KENT
MAP REF: TR 066533

CLARE

This was a motte of the late 11th century with two baileys: a 19th-century railway station was built in one. A polygonal shell enclosure was built round the motte top in the 12th century. Some remains are visible in Clare Park.

LOCATION: SUFFOLK
MAP REF: TL 772452

CLAVERING

The enclosure at Clavering was thought to have been raised before the Conquest at the encouragement of Edward the Confessor: the moat was fed by the River Stort. Earthworks remain on private land.

LOCATION: NR NEWPORT, ESSEX
MAP REF: TL 471320

CLAXTON

This enclosure castle, whose remains consist of a long stretch of wall with six flanking towers, was started in 1333. Traces of a hall, with staircases and upper rooms remain. The ruins are partly surrounded by a moat and the site is private.

LOCATION: NR NORWICH, NORFOLK
MAP REF: TG 335038

COLCHESTER

LOCATION: CASTLE PARK, COLCHESTER, ESSEX
MAP REF: TL 998254
OPEN: COLCHESTER COUNCIL: DAILY
SEE PAGE: 60

COOLING

Cooling Castle was built near Cliffe Marshes in the 1380s to protect the approaches to the Thames. Henry Yevele, the 14th-century architect/master-mason, worked on the castle. Little remains today although the gatehouse is in good condition and can be seen from the road. Cooling was taken by Sir Thomas Wyatt in 1554 during his rebellion against Mary I in protest against her planned marriage to Philip II of Spain.

LOCATION: KENT
MAP REF: TR 755760
OPEN: PRIVATE

DOVER

LOCATION: DOVER, KENT
MAP REF: TR 324419
OPEN: ENGLISH HERITAGE: FEB–OCT DAILY; NOV–JAN THU–MON
SEE PAGE: 62

EATON SOCON

Beside the Ouse, this Norman double enclosure was surrounded with moats filled with water from a diversion of the river, which also operated a watermill. Its origins are uncertain, but by 1156 it was held by the Beauchamp family. Some earthworks remain.

LOCATION: CAMBRIDGESHIRE
MAP REF: TL 173588

ELY

Cherry Hill mound is probably the remnant of the very early motte castle raised by the Conqueror during his campaign against Hereward the Wake.

LOCATION: CAMBRIDGESHIRE
MAP REF: TL 541799

EYE

Eye Castle is a motte and bailey castle built in the 11th century. The mound is about 15m (50ft) tall with some traces of medieval masonry on the motte slopes. A ruined Victorian folly perches on top of the motte. The site is accessible.

LOCATION: SUFFOLK
MAP REF: TM 148738

EYNSFORD

One of the first stone castles, Eynsford was constructed on a low artificial platform of earth originally with a wooden tower. In about 1088, a 2m (6ft) thick curtain of coursed flint rubble was put up around the platform, which was further altered early in the 12th century when the enclosure received stone buildings. The principal building was a rectangular hall with solar c.1130. Remains of the curtain, hall and moat still exist on the site.

LOCATION: KENT
MAP REF: TQ 542658
OPEN: ENGLISH HERITAGE: FEB–NOV DAILY; DEC–JAN WED–SUN

FOLKESTONE

Little evidence exists of the enclosure castle erected on this site, excavated at the end of the 19th century, which sits at the end of a natural mound on the North Downs. Some rubble masonry

has been found which may have been part of a stone structure here, possibly of the early 12th century.

LOCATION: KENT
MAP REF: TR 214380

FRAMLINGHAM

Framlingham Castle was built between 1189 and 1200 by Roger Bigod, Earl of Norfolk, on the site of an earlier castle destroyed on the orders of Henry II in 1175. The enclosure is an excellent early example of this type of castle, which never had a keep: the walls are about 13.5m (44ft) tall and the flanking towers (now with ornate Tudor chimneys) rise about another 6m (20ft). Most of the towers were open-backed, and designed entirely for military purposes.

The castle was besieged in 1216 and taken on behalf of King John, but as there is no evidence of major siege damage, it is likely that the defenders gave in without much of a fight. A great hall, built by the Bigods, was pulled down in the 17th century and has disappeared into the masonry of a poorhouse. In 1553 Mary Tudor learned she was the Queen of England after her brother had died while she was staying at Framlingham. A variety of events for all age groups take place here throughout the year, including plays, and displays of birds of prey.

LOCATION: SUFFOLK
MAP REF: TM 287637
OPEN: ENGLISH HERITAGE: DAILY

Colchester

Colchester was the first of the great keeps and the largest built by the Normans in Europe: its dimensions are a powerful 46 x 33.5m (151 x 110ft). The castle was begun by 1076 and probably built under the supervision of Gundulf, Bishop of Rochester, the builder of the White Tower at London, which he completed a short while later. William I ordered a stone castle on the strategic route between East Anglia and London. Due to a lack of local quality stone the Norman builders plundered Roman Colchester to build their keep and chose a site over the ruined Roman Temple of Claudius, incorporating its base into the foundations of the great tower. Colchester had been the first Roman capital of Britain.

Colchester and the White Tower in London were built to much the same plan, both with an apsidal extension although Colchester's corner turrets are more pronounced and its main staircase is the largest diameter newel

Roman Colchester

The Romans built a small wooden fort at Colchester in around 43 CE. They named the settlement Camulondunum. A more permanent settlement established by 100 CE had around 10,000 inhabitants. This important town and port had temples, villas and a chariot-racing track.

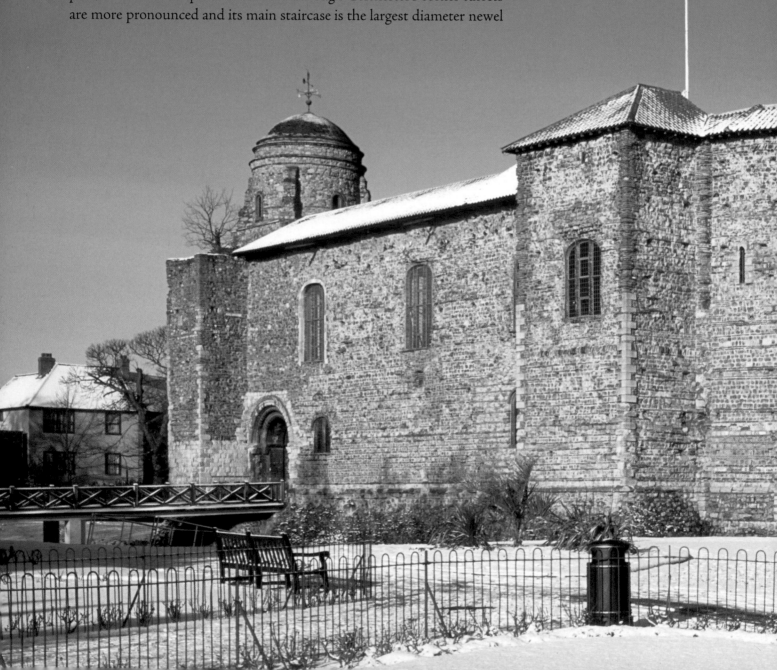

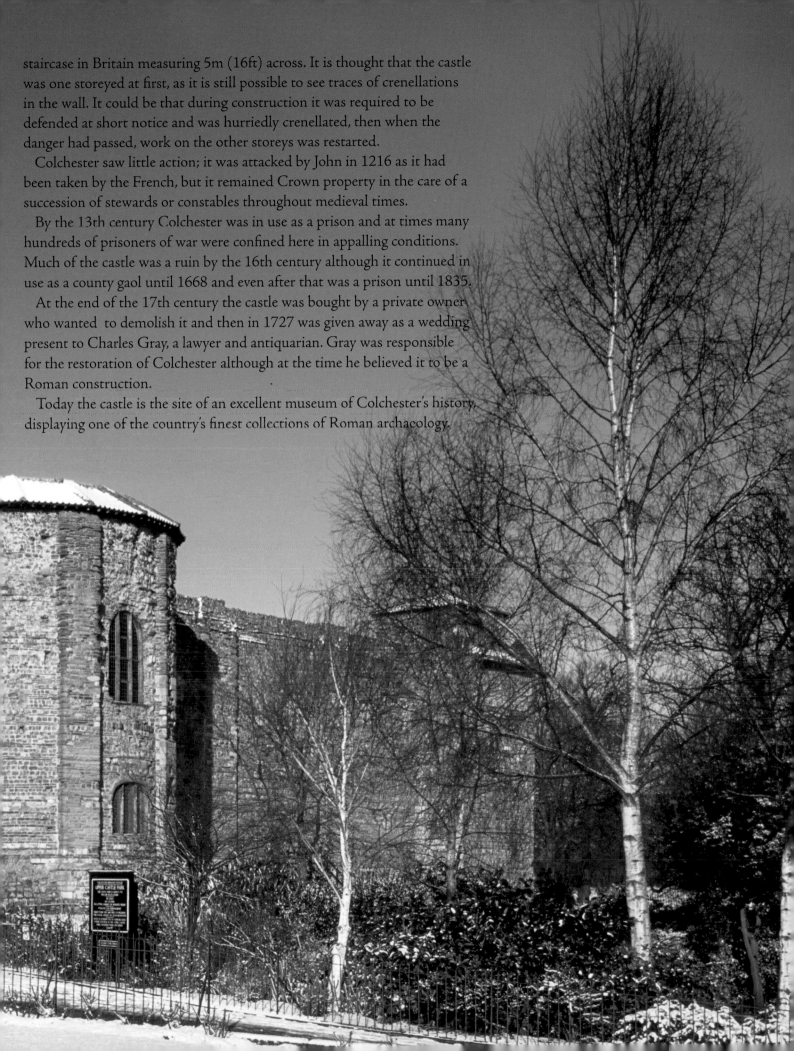

staircase in Britain measuring 5m (16ft) across. It is thought that the castle was one storeyed at first, as it is still possible to see traces of crenellations in the wall. It could be that during construction it was required to be defended at short notice and was hurriedly crenellated, then when the danger had passed, work on the other storeys was restarted.

Colchester saw little action; it was attacked by John in 1216 as it had been taken by the French, but it remained Crown property in the care of a succession of stewards or constables throughout medieval times.

By the 13th century Colchester was in use as a prison and at times many hundreds of prisoners of war were confined here in appalling conditions. Much of the castle was a ruin by the 16th century although it continued in use as a county gaol until 1668 and even after that was a prison until 1835.

At the end of the 17th century the castle was bought by a private owner who wanted to demolish it and then in 1727 was given away as a wedding present to Charles Gray, a lawyer and antiquarian. Gray was responsible for the restoration of Colchester although at the time he believed it to be a Roman construction.

Today the castle is the site of an excellent museum of Colchester's history, displaying one of the country's finest collections of Roman archaeology.

Dover

When the Conqueror landed at Pevensey with his invading army in September 1066 he quickly pushed on and by November reached Dover, leaving garrisoned timber strongholds in his wake. Nothing remains of these fortifications at Dover, and it was more than a century later when Henry II began to rebuild and transform this castle into a powerful medieval stronghold. Military engineer Maurice (the 'Ingeniator') designed Dover as the first fortress in Western Europe with concentric defences. Henry II also built the massive keep, completed c.1190, which continued to be used in a military capacity until the middle of the 20th century. Dover's defences were severely tested when the castle was besieged and undermined by the French in 1216. After this Henry III commissioned the strengthening of the northern defences and these included a unique system of tunnels. He also built accommodation including a great hall. Edward IV modernized the keep in the second half of the 15th century. Although Dover was built primarily for defence it also had to accommodate royalty and VIPs who were travelling overseas. The castle remained in constant use but after the 1500s Dover's defensive importance diminished as artillery power increased.

Above: **Dover Castle by Theodore Henry Fielding (1825).**

The five port towns of Hastings, Romney, Hythe, Dover and Sandwich formed an alliance in the 11th century to provide ships and men to defend the south-east coast and protect trade routes across the Channel. In return, the towns received privileges from the Crown such as exemption from taxes. A warden was appointed to control the alliance and in the 13th century Henry III combined this post with constable of the castle. The appointment of Lord Warden of the Cinque Ports – as they are known – is in the hands of the monarch: Sir Winston Churchill and HM The Queen Mother were holders of the title.

The fortress enjoyed a renaissance during the 18th century when its role as a defence against land assaults on Dover and its harbour was increased. New barracks were added and most of the inner bailey's buildings date from then. The growing threat from France during the Napoleonic Wars led to more defences. Throughout the 19th century the garrison continued to swell and so did its buildings.

Dover remained highly important through both world wars. In May 1940 the operations room beneath the castle was the control centre for Operation Dynamo: the evacuation of Dunkirk, which rescued 338,000 troops. For the rest of World War II, Dover continued as a vital control centre. A garrison was maintained here until the late 1950s. Few castles have maintained such an active role across so many centuries.

Dover Castle from the Sea *by JMW Turner (1822).*

FRAMPTON

Scant remains of a rectangular moated enclosure here may have belonged to the castle mentioned c.1216.

LOCATION: LINCOLNSHIRE
MAP REF: TA 327391

GODARD'S

Fragments of the gatehouse and portions of curtain wall still survive from this 12th-century enclosure castle built of flint masonry.

LOCATION: NR THURNHAM, KENT
MAP REF: TQ 808582
OPEN: KENT COUNTY COUNCIL: OPEN ACCESS

GREAT CANFIELD

The de Vere family, who also built Hedingham great tower, raised a substantial motte castle here. The moats were fed from a diversion from the River Roding. The mound and moats remain.

LOCATION: NR DUNMOW, ESSEX
MAP REF: TL 595179

HADLEIGH

Building was begun in the 13th century by Hubert de Burgh, minister to John and Henry III. Edward III took an interest in Hadleigh and spent £2,300 converting and improving the castle, with several drum towers and a large cylindrical tower. Domestic buildings included a great hall, a chapel, and royal suites. The remains are chiefly of the mid-14th century.

LOCATION: NR LEIGH ON SEA, ESSEX
MAP REF: TQ 810860
OPEN: ENGLISH HERITAGE: OPEN ACCESS

HAUGHLEY

This site has one of Britain's largest surviving mottes, 24.5m (80ft) tall and around 24.5m in diameter. Studies suggest that the outer bailey enclosed Haughley church and much of the village. Stonework remains on the motte may be from a shell enclosure. The castle was dismantled c.1173.

LOCATION: SUFFOLK
MAP REF: TM 025624

HEDINGHAM

A place of superlatives, Hedingham great tower is one of the most famous Norman keeps in the country. In 1140, Aubrey de Vere II built the tower on the flat, raised platform that was the site of an earlier timber fortress. William de Corbeuil, Archbishop of Canterbury and architect of Rochester Castle and Cathedral, is believed to have been its designer. The tower today stands at over 33m (110ft), its walls filled at every storey with chambers and passages. Considered one of the finest Norman domestic interiors still existing, the banqueting hall is spanned by a vast Norman arch.

The de Veres were an important family from the time of the Conquest, and favourites in the Tudor court. Aubrey de Vere III was created 1st Earl of Oxford by Queen Matilda and a later de Vere was one of the barons who compelled King John to consent to the Magna Carta: he was then besieged at Hedingham in the ensuing war. There were many later alterations to the castle buildings but only the Norman great tower remains. In the 18th century Hedingham was sold to Sir William Ashurst, Lord Mayor of London, who built a large country house in the grounds. The estate later passed into the possession of descendants of the de Vere family, through marriage.

LOCATION: CASTLE HEDINGHAM, ESSEX
MAP REF: TL 787359
OPEN: PRIVATE: MID-APR TO SEP SUN–THU

The Real Bard?

There has long been speculation about the identity of William Shakespeare and clues suggest that Edward de Vere of Hedingham, 17th Earl of Oxford, was the real Bard. In Elizabethan times courtiers could only publish poetry and plays anonymously: it was considered a lowly occupation. Edward had a brilliant mind and was the most accomplished poet of his time. De Vere was granted a mysterious annual payment from the queen, and the locations, characters and events in William Shakespeare's plays are subjects about which the earl would have had an intimate knowledge.

An enchanting, fortified manor house with a massive gatehouse, walled bailey and double moat, Hever was begun in the 1270s: a licence to refortify the manor house was granted in 1340 to the owner, William de Hever. In around 1460 Geoffrey Bullen, Lord Mayor of London and great-grandfather to Anne Boleyn, acquired the castle. Hever was greatly modified by the Bullen family who created a comfortable Tudor home in which

Anne, the ill-fated second wife of Henry VIII and mother of Elizabeth I, spent her childhood and much of her youth: after Anne's execution and on the death of her father, Henry VIII appropriated the castle and passed it to Anne of Cleves as part of their divorce settlement. In 1903 its new owner, statesman and financier William Waldorf Astor, lavished money and attention on the by now neglected buildings and restored Hever to its

former glory: he added a number of Tudor-style houses nearby to form a 'village', and the magnificent gardens. The work included digging out the 14ha (35 acre) lake. The peerless Italian Garden is the setting for a collection of classical statuary. The Loggia beside the lake was inspired by the Trevi fountain in Rome.

LOCATION: NR EDENBRIDGE, KENT
MAP REF: TQ 478452
OPEN: PRIVATE: MAR–NOV DAILY

HORSFORD

A motte with some ditching is all that remains today of this Norman earthwork castle, possibly built soon after the great motte castle was raised at Norwich in around 1070.

LOCATION: NR NORWICH, NORFOLK
MAP REF: TG 205156

HUNTINGDON

This is a two-bailey motte castle built by the de Bohun family. The Duke of Buckingham was caught here in 1484 after betraying King Richard. There are stone remains.

LOCATION: CAMBRIDGESHIRE
MAP REF: TL 240714

KINGERBY

This was a motte castle inside a rectangular-plan enclosure that was surrounded by a ditch. The castle was burned at the beginning of the 13th century. A later mansion was built next to the site.

LOCATION: LINCOLNSHIRE
MAP REF: TF 056928

KINNARD'S FERRY

Also known as Owston Ferry Castle, this is the site of a motte castle from the 12th century. It was dismantled on the orders of Henry II in 1175–6, probably following the rebellion of his son.

LOCATION: LINCOLNSHIRE
MAP REF: SE 806002

LEYBOURNE

A circular enclosure with banked ditch and an additional banked area adjacent to it, with masonry remains, are the only remnants of a castle here, which has been incorporated in a 20th-century house.

LOCATION: KENT
MAP REF: TQ 688589

LEEDS CASTLE

LOCATION: NR MAIDSTONE, KENT
MAP REF: TQ 836533
OPEN: LEEDS CASTLE FOUNDATION (A CHARITABLE TRUST): DAILY
SEE PAGE: 68

LIDGATE

This was a rectangular motte with one bailey and a ditch and rampart on the south side. There were two other baileys, one encircled by a wet moat and the other by a dry moat. There is some flint masonry that may be part of a gatehouse.

LOCATION: NR NEWMARKET, SUFFOLK
MAP REF: TL 722583
OPEN: PRIVATE

LINCOLN

Lincoln Castle is built on a site of a Roman fort and like Lewes it has two mottes associated with one bailey. It was started in 1068 on the Conqueror's orders and 166 Saxon houses were cleared to enlarge the site and allow the castle with its earthworks to be erected. The western motte is topped with an interesting 12th-century shell keep known as the Lucy Tower. Ranulf, Earl of Chester, held the castle in the 1140s and was granted leave to refortify it by Stephen: the name Lucy stems from Ranulf's mother, Lucy, Countess of Chester, who died c.1136, passing the castle to her son. The second motte carries a square-plan tower with a 19th-century observatory. The immense 12th-century curtain remains in excellent preservation, the wall-walks give good views of the castle site and surrounding town and countryside. Lincoln was besieged during the Barons' War in the 13th century but its main use has been as a court and a prison; many prisoners were executed on the ramparts and buried in the castle precincts.

One of the four remaining original copies of the Magna Carta is on display at the castle.

LOCATION: LINCOLNSHIRE
MAP REF: SK 974718
OPEN: LINCOLNSHIRE COUNTY COUNCIL: DAILY

LONGTHORPE TOWER

A square great tower of c.1300, supported by angled buttresses at the lower part. The most notable feature of Longthorpe is a series of fine medieval wall paintings in the great chamber.

LOCATION: NR PETERBOROUGH, CAMBRIDGESHIRE
MAP REF: TL 163983
OPEN: ENGLISH HERITAGE: APR–SEP (PRE-BOOKED TOURS ONLY)

LYMPNE

Built on the cliff-top site in the 14th century, Lympne was probably raised as a defence against raiders crossing the Channel, over which the site commands a splendid view. It is also known as Stutfall Castle.

LOCATION: NR HYTHE, KENT
MAP REF: TR 117342
OPEN: PRIVATE

MILEHAM

Mileham is a 12th-century motte castle with a later square great tower built of flint rubble with a splayed plinth. The mound and some stone fragments remain. It is privately owned.

LOCATION: NR LITCHAM, NORFOLK
MAP REF: TF 916193

MOUNTFICHET

Robert Gernon, Duke of Boulogne, founded this enclosure fortress with bailey, surrounded with extensive ditching and ramparts. A small tower was raised inside the enclosure and stone fragments suggest there were additional buildings. Richard Montfitchet II was one of the barons who tried to enforce the Magna Carta and the castle was dismantled by King John in c.1215. The site has now been impressively reconstructed as an earth and timber castle and Norman village.

LOCATION: STANSTED MOUNTFICHET, ESSEX
MAP REF: TL 516249
OPEN: PRIVATE: MID-MARCH TO MID-NOV DAILY

William I

The man who became the first Norman King of England began life as the illegitimate son of the Duke of Normandy. William inherited the dukedom on his father's death in 1035 – he was about seven years old at the time. By 1066 he had fought to establish his dominion over Normandy and was ambitious to claim the English throne, which he said Edward the Confessor had promised to him. William and a sizeable army of men and equipment landed at Pevensey in September and defeated Edward's successor, Harold, in battle at Hastings in October. The army moved towards London, building fortresses in their wake. On Christmas Day 1066, William was crowned King of England.

NORWICH

The first castle at Norwich was raised shortly after the Conquest, at the expense of William I, on a vast mound, part natural and part artificial. A large stone keep, one of the largest in the country, was added during the reign of Henry I c.1125–35 and built in a similar style to the king's tower at Falaise in Normandy. Possibly due to its status as a royal palace, the outside walls at Norwich were unusually decorated with arcading. By 1345, when the castle's baileys were handed to the city of Norwich, the keep was in use as the county gaol, and it remained a prison until 1887 when it was converted into a museum and art gallery. Architect Anthony Salvin carried out a faithful restoration on the tower's exterior in the 1830s when Bath stone was used to replace the original and decaying Caen blocks. A museum is housed in the keep.

LOCATION: CASTLE MEADOW, NORWICH, NORFOLK
MAP REF: TG 232085
OPEN: NORFOLK COUNTY COUNCIL:MUSEUM AND ART GALLERY: DAILY

ONGAR

A motte-and-bailey castle built in the early 12th century by the de Lucy family, Ongar has a substantial motte, 15m (50ft) tall. The motte is 61m (230ft) in diameter at the base and was surrounded by a wet moat.

LOCATION: ESSEX
MAP REF: TL 554031

Leeds Castle

Leeds Castle's origins as a royal fortress date back to Saxon times when it was known as Esledes. Robert de Crevecoeur built the first stone castle here in 1119, on a site near an earlier fortified mill. It was handed to Edward I and his wife Eleanor of Castille at the end of the 13th century and remained in royal ownership (although not entirely unbroken) for the next 300 years. Edward and his queen made many improvements, both defensive and domestic: the first building, the keep (or gloriette as it is called here), stands on its own small island. Other buildings were erected on the main island and the two were connected

Old Gateway at Leeds Castle, Kent (1907) by WB Gardner

Leeds Castle is regarded as one of the world's most beautiful palaces. The castle, owned by six queens and one of Henry VIII's favourite residences, has been developed across 900 years. A vibrant social powerhouse from the 1930s, its owner Lady Baillie established its reputation as one of the 20th century's great English houses, where foreign royalty and leading figures in politics, theatre and film were magnificently entertained. Lady Baillie died in 1974 but the castle continues as a meeting place for history makers: as well as a popular visitor attraction the castle is a top-level conference venue welcoming delegates from all over the world.

originally by drawbridge and later bridged with a corridor. After Eleanor died, Edward granted Leeds to his new queen, Margaret. From then on Leeds Castle was often given to the Queens of England as a part of their dower. Edward III continued work on the castle but it was Henry VIII , when he married his first wife, Catherine of Aragon, who transformed it into a magnificent palace. The end of Henry's reign was to mark the end of the royal ownership of Leeds Castle as Edward VI's Protectors granted it to St Anthony St Leger (Sheriff of Kent) and it then passed through various interconnecting families including the Fairfaxes, some of whom carried out alterations and modifications to the castle. The 19th-century work by Wykeham Martin left Leeds' exterior largely as it stands today (Wykeham built the Tudor-style New Castle which was completed in 1823) then in the 1920s a wealthy Anglo-American, Lady Baillie (as she was to become) bought the castle and transformed its interior with the help of the French designers Rateau and Boudin. It is Lady Baillie's legacy, the result of a life's work and passion, on show at Leeds Castle today.

The 16th-century-style staircase in the gloriette, designed by Rateau in 1929, is part of the spectacular works carried out by Lady Baillie to transform and restore Leeds Castle. The centrepiece of the staircase is the carved Laughing Crusader standing on a newel post hewn out of a single tree trunk. Lady Baillie's remodelling included the gloriette which was transformed in the French Gothic style.

ORFORD

Orford Castle stands on the Suffolk coast, once guarding what was a major port. The only remaining structure is the fine keep, which is still remarkably intact. Orford was built by Henry II, between 1165–73, as part of his programme of stone castle construction which was designed to assert his authority over the barons, particularly Hugh Bigod in East Anglia, the most powerful magnate in the district. Henry's work at Orford was swift and remains well documented; the innovative great tower was up and complete within two years and the castle was ready and garrisoned by the time of the 1173–4 revolt led by his son. Totally unique in Britain or Ireland, the tower is 21-sided on the exterior and cylindrical inside, with three rectangular buttress turrets. Orford was captured towards the end of the Barons' War, but not seriously harmed and thereafter its history is uneventful. The curtain, towers and gatehouse that originally surrounded the keep gradually decayed and collapsed.

LOCATION: SUFFOLK
MAP REF: TM 419499
OPEN: ENGLISH HERITAGE: APR–SEP DAILY; OCT–MAR THU–MON

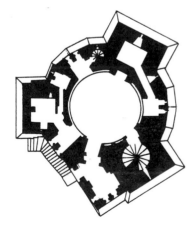

PETERBOROUGH

In the deanery garden here are the remnants of a motte called Tout Hill. It was probably raised in the late 11th century, before the foundation of the present cathedral. It is privately owned.

LOCATION: CAMBRIDGESHIRE
MAP REF: TL 195987

PLESHEY

A figure-of-eight motte castle with a large outer bailey whose remnants include a chapel and round towers. The brick-built bridge across the ditch to the motte probably dates from the 13th century. Aerial views show what an early Norman motte castle looked like before the tower and palisades were erected.

LOCATION: NR CHELMSFORD, ESSEX
MAP REF: TL 666144
OPEN: PRIVATE: ACCESS BY APPOINTMENT

RAYLEIGH

This is an 11th-century motte castle whose motte slopes were revetted with ragstone and flint rubble. The motte, 15m (50ft) tall, was given a substantial wooden tower. No stone buildings were erected, although the castle was in use until the middle of the 13th century.

LOCATION: RAYLEIGH, ESSEX
MAP REF: TQ 805909
OPEN: NATIONAL TRUST: OPEN ACCESS

ROCHESTER

Rochester stands on an important site where the Roman Watling Street crosses the River Medway. The first motte castle, mentioned in Domesday, was held by the Conqueror's half-brother, Odo, Bishop of Bayeux, but taken in 1088 by William Rufus when Odo surrendered and returned to France. Gundulf, Bishop of Rochester and prolific builder, began the first stone castle here. A stone curtain was built, probably c.1088, but the keep, one of the largest in England, wasn't constructed until c. 1127 when Henry I granted Rochester Castle to Archbishop William de Corbeil and his successors at Canterbury and gave him permission to build a tower. In 1215, King John took the castle after a long siege: he undermined the south corner turret and it collapsed. It was later rebuilt in a cylindrical shape with the addition of a drum tower. Further damage was inflicted when Simon de Montfort attacked in 1264; however, the garrison held out for the king. Edward III carried out repairs and restoration in the 14th century but the castle was later abandoned and fell into decay. The remains are substantial.

LOCATION: CASTLE HILL, ROCHESTER, KENT
MAP REF: TQ 742686
OPEN: ENGLISH HERITAGE: DAILY

SAFFRON WALDEN

A late 11th-century motte castle built on a natural hill, with a substantial rectangular great tower added in the 12th century. The tower is partly standing, although ruined to two-thirds of its height. There was a forebuilding on the west wall of the great tower. Two floors, with round-arched recesses in the western and southern walls, remain.

LOCATION: ESSEX
MAP REF: TL 538385
OPEN: LOCAL AUTHORITY: OPEN ACCESS

SALTWOOD

This was a military enclosure surrounded by an oval curtain with open-backed square flanking turrets and square-plan interior towers, joined to the east by a triangular bailey surrounded by banking. The inner enclosure was first raised in the 1150–60s by Henry of Essex. Further buildings were added and it became the residence of the Archbishop of Canterbury. Restored in the 19th and 20th centuries, it was the home of the late Alan Clark MP.

LOCATION: NR HYTHE, KENT
MAP REF: TR 161359
OPEN: PRIVATE

SCOTNEY

The very small, cylindrical turret at Scotney, with machicolation and a conical roof on its top, standing half surrounded by water in a lake, is all that remains of a late 14th-century fortified moated castle/manor house on the south-east coast. The original irregular quadrangle castle was set on two islands and is attributed to Roger de Ashburnham, Conservator of the Peace in Kent and Sussex. The castle was connected to a range of domestic buildings, dating mostly from the 17th century and now a shell; together they form a picturesque feature in the magnificent gardens of a grand country house, built in the 19th century, a short distance from the castle.

LOCATION: NR LAMBERHURST, KENT
MAP REF: TQ 689353
OPEN: NATIONAL TRUST. CASTLE & GARDEN: MAY–OCT. ESTATE WALKS DAILY

SLEAFORD

A rectangular enclosure was erected here probably early in the 12th century. It was surrounded on three sides by a moat and had an additional bailey. Fragments remain.

LOCATION: LINCOLNSHIRE
MAP REF: TF 064455

STAMFORD

Originally a motte castle of the late 11th century, Stamford motte received a shell enclosure before 1153, which may have been the tower surrendered to Henry of Anjou (who later became Henry II) in the same year. The castle was extended in several stages, adding a hall with attached kitchens, cellars and chambers. Fragments remain beside a car park.

LOCATION: LINCOLNSHIRE
MAP REF: TF 027073

TATTERSHALL

Tattershall Castle was first built of stone in the 13th century but just about all that remains now is the remarkable 15th-century great tower erected by Ralph, 3rd Baron Cromwell, Lord Treasurer to Henry VI from 1433 to 1443. It is a masterly example of medieval brickwork, which was, at the time, a relatively new building material. Lord Cromwell intended that the tower should not only proclaim his status (accounts for the work survive and show that nearly one million bricks were made for Tattershall) but should also provide agreeable living accommodation. The large traceried window openings, a serious weak point during a siege, illustrate the shift in priorities from designing serious defensive strongholds to a style that was more illusionary and comfortable: the gatehouses, curtain walls and moat from the earlier castle would have provided defences if required. Tattershall passed to the Crown during the reign of Edward IV and then in the 16th and 17th centuries to the Earls of Lincoln, who eventually abandoned it as a residence.

Lord Curzon, a vigorous campaigner for the preservation of Britain's ancient monuments, rescued the tower from complete ruination in 1910.

LOCATION: LINCOLNSHIRE
MAP REF: TF 211575
OPEN: NATIONAL TRUST: NOT DAILY; WINTER, WEEKENDS ONLY (CLOSED MID-DEC TO MAR)

STANSTED MOUNTFICHET

This was an enclosure with a bailey, surrounded by extensive ditching and ramparts. A reconstruction here is now open to the public.

LOCATION: STANSTED, ESSEX
MAP REF: TL 526249

SUTTON VALENCE

A great tower was built here in the mid- to late 12th century although it was of limited size and had angle buttresses on the corners. The walls, about 2.5m (8ft) thick, contained chambers and passages. A forebuilding was added, but appears to have been demolished and then replaced by a staircase. The castle was abandoned in the 13th century. Fragments remain.

LOCATION: NR MAIDSTONE, KENT
MAP REF: TQ 815491
OPEN: ENGLISH HERITAGE: OPEN ACCESS

SWINESHEAD

Earthworks of the 12th-century motte castle can be seen near the remains of the medieval abbey.

LOCATION: LINCOLNSHIRE
MAP REF: TF 243410

THETFORD

Thetford has one of the tallest mottes in Britain, about 24.5m (80ft) high. The motte, of chalk rubble, was raised before 1086 on the site of an Iron Age fort. Thetford was an important castle and yet it does not appear to have had any stonework additions. The surrounding double ditches and ramparts are impressive. Henry II destroyed the castle in 1174.

LOCATION: NORFOLK
MAP REF: TL 874828

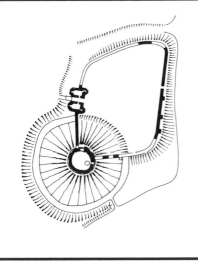

TONBRIDGE

It was probably the 11th century when the motte of an earlier fortress at Tonbridge received an oval shell enclosure of walls with buttressing on the south-east. Gilbert de Clare built the impressive tower gatehouse at the end of the 13th century. The tower contained sumptuous residential accommodation and noble apartments. Edward I visited the castle and handed the Great Seal of England to his son here.

LOCATION: KENT
MAP REF: TQ 589466
OPEN: LOCAL AUTHORITY: DAILY

TONGE

An earthwork castle of Norman origin with stonework added in the 13th century. Some fragments were discovered in two excavations.

LOCATION: KENT
MAP REF: TQ 933636

WEETING

Weeting was a moated, fortified, late 12th-century manor house with a substantial tower and shallow moat. Ruins remain.

LOCATION: NR BRANDON, NORFOLK
MAP REF: TL 778891
OPEN: ENGLISH HERITAGE: OPEN ACCESS

WEST MALLING

This is an interesting medium-sized great tower (known as St Leonard's Tower), built of Kentish ragstone c.1100. The four-storey structure has corner pilaster buttresses (and one mid-wall) and a spiral staircase in the north-west corner; ruins remain.

LOCATION: KENT
MAP REF: TQ 675570
OPEN: ENGLISH HERITAGE: OPEN ACCESS TO EXTERIOR. INTERNAL VIEWING BY APPOINTMENT (TEL 01732 870872)

WOODWALTON

This falls into the enclosure class of early earthwork castles. The earthworks are now known as Castle Hill.

LOCATION: CAMBRIDGESHIRE
MAP REF: TL 211827
OPEN: LOCAL AUTHORITY: OPEN ACCESS

ACTON BURNELL

Acton Burnell is known as a castle, but was a magnificent manor house whose builder, Robert Burnell, Chancellor of England, obtained a licence to fortify in the 1280s.

It is a huge, two-storeyed rectangular tower hall, now roofless, with smaller square towers on the corners and a projecting block between the two west towers. Built of local red sandstone, these ruins are of a building more akin to a palace than a castle.

LOCATION: SHROPSHIRE
MAP REF: SJ 534019
OPEN: ENGLISH HERITAGE: OPEN ACCESS

ALDERBURY

Alderbury was a small 13th-century stone polygonal enclosure castle with a rectangular great tower, and is now all in ruins.

LOCATION: NR SHREWSBURY, SHROPSHIRE
MAP REF: SJ 35814

ALDFORD

A stone motte and bailey castle, built by Richard de Aldford in the 12th century, overlooked a ford across the River Dee. A few fragments of stonework round the bailey still survive. The site is accessible.

LOCATION: NR CHESTER, CHESHIRE
MAP REF: SJ 419596

ALTON

Bertraum de Verdun built Alton in the time of Henry II in the 12th century and further alterations were made to the castle in the 13th and 14th centuries. The slopes provided defence to most sides and a ditch was cut into the rock. It was dismantled after the Civil War and some of the stone was used for local buildings.

Augustus Pugin worked on the castle in the 19th century, and it was his reconstruction that gave Alton its Gothic appearance.

LOCATION: STAFFORDSHIRE
MAP REF: SK 074425
OPEN: PRIVATE (WEDDING VENUE)

ASHBY DE LA ZOUCH

Ashby was a Norman hall begun in the 12th century but extended over the next three centuries to become a fair-sized manor house. In 1464 it was then given by Edward IV to his Lord Chamberlain, William, Lord Hastings. Hastings set about converting the manor into a castle after a licence was granted a decade later. The principal buildings of Hastings' time were the chapel and the great tower, known as Hastings' Tower. This formidable structure was a fortress-cum-residence and unusual in two respects: most towers at the time were built to a cylindrical design, and it was set on the edge of the castle site rather than in the centre. The four-storeyed tower originally reached about 27.5m (90ft) to its semi-octagonal angle turrets with a seven-floor extension. Hastings Tower was blown in two during the Civil War but visitors can still enjoy fine views from the top of this majestic ruin. Mary, Queen of Scots was kept at Ashby on two occasions and the castle features in the classic 19th-century novel, Sir Walter Scott's *Ivanhoe*.

LOCATION: LEICESTERSHIRE
MAP REF: SK 363167
OPEN: ENGLISH HERITAGE: JUL–AUG DAILY; SEP– JUN THU–MON

ASLOCKTON

The moat at Aslockton, a large rectangular earthwork enclosure, was fed from a nearby stream. There was a low motte, about 5m (16ft) high, and two baileys. Some earthworks remain although its history is unknown.

LOCATION: NR NOTTINGHAM, NOTTINGHAMSHIRE
MAP REF: SK 744402

BAKEWELL

There was a motte castle here in the 12th century; it may have been raised illegally in the time of King Stephen. The motte appears to have been added to an earlier rubble-built, ramparted enclosure. The site is accessible.

LOCATION: DERBYSHIRE
MAP REF: SK 221688

BARNWELL

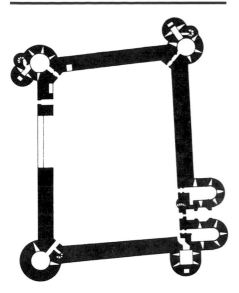

Traces of a possibly 12th-century motte castle lie beside the 13th-century ruined building that is Barnwell Castle. The stone structure, started c.1265 and built by the family of Berengar Le Moine, is quadrangular with cylinder towers on the north-east, north-west and south-west corners. The castle stands in the grounds of the Elizabethan Barnwell Manor. Barnwell is ruinous.

LOCATION: NR OUNDLE, NORTHAMPTONSHIRE
MAP REF: TL 049853
OPEN: PRIVATE: GARDENS OPEN OCCASIONALLY

BEDFORD

Bedford began as a motte castle of the late 11th century. Late in Henry I's or early in Stephen's reign, the castle received stonework including a shell enclosure on the motte. Bedford Castle was besieged on behalf of Henry III in the 13th century. The holder, Faulkes de Bréauté, set out to seek military support, leaving his brother in control. Henry's men undermined the castle's defences and were victorious: the castle was slighted and the leaders executed. De Bréauté returned to see his brother's and supporters' bodies. He begged for mercy and was spared. The site is being restored as a cultural and natural history centre.

LOCATION: CASTLE MOUND, BEDFORD, BEDFORDSHIRE
MAP REF: TL 053497

BEESTON

In the early 12th century the site at Beeston belonged to the powerful Ranulf, Earl of Chester, who, c1220, began to build the castle here. He designed the fortress in two parts, with a small inner bailey and an outer bailey surrounded by towers and walls and guarded by a massive gatehouse, but there was no keep. In 1237 Beeston passed to Henry III, who enlarged it; and in the first years of the 14th century major new works were undertaken by Edward I. However, during the following centuries, the castle became neglected and was in ruins by the 1500s. Nevertheless, Beeston was garrisoned during the Civil War, first by Parliamentarians and then the Royalists, until finally slighted. Stone from the castle was used for buildings elsewhere but even in its present ruinous state, the castle's former strength is still detectable.

LOCATION: TAPORLEY, CHESHIRE
MAP REF: SJ 537593
OPEN: ENGLISH HERITAGE: DAILY

BELVOIR

A motte castle was built on a natural mound by Robert de Todeni in the late 11th century: the Belvoir name dates from this time and means 'beautiful view' but the name is all that is left of the Norman castle. These days Belvoir is known as the grand stately home of the Duke of Rutland and is the fourth building to stand on the original site. It is home to the Queen's Royal Lancers Museum and the stunning interiors also house a magnificent collection of furniture, paintings, porcelains, silks and tapestries.

LOCATION: NR GRANTHAM, LEICESTERSHIRE
MAP REF: TL 296236
OPEN: PRIVATE: EASTER–SEP SAT–SUN, TUE–THU; MAR & OCT SUN.

BENEFIELD

Benefield was a rectangular moated enclosure site, dating from the 12th century. It was confiscated by John in c.1208.

LOCATION: NORTHAMPTONSHIRE
MAP REF: SP 987884

BISHOP'S CASTLE

Probably of 12th-century origin, this was a motte castle with a shell enclosure constructed at a later date. Remaining fragments of stonework on the motte slope suggest that there was probably a wall connecting the shell to a curtain round the bailey. Remnants can be seen near the Castle Hotel.

LOCATION: NR CLUN, SHROPSHIRE
MAP REF: SO 323891

BOLSOVER

Bolsover was built in the 12th century and it received a great tower of stone c.1173–4. More domestic buildings were added in the 13th century but the castle was allowed to deteriorate during the reign of Edward I, when the buildings were leased. What can be seen today at Bolsover is the building project Sir Charles Cavendish started in the 17th century. The 'Little Castle' he and his son built was designed purely for elegant living.

LOCATION: NR CHESTERFIELD, DERBYSHIRE
MAP REF: SK 471707
OPEN: ENGLISH HERITAGE: MAY–AUG DAILY; SEP–APR THU–MON

BRAMPTON BRYAN

Early in the 14th century this 12th-century motte castle received a curtain with towers and a square-plan gatehouse with a long barbican projecting outwards. The castle was more or less destroyed in the Civil War but the gatehouse and twin towers of the barbican survive, along with some remnants of the quadrangular castle. Sited on a floodplain of the River Tene, the castle at Brampton Bryan would have guarded part of the important route from Ludlow into central Wales.

LOCATION: HEREFORDSHIRE
MAP REF: SO 370726
OPEN: PRIVATE: OPEN OCCASIONALLY

BRANDON

Brandon is an early 12th-century earthwork enclosure; excavations revealed it had a rectangular keep. The castle was founded by Geoffrey de Clinton and held for Henry III during his war with Simon de Montfort and the barons. The scant remains can be seen from the road.

LOCATION: NR WOLSTON, WARWICKSHIRE
MAP REF: SP 408759

BREDWARDINE

The manor here was granted to John de Bredwardine during the Conquest. Traces of the stone walls of a rectangular great tower can be seen on a platform near the River Wye. Beside it is an earlier mound, which also had stonework.

LOCATION: HEREFORDSHIRE
MAP REF: SO 335444

BRIDGNORTH

An enclosure castle, first recorded in 1102, was built on the narrow ridge of rock in Bridgnorth beside the River Severn. The castle's principal feature, a square great tower, was built in the reign of Henry II who had taken the castle from the Mortimers (they were supporters of King Stephen) in 1155. The little that is left of the tower was so damaged in the Civil War that it leans at a greater angle than the tower in Pisa. The castle gardens are renowned for their floral displays.

LOCATION: SHROPSHIRE
MAP REF: SO 717927
OPEN: LOCAL AUTHORITY: OPEN ACCESS

BRINKLOW

A motte castle was raised at Brinklow early in the 12th century. The motte was about 12m (40ft) high and the bailey, surrounded by ditch and ramparts, was divided by another ditch with ramparts.

LOCATION: WARWICKSHIRE
MAP REF: SP 438796

BRONSIL

A few remains of a fortified quadrangular manor house, with corner and mid-wall towers, have been dated to the 15th century. The castle was surrounded by a moat.

LOCATION: NR BROMSBERROW, HEREFORDSHIRE
MAP REF: SO 749372

BRYN AMLWG

There are some remains of stone walling round the enclosure castle of the 12th and 13th centuries, which had towers and a gatehouse, at Bryn Amlwg. The castle was also known as Cefn Fron.

LOCATION: SHROPSHIRE
MAP REF: SO 167846

CAINHOE

Cainhoe was an earthwork castle of the late 11th or early 12th century, with a motte and three baileys well protected by ditches. The local population appears to have been decimated at the time of the Black Death, after which the castle fell into decay. Access to the remains is by public footpath

LOCATION: NR CLOPHILL, BEDFORDSHIRE
MAP REF: TL 097374

CAUS

An 11th-century castle covering an area of about 2.5ha (6 acres), Caus received a shell enclosure on its motte in the following century, as well as a rectangular curtain round the inner bailey. The castle was demolished during the Civil War and there are very few remains still visible on the tree-covered site.

LOCATION: NR WESTBURY, SHROPSHIRE
MAP REF: SJ 337078

CHARLTON

There are fragments of earthworks of a 13th- to 14th-century castle here. John, Lord Charlton obtained a licence to crenellate in 1316.

LOCATION: NR THE WREKIN, SHROPSHIRE
MAP REF: SJ 597112

CHARTLEY

This 13th-century motte castle had two baileys and a cylindrical tower on its summit. Around the inner bailey was a rectangular-plan curtain with turrets. The castle was abandoned by 1485 but there are masonry remnants of this once large and impressive castle, founded by the Earl of Chester.

LOCATION: STOWE-BY-CHARTLEY, STAFFORDSHIRE
MAP REF: SK 101285
OPEN: PRIVATE: VISIBLE FROM THE ROAD

CHENEY LONGVILLE

Originally a 14th-century moated fortified manor house built by the Cheney family. The farm buildings here incorporate many of the original medieval features. Privately owned.

LOCATION: SHROPSHIRE
MAP REF: SO 417847

CHESTER

The Conqueror raised a motte castle at Chester with an inner and outer bailey, just outside the site of the old Roman town, in 1069–70. In 1237 the castle came into royal ownership and successive kings enlarged and improved the fortress over several centuries: there are still the remains of the 12th-century square tower on the motte known as the Flag Tower. It was Henry III who built the outer bailey curtain with the gate towers and he also rebuilt the great hall. All that remains of the original Norman building are parts of the Flag Tower, the inner bailey wall and gateway known as the Agricola Tower, which has some fine 13th-century frescoes. Most of the site was levelled and remodelled by Thomas Harrison early in the 19th century.

LOCATION: CHESHIRE
MAP REF: SJ 404657
OPEN: CHESTER CITY COUNCIL: DAILY

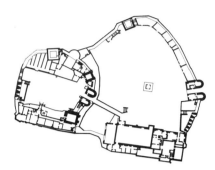

CHURCH STRETTON

Church Stretton was also known as Brockhurst Castle, a motte castle built c.1154 overlooking the land between Shrewsbury and Ludlow. It was destroyed in the following century. Stone curtain walling was found when it was excavated.

LOCATION: SHROPSHIRE
MAP REF: SO 448926

CLEOBURY

Earthworks beside the river here are possibly the remains of an early 12th-century castle, which is recorded as having been pulled down, perhaps by Henry II, in 1155.

LOCATION: CLEOBURY MORTIMER, SHROPSHIRE
MAP REF: SO 681761

CLIFFORD

William FitzOsbern built the motte and bailey of Clifford Castle in around 1080. There are additional 13th-century fortifications in stone. Clifford was held by the Clifford family and later passed to the Mortimers. The site has been excavated and ruins remain.

LOCATION: HEREFORDSHIRE
MAP REF: SO 243457

THE ENGLISH CIVIL WAR

IF EVER THERE WAS A WAR THAT NO ONE WANTED, IT WAS THE CIVIL WAR OF 1642 TO 1646. THE CLOSEST THAT ENGLAND HAS EVER COME TO A REVOLUTION, IT WAS ABOUT VERY DEEP AND PASSIONATELY HELD DIFFERENCES BETWEEN THOSE SUPPORTING THE MONARCHY AND THOSE WISHING TO EXTEND WHAT WE WOULD NOW CALL DEMOCRACY. BUT THAT IS A GROSS OVER-SIMPLIFICATION OF A TIME THAT TORE COMMUNITIES AND EVEN FAMILIES APART.

If the monarch of the time, Charles I, had been prepared to compromise it is possible that war would not have become inevitable, but not only would he not compromise, he also said one thing while doing something quite different behind the scenes. Negotiations between Charles and Parliament went on for an interminable time, with Parliament becoming more and more angry with what it saw as the king's double dealing.

In a deeply conservative country, with a monarchy that had been in place since the foundations of the nation, it was inconceivable to many that they could be disloyal to the king. For others, the king needed only to talk openly and to compromise, and then all might be well.

The king's heartlands were in the West, Midlands and North; the parliamentary supporters had London as their core, with much of the South and East in support. But individual towns and cities might be in either 'camp', depending upon the leanings of their local leaders.

Many areas tried to be impartial, and did their best to keep out both Royalists and Parliamentarians. As the conflict spread, their position became impossible, and eventually, almost every part of the country became embroiled. As all attempts at agreement collapsed, armed conflict seemed to be the only option and war began.

Prevented from entering London by the 'London Trained Bands', the king and his army made Oxford their southern base, and it remained so for the rest of the war. The king's armies and the Parliamentarians (later popularly known as 'Roundheads') ranged far and wide over the country, fighting for advantage and for territory. Ports were hotly contested, as they could provide supplies, reinforcements and much else from other parts of the country and from abroad. There were critical nodal points and strategically important places that were fought over time and again. Castles became every bit as important as they had been in medieval times. Some castles held out for very long sieges.

Cromwell emerged from the Parliamentarian army as a bold, clever and ruthless soldier, but it was not clear for a long time that he would eventually replace the king.

Cromwell leads his troops after a crucial victory at the Battle of Marston Moor in 1644. Painting by Ernest Croft.

The war ranged back and forth, with battles lost and won on both sides. Each side had its heroes – Prince Rupert on the Royalist side was an extraordinarily brave cavalry officer, most famous for headlong charges at the enemy which more often than not simply overwhelmed the foe. Parliament had officers such as Waller, a professional soldier whose dogged determination paid off in the end. The war brought out great courage and bravery, but like all wars it brought misery, especially for civilians caught up in a confusing, increasingly cruel and ruthless campaign. Both sides raided the countryside for food and other provisions; taxes were levied that could hardly be paid; the economy slewed out of control.

Eventually the king was captured. He was tried (the War had rekindled and dragged on), sentenced to death, and beheaded on 30th January 1649. True to his style, he died with great dignity.

Cromwell became 'Lord Protector' – dictator in all but name – whose 11-year 'reign' achieved virtually nothing except to earn him almost unanimous vilification.

When the monarchy was restored in 1660, with Charles II as king, there was widespread and genuine jubilation. But nothing could ever be quite the same again.

Elaborate defences were built around Oxford once it had become the headquarters of King Charles. This picture by Jan Wyck shows the city from the position of the besieging parliamentary forces in 1645.

The Battle of Naseby, 14th June 1645. A decisive defeat for the Royalists, it ended in a bloody and murderous rout, with battle-crazed Parliamentarians slaughtering Royalists and their followers without mercy.

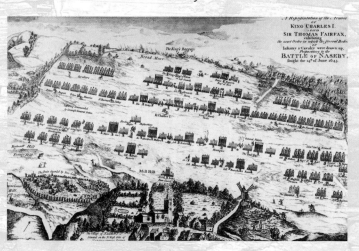

CLUN

The castle at Clun, a substantial motte fortification, was the largest of the Shropshire manors held by 'Picot' de Say. First recorded in 1140, the castle was rebuilt in stone during the 12th and 13th centuries. Clun came under the control of Owain Glyndwr in the early 1400s and it was from this time that it started to fall into decay: by the time of the Civil War, Clun was too ruinous to defend. Lord Clive of India owned the estate for a time but it was the Duke of Norfolk who began conservation work on Clun at the end of the 19th century. Now it is an impressive ruin, with the main survivor being the Great Tower built into the side of the motte.

LOCATION: SHROPSHIRE
MAP REF: SO 298809
OPEN: ENGLISH HERITAGE: OPEN ACCESS

COVENTRY

Coventry was a rectangular enclosure castle with surrounding ditchwork. Originally built as a priory it was taken by Robert Marmion during the Anarchy of King Stephen and converted into a fortress. The castle was seized by Stephen c.1147 after Coventry sided with Empress Matilda. From the end of the 1100s the castle began to fall into disrepair, although traces of it remained until early in the 16th century.

LOCATION: WARWICKSHIRE
MAP REF: SP 336788

CROFT CASTLE

Built on the remains of a 14th-century quadrangular-plan castle, the Georgian country house at Croft dates from the late 16th and early 17th centuries with later additions. The 14th- to 15th-century castle was dismantled by Royalists in 1645.

LOCATION: LEOMINSTER, HEREFORDSHIRE
MAP REF: SO 449655
OPEN: NATIONAL TRUST: APR–SEP WED–SUN; MAR & OCT SAT–SUN

CUCKNEY

Cuckney was a motte castle, raised on the site that the church now occupies, during the Anarchy of King Stephen's time. The remains consist of a low-level motte surrounded by a dtich.

LOCATION: BASSETLAW, NOTTINGHAMSHIRE
MAP REF: SK 566714

DONINGTON

An earthwork enclosure of the early 12th century, Donington probably had stonework by the time of King John and was attacked during the Magna Carta War. It passed to Thomas, Earl of Lancaster, in 1311, and eventually became Crown property. The castle had disappeared by the 16th century and all that now marks it is a mound.

LOCATION: LEICESTERSHIRE
MAP REF: SK 448276

DORSTONE

Dorstone started as a motte castle of the late 11th or early 12th century and survived into the 13th century without conversion to stone. The mound is over 6m (20ft) high with a dry ditch and an adjoining kidney-shaped bailey.

LOCATION: HEREFORDSHIRE,
MAP REF: SO 312416

DUDLEY

Mentioned in Domesday, Dudley Castle was strengthened with stonework in the 1130s. Destroyed by Henry II in 1175 it lay abandoned until the middle of the 13th century when a rectangular great tower with cylindrical corner turrets was built. Other structures were added in the

14th century. Although garrisoned by Royalists during the Civil War, Dudley's destruction came in the 18th century in a fierce fire. The remains are in the grounds of Dudley Zoo, and various historical events are held throughout the year.

LOCATION: WEST MIDLANDS
MAP REF: SO 947907
OPEN: ZOO: DAILY

DUFFIELD

The tower at Duffield was built in the 1160s–70s on the mound of an earlier motte castle by the de Ferrers family. Only traces now remain of what was once one of the largest fortress-residences in England.

LOCATION: DERBYSHIRE
MAP REF: SK 344441
OPEN: NATIONAL TRUST: OPEN ACCESS

DUNHAM MASSEY

A motte from the 12th century stands in the grounds of Dunham New Park. It may be the castle of Hamo de Masci held against Henry III in 1173.

LOCATION: NR ALTRINCHAM, CHESHIRE
MAP REF: SJ 730878

Stephen and Matilda

The war between Stephen, who had usurped the throne of England, and Matilda, daughter of Henry I, lasted almost 10 years. Stephen and Matilda were both grandchildren of William I, but Matilda was in direct line of succession. However, some nobles resented the idea of a woman ruling over them and they supported Stephen when he took the throne. Matilda failed to win the Crown, but when Stephen's own son died, her son was named successor and became Henry II.

ECCLESHALL

The ruins of Eccleshall Castle stand in the grounds of a 17th-century house. In c.1200 Bishop Muschamp of Lichfield was granted a licence to fortify his house. The resulting castle was besieged and demolished by Parliamentarians during the Civil War and there are only a few remains.

LOCATION: STAFFORDSHIRE
MAP REF: SJ 827295
OPEN: PRIVATE

ELLESMERE

Possibly built by Roger de Montgomery who led the Norman invasion into central Wales, Ellesmere was a motte castle built late in the 11th century. Ownership of Ellesmere alternated between the English and Welsh Crowns up to the 1240s and then passed to the le Strange family.

LOCATION: SHROPSHIRE
MAP REF: SJ 403347

ELMLEY

Little remains of this late 11th-century earthwork castle which received stone additions in the 12th and possibly the 13th centuries. It was built on the site of an Iron Age hillfort. For more than two centuries it was the principal seat of the Earls of Beauchamp before they moved to Warwick.

LOCATION: NR PERSHORE, WORCESTERSHIRE
MAP REF: SO 979403
OPEN: ACCESSIBLE

EWIAS HAROLD

This is one of the few castles built before the Conquest. It is referred to in the Anglo-Saxon Chronicle for 1052, and in Domesday there is a reference to Castellum Ewias. By 1086 Ewias, a motte castle, probably had a stone shell. Below the motte is a kidney-shaped bailey. By 1538 the castle was reported to be completely ruinous.

LOCATION: NR PONTRILAS, HEREFORDSHIRE
MAP REF: SO 385287

FOTHERINGHAY

This was the scene of the execution of Mary, Queen of Scots in 1587. The only thing that now marks the site and the existence of the once-imposing edifice of Fotheringhay is a mound and a small pile of stones. Fotheringhay had begun as a simple motte castle on the north of the River Nene.

LOCATION: NORTHAMPTONSHIRE
MAP REF: TL 061930
OPEN: ACCESSIBLE ON FOOT

FRODSHAM

Stones from the Norman castle were used in the building of the 18th-century Castle Park House at Frodsham. There are indications that a tower was built on the high ground and that this early Norman castle was burned down in the middle of the 17th century.

LOCATION: CHESHIRE
MAP REF: SJ 514775

GOODRICH

Goodrich Castle is set on a high rocky spur over the right bank of the River Wye, commanding a crossing of the river. It is protected partly by a natural steep slope and valley and partly by a moat cut out of the rock. By 1102, it was known as Godric's Castle, after Godric the first lord here. A square great tower was the first stone building at Goodrich put up in the middle of the 12th century.

The tower stood alone for a time, then late in the 13th century, when Goodrich was held by the de Valence family, the fortress was substantially renovated. It was converted into a formidable quadrangle with massive cylindrical towers on three corners, and a vast gatehouse-tower on the fourth (north-east) corner. The cylindrical towers were raised on square bases with spurs that clamped the towers to their rock bases. Elaborate apartments were built inside the quadrangle, including a great hall, a solar and kitchens. The north-east corner tower was built as a gatehouse which included a chapel.

Goodrich was held for Parliament at the start of the Civil War and garrisoned with 100 men. The Royalists then held it for a time and the castle was partly demolished to remove its defences.

LOCATION: NR ROSS-ON-WYE, HEREFORDSHIRE
MAP REF: SO 579199
OPEN: ENGLISH HERITAGE: MAR–OCT DAILY; NOV–FEB THU–MON

GROBY

Groby Castle was given stonework in the 12th century but it was destroyed in the 1170s after the rebellion of Prince Henry against his father Henry II (1173–4); nothing remains.

LOCATION: LEICESTERSHIRE
MAP REF: SK 525076

HALLATON

This is an interesting motte castle, whose motte area occupied hardly less space in circumference than its inner bailey. Excavations in the 19th century revealed tree trunks bearing axe marks, boulders and clay lumps. There are no remains today.

LOCATION: LEICESTERSHIRE
MAP REF: SP 780967

HALTON

Hugh Lupus, Earl of Chester, put up a timber-and-earth fortification at Halton c.1071. Late in the 12th century it was converted into a stone enclosure with flanking towers, and then a large gatehouse was constructed in the 15th century. The castle continued in use, mainly as a prison, into the 1700s. Halton was in the hands of two of England's most powerful families, the de Lacys and the Lancasters, and when Henry Bolingbroke became Henry IV, the Barony of Halton became the property of the Crown. Today the ruins are managed by a trust and are the setting for various historical and cultural events.

LOCATION: NR FRODSHAM, CHESHIRE
MAP REF: SJ 537820
OPEN: NORTON PRIORY MUSEUM TRUST LTD:
OUTSIDE WALLS ACCESSIBLE

HANLEY

King John built Hanley Castle between 1207–12, possibly on the site of an earlier rectangular-moated enclosure. Edward II carried out extensive work and a description of 1416 indicated the existence of several stone towers, a palisade and a chapel.

LOCATION: HANLEY CASTLE, WORCESTERSHIRE
MAP REF: SO 837415

HARTSHILL

There are the remains of a Tudor timber-framed house in the 14th century bailey at Hartshill, which began as a motte castle that later received a stone curtain round the bailey. The site is in woods.

LOCATION: WARWICKSHIRE
MAP REF: SP 325942

HEREFORD

Hereford was one of the few castles thought to have been erected by Norman lords during the reign of Edward the Confessor. It was then held by William FitzOsbern, one of the Conqueror's principal lords, and the post-Conquest castle consisted of a motte and a kite-shaped bailey.

Royal visitors frequently came to stay at Hereford, which was a grand and important castle in its heyday. During the Barons' War it served as the headquarters of the Baronial Party and when Prince Edward was taken prisoner at Lewes he was brought to Hereford. Nothing remains today and the site is a landscaped park.

LOCATION: CASTLE GREEN, HEREFORD,
HEREFORDSHIRE
MAP REF: SO 509395

HOPTON

Hopton was a motte castle of the 11th and 12th centuries with a rectangular great tower not built until some time in the 13th century. The stonework was surrounded by wet moats. It was captured by Royalists in the Civil War and was the scene of the cold-blooded murder of 28 men. The remains of the great tower still stand on a low-level mound in the village.

LOCATION: HOPTON CASTLE, SHROPSHIRE
MAP REF: SO 367779

HORSTON

Only fragments of this early Norman castle have survived. Built on a spur of rock, the principal feature was a rectangular great tower with ashlar masonry dressings. Further works were carried out in Henry III's time and in

1264 Horston was captured and dismantled by the de Ferrers family. The site is in woodland and is accessible by a footpath. The castle is also known as Horsley or Horeston.

LOCATION: NR COXBENCH, DERBYSHIRE
MAP REF: SK 375432

HUNTINGTON

The powerful de Bohuns built a motte castle with two baileys on this site and a stone tower was raised during the late 12th century. Henry Stafford, Duke of Buckingham, was captured here when he was found out for his treachery to Richard III. Some fragments of walling still remain but the site, next to a footpath, is overgrown.

LOCATION: NR KINGTON, HEREFORDSHIRE
MAP REF: SO 249539

Major Battlefields

Some of England's largest battles have been fought in the Midlands.

Evesham was the site for the last battle of the Barons' War in 1265. The rebels, led by Simon de Montfort, were defeated by the forces of Prince Edward (later Edward I). Many of the barons, including de Montfort, were killed on the battlefield.

The Battle of Shrewsbury was fought between Henry IV and Henry Percy (Hotspur). The Percys had supported Henry against Richard II in return for lands and money. When neither were delivered, the Percys rebelled and met Henry at Shrewsbury. Henry Percy was killed and his forces were routed: thousands died.

The Battle of Bosworth Field in 1485 was the final encounter in the Wars of the Roses. Henry Tudor defeated Richard III, the last Plantagenet king, and claimed the Crown for the House of York.

This is one of the grandest ruined castles in England. Henry I granted Kenilworth to his chamberlain, Geoffrey de Clinton in 1120, and later in the century a substantial great tower and a stone curtain were built. The castle was favoured by royalty and greatly enhanced by various royal patrons, but in 1253 Henry III passed Kenilworth to the de Montforts under a lifetime grant. The siege at Kenilworth, between the de Montfort supporters and Prince Edward's army, was a major incident of the Barons' War. John of Gaunt added a range of palatial buildings and in the 16th century, when the castle was home to Robert Dudley, Earl of Leicester, and a favourite of Queen Elizabeth I, Kenilworth was further embellished. Elizabeth was a frequent visitor to the castle during this time and was lavishly entertained on her visits. The castle changed hands twice during the Civil War and was slighted, but only minimally. It was after this that the ingenious and magnificent great moat/lake, created by damming the streams flowing through the marshy land below the castle, was lost. Such was the impact and history of this grand and important castle that, in 1821, Sir Walter Scott wrote a two-volume novel named after it.

LOCATION: WARWICKSHIRE
MAP REF: SP 278723
OPEN: ENGLISH HERITAGE: DAILY

KILPECK

William FitzNorman built the castle at Kilpeck and his son built the 12th-century Romanesque church which stands, virtually unchanged, near the castle ruins. Kilpeck Castle and its massive keep was demolished during the Civil War but the site, together with the church and the medieval village are an excellent illustration of rural medieval life.

LOCATION: NR HEREFORD, HEREFORDSHIRE
MAP REF: SO 444305
OPEN: DAILY

KINGTON

The remnants of an earthwork castle of mound and ditch, dating possibly from the 12th century, are near the church at Kington. The castle was taken from its holder, Adam de Port, in 1172 by Henry II and then after a short but fairly turbulent history, was destroyed by King John in 1216.

LOCATION: HEREFORDSHIRE
MAP REF: SO 291569

KIRBY MUXLOE

Lord Hastings, who built Hastings' Tower at Ashby de la Zouch, began to build this attractive fortified house in brickwork c.1480 but was executed before it was finished. All that remains today are the gatehouse and one corner tower, still grandly surrounded by a wet moat.

LOCATION: NR LEICESTER, LEICESTERSHIRE
MAP REF: SK 524046
OPEN: ENGLISH HERITAGE: REOPENS 2006 AFTER RENOVATION

KNOCKIN

Knockin was a motte castle with a low motte, probably dating from the 12th century and reinforced with stone. There are traces of curtain wall round part of the bailey. All that remains is a tree-covered mound and a church which was once the castle chapel and, although restored in the 19th century, it retains some of its Norman features.

LOCATION: SHROPSHIRE
MAP REF: SJ 334223
OPEN: CHURCH: DAILY. CASTLE: SITE ACCESSIBLE

LEICESTER

Leicester Castle was a motte castle with inner and outer bailey raised in around 1068. Simon de Montfort, Earl of Leicester had it for a time but when he was killed at the Battle of Evesham in 1265, the castle was taken over by Henry III. During the 15th century the fortunes of the castle declined but Richard III, the last Yorkist king, stayed here a few days before the Battle of Bosworth in August 1485. Today the site of Leicester Castle, which includes remains of the great hall and the original motte, is a conservation area, although what remains of the medieval castle has been dramatically changed over the centuries.

LOCATION: LEICESTERSHIRE
MAP REF: SK 585040
OPEN: LEICESTER CITY COUNCIL: OCCASIONAL TOURS OF HALL AND MEDIEVAL CELLAR. MOUND ACCESSIBLE

LONGTOWN

A motte with a rectangular double bailey, built by the de Lacys late in the 12th century and later crowned with a cylindrical great tower of sandstone rubble on a battered plinth with 4.5m (15ft) thick walls. The tower is interesting: its three lobes project slightly at 120 degrees from each other and from the cylindrical plan, the lobes acting as buttresses and one has a staircase. Longtown, decaying during the 14th century, was refortified during Owain Glyndwr's rebellion in 1402.

LOCATION: NR ABBEY DORE, HEREFORDSHIRE
MAP REF: SO 321291
OPEN: ENGLISH HERITAGE: OPEN ACCESS

LOWER DOWN

The early motte castle here is believed to have received a polygonal shell enclosure in the 12th century. Only fragments remain.

LOCATION: LYDBURY, SHROPSHIRE
MAP REF: SO 336846

LUDLOW

LOCATION: SHROPSHIRE
MAP REF: SO 508746
OPEN: PRIVATE: DAILY.
SEE PAGE: 86

LYONSHALL

Lyonshall was an earthwork enclosure with bailey, the remains of which are near the church. The castle had a cylindrical tower, erected on a low platform, probably in the 13th century and a stone curtain was put up around the enclosure.

LOCATION: NR MADLEY, HEREFORDSHIRE
MAP REF: SO 331563

MAXSTOKE

A licence was granted c.1345 for this quadrangular fortified house with corner polygonal towers and a gatehouse. It was one of the earliest fortified houses of this kind to be built although it has been considerably altered since the 14th century. Maxstoke is surrounded by a wide, deep moat.

LOCATION: COLESHILL, WARWICKSHIRE
MAP REF: SP 224891
OPEN: PRIVATE: GOLF CLUB IN THE GROUNDS

MEPPERSHALL

A motte castle with two baileys, all ditched and banked. These are inside a larger rectangular moated enclosure split into segments. The motte may have been one of those besieged by King Stephen in 1138.

LOCATION: BEDFORDSHIRE
MAP REF: TL 132358

MORETON CORBET

A sandstone-and-rubble great tower of diminutive size was built here c.1200, inside a roughly triangular stone enclosure. Unusually, this castle was built by the head of an old Saxon family. Remains of the castle can be seen beside the dramatic ruins of an Elizabethan manor house built for Robert Corbet c.1579.

LOCATION: SHROPSHIRE
MAP REF: SJ 562232
OPEN: ENGLISH HERITAGE: OPEN ACCESS

MOUNTSORREL

Mountsorrel began as a motte castle on a natural rock overlooking the town and the River Soar. It was held by the Earls of Leicester from c.1140 until taken by Henry II after the revolt of his son, Prince Henry. Richard I and John both made improvements to the buildings. The castle was besieged in 1216–17 and razed to the ground.

LOCATION: LEICESTERSHIRE
MAP REF: SK 578148

MYDDLE

Myddle was a small quadrangular castle with an outer bailey built in the 14th century. It was almost completely destroyed in the 17th century, reputedly as a result of earth tremors. There are the remnants of one turret on the site, which can be seen from public footpaths.

LOCATION: SHROPSHIRE
MAP REF: SJ 469235

NEWCASTLE-UNDER-LYME

The motte castle at Newcastle-under-Lyme was built in the 12th century and protected by damming the River Lyme to produce a sizable lake. Remains have been found of a long and narrow building with pilaster buttresses, of the 12th century. King John spent more than £200 on the castle. The mound is visible.

LOCATION: STAFFORDSHIRE
MAP REF: SJ 845459

NORTHAMPTON

There is nothing left to see of this once important medieval castle which, from 1131 to 1380, became the seat of the national parliament. The first motte castle here was built in the 1080s and Northampton expanded rapidly so that by the 12th century it was the third largest town in England. Henry I enlarged the castle in c.1110 and by 1164 it had a great hall, a gateway, curtain walling and a chapel and soon afterwards a great tower was built. It was at Northampton that Thomas Becket, Archbishop of Canterbury, was tried and found guilty for his opposition to King Henry II. The castle was besieged during the Magna Carta war but King John relieved the garrison and forced the attackers to withdraw.

LOCATION: NORTHAMPTONSHIRE
MAP REF: SP 748604

NOTTINGHAM

The present castle at Nottingham has little to do with the medieval structure that began as a motte castle c.1068. The motte was raised on what is now called Castle Rock. Henry II appropriated the castle in the 1150s and spent about £900 on it in the years 1170–5. The castle remained as a property of the Crown for centuries, during which time it grew in magnificence and became one of the four principal English castles. Queen Isabella (widow of Edward II) and her paramour Roger Mortimer attempted to hold out against the young Edward III at Nottingham. However, he entered the fortress through a secret tunnel running through the rock beneath the castle and captured the pair who were implicated in the murder of his father. All that survived after the castle was destroyed in 1651, on the orders of Cromwell, was the gatehouse and the base of a tower built by Edward IV. The site of the medieval castle is now a museum and art gallery.

LOCATION: NOTTINGHAMSHIRE
MAP REF: SK 569394
OPEN: NOTTINGHAM CITY COUNCIL: CASTLE MUSEUM DAILY

OAKHAM

Oakham has one of the best-preserved examples of a free-standing hall of a Norman fortified manor house. Built late in the 12th century, the hall is adorned with splendid 12th-century carvings. Oakham has a collection of over 200 horseshoes: it is the custom that every peer, on a first visit, must give up a horseshoe to the lord of the manor. The oldest horseshoe here belonged to Edward IV; the tradition continues. Oakham began as a motte castle and acquired stonework in the 12th century, but fell into decline during the 15th century. Only grassy mounds indicate the other castle buildings: there were at least two towers. Oakham's great hall, mentioned in Domesday, survived intact and today it is used as an occasional Crown or Coroner's Court.

LOCATION: RUTLAND
MAP REF: SK 861090
OPEN: RUTLAND COUNTY COUNCIL: DAILY

Ludlow

Arthur, Prince of Wales and brother to Henry VIII, depicted in a stained-glass window at Great Malvern Church. Arthur died at Ludlow Castle in 1502.

Described by Daniel Defoe in 1722 as 'the very perfection of decay' Ludlow Castle was begun by the de Lacys in the 11th century, one of a string of fortresses along the borderlands between England and the yet unconquered Welsh territories. Some of the earliest surviving parts of the castle are remnants of their work, including the unusual gatehouse/keep and a Norman chapel in the inner bailey. Among the earliest castle chapels to be built in Britain, its circular nave is still standing. Round chapels were associated with the Knights Templar. The de Lacys held Ludlow until the end of the 13th century when the castle came into the possession of the de Genevilles and then at the beginning of the 14th century, the infamous Roger Mortimer. Mortimer's Tower, which stands out at the castle for its semicircular design, takes its name from its treacherous occupant but was, in fact, built by the de Genevilles. Roger Mortimer did build the Chapel of St Peter, to celebrate his escape from the Tower of London. Mortimer was imprisoned after he and his lover Queen Isabella were implicated in the murder of Edward II. Eventually becoming too powerful, Roger Mortimer was arrested at Nottingham and put to death in 1330.

In 1461 Ludlow began more than three centuries of royal ownership and the castle gradually became the centre of administration for the Marches and for Wales. Edward IV's son was sent to live here and a Prince's Council was formed from members of his household. Prince Edward was at Ludlow

when his father died. The new king and his brother travelled to London but were imprisoned in the Tower of London by their uncle, the Duke of Gloucester. Edward and his brother disappeared and their uncle was crowned King Richard III. The story of the princes has become one of the Tower's most famous legends, and even today their fate remains uncertain. Ludlow also had a cameo role in the years leading up to the Reformation as Henry Tudor's eldest son Prince Arthur died here in 1502. Arthur's wife, Catherine of Aragon, was to become the first wife of Arthur's brother, Henry VIII; it was the separation of this union that led to one of the most momentous periods of British history.

The last few decades of the 16th century saw a period of massive building work. Ludlow wasn't just a royal residence, but a regional government office, court and prison. Both town and castle were besieged by the Parliamentarians during the Civil War when its loyalties lay with the Royalists, but the castle suffered little damage. Its demise came later in the century when government control was centralized in London and Ludlow was abandoned.

Today there are substantial ruins of this once bustling and important administrative centre and royal castle. Ludlow developed over many centuries; its gatehouse keep was first built in the 11th century, altered to include residential accommodation and altered again in the 12th century. The north range, dating mainly from the 14th century, survives as a largely intact shell: the Judges' Lodgings date from the 16th century and were used to house the many officials who came to the castle.

OSWESTRY

The Norman Lord, Rainald de Baliol, an ancestor of King John Baliol of Scotland (1292–6), erected a motte castle at Oswestry late in the 11th century. Stonework was added on the motte in the form of a shell wall, some time in the 12th century. The castle was so throughly destroyed in the Civil War that only piles of stonework and the mound remain. The council maintain the ruins which are now in a public park.

LOCATION: SHROPSHIRE
MAP REF: SJ 290298

PEMBRIDGE

Pembridge Castle, also known as Newland Castle, was built on a rectangular site, partly surrounded by a wet moat. A cylindrical great tower, three storeys high, was erected, probably in the early 13th century. The castle also had a two-storey gatehouse, a separate hall block and a chapel. Held for the king in the Civil War, the Pembridge was besieged and slighted but repaired and then it was restored in Victorian times.

LOCATION: NR WELSH NEWTON, HEREFORDSHIRE
MAP REF: SO 448193
OPEN: PRIVATE

The Earl of Warwick, the Kingmaker

Richard Neville (1428–71) gained lands and the earldom of Warwick through marriage. When his father died he acquired more wealth and power. Warwick helped his cousin to become Edward IV by deposing Henry VI. But Edward displeased Warwick, who then schemed to replace Edward with Henry VI. Edward fought Warwick in battle and killed him.

PEVERIL

Sometimes known as Castle Peak, the castle at Peveril was a very early example of castle-building. Raised on a natural, easily defendable ridge with two precipitous sides, the first building was a stone curtain, which contained herringbone masonry, along the north side of a triangle; it was continued along other sides in the 12th century. After the revolt of his son Prince Henry, Henry II fortified the castle by adding a 18.5m (60ft) square great tower in 1176. The tower was a simple structure and not really intended to be residential: it was faced with ashlar and cost a little under £200.

Peveril is named after its original owners, the Peverel family. William Peverel forfeited it to Henry II in 1155 after he was disgraced, it is said, for having been involved in the murder of the Earl of Chester. The king took a liking to the site, and the great tower was perhaps intended to be a kind of pied-à-terre for visits to Derbyshire and the Peak District. By 1400 the castle's strategic importance had diminished and the keep was used as a courthouse and prison. By the 19th century the castle was ruinous. Extensive renovation works have been carried out on the keep. The setting is magnificent.

LOCATION: CASTLETON, DERBYSHIRE
MAP REF: SK 149826
OPEN: ENGLISH HERITAGE: APR–OCT DAILY; NOV–MAR THU–MON

PRESTON CAPES

Probably late in the 11th century a motte castle was built at Preston Capes on a natural sandstone mound. The mound was surrounded on three sides by a ditch; it seems that the masonry wall may have protected the southern side.

LOCATION: NORTHAMPTONSHIRE
MAP REF: SP 576549

PULVERBATCH

There are two motte sites at Pulverbatch, one at SJ 433016 and visible by Wilderby Hall, and the other, which has its bailey at SJ 423023. The latter may be that mentioned in 1205. It is known locally as Castle Pulverbatch and the earthworks are visible. Both sites are accessible.

LOCATION: CASTLE PULVERBATCH, SHROPSHIRE
MAP REF: SJ 423023

QUATFORD

One of the Conqueror's principal earls and commanders, Roger Montgomery, built a motte castle here on a cliff beside the River Severn some time between 1066–86. It is mentioned in Domesday and some stonework was added, but early in the 12th century the buildings were dismantled. There are traces of the original motte.

LOCATION: NR BRIDGNORTH, SHROPSHIRE
MAP REF: SO 738907

Rockingham is mentioned in the Domesday Book. It was a motte castle built by the Conqueror on a steep hill overlooking the Welland valley, with two quadrilateral baileys. The early castle was probably residential rather than military but it was an important site nevertheless: the Great Council of Rockingham was held here in 1095. The castle was taken over by Henry II c.1156 and from then on, over at least two centuries, many new works and repairs were recorded. Among the major features of this castle was its twin cylindrical-towered gatehouse built by Edward I (c.1280–90) and still an impressive sight. Little of the original Norman castle remains and the main influence today is of the Tudor period. Henry VIII granted the castle to Edward Watson, an ancestor of the present owner and he converted the castle into a more comfortable mansion. Charles Dickens was a frequent visitor here and used it as a model for Chesney Wold in his novel *Bleak House*. The castle displays a fine collection of 20th-century paintings among its many treasures, and hosts many events.

LOCATION: RUTLAND
MAP REF: SP 867913
OPEN: PRIVATE: MAY–SEP SUN–TUE PM; EASTER–END APR SUN & HOLIDAY MON

SAUVEY

Sauvey is a very late motte castle built by King John in the early 13th century and placed in the path of a stream to provide water for a wet moat. The castle remained in royal hands, although granted to the Count of Aumale for a few years. Earthwork remains can be seen.

LOCATION: WITHCOTE, LEICESTERSHIRE
MAP REF: SK 787053

SHOTWICK

Shotwick was a motte castle, enlarged in the 12th and 13th centuries into a roughly hexagonal enclosure of stone with a great tower inside. The curtain had four rounded flanking turrets, a gate-tower and a rectangular great tower with pilaster buttresses. The castle controlled a ford across the Dee. Only earthworks remain today.

LOCATION: NR CHESTER CHESHIRE
MAP REF: SJ 350704

SHRAWARDINE

Shrawardine is a 12th-century motte castle built at a crossing point of the River Severn. The castle was attacked and severely damaged by the Welsh in 1215 and then handed to the FitzAlans in the middle of the 13th century: they rebuilt and renamed the fortress Castle Isabel. The site, razed in the Civil War, is accessible.

LOCATION: NR SHREWSBURY, SHROPSHIRE
MAP REF: SJ 400154

SHREWSBURY

Roger de Montgomery built the motte castle here in 1067–9. A gatehouse and barbican were built in the time of Henry III. Thomas Telford remodelled the castle as a private house in the 18th century; today it houses the Shropshire Regimental Museum.

LOCATION: SHROPSHIRE
MAP REF: SJ 495128

SNODHILL

Fragments of an unusual octagonal tower dating from the 13th century and a gateway flanked by drum towers remain on the top of this motte castle.

LOCATION: NR DORSTONE, HEREFORDSHIRE
MAP REF: SO 322404

Stafford began as a large motte castle of c.1070 and was held by the Stafford barony by the middle of the 12th century. Ralph, 1st Earl of Stafford, invited master-mason John of Burcestre to build a great tower on the old motte in 1347 and up went a rectangular core of three storeys, with octagonal corner turrets rising an extra storey above. The upper storey contained a Great Hall and a Great Chamber. Rooms for the owners, wardrobes, chapel and garderobes were all in the towers. A century later, Stafford enjoyed its heyday as by then it belonged to Humphrey Stafford who had married into the Buckingham family. However, the 3rd Duke of Buckingham, Edward Stafford, was put to death by Henry VIII in 1521 and the castle was left to deteriorate: one owner early in the 17th century, referred to it as 'my rotten castle of Stafford'. It was slighted during the Civil War but the remains were reconstructed in the 19th century. Ruins of this rebuilding, together with medieval stonework and the earthworks of two large baileys, can still be seen. The site has been extensively excavated and details of the findings are displayed on interpretive panels on the site. There is a visitor centre and a full programme of events.

LOCATION: STAFFORDSHIRE
MAP REF: SJ 902222
OPEN: STAFFORD BOROUGH COUNCIL: OPEN ACCESS

STOKESAY

Stokesay is one of the best-preserved medieval fortified manor houses in England. Built by the de Say family, the first structure was a simple two-storey 12th-century pentagonal tower with a projecting square wall-turret on the north angle, both with a timber-framed gallery. In the late 13th century, the new owner, a rich wool merchant called Lawrence of Ludlow built a long hall with gabled windows on to the tower's south wall and at the south end of the hall a three-storey multangular tower; these buildings formed one side of an enclosure of stone which was surrounded by a moat. Most of the surviving structures at Stokesay date from de Ludlow's ownership although the de Say tower still survives and a charming Jacobean gatehouse was added in the 17th century. Only moderately slighted during the Civil War, having avoided a siege by quickly surrendering to the Parliamentarians, Stokesay has survived in much the same condition as it was in its medieval and 17th-century heydays. It is a wonderfully evocative and romantic place to visit.

LOCATION: NR CRAVEN ARMS, SHROPSHIRE
MAP REF: SO 436817
OPEN: ENGLISH HERITAGE: JUN–AUG DAILY; SEP–MAY THU–MON

SULGRAVE

Earthworks next to the church are all that remain of Sulgrave Castle, a fortified enclosure of triangular shape probably built soon after the Conquest. A hall of stone was discovered during excavations but it thought the site was abandoned by the mid-12th century.

LOCATION: NORTHAMPTONSHIRE
MAP REF: SP 556452
OPEN: ACCESSIBLE

TAMWORTH

There is still much to see of Tamworth Castle, which is most notable for its robust shell enclosure wrapped round the tall 11th-century artifical motte. One wing wall remains in part on the motte slope with some familiar Norman herringbone pattern masonry. The castle received stonework c.1180 and the oldest suriviving parts of the castle today are the tower and the north wing. The hall was added early in the 15th century and at the entrance to the courtyard is a Tudor warder's lodge. Tamworth, a castle which frequently hosted royalty, has twice survived destruction; by King John in 1215 and again by the Parliamentarians in 1645.

LOCATION: STAFFORDSHIRE
MAP REF: SK 206037
OPEN: TAMWORTH BOROUGH COUNCIL: FEB–OCT TUE–SUN; NOV–FEB THU–SUN

TOTTERNHOE

On the edge of a chalk down, 3km (2 miles) from Dunstable, a motte castle was built using the promontory for part of the motte which was enclosed on three sides by a wide ditch. Some stonework pieces were found in excavations.

LOCATION: NR DUNSTABLE, BEDFORDSHIRE
MAP REF: SP 979221

TUTBURY

The imposing ruins of Tutbury started as a motte castle built on a natural hill of rock, overlooking the River Dove and on the site of much earlier occupation: it was the principal residence of the de Ferrers. The work at this time included the moat and three baileys but the early fortress was dismantled by Henry II in c.1175. Rebuilt shortly after its dismantling, Tutbury was a grand castle: Henry III visited in 1251, Queen Eleanor was here in 1257 and in the second half of the 13th century the castle became a Lancaster stronghold.

Although at times the buildings were rather neglected, the site retained its importance and Elizabeth I chose it as a place of imprisonment for Mary, Queen of Scots who arrived here in 1569. Severely slighted after the Civil War for harbouring Charles I and his army, the castle is now mainly a shell and the motte is topped with an 18th-century folly. The Great Hall has been restored and opened to the public and events are staged in the grounds.

LOCATION: TUTBURY, STAFFORDSHIRE
MAP REF: SK 209291
OPEN: DUCHY OF LANCASTER: EASTER–SEP WED–SUN; REST OF YEAR SPECIAL EVENTS AND BOOKED PARTIES ONLY

WARWICK

LOCATION: WARWICKSHIRE
MAP REF: SP 284047
OPEN: PRIVATE: DAILY
SEE PAGE: 92

WATTLESBOROUGH

The three-storeyed stone great tower at Wattlesborough appears to have been enclosed by wooden palisading: the tower probably dates from the late 12th century. The castle became part of an 18th-century manor house.

LOCATION: SHROPSHIRE
MAP REF: SJ 355126

WEOBLEY

Weobley was an earthwork enclosure which was captured in 1138. Later stonework probably consisted of a quadrangle with corner and mid-wall towers, gateway and a great tower. It was decaying by the 16th century.

LOCATION: HEREFORDSHIRE
MAP REF: SO 403514

WHITTINGTON

Henry III licensed this castle in 1220 and it received a stone rectangular tower. Only the foundations remain. The site was protected by marshlands. A gatehouse was inserted in the outer enclosure, along with other towers and this was restored in the 19th century.

LOCATION: SHROPSHIRE
MAP REF: SJ 325311
OPEN: WHITTINGTON CASTLE PRESERVATION TRUST: ACCESS TO GROUNDS

WIGMORE

A motte castle was raised here c.1067 by William FitzOsbern and later Wigmore became the main power base of the Mortimers. Reconstruction was carried out in the 14th century and also later between 1461–85. The castle was used as a prison for part of the 16th century. Wigmore's ruins are reasonably substantial.

LOCATION: HEREFORDSHIRE
MAP REF: SO 408693
OPEN: ENGLISH HERITAGE: DAILY

WILTON

Dating from King Stephen's time and sited near the Wye, the ruins from the 13th and 14th centuries are of an irregular quadrilateral curtain wall, with towers at each angle and an additional one in the east wall. An Elizabethan mansion was built on the site of the keep but replaced with a new house in the 19th century.

LOCATION: BRIDSTOW, HEREFORDSHIRE
MAP REF: SO 590244
OPEN: PRIVATE: VIEWING BY APPOINTMENT ONLY

WORCESTER

The original motte castle c.1069 was burned down in 1113. It was rebuilt, part in wood, part in stone, and a stone gateway was added by John in 1204. The castle was in ruins by the 16th century; there are no visible remains.

LOCATION: WORCESTERSHIRE
MAP REF: SO 847550

Warwick

Warwick was sold by the Grevilles in 1978 to The Tussaud's Group which has put much effort into restoring and developing the castle, now one of the country's top tourist attractions. Displays in the castle include period furnishings and the extraordinarily life-like waxwork models, and show the life of the castle through the ages up to the late Victorian era. Parts of the medieval castle are incorporated into the state rooms which were refurbished mainly in the 17th and 18th centuries.

As medieval castles go, Warwick has to be one of England's most evocative, redolent of the history that shaped it since William the Conqueror first built his motte and bailey fortress here in 1068. William's mound is all that survives of that fortification but over the centuries the castle grew into an impressive stronghold to reflect the status of its owners. By 1088 this was the seat of the Earls of Warwick who were to become significant figures in Britain's story.

By the middle of the 13th century the castle had an imposing gatehouse inserted into its stone curtain and a shell keep crowning the motte. The main protagonist in the the Barons' War, Simon de Montfort, lived at neighbouring Kenilworth Castle, so attack was almost inevitable when Warwick sided with Henry III.

Four years later the de Beauchamps inherited the earldom: it was Guy de Beauchamp who helped to seize and trick Edward II's favourite, Piers Gaveston, leading to Gaveston's trial and execution at Warwick in 1312. Early in the 15th century the family's influence at Court was great enough for Henry V to appoint Richard de Beauchamp as tutor to his son Prince Henry (Henry VI), but the dynasty ended in 1449 when Richard Neville gained the title through marriage. He was the most powerful of all the Earls of Warwick.

So great was Neville's influence over the English monarchy that he was called 'Kingmaker'. After Neville was killed at the Battle of Barnet in 1471,

the castle entered a period when it was affiliated even more closely with the Crown. Through the 14th and 15th centuries Warwick was greatly extended, works that included the construction of Guy's Tower and a barbican. Under royal ownership the castle was embellished further.

In 1547 Warwick was granted to another influential family, the Dudleys, key players in the Lady Jane Grey/Mary Tudor struggle and through the reign of Elizabeth I. The Dudleys' possession of Warwick ended in 1590. Early in the 17th century the castle passed into the hands of the Rich and Greville families who inhabited Warwick up to the end of the 20th century. It was lavishly refurbished in the 18th century, and the peerless landscaper 'Capability' Brown was commissioned to design the grounds. Today the castle is one of the best places in England to get a flavour of life in a medieval castle. There is a full calendar of events as well as the display in the castle itself.

WAR GAMES

The Sealed Knot stages re-enactments of Civil War battles at period houses. Audiences are encouraged to talk to the participants who will explain about their weapons, clothes, living conditions and the battles. Members of the Sealed Knot belong to Parliamentarian or Royalist companies and stage battles with attention to detail. A commentary explains exactly what is happening during the battle

ALDINGHAM

Earthwork remains of a motte and bailey castle from the 13th century overlay an earlier ringwork here. The motte and a number of ditches are all that remain on a steep cliff that is gradually eroding.

LOCATION: LANCASHIRE
MAP REF: SD 278698

ALNWICK

LOCATION: NORTHUMBERLAND
MAP REF: NU 187137
OPEN: PRIVATE: APR–OCT DAILY
SEE PAGE: 96

ALMONDBURY

A motte castle was raised here on the site of an Iron Age hill fort in the 11th or 12th century, but there are no remains and the motte is now topped by a tower erected to celebrate Queen Victoria's Golden Jubilee. There is a small exhibition on site.

LOCATION: WEST YORKSHIRE
MAP REF: SE 152140

ANCROFT

Described in the 1540s as a 'little fortress', this interesting three-storey tower was constructed in the 13th century as an integral part of St Anne's, the Anglican church at Ancroft. The chapel dates from the 12th century and was established by monks from the 'Holy Island' of Lindisfarne. The later tower was built as a residence for the curate and to protect the villagers during border raids.

LOCATION: NR BERWICK-ON-TWEED, NORTHUMBERLAND
MAP REF: NV 043437

APPLEBY

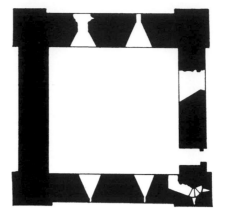

Built in the 12th century, Appleby was an impressive enclosure castle with a sandstone rubble curtain around the bottom of the motte. The square keep, erected in about 1170 and little altered, is one of the best-preserved examples of its type and, unusually, the entrance is not protected by a forebuilding. When William the Lion attacked the castle, the constable here surrendered immediately and without a fight, for which he was heavily fined by Henry II. Lady Anne Clifford restored and improved the castle in the 17th century.

LOCATION: CUMBRIA.
MAP REF: NY 685200
OPEN: PRIVATE. NOT OPEN TO PUBLIC

ARMATHWAITE

Armathwaite is a four-storey 15th-century pele tower overlooking the Eden river. It received 18th- and 19th-century alterations. The castle was home to John Skelton, Poet Laureate in Henry VIII's time.

LOCATION: CUMBRIA
MAP REF: NY 506459

AYDON

A wealthy Suffolk merchant built this fine example of a 13th-century manor house. Aydon was originally intended to be an undefended dwelling but was fortified early in the 14th century when troubles over border territories worsened. It was attacked by the Scots twice, in 1315 and again in 1346. From the 17th century until the 1960s the castle was used as a farm but it has now been restored to its original medieval appearance.

Visitors today can walk through the great hall, chambers, service rooms, and kitchen and servants' accommodation, seeing them just as they would have been in medieval times.

LOCATION: NR CORBRIDGE, NORTHUMBERLAND
MAP REF: NZ 001663
OPEN: ENGLISH HERITAGE: APR–SEP DAILY

BAMBURGH

LOCATION: NORTHUMBERLAND
MAP REF: NU 184351
OPEN: PRIVATE. MID-MAR–OCT DAILY
SEE PAGE: 98

Overlooking the Tees, Barnard Castle began as a small, fortified enclosure of the late 11th century belonging to the Baliol family. It developed into a considerable oblong enclosure site divided into four stone-walled wards and, despite being little more than an imposing ruin today, was once one of the largest castles in the North. The most interesting feature of Barnard is its 13th-century cylindrical great tower built of sandstone blocks, which contrast with the rougher masonry of the curtain. Nearby lie the remains of a 13th- to 14th-century great hall. When the castle was besieged by Alexander I of Scotland in 1216, Barnard was held by Hugh de Baliol. Much later in the century his grandson John became King of Scotland, but only for four years as John was deposed in 1296 and retired to his estates in Picardy. Barnard passed to the Bishop of Durham, but was claimed back by the Crown c.1300. Later still the castle was owned by the Earls of Warwick and was kept on a strong defensive footing against attack from the Scots. During the Rising of the North in the 16th century, Barnard was besieged by 5,000 rebels and from then fell into a state of decay. Sir Henry Vane bought the castle in 1630; he dismantled the buildings and used the materials to build his grand residence at Raby.

LOCATION: BARNARD CASTLE, DURHAM
MAP REF: NZ 049165
OPEN: ENGLISH HERITAGE: APR–OCT DAILY; NOV–MAR THU–MON

BARWICK-IN-ELMET

Built on the site of an Iron Age hill fort, this 12th-century motte and bailey castle was held by the de Lacy family who had the Honour of Pontefract (several estates in Yorkshire) and used it as the administrative centre of the northern part of the Honour. The site is accessible.

LOCATION: WEST YORKSHIRE
MAP REF: SE 398375

BELSAY

Belsay is a substantial stone tower house built in the mid-14th century during a period of turbulence in the borders. The large three-storey tower has a tunnel-vaulted ground floor (probably used as the kitchen) and a great hall with traces of 15th-century painted wall plaster. A Jacobean two-floor range, remodelled in the 19th century, adjoins the tower which has also been repaired. The castle stands in the grounds of Belsay Hall, which was built in Greek Revival style in 1807. The magnificent gardens make for a pleasant walk between the 19th-century hall and medieval castle.

LOCATION: NORTHUMBERLAND
MAP REF: NZ 086785
OPEN: ENGLISH HERITAGE: APR–OCT DAILY; NOV–MAR THU–MON

BERWICK-UPON-TWEED

Berwick, first mentioned in documents dating from the 12th century, was built on rising ground between the east bank of the Tweed and the North Sea. Edward I strengthened the castle and town walls when he seized Berwick from the Scots in 1296 but nothing remains of the castle; the ramparts date largely from the 16th century.

LOCATION: NORTHUMBERLAND
MAP REF: NT 994535
OPEN: ENGLISH HERITAGE: RAMPARTS DAILY

BEW CASTLE

Built on the site of a Roman fort in 1092, Bew was destroyed in 1173 but was rebuilt towards the end of the 14th century. By the 17th century it was ruinous and much of the stone was removed for nearby buildings. Part of the gatehouse remains.

LOCATION: CUMBRIA
MAP REF: NY 566747
OPEN: BY PERMISSION OF LANDOWNER

BITCHFIELD

This rectangular-plan tower had a mansion built beside one of its walls during the late 14th century. The tower is three storeys, each floor containing one main room, with stairs to the next.

LOCATION: NR BELSAY, NORTHUMBERLAND
MAP REF: NZ 091771

Alnwick

One of the best known castles in Britain, its current popularity partly attributable to its starring role in the Harry Potter films, Alnwick's history is as interesting as any work of fiction. The castle is still the seat of the Dukes of Northumberland and is the second-largest inhabited castle in the country.

Yves de Vescy built the earliest parts of the fortress in 1096 and by the middle of the 12th century the castle had taken on the basic plan that remains today. It was one of the earliest Norman fortresses to have been built without a square keep, and fragments of the Norman masonry still exist in the curtain walls.

The de Vescys held Alnwick through several sieges and periods of turbulence (Eustace de Vescy was a ringleader of the Barons' Revolt in 1212; the castle was ordered to be destroyed, but this wasn't carried out) until early in the 14th century when the fortress and manors of Alnwick were handed to Anthony Bek, the Bishop of Durham. The direct male line of the de Vescys died out in 1314 at the Battle of Bannockburn and the Percy family, who became one of England's most powerful dynasties, came to Alnwick in 1309.

The Percy family were instrumental in Henry Bolingbroke's accession to the throne and Hotspur Percy (who earned his nickname at the siege of Berwick Castle) became guardian the young Henry V.

The de Percys were already important English landowners when Henry de Percy bought the castle. Henry, the 1st Lord Percy of Alnwick, started to transform the castle into a formidable stronghold and palatial residence: he reconstructed the keep and rebuilt most of the towers on the curtain wall. His son carried on with the reconstruction – the octagonal towers on either side of the keep's entrance are his and date from c.1350. Generations of Percys made their mark on Alnwick but during the second half of the 18th century the castle was radically altered by architect Robert Adam in the Gothic Revival style (much of this work was later removed). Around the same time Alnwick first became home to the Dukes of Northumberland.

The Percys and Alnwick were often intertwined with many of the pivotal events of British history. Contemporary invaders of Alnwick are visitors who come to view this important part of the nation's heritage and to be reminded of the ancestry of the present 12th Duke of Northumberland, Ralph Percy.

The capture of William the Lion, King of Scotland, depicted in an illustration in A Chronicle of England *(1864) by James Doyle. William planned to extend his lands into Northumberland but Alnwick resisted his first siege in 1172. William was captured during a second siege in 1174, when it is said that he was riding in heavy fog and saw some soldiers on horseback. Believing they were his own men, he approached them and was taken by the English knights.*

THE ALNWICK GARDEN

The Duchess of Northumberland has led the drive to convert a formerly derelict area into the leading garden in Britain. The charitable trust that manages the garden is in the process of creating a place of enjoyment, inspiration and contemplation. Leading garden designers and architects have come together to transform 16ha (40 acres) of parkland. So far 65,000 shrubs, trees and flowers have been planted, and the Grand Cascade has been regenerated. Plans include a visitor centre, extensive pathways and ponds. The garden was opened in 2002 and welcomes more than half a million visitors a year.

The magnificent Grand Cascade

Bamburgh

Bamburgh was an impregnable fortress and royal stronghold virtually from the time it was built by the Norman invaders in the 11th century for around 400 years. In 1464, during the Wars of the Roses, this was the first English castle to fall to artillery which was ranged against this Lancastrian stronghold by the army of Edward IV. The earliest of the many sieges and skirmishes at the fortress came in 1095 when William II attacked Bamburgh using a siege-castle nicknamed Malvoisin (Evil Neighbour): the holder, Robert de Mowbray, was imprisoned for conspiring against the king, and from then until around the early 17th century, Bamburgh remained for the most part in royal hands, maintained as a fortress crucially sited for defence against Scottish invaders. Its great keep is attributed to Henry II and the fortress hosted many visits of the English monarchs.

The castle's formidable outline is still silhouetted against the skyline, much as it would have been when it was one of the most important northern strongholds. Its current grandeur owes more to the 18th and 19th centuries. Bamburgh was ruinous by the end of the 1600s with only the keep remaining intact. It was bought by the 1st Lord Armstrong, a noteworthy industrialist, shipbuilder and engineer, towards the end of the Victorian era, and he began a massive programme of reconstruction and restoration at the fortress.

Bamburgh's origins go back far beyond the Norman castle. Its site has been occupied since the 1st century BC when the lands belonged to a British tribe. A citadel was established here throughout the Roman occupation and when they left Britain there is evidence that Bamburgh was used as the stronghold of a local chieftain. In 547CE Bamburgh was the seat of the Anglo-Saxon king, Ida. During the 7th century it came into the hands of Edwin of Northumbria, a Christian who brought the Roman missionary Paulinus to preach around Bamburgh. After Edwin's death, Oswald, the son of Edwin's adversary Ethelfrith, took Bamburgh and established a monastery on Lindisfarne (Holy Island) in 625; this became one of the world's great centres of learning, art and Christianity.

Viking raids were a constant threat on the north-east coast of England for hundreds of years. Castles such as Bamburgh were intended to protect from invaders of all sorts.

BLENKINSOP

This is a 19th-century house that incorporates the ruined remains of a medieval L-plan tower house, which was licenced to be fortified in 1349. Masonry ruins remain.

LOCATION: NR HALTWHISTLE, NORTHUMBERLAND
MAP REF: NY 664645

BOTHAL

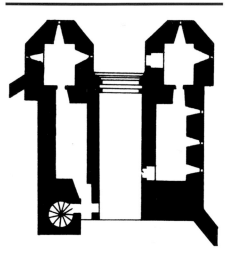

Possibly built on the site of a Norman castle, this 14th-century manor house was fortified in 1343 when the owner Sir Robert de Ogle was granted a licence to crenellate. It consisted of a walled enclosure with towers and buildings. The main feature remains a splendid square gatehouse tower with twin turrets with semi-octagonal front ends flanking the entrance. The castle can be seen near the river.

LOCATION: NR MORPETH, NORTHUMBERLAND
MAP REF: NZ 240866
OPEN: PRIVATE

BOWES

One of Henry II's great tower castles, Bowes was built in a corner of the Roman fort of Lavatrae and was a massive structure for its time. The original fortification was built soon after the Conquest and the keep, of which there are substantial remains, was erected towards the end of the 12th century.

LOCATION: DURHAM
MAP REF: NY 992135
OPEN: ENGLISH HERITAGE: DAILY

BRANCEPETH

A castle at Brancepeth was originally built in the 12th century by the Bulmer family, but the present building is a 19th-century restoration of a 14th-century fortification built by the Earls of Westmoreland. Confiscated by Elizabeth I after the Rising of the North – the rebellion had been partly planned at the castle – Brancepeth became a hospital during World War I and was later the headquarters of the Durham Light Infantry.

LOCATION: DURHAM
MAP REF: NZ 223377
OPEN: PRIVATE (GOLF CLUB)

BROUGH

Brough stands in one corner of the remains of the Roman fort of Verteris, guarding the routes south and across the Pennines against the Scots. The first work was a roughly triangular enclosure of stone begun late in the 11th century, making Brough one of the earliest castles in Britain to have stonework. During the mid-13th century the fortress was owned by the Clifford family who were responsible for building a new hall, tower and range of domestic buildings, and it remained their family home until 1521 when the place was rendered unusable by an accidental fire. Lady Anne Clifford restored Brough in the 17th century, but after her death the castle was left to decay, and all that is left is an interesting ruin.

LOCATION: CUMBRIA
MAP REF: NY 791141
OPEN: ENGLISH HERITAGE: DAILY

BROUGHAM

Robert de Vieuxpont built this castle early in the 13th century on the site of a Roman fort. The Clifford family held Brougham from the 1260s. Late in the 13th century the castle and its defences were much improved by Robert Clifford, a leading figure in Edward I's campaigns in Scotland. Like Brough and various other castles, Brougham was restored by Lady Anne Clifford. She died in the castle, after which it was left to decay by the Earls of Thanet.

LOCATION: NR PENRITH, CUMBRIA
MAP REF: NY 537290
OPEN: ENGLISH HERITAGE: APR–SEP DAILY; OCT THU–MON

BURTON-IN-LONSDALE

A motte castle with two baileys, probably dating from early in the 12th century, the estate was listed in Domesday but the castle here was not recorded until 1129. All that survives are the mound and earthworks. In 1322 the castle was confiscated from the Mowbrays who held it in opposition to Edward II.

LOCATION: NORTH YORKSHIRE
MAP REF: SD 649721A
OPEN: PRIVATE

BUTTERCRAMBE

Thought to date from the 12th century the castle at Buttercrambe is reduced to earthwork traces of a mound and bailey situated in Aldby Park.

LOCATION: NR YORK, NORTH YORKSHIRE
MAP REF: SE 733584

BYWELL

Bywell Castle was built by the de Nevilles, probably during the 1430s although the earliest reference to the castle is 1464 and it was never completed. What still remains is the huge gatehouse tower, a three-storey structure about 18.5m (60ft) wide and 11.5m (38ft) tall.

LOCATION: NR CORBRIDGE, NORTHUMBERLAND
MAP REF: NZ 049618
OPEN: PRIVATE

CALLALY

The present mansion at Callaly stands near the site of a motte castle raised in the 12th century. A pele tower was built in the 15th century and this forms part of the present 17th- and 19th-century mansion.

LOCATION: NR WHITTINGHAM, NORTHUMBERLAND
MAP REF: NU 051099
OPEN: PRIVATE

CARLISLE

The earliest castle structure at Carlisle was a wooden, palisaded enclosure, raised by William Rufus c.1092 on the high bluff overlooking the River Eden. Henry I is then recorded as having ordered a 'castle and towers' to be raised to fortify the city in 1122 and the first stone buildings were begun. The massive great tower was built later in the same century and is the oldest surviving part of the fortress. King David I of Scotland seized Carlisle but Henry II reclaimed the castle in 1157. Its position, at the western end of the border with Scotland, ensured that this fortress was a frequent scene of conflict and change of ownership.

Edward I renovated it and used Carlisle as his seat of government and headquarters when he invaded Scotland. Mary, Queen of Scots was held prisoner here following her abdication from the Scottish throne and the castle was also subjected to an eight-month siege when it was held for the Royalists during the Civil War. In 1746, the final time Carlisle was involved in clashes, supporters of 'Bonnie' Prince Charlie had to defend the castle against the Hanoverian army. It continued to be used as barracks late into the 20th century and houses the museum of the King's Own Royal Border Regiment and much else of interest. Events are held in the grounds.

LOCATION: CUMBRIA
MAP REF: NY 397563
OPEN: ENGLISH HERITAGE: DAILY

CARTINGTON

Now in ruins, there was once a large complex of buildings associated with the castle at Cartington, including a 14th-century tower and great hall. As a Royalist headquarters it was dismantled after the Civil War but partially rebuilt in the 19th century.

LOCATION: NR ROTHBURY, NORTHUMBERLAND
MAP REF: NU 039045
OPEN: ON PRIVATE LAND BUT CAN BE VIEWED FROM A DISTANCE

CHILLINGHAM

A licence to crenellate Chillingham was granted in 1344. The licence, drawn up by William Wakefield, secretary to Edward III, is on display at the castle. What was little more than a single tower built in the previous century became an extensive but compact quadrangular castle with square-angle towers, and a curtain of which there are scant remains. Somewhat altered over the centuries and the subject of wide-ranging restoration by its present occupants, Chillingham is, nevertheless, a fine example of a medieval castle with Tudor additions and is still the family home of descendants of the original owners. Chillingham has the reputation of being one of the most haunted castles in England.

The castle came under attack in 1536 and suffered some damage during the Pilgrimage of Grace rebellion but was successfully defended. Later in the 16th century the main entrance was moved in preparation for a visit to the castle by James VI of Scotland; further alterations were carried out in the 18th and 19th centuries. The grounds were laid out by Sir Jeffrey Wyatville; who worked at Windsor Castle.

LOCATION: NORTHUMBERLAND
MAP REF: NU 061257
OPEN: PRIVATE: EASTER–SEP SUN–FRI

CHIPCHASE

Chipchase Castle sits on the western bank of the North Tyne. The fortified part is principally the 14th-century rectangular tower, which is at one end of the later 17th-century mansion. The four-storeyed tower has machicolated cylindrical turrets on the angles with machicolation along the walls between. The entrance was guarded by an oak portcullis which is still there. Further additions were made in the early part of the 19th century. The castle is private and open briefly in summer but the gardens and a nursery are open all summer

LOCATION: NR CHOLLERTON, NORTHUMBERLAND
MAP REF: NY 882757

CLIFFORD'S TOWER AND BAILE HILL

The Conqueror built two motte castles in York on opposite banks of the River Ouse. Attacked by the Vikings, both were destroyed in 1069 and both were later rebuilt. The motte on the north side of the Ouse – built of marl and clay in layers, with gravel and stones above and with layers of timber – supported a timber great tower, but it was burned down during the anti-Jewish riots in York in 1190. Henry III ordered a rebuild in 1245 and over the next 25 years a curtain with several towers and two gateways was raised round the bailey while the huge motte was adorned with an unusual great tower, now called Clifford's Tower. The plan of the tower is quatrefoil and similar to the great tower of Étampes, south of Paris, where Henry had stayed and which was dated c.1130–50. The motte on the south side of the river was described in the 14th century as 'vetus ballium' (Old Baile) and it is known as Baile Hill. Excavations have revealed remains of 12th-century buildings but nothing survives today.

LOCATION: YORK, NORTH YORKSHIRE
MAP REFS: CLIFFORDS TOWER: SE 605515;
BAILE HILL: SE 602512
OPEN: CLIFFORD'S TOWER (ENGLISH HERITAGE):
DAILY

CLITHEROE

Built around 1186 by Robert de Lacy to protect the administrative centre of his vast estates, the surviving medieval parts of the castle include the stone keep and the adjacent curtain wall that surrounds it. It is said to be the smallest keep in England, the rooms are only about 2sq m (20sq ft) and is also claimed to be the oldest surviving building in Lancashire. Open access.

LOCATION: CLITHEROE, LANCASHIRE
MAP REF: SD 742416

COCKERMOUTH

This is mainly a 13th-century structure built on the site of the original 12th-century castle. It was further fortified in the 14th century. The castle played an important role in the Wars of the Roses and the Civil War, after which it was dismantled. Partly restored in the 19th century, much of Cockermouth is still in ruins. Privately owned.

LOCATION: CUMBRIA
MAP REF: NY 123309

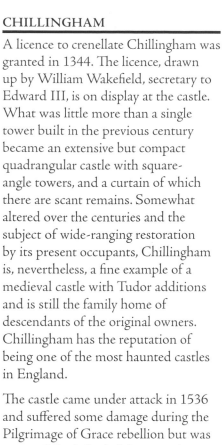

COCKLE PARK TOWER

An interesting three-storey tower house of the 15th century with machicolated embellished corners on one end and machicolated bartizans at the wallhead. A domestic building on one end later extended the tower house. The site, within land now owned by Newcastle University, can be seen from the road.

LOCATION: NR MORPETH, NORTHUMBERLAND
MAP REF: NZ 202910
OPEN: PRIVATE

Pilgrimage of Grace
In 1536 Roman Catholics resisted Henry VIII's abolition of papal supremacy. Protesters in the North occupied several cities in defiance of the king but they were promised a parliament in York within a year if they dispersed. However, this did not prevent unrest and the leaders were tried and executed. Harsh repression in the North quashed further protests.

CONISBROUGH

Conisbrough Castle was built around 1180–1200 by Hamelin Plantagenet, illegitimate half-brother to Henry II. It stands on the site of an earlier fortress, which was held by William de Warenne and probably built c.1070: Hamelin was the 5th Earl de Warenne and he built a great tower castle enclosed in a curtain wall with flanking solid half cylindrical towers and a gatehouse with projecting barbican (of which there are a few remains). The principal feature of the castle is the uniquely shaped great tower (unique, that is, in Britain as there is a similar De Warenne stronghold at Mortemer near Dieppe in France). Constructed from limestone ashlar, the tower is cylindrical with six wedge-shaped buttresses placed equidistantly round the outer wall and is notable for the scarcity of window openings and arrow-loops. It had the disadvantage of most cylindrical towers in that the entrance was not protected by a forebuilding. However, the castle was not put to the test of a siege and Conisbrough remained mostly in the hands of the de Warenne family until the 14th century when it passed to the Crown. It was quite ruinous by the 16th century and this probably saved it from further destruction after the Civil War. Conisbrough has been made more famous by inspiring Sir Walter Scott to write his epic novel *Ivanhoe*.

LOCATION: NR DONCASTER, SOUTH YORKSHIRE
MAP REF: SK 515989
OPEN: ENGLISH HERITAGE/IVANHOE TRUST: OPENING TIMES VARIABLE (TEL 01709 863329)

CORBRIDGE VICAR'S PELE

One of the few fortified vicarages in the country, the Vicar's Pele is built largely of stone taken from the nearby Roman fortress at Corstopitum.

LOCATION: CORBRIDGE, NORTHUMBERLAND
MAP REF: NY 987644

COTTINGHAM

Originally known as Banyard's Castle, a licence to fortify Cottingham was granted c.1202. Later, the manor was turned into a castle. One owner, Lord Wake, deliberately burned down Cottingham just before a visit from Henry VIII: it is said that he was worried the amorous attentions of the king would be turned on his wife. Nothing remains of the castle today.

LOCATION: BEVERLEY, HUMBERSIDE
MAP REF: TA 041330

COUPLAND

This Grade1 listed country house incorporates an L-plan tower house dating from the very early 17th century. The building was extended in the 18th century and further developed between 1820 and 1825.

LOCATION: NR MILLFIELD, NORTHUMBERLAND
MAP REF: NT 936312
OPEN: PRIVATE

CRASTER

Craster castle has a medieval tower documented from the 15th century, now part of a mansion built in the late 1700s. The tower has been altered and has Gothic-style windows.

LOCATION: NR DUNSTANBURGH, NORTHUMBERLAND
MAP REF: NU 251196
OPEN: PRIVATE

DACRE

Dacre has a very fine pele tower, which is still occupied. It was first constructed in the 13th century by the Dacre family and rebuilt in the mid-14th century after being attacked by the Scots. Given two wings, its design follows in the Scottish tower-house manner. The 5th Lord Dacre altered and renovated the tower in the late 17th century and added the large windows.

LOCATION: CUMBRIA
MAP REF: NY 462265
OPEN: PRIVATE VISITS BY ARRANGEMENT

DRIFFIELD

A 12th-century motte castle was built here at what came to be called Moot Hill. The site has been excavated.

LOCATION: EAST RIDING OF YORKSHIRE
MAP REF: TA 023583

DUNSTANBURGH

Dunstanburgh was a lavish stonework enclosure castle whose main feature was the huge gatehouse tower at the extreme southern end. The first buildings were erected in the early 14th century and included the massive three-storey gatehouse, with its cylindrical towers rising another two storeys. Now in ruins, the gatehouse contained a great hall on the second floor, with tall, mullioned and transomed windows positioned at each end. Built by Thomas, Earl of Lancaster who opposed Edward II for his bad government and his infelicitous choice of friends, particularly Piers Gaveston, Dunstanburgh passed in due course to John of Gaunt. It was John who, in the 1370s and 1380s, closed up the entrance to the gatehouse with a stone wall and a forebuilding (now disappeared) and turned it into a residential great tower, building an alternative gateway with barbican. Dunstanburgh, a Lancastrian stronghold, was besieged during the Wars of the Roses and suffered much damage from the Yorkist cannons. It is now an impressive ruin standing high on the cliffs above the sea.

LOCATION: NR CRASTER, NORTHUMBERLAND
MAP REF: NU 257219
OPEN: ENGLISH HERITAGE: APR–OCT DAILY; NOV–MAR THU–MON

DURHAM

A motte castle erected in a loop of the River Wear in 1072 was granted to the Prince-bishop of Durham and the chapel of 1080 still survives. In the early 12th century a shell enclosure of sandstone in roughly octagonal plan was erected on the motte around the wooden tower and this may have been retained for some time; the shell was destroyed in 1340 and rebuilt. Domestic buildings were gradually added within the banked, ditched and partly curtained bailey, including a range to the north, a 13th–14th century great hall, a gatehouse and a kitchen. Although primarily a bishops' palace rather than a fortress, the castle was always kept ready for defence. Prince-bishops were expected to levy an army in times of threat, in return for absolute power over their bishopric. The keep was rebuilt in the middle of the 19th century when the castle became the site of Durham University but the great hall, used as the dining hall of University College, is medieval: it was first built by Bishop Antony Bek (1284–1311) and then altered by Bishop Thomas Hatfield later in the 14th century. The walls of the palace/castle were connected with the city's walls, and the entire peninsula was enclosed by the river, with the magnificent cathedral included. Together with the cathedral, the castle at Durham has been declared a World Heritage Site.

LOCATION: CITY OF DURHAM, DURHAM
MAP REF: NZ 273423
OPEN: UNIVERSITY OF DURHAM: GUIDED TOURS ALL YEAR, DAILY DURING SUMMER. CONTACT THE CASTLE PORTER OR TOURIST INFORMATION

EDLINGHAM

A picturesque ruin set in a ruggedly attractive valley site, Edlingham Castle was first begun at the end of the 13th century and building continued until the 14th century. It began as a long rectangular hall to which a gatehouse, a small tower/keep and curtain was added. By the middle of the 17th century the castle was abandoned and a great deal of the stone had been removed for other buildings. The ruins date from the 13th–14th centuries.

LOCATION: NR ALNWICK, NORTHUMBERLAND
MAP REF: NU 116092
OPEN: ENGLISH HERITAGE: ALL REASONABLE TIMES

EGREMONT

Egremont was erected in the 12th century with a circular keep and gatehouse added later in the same century. Robert the Bruce raided the castle in 1314. The gatehouse and parts of the walls (some with herringbone

masonry) are still standing beside a public footpath.

LOCATION: CUMBRIA
MAP REF: NY 010105
OPEN: ACCESS AT ANY TIME

EMBLETON TOWER

Not far from the ruins of Castle Dunstanburgh, this three-storey stone tower, complete with crenellations and a double vaulted basement, is a fine example of a 14th-century vicar's pele. Later additions include the Elizabethan windows, and further alterations were made in the 18th and 19th centuries.

LOCATION: EMBLETON, NORTHUMBERLAND
MAP REF: NU 231225
OPEN: PRIVATE

ETAL

In 1341 Robert Manners was granted permission to crenellate his three-storey tower house. The castle fell to

the army of James IV of Scotland during his invasion of England in 1513 but the Scots were defeated at the Battle of Flodden Field. On the site of the ruins of Etal Castle is an award-winning exhibition about the battle and the border warfare before the union of the English and Scottish crowns early in the 17th century.

LOCATION: NORTHUMBERLAND
MAP REF: NT 925394
OPEN: ENGLISH HERITAGE: APR–SEP DAILY

FEATHERSTONE

The mansion at Featherstone, built in the 17th century, incorporates some much earlier stone building, including a handsome square pele tower, with an arm to make it L-plan, erected c.1330 by Thomas de Featherstonehaugh. The house was remodelled in the 17th and 19th centuries.

LOCATION: NR HALTWHISTLE, NORTHUMBERLAND
MAP REF: NY 674610
OPEN: PRIVATE

KINGS, BARONS AND SOCIETY

The lord and lady had the best rooms in their castle. It is not unusual to see pictures of couples like this in bed in medieval manuscripts; they reflect a society where privacy was not always available or sought.

THE MONARCH WAS AT THE PINNACLE OF MEDIEVAL SOCIETY. HIS RULE WAS ABSOLUTE, BUT HE COULD ONLY RULE WITH THE ACTIVE HELP OF LORDS AND BARONS. THE BARONS THEMSELVES WERE OFTEN IMMENSELY POWERFUL, ESSENTIALLY RULING THE LANDS THEY CONTROLLED. SOMETIMES THEY WORKED TOGETHER FOR THE GOOD OF THE COUNTRY, BUT THERE WERE TIMES WHEN THE BARONS SEEMED THE CREATORS OF ANARCHY AND MISERY.

Feudal society was pyramidal: at the top was the monarch, next came the barons, who were given land by the king in return for loyalty and help in times of strife and war. Next were the knights, who were given land by the barons in return for service. At the bottom of the pyramid were the peasants, or villeins, who did all the manual work. Villeins had few rights: the baron or knight could order them to work without pay, and they were sometimes little better than slaves. But society would have collapsed entirely without their work, and the lords knew that.

Later in the Middle Ages, society gradually moved from a service-based structure to one based on money. A new class arose called freemen who were better off than villeins, and were usually the skilled workers and tradesmen.

The fortunes of the times depended very much on individual monarchs. If they were strong they could hold society together; if weak, then things could unravel very quickly. An example of this is the reign of King Stephen from 1135 to 1154. Stephen was the nephew of the previous king, Henry I, and was

The king was powerful only if he had the support of his nobles. If they changed their allegiance they could threaten the security of the monarch and thus the country.

crowned by barons who did not like the idea of Henry's rightful heir – Matilda – coming to the throne because she was a woman. Matilda did not accept this, and the ensuing civil war lasted for most of Stephen's reign. Each side courted the barons, who took advantage of the situation.

Castles were central in this struggle. A contemporary account describes the misery created: 'when the castles were built they filled them with devils and wicked men … At regular intervals they levied a tax known as protection money on the villages. When the wretched people had no more to give they plundered and burned all the villages … the land was ruined by such doings and men said openly that Christ and His Saints slept.'

In the reign of King John (1199–1216), the barons showed themselves in a better light, through their insistence on the drawing up of Magna Carta. Although it worked to the advantage of the barons, it put in writing some of the basic tenets of society, and formed the foundation for England's unwritten constitution. A key passage reads: 'No free man shall be taken or imprisoned … or in any way ruined … except by the lawful judgement of his peers or the law of the land.'

Such statements showed that society could draw towards civilization and ideas of justice for all.

Cleanliness and hygiene were variable in medieval times. A special official was responsible for water and the necessary equipment for royal baths. Henry I paid three pence each for his (infrequent) baths.

FORD

Ford Castle was once an extensively fortified quadrangular castle c.1400 but captured by the Scots and dismantled. By the beginning of the 16th century it had been rebuilt and was converted into a mansion at the end of the 17th century. Ford was captured by James IV of Scotland just before the Battle of Flodden in 1513.

LOCATION: NR ETAL, NORTHUMBERLAND
MAP REF: NT 944375
OPEN: PRIVATE

GILLING

Now part of the famous Catholic school of Ampleforth, this impressive building was first erected in the 14th century as a fortified tower house by the de Etton family and extended in the 16th century by Sir William Fairfax. The castle was remodelled in the 18th century. Gilling Manor belonged to Alan the Red who built Richmond Castle.

LOCATION: GILLING EAST, NR HELMSLEY, NORTH YORKSHIRE
MAP REF: SE 611768
OPEN: HALL OPEN TO PUBLIC

GLEASTON

A simple quadrangle castle, Gleaston was built in the early 14th century by the de Harrington family. At one time it was owned by the great-grandfather of Lady Jane Grey. It had four corner towers, three of which still stand but in a very ruinous state. The castle was dismantled in 1458.

LOCATION: ULVERSTON, CUMBRIA
MAP REF: SD 261715
OPEN: CAN BE VIEWED EXTERNALLY FROM A DISTANCE ONLY AS UNSAFE

HALTON

The tower here, Aydon's sister castle, was erected in the 14th century and is attached to a later hall. The rectangular tower is four-storeyed with cylindrical bartizans topping the corners.

LOCATION: NR AYDON, NORTHUMBERLAND
MAP REF: NY 997678

HARBOTTLE

The castle here was raised in about 1157 and this motte castle was rebuilt in stone c.1200. In 1515, Queen Margaret of Scots gave birth to her daughter here. It was used as a prison for border reivers in the 16th century. There are very few remains.

LOCATION: NR ROTHBURY, NORTHUMBERLAND
MAP REF: NT 932048
OPEN: NORTHUMBERLAND NATIONAL PARK: OPEN ACCESS

HELMSLEY

The most striking thing about this stone enclosure castle of the late 12th to early 13th century are the huge earthwork ditch-and-bank defences. Built to a simple enough design as a quadrangle inside another quadrangle, the castle was extremely well defended: the ditches are over 9m (30ft) deep. These earthworks are related to an earlier castle on the site built some time in the first half of the 12th century. Robert de Roos rebuilt the castle in stone and erected a thick curtain wall with D-end and round flanking towers along the edge of the platform in the inner quadrangle. On the north east of the wall he inserted, c.1200, a rectangular great tower and another great tower in the west which remains. The Lordship of Helmsley stayed with the de Roos name until 1478; the castle was much improved and altered by members of the family. Eventually the Manners family inherited the lordship and created a fashionable Elizabethan residence. Helmsley was never a site of siege or battle until the Civil War when it was garrisoned for the king and besieged by Parliamentarians: this was a relatively peaceful affair with the defenders finally surrendering through lack of food. Sir Thomas Fairfax dismantled most of the fortress but kept the Elizabethan west range intact.

LOCATION: NORTH YORKSHIRE
MAP REF: SE 611836
OPEN: ENGLISH HERITAGE: APR–SEP DAILY; OCT–MAR THU–MON

HORNBY

This is a large privately owned house which includes the 13th-century keep from the orginal motte castle. The house, built in the 16th century, was altered early in the 18th century and remodelled again in the 1850s.

LOCATION: LANCASHIRE
MAP REF: SD 587685
OPEN: PRIVATE

HUTTONS AMBO

A rectangular enclosure raised on a spur above the River Derwent. The earliest building was a timber hall replaced by a stone hall in the 13th century. The site was excavated in the middle of the last century.

LOCATION: NORTH YORKSHIRE
MAP REF: SE 763674

HYLTON

Hylton consists of the repaired ruin of a substantial gatehouse tower which was used as a residence by Sir William Hylton from the end of the 14th to the early 15th centuries. The tall great hall rose up the centre of the tower, which is now a shell, all the way to the roof. The exterior of the castle displays medieval heraldic shields.

LOCATION: NR SUNDERLAND, TYNE AND WEAR.
MAP REF: NZ 358588
OPEN: ENGLISH HERITAGE: REASONABLE ACCESS

KENDAL

Kendal was an enclosure with earth banking which received stone additions in the 12th century. The castle was built by the de Lancasters, Barons of Kendal, and passed to the Parr family during the time of Richard II. Kendal was derelict by the end of the 16th century and only the remains of two towers and some walls are still extant, as much of its stone was used for other buildings. Excavations revealed two vaults beneath the hall. Visitors can explore the ruins by using the specially built wooden steps, and look over the town from the walls.

LOCATION: CUMBRIA
MAP REF: SD 522924
OPEN: OPEN SITE

KIRKOSWALD

Owned by Simon de Morville, Kirkoswald was fortified in the early 13th century, but more or less destroyed in 1314 when it was burned down during a Scottish border raid. Rebuilt, for a time it was in the possession of Lord Dacre who made numerous alterations and additions. In the 17th century the site was plundered for materials and only the partial remains of one tower can be seen today.

LOCATION: CUMBRIA
MAP REF: NY 560410
OPEN: ON PRIVATE LAND BUT CAN BE VIEWED FROM A PUBLIC FOOTPATH

KNARESBOROUGH

Knaresborough Castle stands on a high rock overlooking the town and the Nidd valley. The fortress was mainly in royal hands right through to the end of the 15th century and much of the building here was carried out by the kings. King John held Knaresborough as one of his main administrative strongholds in the North: he spent a great deal of money on the castle and in return it stayed loyal to the Crown during the Barons' Revolt.

The most extensive work, though, was under the patronage of Edward II and Edward III between 1307–50, and the remains are chiefly from this period. Edward II built the great tower, and it was Edward III's wife, Queen Phillipa, who received the Honour and Castle of Knaresborough as part of her marriage settlement and turned the castle into a proper royal residence: she spent many of her summers here. Knaresborough was defended during a siege of six months during the Civil War but the Royalist garrison finally capitulated and much of the castle was slighted. The great tower was saved at the request of the local population and used as a prison.

LOCATION: CASTLE YARD, KNARESBOROUGH, NORTH YORKSHIRE
MAP REF: SE 348569
OPEN: HARROGATE BOROUGH COUNCIL: EASTER– SEP DAILY WITH GUIDED TOURS. GROUNDS: ALL YEAR

LANCASTER

Lancaster Castle is not only a fortress but also one of Europe's longest serving prisons: the first reference to the castle gaol is dated 1196. Huge crowds used to gather outside the castle walls to watch executions. The Pendle witches were tried, convicted and died at Lancaster, and the founder of the Quaker movement, George Fox, spent two years imprisoned here. The castle today is still the site of a prison and a County Court.

Lancaster stands on a knoll overlooking the River Lune and began as a motte castle, erected on the site of an earlier Roman fortress. It was rebuilt in stone during the late 11th and early 12th centuries by Roger de Poitou. When the castle came into the possession of Henry IV in 1399 he began major new works. These included the handsome and formidable twin semi-octagonal-turreted gatehouse, which is still extant and named after his father John of Gaunt. The Royalists besieged Lancaster during the Civil War (having first lost it to the Parliamentarians) and they also set fire to the town. The castle has been used as a prison proper since the mid-18th century, which led to major additions in the 19th century, including the Shire Hall which is still sometimes in use as a courtroom.

LOCATION: LANCASHIRE
MAP REF: SD 473620
OPEN: LANCASHIRE COUNTY COUNCIL: MAR–DEC DAILY

LANGLEY

Built by Thomas de Lucy in the mid-14th century, Langley is one of the finest tower houses in Northumberland. Built to an H-plan design, it is four storeys high and with four substantial turrets. Attacked and severely damaged by Henry IV during his campaign against the Percys and Archbishop Scrope in 1404, it had fallen into ruins by the mid-16th century. However, in the late 19th and early 20th century the castle was lovingly restored by local historian Cadwallader Bates and his wife.

LOCATION: NR HAYDON BRIDGE, NORTHUMBERLAND
MAP REF: NY 835624
OPEN: HOTEL

LUMLEY

A fortified manor house of the 1390s, quadrangular with substantial square towers at the corners. Alterations were made c.1580 and again in the 18th century. The east wing has an interesting gatehouse.

LOCATION: NR CHESTER-LE-STREET, DURHAM
MAP REF: NZ 287510
OPEN: HOTEL

MIDDLEHAM

A motte castle was put up at Middleham but the motte was abandoned and is known today as William's Hill. In c.1170, Robert FitzRanulph was granted leave to build a great tower on a site south-west of the motte and a surprisingly substantial structure with palatial accommodation emerged. In the 13th century, the magnificent great tower was enclosed in a quadrangular curtain with buildings ranged along three sides, including corner towers and gatehouse, and yet more buildings were added in the 14th and 15th centuries. The castle was also surrounded by a moat. Middleham came into the possession of the Nevilles, passing eventually to the Earl of Warwick, and for ten years before his death in 1471 the castle was a political and social powerhouse. Warwick's daughter married the Duke of Gloucester, who later became Richard III, and it was here that their only son was born and then died at age ten. Henry VII seized Middleham after Richard's death and it remained a royal castle until very early in the 17th century but no royal visits are recorded. Although it was garrisoned during the Civil War, Middleham was never besieged. Nevertheless the castle was ruinous by the 19th century although the extensive remains imply its former grandeur.

LOCATION: NR LEYBURN, NORTH YORKSHIRE
MAP REF: SE 128875
OPEN: ENGLISH HERITAGE: APR–SEP DAILY; OCT–MAR THU–MON

MITFORD

Early motte castles were few and far between in Northumbria but this was erected at Mitford prior to the 1100s. The motte eventually received a unique five-sided keep and the castle here was home to the Barons of Mitford. Burned down by King John and confiscated by Henry III, in 1318 the castle was attacked by the Scottish led by 'Black Douglas' on behalf of Robert the Bruce. Only ruins remain.

LOCATION: NORTHUMBERLAND
MAP REF: NZ 170855
OPEN: NORTHUMBERLAND COUNTY COUNCIL. ACCESSIBLE

MORPETH

A gatehouse belonging to the second of the two castles built on this site is all that remains. The first started as a motte and bailey in the 11th century and the second castle, in the bailey of the orginal, was built in the 13th century. Five hundred Scots held out against a siege here in the Civil War.

LOCATION: NORTHUMBERLAND
MAP REF: NZ 200857
OPEN: PRIVATE

MULGRAVE

A polygonal-plan curtain enclosure, Mulgrave's gateway with two drum towers encircled a great tower which had round angle turrets and a forebuilding. The castle was begun c.1215 and the great tower dates from c.1300. Additions include large mullioned windows from the 16th century. Mulgrave was slighted after the Civil War and is now in ruins.

LOCATION: NR LYTHE, NORTH YORKSHIRE
MAP REF: NZ 840117
OPEN: ACCESSIBLE AT WEEKENDS ONLY

MUNCASTER

The castle at Muncaster was originally built c.1258 on a remote site beneath England's tallest peak, Scafell Pike. In the 14th century a pele tower was put up on Roman foundations. This is incorporated into the present castle whose buildings were reconstructed in the 1850–60s by Anthony Salvin. Muncaster has been in the possession of the same family for nearly 800 years. Legend has it that when Sir John Pennington gave shelter to Henry VI after the Battle of Hexham, Henry left his drinking bowl at the castle saying that as long as it remained whole the Penningtons would live and thrive at Muncaster: the bowl is intact and known as the 'Luck of Muncaster'. The castle is a family home and has large collections of furniture, paintings and artefacts gathered by the Penningtons.

LOCATION: RAVENGLASS, CUMBRIA
MAP REF: SD 103964
OPEN: PRIVATE. CASTLE: SUN–FRI PM

NAFFERTON

Known locally as Lonkin Hall, only earthworks remain of the enclosure castle here which sat on the edge of Whittle Burn not far from Prudhoe. There are the remains of a tower house thought to date from the 15th or 16th century.

LOCATION: NORTHUMBERLAND
MAP REF: NZ 072657

NAWORTH

Naworth castle, built in the early 14th century, appears to have been a simple walled quadrilateral enclosure with a great tower in the wall at one end and a gateway at the other, and then extended into a border fortress during the hostilities between England and Scotland later that century. A deep moat was cut on three of the four sides. The present appearance is due largely to restoration by Anthony Salvin after a fire in the 1840s.

LOCATION: CUMBRIA
MAP REF: NY 560626
OPEN: PRIVATE: APR–OCT

NEWCASTLE

Newcastle began as a motte castle with a bank and ditch, built by Robert Curthose, the Conqueror's eldest son, in 1080. During the late 11th and early 12th centuries the ownership of the northern counties of England was often disputed with Scotland and for a time Newcastle was held by the Scottish kings, most notably David I (1124–53). A new, stone castle was begun by Henry II in 1168. Works continued for about ten years under Mauricius Caementarius (Maurice the Engineer), and included a substantial rectangular great tower enclosed within a curtain wall. The great tower with its vaulted basement was restored in the middle of the 19th century and now houses a museum. It is one of the best surviving examples of a Norman keep in the country.

The curtain enclosure was many sided, with postern gates and rectangular flanking towers. Additional buildings raised against the inside in later years include the aisled great hall of c.1210 which was dismantled in 1809. In 1247–50 a tower gatehouse, the Black Gate, which survives, was added to the more vulnerable western edge of the castle site. Once the town walls were completed in the middle of the 14th century the castle's defensive significance declined. It was garrisoned again briefly during the Civil War.

LOCATION: NEWCASTLE UPON TYNE
MAP REF: NZ 250638
OPEN: NEWCASTLE SOCIETY OF ANTIQUARIES OF NEWCASTLE UPON TYNE: DAILY

NORHAM

Set at a strategic crossing point of the south bank of the River Tweed, Norham's site is protected by a steep cliff forming part of the river bank, a ravine and an artificially deepened hollow leading into the river. A D-shaped inner bailey contains the ruins of a massive great tower. Founded by Bishop Flambard of Durham c.1120, the first castle here was destroyed by the Scots but rebuilt in stone in the 1160s on the orders of Henry II: the great tower was built at this time. Norham stood in the front line of attack by the Scots and on numerous occasions it was besieged, and even captured. There is evidence of new building and repair work in nearly every generation between the 12th and

the 16th centuries. The Scots employed the famous siege gun Mons Meg (now on display at Edinburgh Castle) during one of their attacks on the castle. In 1513, James IV of Scotland besieged, captured and virtually destroyed the fortress but following the defeat of the Scots at Flodden Field the castle was returned to the English and repaired. Early in the 17th century Norham lost its already declining strategic importance and the ruins were left to become a favourite subject of the 19th-century Romantic artist JMW Turner.

LOCATION: NR BERWICK UPON TWEED, NORTHUMBERLAND
MAP REF: NT 907476
OPEN: ENGLISH HERITAGE: APR–SEP SAT–SUN

MONS MEG

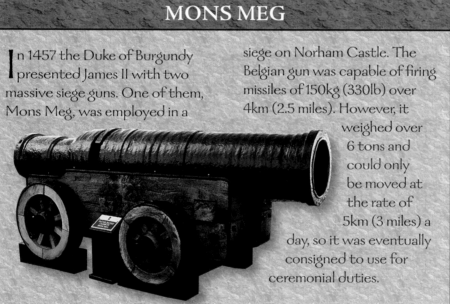

In 1457 the Duke of Burgundy presented James II with two massive siege guns. One of them, Mons Meg, was employed in a siege on Norham Castle. The Belgian gun was capable of firing missiles of 150kg (330lb) over 4km (2.5 miles). However, it weighed over 6 tons and could only be moved at the rate of 5km (3 miles) a day, so it was eventually consigned to use for ceremonial duties.

PENDRAGON

A square great tower with intramural passaging and angle buttressing was built late in the 12th century, inside an enclosure here, beside the River Eden. Just the ruined base remains today. According to legend this is the place where King Arthur's father, Uther Pendragon, died. Lady Anne Clifford restored the castle in the 17th century but it fell into decay after her death.

LOCATION: MALLERSTANG, CUMBRIA
MAP REF: NY 782026
OPEN: PRIVATE

PENRITH

The beginnings of Penrith Castle are obscure, but permission to crenellate was granted in 1397 to William Strickland, later Bishop of Carlisle; Penrith was extended further in the 15th century. Much of the stone has been removed but some of the walls and the motte remain set in a park on the edge of the town.

LOCATION: PENRITH, CUMBRIA
MAP REF: NY 513299
OPEN: ENGLISH HERITAGE: DAILY

PENWORTHAM

This motte castle, which now survives as earthworks, was mentioned in the Domesday Book and possibly dates from the early 11th century. The motte was raised around the base of the wooden tower in the same way as those at Totnes and South Mimms. The castle guarded the estuary of the River Ribble.

LOCATION: LANCASHIRE
MAP REF: SD 524290

PIEL

Known also as the Peel of Fouldry, this castle sits on an island at the mouth of the deep-water harbour of Barrow-in-Furness: it was built to protect the monks at Furness Abbey. In the 1320s a licence to crenellate was granted and a concentric castle was erected consisting of a great tower inside an inner bailey and surrounded by an outer ward with broad ditches and thick stone walling, towers and moats. The castle was dismantled in 1403 but partly rebuilt c.1429. The great tower is square, with pilaster buttresses on the corners, and remains relatively well preserved as the castle was in ruins by the 16th century. Some renovation was undertaken in the 19th century. In 1805, having stayed in the district for a while, William Wordsworth wrote about Piel :

> "I was thy neighbour once,
> thou rugged Pile!
> Four summer weeks I dwelt
> in the sight of thee:
> I saw thee every day; and all the while,
> Thy form was sleeping on a glassy sea."

LOCATION: PIEL ISLAND, NR BARROW-IN-FURNESS, CUMBRIA
MAP REF: SD 233636
OPEN: ENGLISH HERITAGE: DAILY (ACCESS BY FERRY ONLY)

PICKERING

This was a motte castle built soon after the Conquest, during William I's northern campaign. The motte was surrounded by a ditch with two baileys enclosing it, in two curved halves. Stone was added between 1180 and 1236: a stone curtain was built and c.1218–36 work was done on constructing a circular shell keep on top of the motte, which was replaced in the 13th century. Various buildings were raised in the two baileys, including a new hall of c.1314, a chapel of c.1227 and the constable's lodgings. Pickering was besieged in the Magna Carta war of 1215–16. Edward II was fond of the castle and lavished nearly £1,000 on it in 1323–6, including replacing the timber palisade around the outer bailey with stone. This outer curtain had three towers, one of which was built as a prison, and the order for this work is preserved in the Public Record Office. By the 17th century the chapel was the only usable building; today it serves as an exhibition space. Much of the keep, towers and walls remain as substantial ruins.

LOCATION: NORTH YORKSHIRE
MAP REF: SE 800845
OPEN: ENGLISH HERITAGE: VARIED OPENING TIMES

PONTEFRACT

Pontefract was for a long time the principal royal castle in northern England. Used as a residence, arsenal, court and prison, its end came after it was besieged three times during the Civil War and then so severely slighted by Parliament that this once great fortress has almost disappeared. Originally a de Lacy holding, Pontefract began as a motte castle of c.1086. Over the next two centuries it acquired two more baileys, and all three of these received buildings and walls, timber first and then stone. Through marriage, the castle came into the possession of Thomas Plantagenet, Earl of Lancaster and extensive additions were made during his tenure, but in 1322 Thomas was tried for treason and beheaded at the castle: his lands were eventually restored to his heirs and Pontefract became and still remains a part of the Duchy of Lancaster. At the end of the 14th century Richard II was imprisoned and died here after Henry Bolingbroke forced his abdication and the House of Lancaster came to the throne. Unsurprisingly the castle was an important Lancastrian stronghold during the Wars of the Roses. However, its significance declined somewhat during Tudor times. Nevertheless it was an important arsenal after the Pilgrimage of Grace in 1536. Major repairs and renovations were made early in the 17th century prior to the Civil War, and when it fell in 1649, the fortress was the last Royalist stronghold to surrender.

LOCATION: WEST YORKSHIRE
MAP REF SE 460224
OPEN: CITY OF WAKEFIELD METROPOLITAN DISTRICT COUNCIL: OPEN ACCESS

PRUDHOE

Prudhoe is a motte castle of c.1080s which developed into a roughly figure-of-eight plan enclosure. Set on a natural spur on the south bank of the River Tyne, the site was well defended by a deep ravine on the south and east sides, with ditches to south and west. A second structure was an early 12th-century earthwork, and around c.1175 a great tower was raised in the western part of the enclosure. The tower was almost square, three storeys tall, with 3m- (10ft-) thick walls. The gatehouse was also built in the 12th century and this, together with the curtain wall, are the best preserved parts of the castle. Prudhoe was unsuccessfully besieged in 1173, and then again a few years later, by William the Lion, King of Scotland.

In the 13th or very early 14th century a barbican was added which led to a drawbridge across the moat, and the gatehouse was given a vaulted basement and a chapel on the first floor which is noted for the oriel window. Prudhoe became a possession of the Percy Earls of Northumberland at the end of the 14th century. A manor house was built across the middle of the castle, inside the defensive ditches and walls, by the 2nd Duke of Northumberland in the 19th century.

LOCATION: NORTHUMBERLAND
MAP REF: NZ 092634
OPEN: ENGLISH HERITAGE: APR–SEP DAILY

RABY

First built by the powerful Neville family as a quadrangular structure with high towers and a lower crenellated curtain wall, Raby evolved over the centuries to become a large, palatial residence of towers and ranges of apartments clustered round a small courtyard. The tallest of the towers is Clifford's standing at 25m (81ft). The licence to fortify was granted in 1378 and the house remained as one of the main Neville residences until the 16th century and the Rising of the North. Raby then became the property of Sir Henry Vane and was a Parliamentary stronghold in the Civil War, attacked repeatedly by Royalist forces. During the 18th and 19th centuries the castle was much altered although the kitchen tower, dating from the mid-1300s, retains its original medieval form. Set in lovely parkland, this castle has become a grand house; the interior displays an important collection of china, art and fine furnishings.

LOCATION: STAINDROP, DURHAM
MAP REF: NZ 129217
OPEN: PRIVATE: JUN–AUG DAILY; MAY & SEP WED & SUN

RICHMOND

This is an interesting very early castle, of formidable aspect which dominates Swaledale from a great height, but never saw military action. The site was granted to Alan the Red in the 1080s and he erected a triangular curtain and possibly one of the earliest stone hall keeps in England, known as Scolland's Hall; this might have been built soon after Alan's death in 1089 but the name comes from Alan the Red's steward, Scolland. The gate-tower was also begun in the 11th century, and appears to have been similar to the one at Exeter in Devon. Joining the hall on the extension of the curtain is the massive keep: the lower part is 11th century, the remainder from the 13th century. It was built as an extension of the original gate-tower c.1150–70, and it reached 30.5m (100ft), retaining the fine archway of the earlier gateway. It was built by Conan 'the little' Earl of Brittany. Henry II took the castle after Conan's death and may have altered the tower more as he carried out various other alterations. By the early 16th century the castle was decaying, but it was converted into a military headquarters in 1855 and was in use during both world wars.

LOCATION: NORTH YORKSHIRE
MAP REF: NZ 174006
OPEN: ENGLISH HERITAGE: MID-MAR–SEP DAILY: OCT–MAR THU–MON

RIPLEY

Ripley Castle is an 18th-century mansion incorporating some much earlier structures of a tower castle, and has been the home of the Ingilby family since the 1320s.

LOCATION: RIPLEY, NORTH YORKSHIRE
MAP REF: SE 283606
OPEN: PRIVATE: JUL–AUG DAILY; SEP–JUN TUE–THU, SAT–SUN & HOLIDAYS. TIMES CAN VARY

SANDAL

One of the most dramatic castle excavations of the 20th century revealed the ruins of a complete medieval castle here, which had all but disappeared in 2.5ha (6 acres) of earth and scrub. Sandal began as a motte castle c.1150, built by William de Warrenne who received the Manor of Wakefield from Henry I, and substantial traces of timber buildings, including a hall, were found in the excavations. In c.1200 conversion to stone began and continued to about 1280. One of the early stone buildings is the barbican dated c.1250. The masonry round its base is of the highest quality, cut and beautifully shaped. The de Warrennes held the castle until 1361, when it became a possession of the Crown. Remains of a complex keep, added in 1484 by Richard III, were uncovered: Richard developed the castle as a suitable northern base but despite its royal patronage, the history of Sandal was relatively uneventful, although the Battle of Wakefield was fought below the castle in 1460. The castle appears to have been neglected from the end of the 15th century, and entirely unoccupied from about 1600. It was refortified and garrisoned by Royalists in the Civil War, besieged twice in 1645, and then ordered to be slighted the following year.

Finds from the castle site are on display at nearby Wakefield Museum.

LOCATION: NR WAKEFIELD, WEST YORKSHIRE
MAP REF: SE 337182
OPEN: CITY OF WAKEFIELD METROPOLITAN DISTRICT COUNCIL: DAILY

SCALEBY

Scaleby began as a pele tower in the 13th century and when Robert de Tilliol was granted a licence to crenellate, it grew into a fortified house with extra towers and a 14th-century gatehouse. Scaleby was garrisoned during the Bishops' War (1638–9).

LOCATION: NR CARLISLE, CUMBRIA
MAP REF: NY 449624
OPEN: PRIVATE

SCARBOROUGH

Standing proudly on a cliff edge are the ruins of the important northern royal power base of Scarborough Castle, begun in the 1130s by William le Gros, Count of Aumale. He built a stone curtain and the first stage of the great tower: the curtain together with the steep slopes of the cliffs formed a roughly triangular site.

Then in 1154 Henry II claimed Scarborough for the Crown, improved the fortifications and raised the keep on the site of the first tower. It is now ruinous, but was a square building, rising to over 30.5m (100ft) and built of rough stone and mortar, faced with fine ashlar laid in beautiful courses. King John made further improvements but the castle is noted for its barbican, built by Henry III in the 1240s. Scarborough remained a royal castle until the reign of James I. A bombardment by Parliamentarians during 1645 badly damaged the keep, and after the Civil War the castle was used as a prison and barracks. The barracks were virtually destroyed during a shell attack in 1914. The castle was the site of a secret listening post during World War II.

LOCATION: CASTLE HILL, SCARBOROUGH, NORTH YORKSHIRE
MAP REF: TA 050893
OPEN: ENGLISH HERITAGE: MID-MAR TO SEP THU–MON

SHERIFF HUTTON

Masonry remains of a large 14th-century fortified house built by the powerful Neville family close to the site of an earlier motte and bailey castle can be seen here. In ruins by the 17th century, the two western towers remain together with the gatehouse.

LOCATION: NR YORK, NORTH YORKSHIRE
MAP REF: SE 652661

SIZERGH

Sizergh Castle started its life as a pele-tower, built in the mid-14th century for defensive purposes. South of the pele is a rectangular turret called the Deincourt Tower, named after the the original owners of the land, and both towers are battlemented. A great hall was added in 1450 and forms part of the entrance hall of the house today. Sizergh is part 14th-century pele tower, part Tudor/Elizabethan mansion and further alterations were made in the 18th century when the great hall was enlarged. The castle has been in the possession of the same family, the Stricklands, for well over 700 years after a Deincourt married a Strickland in the 13th century.

The series of oak-panelled rooms are notable, in particular the Inlaid Chamber which is a spectacular restoration with an ornate plaster ceiling. Sizergh has a fine collection of family portraits, furniture and 5.5ha (14 acres) of gardens, including lakes, which were laid out in the 18th century. The beautiful estate grounds are famous for their views of the Lake District.

LOCATION: NR KENDAL, CUMBRIA
MAP REF: SD 498878
OPEN: NATIONAL TRUST (CASTLE): LATE MAR–OCT SUN–THU

SKIPSEA

The earthwork remains of a motte and bailey castle built by Drogo de Beauvrière towards the end of the 11th century. This is one of the few motte castles where the motte is surrounded by its own ditch and rampart. Henry III ordered the destruction of the castle. It is possible there was once a harbour associated with this castle.

LOCATION: NR BRIDLINGTON, HUMBERSIDE
MAP REF: TA 163551
OPEN: ENGLISH HERITAGE: DAILY

SKIPTON

This was initially an earthwork castle built soon after 1090 by Robert de Romille. Late in the 12th century the castle received the beginnings of the stonework which turned it into a formidable fortress set on top of a rocky bluff backed by the Eller Beck. The Clifford family were granted the site in 1310 by Edward II, and Skipton remained their principal family seat until the 17th century. The castle was besieged and partially slighted in the Civil War but restored in 1658 by Lady Anne Clifford, born here in 1590.

LOCATION: NORTH YORKSHIRE
MAP REF: SD 995519
OPEN: PRIVATE: DAILY

SPOFFORTH

Still an imposing sight, a rectangular hall-tower range of 13th-century beginnings with 14th- and 15th-century enlargements is all that remains of Spofforth. The 13th-century part is the ground floor undercroft to the later hall, whose eastern side is rock face. The site was one of the holdings of the Percy family.

LOCATION: NR HARROGATE, NORTH YORKSHIRE
MAP REF: SE 360511
OPEN: ENGLISH HERITAGE: DAILY

THIRLWALL

This mid-14th-century tower was built largely of stone quarried from a nearby section of Hadrian's Wall and extended into a fortified hall-house. Now it is a derelict shell sited in Northumberland National Park.

LOCATION: NR GREENHEAD, NORTHUMBERLAND
MAP REF: NY 660662
OPEN: NORTHMBERLAND NATIONAL PARK: ACCESSIBLE BY PUBLIC FOOTPATH

THIRSK

Thirsk Castle, c.1100, was destroyed in 1176 on the orders of Henry II following the collapse of the revolt of his son Prince Henry, whom the castle's owners, the Mowbrays, supported.

All that remains are traces of the moat around part of the bailey site.

LOCATION: NORTH YORKSHIRE
MAP REF: SE 428820

TICKHILL

Tickhill was a motte castle, raised at the end of the 11th century by Robert de Belleme. On the tall motte an unusual eleven-sided great tower was raised by Henry II at the end of the 12th century although little remains of this. The bailey wall survives for long stretches and its north side, with an early square-plan gatehouse, can be seen from the road.

LOCATION: SOUTH YORKSHIRE
MAP REF: SK 594928
OPEN: DUCHY OF LANCASTER: OPEN ONE DAY A YEAR

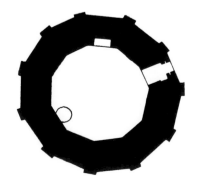

TOPCLIFFE

Set beside the River Swale, part of the mound of this motte castle is the only thing still visible. Built in the 12th century by the Bishop-elect of Lincoln, a son of Henry II who backed his father against Prince Henry, the castle was later owned by the Percy family.

LOCATION: NR THIRSK, WEST YORKSHIRE
MAP REF: SE 410750

TYNEMOUTH

Tynemouth Castle was integrated with Tynemouth Priory, a Benedictine monastery founded by the Earl of Northumberland in 1085. Both castle and priory were interdependent. When there was a royal visit, or turbulence between England and Scotland and the castle played a role as a border fortress, the monks of the priory had to contribute towards the associated costs of provisioning and garrisoning the castle. Fortunately they had income from their coal industries. The only remains of the priory now are of the majestic priory church, which was started in 1090 but largely rebuilt in the 13th century.

The castle, which began as an earthwork enclosure, stood on a prominent headland with steep cliffs on three sides and commanded the northern approaches of the River Tyne. Its late 13th-century curtain wall, with towers, also surrounded and protected the priory. Still extant is a substantial gatehouse-tower and barbican built in the 1390s: the outer walls continue back to the rectangular-plan gatehouse-tower with walls 1.5m (5ft) thick and rising three storeys. The first floor was used as the great hall. Tynemouth was one of the largest fortified sites in England, and possibly because of this, was retained by Henry VIII after the Dissolution of the Monasteries (1536–1540).

LOCATION: NR NEWCASTLE UPON TYNE, TYNE & WEAR
MAP REF: NZ 374695
OPEN: ENGLISH HERITAGE: APR–OCT DAILY; NOV THU–MON

WAKEFIELD

The earthwork remains of this medieval motte and bailey castle are covered by trees and it is best viewed in the winter. It seems that the motte with two baileys probably remained an earthwork and timber castle for its entire existence: excavations on the site have shown no stonework. The castle has been dated to the mid-12th century by pottery finds.

LOCATION: LOWE HILL, WAKEFIELD, WEST YORKSHIRE
MAP REF: SE 327198
OPEN: ACCESSIBLE IN DAYLIGHT HOURS

WARKWORTH

A late motte castle of the mid-12th century, this eventually developed into a masterpiece of late medieval architecure and household to the most powerful family in the North. One part of the castle was ranged around the outer bailey and the other was contained within a magnificent multiangular keep. David I of Scotland's son, Henry, probably built the earliest castle but it was the English Clavering (or FitzRoger) family who built the great gateway and massive curtain with flanking towers. By the end of the 13th century the castle was visited by Edward I. Warkworth was granted to the de Percys in 1332. The de Percys built the polygonal Grey Mare's Tail Tower and much later, in the 14th century the keep was erected: its apartments were grouped round a square lantern turret which ingeniously collected rainwater, channelled it to a tank in the basement and then distributed it to garderobes and basins. The Percys remained at the castle until the Reformation when the castle was pillaged. In the 19th century Anthony Salvin carried out some restoration.

LOCATION: NORTHUMBERLAND
MAP REF: NU 247057
OPEN: ENGLISH HERITAGE: APR–OCT DAILY; NOV–MAR SAT–MON

WARK

Wark Castle was started early in the 12th century. It was besieged and captured by David I of Scotland, and dismantled in 1138. Henry II recaptured it c.1158 and refortified it. Most of the castle was demolished in the 16th century; the scant remains give little clue to its turbulent past for it blocked the main Scottish invasion point on the river and became the object of frequent attacks and sieges.

LOCATION: CARHAM, NORTHUMBERLAND
MAP REF: NT 824387)

WHORLTON

This was an earthwork enclosure that received later stonework. Edward II stayed here and it was a Royalist stronghold during the Civil War. There are remains of the 14th-century gatehouse.

LOCATION: NR SWAINBURY, NORTH YORKSHIRE
MAP REF: NZ 481025

Scotland

Scotland's first castles were built by Normans, often at the invitation of the Scottish kings, and by the Scots themselves copying the idea. The 'classic' Scottish castle is the tower, a design that became widespread in the 14th century and was developed in the centuries that followed.

Strongly fortified residences were still being built in large numbers in Scotland after the majority of English castle owners felt able to relax and introduce such things as windows on outside walls. This was because Scotland could still be a dangerous and insecure place. Often the threats were from other Scots – intransigent Highland clans were frequent culprits.

Edinburgh and Stirling are Scotland's most famous castles. These two mighty complexes developed as royal palace-fortresses over many centuries and are unlike anything else in the country.

ABERDOUR

Aberdour is an assemblage of ruins from several periods. It began as a hall house built by Andrew Mortimer and passed through the Earl of Moray and the Douglas family until the 16th century when it belonged to the Regent Morton. After centuries of improvements the castle was damaged by fire towards the end of the 17th century and from then much of it was allowed to deteriorate. For today's visitors, there are substantial remains with a painted ceiling and a lovely walled garden.

LOCATION: ABERDOUR, FIFE
MAP REF: NT 193854
OPEN: HISTORIC SCOTLAND: APR–OCT DAILY; NOV–MAR SUN–THU

ACHADUN

This was an irregular quadrilateral stone enclosure of the early 13th century. The castle had a small rectangular turret projection in one corner, and a garderobe built into the curtain wall itself. Achadun was held by the Bishops of Argyll until the mid-16th century and is also known as the Bishop's Castle. The ruins stand to the south-west of the island of Lismore.

LOCATION: LISMORE, ARGYLL & BUTE
MAP REF: NM 804392

AFFLECK

Affleck started as an L-plan tower house in the late 15th century and was built of local reddish sandstone rubble with fine quality dressings. It is four floors to the parapet which has two square corner turrets and two small corner roundels. With elaborate internal accommodation, the tower house includes a chapel at the top floor and a solar with a remarkable fireplace, a garderobe and several wall chambers, probably bedrooms. This was a fine, well-fortified residence: the walls are thick, with inverted keyhole gun ports at lower levels and battlemented cap-houses acting as watch-turrets at the top on two corners.

LOCATION: MONIKIE, ANGUS
MAP REF: NO 495388
OPEN: NOT OPEN TO PUBLIC

AIRLIE

This renovated castle stands on a promontory over the junction of the Isla and Melgund rivers, belonging, as it has for centuries, to the Ogilvy family. The first building began c.1432 and was probably a large enclosure castle. The Duke of Argyll burned the old castle in 1640 and a more modern mansion, still occupied, was built in part of the original enclosure.

LOCATION: KIRRIEMUIR, ANGUS
MAP REF: NO 293522

AIRTH

Airth Castle dates from the 15th century but was built on an earlier castle site. In the 16th century a wing was added on the east wall of the tower and a further north wing was joined to that. Today it is a grand hotel.

LOCATION: AIRTH BY FALKIRK, FALKIRK
MAP REF: NS 900868

ALDIE

Aldie's was built as a fortified home in the late 15th to early 16th century. The tower is four-storeyed with bartizans that are corbelled out at the corners. Remodelling in the 17th century and also later, converted the castle into a courtyard mansion which can be viewed from the road.

LOCATION: PERTH & KINROSS
MAP REF: NT 050977

ALLARDYCE

A late 16th-century rectangular tower house, now greatly altered and expanded, Allardyce has an unusually profuse cluster of turrets and label-moulding in the corbelling of the turrets and parapet, and there is an interesting old archway into the courtyard. The tower house fell into ruin but has been restored; it is privately owned.

LOCATION: INVERBERVIE, ABERDEENSHIRE
MAP REF: NO 817739

ALLOA TOWER

Alloa is the largest surviving keep in Scotland and dates from the 14th century although it has been greatly altered, particularly c.1700 when an Italianate staircase and dome were added. The tower retains some of its medieval features including a dungeon and, at the top of the tower, the solar, with the original oak roof timbers.

Alloa Tower was home to the powerful Earls of Mar who were guardians to Mary, Queen of Scots when she was a child. The building currently displays a significant collection of family portraits and silver on loan from the Earl of Mar and Kellie.

LOCATION: CLACKMANNANSHIRE
MAP REF: NS 888925
OPEN: NATIONAL TRUST FOR SCOTLAND: APR–OCT DAILY PM ONLY

AMISFIELD

Amisfield Tower, built 1600, embodies the Scottish anxiety to build tall and strong. Erected by the Anglo-Norman Charteris family, it includes a variety of features and could almost be described as having been thrown together, with its lower walls built of random rubble, its higher floors of ashlar work. The odd appearance of Amisfield's design is heightened by the different shades of colour of the stonework. A Victorian mansion house stands beside the tower.

LOCATION: DUMFRIES & GALLOWAY
MAP REF: NX 992837
OPEN: PRIVATE: NO ACCESS

ARDROSSAN

This was a courtyard castle on rock detached from a large promontory. It is ruinous but parts of a large gatehouse at the north-east can be seen, along with the remains of another tower at the south west. The lower level of the gatehouse dates from the late 13th century. In the 15th century the gatehouse was converted into a gatehouse-tower and fortified with gun ports in the 16th century. The castle was destroyed by Cromwell in 1648.

LOCATION: NORTH AYRSHIRE
MAP REF: NS 232422

ARDTORNISH

Built in the 13th century, Ardtornish was a rectangular great tower, of which only the walling of the ground floor remains. Ardtornish belonged to the Macdonalds, Lords of the Isles.

LOCATION: NR LOCHALINE, HIGHLAND
MAP REF: NM 692426

ARDVRECK

Perched on a rocky promontory jutting into the north side of Loch Assynt, Ardvreck is now a picturesque ruin. It was built in the 16th century as a simple rectangular tower with a cylindrical staircase turret at the south-east corner, corbelled out on the upper storeys. The three chambers on the ground floor were vaulted. After his defeat at Invercharron in 1650, James Graham, Marquis of Montrose, took refuge at Ardvreck, but was betrayed and handed over to Parliament, which hanged him in Edinburgh. The castle was sacked in the 17th century.

LOCATION: ASSYNT, NR INCHNAMPH, HIGHLAND
MAP REF: NC 239236
OPEN: PRIVATE: OPEN ACCESS

AUCHINDOUN

Auchindoun was a 15th-century L-plan tower house built inside the earthworks of a prehistoric hill fort. Robert Cochrane, the court mason who was also responsible for the great hall at Stirling Castle, designed Auchindoun. The castle was sacked in 1591 by the Mackintoshes but later restored. It was nevertheless in ruins by the middle of the 18th century.

LOCATION: MONTLACH, NR DUFFTOWN, MORAY
MAP REF: NJ 349374
OPEN: HISTORIC SCOTLAND: OPEN ACCESS TO EXTERIOR ONLY

AUCHTERARDER

This very early rectangular tower of the 11th century was used as a royal hunting lodge. It is now a ruin.

LOCATION: PERTH & KINROSS
MAP REF: NN 943133

AYR

Traces remain here of a 12th-century castle built by William the Lion. It began as an earthwork enclosure and later received stonework.

LOCATION: SOUTH AYRSHIRE
MAP REF: NS 943133

AULDEARN

A castle at the time of William the Lion, Auldearn is mentioned in a charter dated 1187–8 and was still in use in the early 1300s. All that remains today, though, is a raised area enclosed by a rampart and topped by a restored 17th-century doocot or dovecote. The site is accessible.

LOCATION: NR NAIRN, HIGHLAND
MAP REF: NH 917556

BALGONIE

Balgonie was a substantial castle begun in the 14th century, standing beside the River Leven. Once it was a gaunt, dilapidated structure but Balgonie has undergone extensive restoration and is now used for weddings and events. The main rectangular great tower of four storeys plus garret, the oldest still standing intact in Fife, was built of ashlar blocks and is one of the finest 14th-century towers in Scotland. It is around 23m (76ft) tall and the walls on the ground floor are about 3m (10ft) thick. Additional buildings were raised in the 16th and 17th centuries, the latter by the 1st Earl of Leven, and remains of these are still standing. The barmkin wall dates from the 15th and 16th centuries and incorporates the gatehouse and a prison. The castle fell into decay in the 19th century after it was sold to Sir James Balfour and the roofs were removed to avoid the Roof Tax.

LOCATION: MARKINCH, FIFE
MAP REF: NO 313007
OPEN: PRIVATE: OPEN FOR EVENTS ONLY

BALBEGNO

Balbegno was built in the late 1560s on a roughly L-shape plan, and has considerable additions from the 17th, 18th and 19th centuries. The upper hall in the earlier tower part is notable for its ribbed vaulting and armorial paintings.

LOCATION: NR FETTERCAIRN, ABERDEENSHIRE
MAP REF: NO 639729

BALLINDALLOCH

A Z-plan tower house built here in the late 16th and early 17th centuries has been enlarged and modified. The main tower dates from the 16th century and two new wings were added in the 18th century. During the 19th century more renovations were carried out. The Macpherson Grants have lived at the castle since it was first built. Ballindalloch houses a collection of Spanish paintings. The extensive grounds provide fishing and golf.

LOCATION: MORAY
MAP REF: NJ 179365
OPEN: PRIVATE: EASTER–SEP SUN–FRI

BALNAGOWN

This is a great tower castle of the 15th century, standing on the south bank of the River Balnagown. The castle was remodelled in the 17th century and again in the middle of the 19th century in the Gothic style. The greatest changes have been wrought by Mohammed Al Fayed, the businessman and owner of Harrods department store, who bought the castle in the 1970s and has lavished millions of pounds on restorations.

LOCATION: KILDARY, HIGHLAND
MAP REF: NH 763752
OPEN: PRIVATE: NO ACCESS

BALQUHAIN

A large quadrilateral great tower was built here in the 14th century. The walls were thick, with deep recesses and narrow window loops. It was destroyed in 1526 and rebuilt soon afterwards to a smaller plan. The castle was finally destroyed by the Duke of Cumberland in 1746, but there are some remains.

LOCATION: INVERURIE, ABERDEENSHIRE
MAP REF: NJ 731236

BALTHAYOCK

This is the simple but impressive ruin of a 15th-century rectangular great tower. It was the main seat of the Blairs of Perthshire for nearly 500 years.

LOCATION: NR SCONE, PERTH & KINROSS
MAP REF: NO 174230

BALVAIRD

Balvaird is an L-plan tower house perched in the Ochil Hills. Built in 1500 by Sir Andrew Murray, the tower still stands to its full height. The castle was altered and developed over the 16th century, and part of the barmkin, added later than the tower's construction period, remains, along with the ruins of the other buildings that would have served the household. There are also remnants of Balvaird's interesting plumbing arrangement. In the 17th century, when the family inherited the Earldom of Mansfield, they moved to Scone Castle.

LOCATION: BALVAIRD, PERTH & KINROSS
MAP REF: NO 169115
OPEN: TOWER HOUSE JUL–SEP SAT–SUN

BALVENIE

Balvenie began as a substantial stone quadrilateral enclosure built by the Earls of Buchan in the 13th century. There are remnants of a small latrine turret on the north corner and of a larger square-plan tower on the west corner and of other buildings raised inside. The castle once belonged to the 'Black Douglases' but by the middle of the 16th century, it was owned by John Stewart, 4th Earl of Atholl, who completely remodelled the eastern part by constructing a palatial three-storey range with a cylindrical tower, which once had a 'pepper-pot' roof. The castle changed hands many times its last owner was William Duff. The castle was occupied until the 18th century.

LOCATION: DUFFTOWN, MORAY
MAP REF: NJ 326408
OPEN: HISTORIC SCOTLAND: APR–SEP DAILY

BARCALDINE

Barcaldine was built to an L-plan in Scottish Baronial style in the 16th century; the main tower block, rising three storeys plus attic, was 13 x 8m (43 x 26ft), with the walls varying between 1–2m (3–6ft) thick. Home of the Campbells of Barcaldine, the castle has been restored and offers bed-and-breakfast accommodation.

LOCATION: BENDERLOCH, ARGYLL & BUTE
MAP REF: NM 908406

BARHOLM

Until recently Barholm was a ruinous L-plan tower house of three floors plus garret and an added wing containing the staircase. It was built during the late 16th and early 17th centuries and is now undergoing restoration.

LOCATION: KIRKMABRECK, DUMFRIES & GALLOWAY
MAP REF: NX 521529

BARJARG

A 16th-century L-plan tower house forms the eastern wing of an early 19th-century mansion here. It was built of red rubble and has corbelled angle turrets on the parapet corners.

LOCATION: NR PENPONT, DUMFRIES & GALLOWAY
MAP REF: NX 878901

BASS OF INVERURIE

The natural mound here, rising some 15m (50ft), was altered into a motte by scarping the sides and excavating a ditch round it. The work was probably done c.1180 by David, Earl of Huntingdon and brother of William the Lion. The remains of an oak gangway were found in excavations.

LOCATION: INVERURIE, ABERDEENSHIRE
MAP REF: NJ 781206

BAVELAW

A 17th-century L-plan tower house was built here around an earlier structure of three storeys with an attic.

LOCATION: PENICUIK, MIDLOTHIAN
MAP REF: NT 167627

BEDRULE

Bedrule began as an oval, stone-wall enclosure. A gatehouse was inserted on the north-west and a cylindrical flanking tower on the south-east, with two further round towers at the west and south-west. The structure was built in the late 13th century by the Comyns. Robert Bruce captured it during the War of Independence and gave it to his friend and counsellor, Sir James Douglas. Scant traces remain.

LOCATION: BORDERS
MAP REF: NT 598180

BEMERSYDE

A modernized mansion which incorporates a 16th-century tower house, Bemersyde has been held by the Haig family for centuries. Its most celebrated occupant was Field Marshal Sir Douglas Haig, 1st Earl Haig of Bemersyde, Commander-in-Chief of the British army in France, 1915–18.

LOCATION: MERTOUN, BORDERS
MAP REF: NT 592333

BLACKNESS

Once an important Scottish fortress by virtue of its position on a rocky outcrop at the end of a promontory jutting into the waters of the Firth of Forth, Blackness was built during the 15th and 16th centuries by the Crichtons, one of Scotland's most powerful families. The rectangular great tower was put up in the 15th century but this stands inside a mainly 16th-century courtyard, built when the castle was brought to its full, impressive defensive capabilities. Blackness was besieged by Cromwell's army and then used as a prison for Covenanters in the 1660s.

LOCATION: NR LINLITHGOW, WEST LOTHIAN
MAP REF: NT 055802
OPEN: HISTORIC SCOTLAND: APR–SEP DAILY; OCT–MAR REDUCED HOURS

BLAIR

This is the palatial home of the Dukes of Atholl; it is largely a late 18th-century reconstruction grafted on to the remains of an earlier complex tower-house castle. The first building was the Comyn Tower, built c.1270. It was subsequently enclosed in a barmkin along with other buildings, including a lord's hall. Bonnie Prince Charlie stayed at Blair during the Second Jacobite Rising, and after the flight of the prince, the castle was taken over by the Hanoverian government. Queen Victoria visited Blair in 1844 and presented Colours to the Atholl Highlanders, Europe's only remaining private army. The castle is still the home of the Dukes of Atholl. Today's visitors will find much of interest: walled gardens, arms and armour, paintings, furniture and memorabilia.

LOCATION: PITLOCHRY, PERTH & KINROSS
MAP REF: NN 866662
OPEN: PRIVATE: APR–OCT DAILY;
NOV–MAR REDUCED HOURS

BORTHWICK

Borthwick is one of the most imposing tower houses in Scotland. It has been in almost continuous occupation since its construction in 1430–2, and today is a fine hotel. A licence to build the castle was granted to the first Lord Borthwick in 1430.

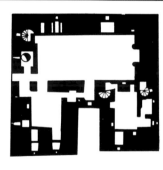

From the great hall ,which has a magnificent 6m (20ft) high canopied fireplace, four spiral staircases wind their way up to chambers and down to dungeons and cellars. The castle was a place of sanctuary for Mary, Queen of Scots and her third husband, the Earl of Bothwell. In 1650, during the war between England and Scotland, Cromwell bombarded the castle: the 9th Lord Borthwick, a staunch Royalist, refused to yield to Cromwell who then demanded surrender in a letter 'if you necessitate me to bend my cannon against you, you may expect what I doubt you will not be pleased with…' Borthwick refused and Cromwell's guns opened fire and fragmented the battlements and some wall stonework on the top of the east main wall. The castle surrendered and the tower house was spared but the damage is still visible.

LOCATION: GOREBRIDGE, MIDLOTHIAN
MAP REF: NT 369597
OPEN: HOTEL. OPEN TO NON-RESIDENTS

BOTHWELL

Bothwell was an important castle and is still a fine ruin. It was built c. 1270 by the Moray (later Murray) family who also owned Duffus Castle. The castle, built on the south bank of the Clyde in red sandstone, had a great tower, or donjon, over 20m (66ft) in diameter and at least 24.5m (80ft) high, with walls about 4.5m (15ft) thick. Although damaged, much of the donjon survives but the original castle was never finished. Foundations have been discovered of parts of a planned curtain wall, twin-towered gatehouse and other towers laid out to form a quadrilateral enclosure. Wide ditches around the area also indicate that a large area was due to be fortified. The castle changed hands often: in the 1290s it fell into English hands after the deposition of John Balliol in 1296 and the next year the Scots

attacked and captured Bothwell after a 14-month siege. By employing a huge 'belfry' or siege tower made of prefabricated parts, Edward I successfully recaptured the castle in 1301. After Bruce's great victory at Bannockburn in 1314, the castle reverted to Scotland. Bothwell was captured by the English again c.1331, this time by Edward III who used it as a headquarters, but a few years later it fell into the Scottish hands of Sir Andrew Murray. Later in the 14th century the castle came into the possession of the 'Black Douglas' family who rebuilt the hall and chapel and erected a new wall from east to west. Bothwell was finally abandoned in the 17th century.

LOCATION: UDDINGSTON, SOUTH LANARKSHIRE
MAP REF: NS 688593
OPEN: HISTORIC SCOTLAND: APR–SEP DAILY; OCT–MAR LIMITED OPENING

BRACO

Braco is a tall, square tower house dating from the 16th century. This was given an extension in the 17th century and a further extension of L-plan in the 18th century. The castle belonged to the Earls of Montrose and then in the late 1700s to the Smythes. The gardens are lovely and offer fine views.

LOCATION: PERTH & KINROSS
MAP REF: NN 823113

BRAEMAR

Braemar is near Balmoral, the Scottish home of the royal family. It is basically an L-plan tower house begun c.1628, but burned in 1689. It was restored in 1748 and later transformed into a family home by the Farquharsons of Invercauld.

LOCATION: ABERDEENSHIRE
MAP REF: NO 156924
OPEN: PRIVATE: JUL–AUG DAILY; APR–JUN SEP–OCT SAT–THU

BRAIKIE

An L-plan tower house built by the Fraser family in 1581 (according to a date stone), Braikie has been little altered and has the usual features of 16th- and 17th-century smaller Scottish tower houses, such as crow-stepped gables, corbelled embrasures and an iron yett at the entrance. It is now derelict but relatively complete.

LOCATION: KINNELL, ANGUS
MAP REF: NO 628508

BREACACHADH

This is a medieval great tower castle with curtain wall and other buildings, mainly of the 15th century, which has been restored as a private residence. It was home to the Clan Maclean until the middle of the 18th century.

LOCATION: ISLE OF COLL, ARGYLL & BUTE
MAP REF: NM 160539

BRODICK

The red sandstone Brodick Castle stands on the site of a Viking fortress. In the 13th or 14th century a stone L-plan tower house was built as a seat for the Dukes of Hamilton. The north wing is all that remains of the original building, and the remainder of the structure, dating mainly from the 19th century, was designed by Gillespie Graham. A collection of furniture, paintings and sporting memorabilia is on display in the house, and the garden has an internationally acclaimed rhododendron collection.

LOCATION: ISLE OF ARRAN, NORTH AYRSHIRE
MAP REF: NS 007379
OPEN: NATIONAL TRUST FOR SCOTLAND: APR–OCT DAILY. COUNTRY PARK ALL YEAR DAILY

BRODIE

This has belonged to the Brodie family since the 12th century. The present Z-plan structure dates from the 16th and 17th centuries, raised on an earlier site. The four-storey tower is incorporated into a fine 19th-century mansion.

LOCATION: NR FORRES, MORAY
MAP REF: NH 979578
OPEN: NATIONAL TRUST FOR SCOTLAND: APR, JUL, AUG DAILY; MAY–JUN, SEP REDUCED OPENING

BROUGHTY

Broughty has been extensively rebuilt and altered as a result of its long history as a scene of sieges and battles. The castle started as a tower house of the end of the 15th century. The English attacked and damaged the castle in 1547 and it was damaged again when it was retaken in 1550. In c.1603 Broughty was restored, but suffered again in 1650, so the shape of the castle in its earlier state has been lost, though the foundations of the main tower block are still visible. In 1855 the castle was purchased as part of the Crimean War effort and rebuilt as a coastal fort. Parts of the east block are the only upright remains of the 15th-century castle. It houses a museum on the history of the local area and Broughty Ferry itself.

LOCATION: BROUGHTY FERRY, CITY OF DUNDEE
MAP REF: NO 465304
OPEN: DUNDEE CITY COUNCIL: APR–SEP DAILY; OCT–MAR TUE–SUN

CAERLAVEROCK

BURLEIGH

Near the north edge of Loch Leven, the early 16th-century tower of Burleigh stands roofless and makes an impressive ruin. A stretch of enclosure wall joins on to a round tower with several interesting features, including gun-ports and shot-holes. The castle was built by the Balfours.

LOCATION: MILNATHORT, PERTH & KINROSS
MAP REF: NO 129046
OPEN: HISTORIC SCOTLAND: KEYS AT THE NEARBY HOUSE

CADZOW

An early 12th-century castle might have stood on this site, used by David I and succeeding kings. Set on a hill overlooking the River Avon, the fortification was later surrounded by a formidable curtain and a wide ditch. Substantial ruins remain of two round towers projecting into the ditch.

LOCATION: HAMILTON, SOUTH LANARKSHIRE
MAP REF: NS 734536

'Caerlaverock was so strong a castle that it feared no siege … it had but three sides round it, with a tower at each corner but one of them was a double one, so high, so long and so wide, that the gate was underneath it, well made and strong, with a drawbridge and a sufficiency of other defences'. This is a translation of *Le Siège de Karlaverock*, a contemporary French rhyming account of the siege in 1300 by Edward I. It was built c.1280–1300 and held by the English for 12 years. The constable then declared for Robert Bruce, dismantling the castle. Caerlaverock was rebuilt in the 15th century, following the original design; the massive gatehouse was strengthened and made residential. In 1630 Lord Nithsdale built a three-storey residential block against the inner eastern wall. The castle was defended for the king against the Covenanters in 1640.

LOCATION: DUMFRIES, DUMFRIES & GALLOWAY
MAP REF: NY 026656
OPEN: HISTORIC SCOTLAND: APR–SEP DAILY; OCT–MAR REDUCED HOURS

CAIRNBULG

Cairnbulg is situated on the bank of Philorth Water near Fraserburgh. It was built in the mid-13th century by the Comyn family and was a rectangular tower, some 21.5m (71ft) tall. The castle was converted to a mansion at the end of the 19th century.

LOCATION: RATHEN, ABERDEENSHIRE
MAP REF: NK 017639

CAKEMUIR

Cakemuir belonged to the Wauchope family. Built in the 16th century as a rectangular four-storey tower house, the castle has since been extended, notably in the 19th century. Cakemuir was restored in the 20th century and is now a private residence.

LOCATION: NR CRICHTON, MIDLOTHIAN
MAP REF: NI 412590

CARBERRY

A small but massive tower of the 15th century was put up on what was probably the site of an earlier building. The original tower is incorporated in the north-west end of a later building. It has four storeys to the heavy rounded parapets, which are supported by corbels bearing carved faces of angels and feature wide-mouthed gun-ports. Mary, Queen of Scots spent her last hours of freedom near the castle.

LOCATION: INVERESK, EAST LOTHIAN
MAP REF: NT 363696
OPEN: PRIVATE. CONFERENCES AND RETREATS

CARDONESS

The ruins of Cardoness stand on a rock platform overlooking the Water of Fleet. The principal feature is a great tower of the 15th century; the basement storey is vaulted. The tower has both wide-mouthed and keyhole gun-ports. Inside its shell the great hall has a fine fireplace with clustered pillars on moulded bases. Cardoness was built for the McCulloch family, and abandoned in the 17th century.

LOCATION: GATEHOUSE OF FLEET, DUMFRIES & GALLOWAY
MAP REF: NX 590553
OPEN: HISTORIC SCOTLAND: APR–SEP DAILY; OCT–MAR REDUCED HOURS

CARNASSERIE

Carnasserie was once the home of John Carsewell, Bishop of the Isles (after the Reformation), who translated John Knox's *Liturgy* into Gaelic. Built of a local stone called schist in the second part of the 16th century, the tower is of architectural interest. The castle was captured during the rebellion of the Duke of Argyll in 1685 and blown up although there are substantial remains.

LOCATION: NR KILMARTIN, ARGYLL & BUTE
MAP REF: NM 838009
OPEN: HISTORIC SCOTLAND: DAILY

CARRICK

The remains of this early 15th-century rectangular four-storey tower house stand on a rock projecting into Loch Goil. It was once a hunting lodge used by the Stewart kings.

LOCATION: CARRICK, ARGYLL & BUTE
MAP REF: NS 193945

CASTLE CAMPBELL

An imposing complex of buildings round a well-preserved, rectangular tower sited on a rocky mound in Dollar Glen. The tower was the earliest stone building and dates from the late 15th century, erected on what may have been a much earlier motte castle site. With four storeys, three of which are vaulted, a pit prison and two entrances, the tower's floors were originally reached by straight-flight mural stairways: in the 16th century a square-plan stair tower with a spiral staircase was built. Further additions were made to the castle in the 16th century but these were ruined when the Royalists sacked Castle Campbell in the 1650s. The castle was a stronghold of the Campbells.

LOCATION: DOLLAR, CLACKMANNANSHIRE
MAP REF: NS 961993
OPEN: HISTORIC SCOTLAND: APR–SEP DAILY; OCT–MAR REDUCED HOURS

CARSLUITH

This basically L-plan tower-house castle of the 16th century stands on a promontory overlooking Wigtown Bay. The main block is rectangular and dates from the 15th century with the wing tower containing the spiral staircase. Other buildings date from the 18th century.

LOCATION: NR CREETOWN, DUMFRIES & GALLOWAY
MAP REF: NX 495542
OPEN: HISTORIC SCOTLAND: DAILY

CARY

An L-shaped tower house built by the Livingstones in the late 15th century, with 17th- and 18th-century additions. The privately owned tower house incorporates some stone from a Roman fort, which had been built on the Antonine Wall nearby.

LOCATION: FALKIRK
MAP REF: NS 786775

LIFE IN A MEDIEVAL CASTLE

CASTLES WERE SYMBOLS OF STRENGTH AND CONQUEST, AND THAT SYMBOLISM REMAINED POWERFUL, BUT AS STABILITY INCREASED AND AS SOCIETY DEVELOPED, CASTLES BEGAN TO EXPRESS THE ASPIRATIONS OF THEIR OWNERS IN DIFFERENT WAYS.

By the 13th century, for example, many lords preferred to have their chamber and hall not high in a tower, but in a range of buildings within a central courtyard. These were nearly always timber-framed rather than of stone, and often these do not survive, making it difficult to imagine what they must have looked like. However, the Tower of London retains a few such buildings, as does Warwick, where great efforts have been made to re-create the feeling of life in the Middle Ages. Notions of living in a civilized way spread, and so the castle courtyard often contained a garden where herbs and flowers would be grown, and where the ladies of the castle might have a bower to retreat from the rough side of castle life. Here also, in clement weather, minstrels might entertain and knights might court the ladies.

Many castles had moats around them. Originally, these were purely defensive in function, but they could also provide food in the form of fish and water fowl. But sanitation was problematic in castles, and so garderobes – lavatories – often consisted of a seat beneath which was a funnel channelling the waste down the walls and directly into the water. Where there was no moat, the waste was collected from the foot of the castle walls and taken to be used as manure on the fields. Clean water was essential, and this was usually taken from wells within the castle walls, but for daily use most people drank either watered wine or 'small' beer. Small beer was a weak beer that could be consumed in quantity without becoming drunk. Making beer was a major industry, usually undertaken by ale wives.

Scenes from 14th-century life. Above, a maid holds a mirror for her mistress. Below, a cook prepares pork and chicken, while wine is poured and servants deliver dishes to the table.

Furnishings and fittings became richer and more widespread. The lord would have had a large bed that was essentially a small room when drapes and hangings were closed around it.

As well as the great bed, the lord and lady would have places to store their clothes and other possessions – the warderobe. But the warderobe could also describe virtually everything the lord owned, and the royal warderobe of the monarch often travelled wherever he or she went, as did the royal bed.

The monarch's retinue on his extensive journeys included people whose job was to transform castles into warm and comfortable places. All these people were under the control of the offical called the marshal.

Hangings were used to disguise bare and unattractive stone walls, and to provide protection from draughts. But one of the greatest luxuries came to be glass in the windows where previously only shutters or hangings had kept out the worst of the weather.

In the hall, centre of castle life for domestic as well as official functions, communal eating was still the norm, but kitchens gradually replaced cooking over fires in the hall itself. Rushes and other plant material remained the best floor covering, since these could be easily and speedily replaced when soiled by food remains or other debris. A favourite floor covering was meadowsweet; as its name conveys it is gently scented and could disguise less pleasant smells. Weapons, armour and coats of arms would be displayed on the hall walls, twinkling in the fire glow and rushlight.

LIFE IN A MEDIEVAL CASTLE 129

CASTLE DONNAN

Also known as Eilean Donan, this much-photographed castle stands on an islet in the Kyle of Localsh at the meeting point of three sea lochs and is joined to the mainland by an arched bridge. It is a major reconstruction of a strong, early 13th-century fortress built by Alexander II. Held by the MacKenzies and later the MacRaes, the original castle, a stone curtain enclosure that received a rectangular great tower, was a stronghold for the Jacobite cause. It was reduced to rubble by a bombardment from British frigates in 1719. Today's castle is the result of an early 20th-century reconstruction by Colonel Jon MacRae Gilstrap, a descendant of the original owners. It is instantly recognizable as the setting of such films as *Highlander* and *The World is Not Enough*.

LOCATION: DORNIE, KYLE OF LOCALSH, HIGHLAND
MAP REF: NG88 1258
OPEN: THE CONCHRA CHARITABLE TRUST: APR–OCT DAILY

CASTLE GRANT

Originally a Comyn stronghold and the ancestral seat of the chiefs of Clan Grant, Castle Grant is an L-plan tower house dating from the 15th or 16th century and absorbed into a later 18th-century mansion. It fell into decay in the 20th century, but has been restored and is privately owned.

LOCATION: NR GRANTOWN-ON-SPEY, HIGHLAND
MAP REF: NJ 041302

CASTLE KENNEDY

Set in outstanding gardens, Castle Kennedy was built in the early 17th century. It was a rectangular tower block with a square wing at one end with dressed quoins. The tower was burned in during the Jacobite Rising in 1716 but the shell makes a picturesque addition to the landscape, which incorporates two lochs and two castles. The second castle is the 19th-century home of the current Earl of Stair.

LOCATION: NR STRANRAER, DUMFRIES & GALLOWAY
MAP REF: NX 111605
OPEN: PRIVATE: GARDENS APR–SEP DAILY

CASTLE FRASER

Castle Fraser is a rectangular tower castle originally built in the 15th century. In the late 16th century it was converted to Z-plan and in the following century the main core was enlarged under the supervision of John Bell, a noted mason. The diagonally opposing four-floor towers are cylindrical (south-east) and rectangular (north-west) and are equipped with ornamented shot-holes. There is also a 'luggie' between the vaulting of the hall and the chamber above, which was formed in the thickness of the wall and reached from behind a window shutter. An eavesdropper could slip into the cubicle by lifting a stone slab, replace it and listen to goings-on in the hall. The castle was restored early in the 20th century by the Cowdray family.

LOCATION: SAUCHEN, INVERURIE, ABERDEENSHIRE
MAP REF: NJ 722125
OPEN: NATIONAL TRUST FOR SCOTLAND: JUL–AUG DAILY; APR–JUN & SEP FRI–TUE

CASTLE LACHLAN

From the outside this interesting ruin appears to be a large, rectangular tower-house keep. But inside it is in two parts round an open inner courtyard. It belonged to the MacLachlans, but during the Second Jacobite Rising in the middle of the 1700s it was fired on by government warships. The castle was abandoned and the MacLachlans built a newer castle nearby which they still own. The old castle ruins, on the shore of Loch Fyne, are accessible.

LOCATION: STRACHUR, ARGYLL & BUTE
MAP REF: NS 005592

CASTLE LEOD

Leod is a handsome, red sandstone, late 16th-century to early 17th-century L-plan tower house with bartizans at the angles and an open parapet, built on the site of, and incorporating, a much earlier fortification. It has been greatly modified and remains the seat of the Clan MacKenzie and home to the Earl of Cromartie.

LOCATION: STRATHPEFFER, HIGHLAND
MAP REF: NH 486593

CASTLE OF PARK

Castle of Park stands over the shore of Luce Bay. It was built c.1590 as a four-storey plus attic tower house, and transformed in the 18th and 19th centuries from a baronial fortress to an elegant country home.

LOCATION: CORNHILL, ABERDEENSHIRE
MAP REF: NX 188571

CASTLE ROY

This castle began in the 13th century as a quadrilateral stone enclosure. There is a square tower on the north west side. The ruins are low level.

LOCATION: NETHY BRIDGE, HIGHLAND
MAP REF: NJ 007219

CASTLE STALKER

You can see this castle on a small island in Loch Laich from the road driving from Ballachulish down towards Oban. Access has always been by boat. The building was a rectangular tower house, about 14 x 11m (46 x 36ft), and with walls about 3m (10ft) thick. The entrance was at first floor level, reached by a wooden ladder and later a stone stairway and the ground level contained a pit prison. Stalker was probably built in the 15th century on the site of a 14th-century fortalice belonging to the MacDougalls. These MacDougall lands later became the property of the Stewarts until the 17th century when they passed to the Campbells after a wager. Castle Stalker fell into disrepair and dereliction in the 19th century when the Campbells built a new home on the mainland, but it was preserved and then fully restored towards the end of the 20th century.

LOCATION: APPIN, ARGYLL & BUTE (LOCH LAICH)
MAP REF: NM 921473
OPEN: PRIVATE: OPEN SUBJECT TO TIDES AND WEATHER BY APPOINTMENT (TEL 01631 730 234)

CAWDOR

This palatial range of buildings belongs to the Earl of Cawdor whose family has owned the castle since the 14th century. It was the seat of the Thanes of Calder, an earlier spelling of the place name. The early stone tower house has been absorbed by a later rectangular great tower built in 1454 following a licence to fortify granted to John Calder by James II of Scotland. This allowed him to erect his castle 'with walls and ditches and [to] equip the summit with turrets and means of defence' but on the understanding that it was always to be open to the king and his successors. The resulting tower was substantial and the lower parts of it have survived, heightened in the 16th century. A deep ditch and a drawbridge were added in the 15th century. The entrance, at first floor level, had an iron yett. Later extensions and improvements were residential and this comfortable castle displays a fine collection of furnishings, paintings and domestic items. It sits in magnificent grounds, with a 9-hole golf course, which are open to the public.

LOCATION: NR NAIRN, HIGHLAND
MAP REF: NH 847499
OPEN: PRIVATE: JUN–SEP DAILY

CESSFORD

Once regarded as one of the strongest castles in Scotland, Cessford, built by Andrew Ker, was a massive L-plan great tower of c.1450 with very thick walls and a vaulted basement. Its position on the Borders made it a target for English attacks. The tower was dismantled in the middle of the 16th century and the castle was abandoned to become the interesting ruin it is today. The ruins are visible but fenced off and entering the area is not advised.

LOCATION: ECKFORD, BORDERS
MAP REF: NT 738238

CLACKMANNAN TOWER

A substantial L-plan tower house stands on the summit of King's Seat Hill on the edge of Clackmannan. The oldest part is the north end of the L-plan, an oblong tower of the late 14th century. The 'L' wing was added in the 15th century and is five floors high. The castle, built by David II, was once surrounded by a moat with a drawbridge across it. The tower has a commanding view of the land towards the Firth of Forth, but it is not possible to view it internally.

LOCATION: CLACKMANNANSHIRE
MAP REF: NS 906919

CLAYPOTTS

Claypotts is one of several dozen Z-plan castles built in Scotland in the 16th and 17th centuries. It was built in the 1570s by John Strachan, Lord of Claypotts, and began as a rectangular, gabled, four-storeyed great tower house of hard local stone with cylindrical towers grafted diagonally on the north-east and south-west corners. The towers were topped with overhanging square cap-houses (with garrets inside) and were large enough to contain rooms all the way up. Each of the towers gives cover to two surfaces of the centre building which in turn covers both towers so, in theory, it was impossible to approach the castle from any angle without being in a direct line of fire.

The all-round defensiveness of Claypotts was never put to the test.

In the 1620s the castle was sold to Sir William Graham of Claverhouse, and it was his great-grandson, John Graham, who was later famous throughout Scotland as Bonnie Dundee. He became 1st Viscount Dundee, and raised an army to help the cause of James II (and VII) who was driven off the English throne late in 1688 by supporters of William of Orange. When James II was deposed, Claypotts was forfeited to William III who gave it to the Marquis of Douglas.

LOCATION: BROUGHTY FERRY, DUNDEE
MAP REF: NO 453318
OPEN: HISTORIC SCOTLAND: EXTERNAL VIEWING ONLY

COMLONGON CASTLE

This splendid four-storey tower house, built c.1435, dominates the north shores of the Solway Firth. It is one of three 15th-century castles in which the great tower predominates and which are the nearest equivalent in Scotland of the English (and Welsh) great towers or keeps. Comlongon was a seat of the Earls of Mansfield (Murrays). There is a great hall on the first floor with a fireplace at each end. Like Borthwick, Comlongon's great tower was not provided with gun-ports or arrow-loops. Next to the tower is a late 19th-century to early 20th-century mansion and both are now incorporated into a grand country house hotel.

LOCATION: CLARENCEFIELD, DUMFRIES & GALLOWAY

CORGARFF

A well-restored, plain, rectangular tower house of the 16th century, Corgarff was modified after the Second Jacobite Rising by the Hanoverian government: a single-level building was added to each short end and the whole tower was enclosed inside a star-shaped barmkin with narrow vertical loops for guns. This provided a useful fortress for guarding crossings of the rivers Dee, Don and Avon. A garrison was maintained at Corgarff for many years, right into the 1830s. The castle was restored in the 1960s and now contains an exhibition and reconstruction of a barrack room.

LOCATION: ABERDEENSHIRE
MAP REF: NJ 255087
OPEN: HISTORIC SCOTLAND APR–SEP DAILY; OCT–MAR REDUCED HOURS

CORSE

This is a 16th-century L-plan tower house built by the Forbes family. Patrick Forbes is quoted as saying, 'I will build me such a house as thieves will need to knock at ere they enter' (SH Cruden). This was after the previous building had been destroyed in a raid. There are substantial remains.

LOCATION: ABERDEENSHIRE
MAP REF: NJ 549074

CORTACHY

This enclosure castle of the 15th century was considerably altered in the 19th century to include towers and decorative turrets. Originally the castle had four cylindrical flanking towers: three of these towers remain, absorbed in the newer work. The castle is the family seat of the Ogilvy clan.

LOCATION: KIRRIEMUIR, ANGUS
MAP REF: NO 398595

CRAIGCROOK

A 16th-century tower house: the three-storeyed main block with wing towers (one cylindrical and one square staircase tower) is incorporated in later renovations and additions.

LOCATION: BLACKHALL, EDINBURGH
MAP REF: NT 210742

CRAIGIE

Most Scottish tower houses were tall, but some were rectangular hall-towers, much the same as Chepstow in Wales. One was Craigie which dates from the early 1200s. Now ruinous, the original long hall was incorporated in a later 15th-century tower house and the castle was enclosed by a moat.

LOCATION: NR KILMARNOCK, SOUTH AYRSHIRE
MAP REF: NS 409317

CRAIGIEVAR

Craigievar, set high on a hill, is a fairy-tale castle and one of the finest baronial tower houses in Scotland. Built c.1620–6 and rather forbidding from the outside, internally Craigievar is luxurious with a lavishly decorated and vaulted roof in the great hall. Built by William Forbes or 'Danzig Willie', it remains true to its 17th-century origins. The simplicity of the lower part of the castle contrasts with the finely corbelled, well-proportioned cylindrical turrets with conical roofs and cupolas above. Palatial rather than military, the castle was fortified with ramparts, and a courtyard wall with towers and an outer gateway. There was only one way in – through a massive iron-studded door, past a yett and through another pair of stout doors. Inside, the castle is a showcase for 17th- and 18th-century furniture and Forbes family portraits.

LOCATION: ALFORD, ABERDEENSHIRE
MAP REF: NJ 566095
OPEN: NATIONAL TRUST FOR SCOTLAND: APR–SEP, FRI–TUE PM. GUIDED TOURS ONLY. GROUNDS: DAILY

CRAIGMILLAR

This castle is famous as the place where the murder of Darnley, husband of Mary, Queen of Scots, was planned while the queen was staying there in 1566–7. The castle began in the late 14th century as a large L-plan tower house and was built with close-texture rubble of red-grey sandstone, with long, dressed quoins. The great tower house was fortified in the 1420s by the addition of a massive fortified enclosure with round flanking towers and other additions were made in the 16th and 17th centuries. Craigmillar was attacked and burned by the Earl of Hertford (later the Duke of Somerset) on behalf of Henry VIII in 1544, but it was restored in time for Mary, Queen of Scots to reside there from 1566–7 after the murder of her Italian secretary, David Rizzio. During her stay, a band of conspirators, Argyll, Huntly, Bothwell, Maitland and Gilbert Balfour, met and plotted to ensure that 'sic ane young fool and proud tirrane suld not reign nor bear reull over thame: and that … he sould be put off, by ane way or uther …': Darnley was to be dispatched. Today the castle is an impressive and substantial ruin.

LOCATION: EDINBURGH
MAP REF: NT 285710
OPEN: HISTORIC SCOTLAND: APR–SEP DAILY; OCT–MAR REDUCED HOURS

CRAIGNETHAN

Craignethan stands on a rocky promontory overlooking the Clyde. Although a ruin now, this was was once an impressive structure built to incorporate artillery defences. It consists of a 16th-century rectangular outer courtyard surrounded on three sides by a curtain wall; on the east side the yard is protected by a ditch. In the west wall is a fine battlemented gateway defended at low level by gun-ports. A century after the courtyard was built a private house was erected in the south-west corner: to the east of this courtyard is the older part of the castle, built mostly between c.1530 and 1545, which consists of a second courtyard surrounded by a thick barmkin with towers on the east. The principal feature of the inner courtyard was the substantial tower house which still stands. Craignethan was built by Sir James Hamilton, the illegitimate son of the 1st Earl of Arran, but as the Hamiltons backed Mary, Queen of Scots against the forces of the regent, the castle was slighted in 1579.

LOCATION: NR LANARK, SOUTH LANARKSHIRE
MAP REF: NS 815463
OPEN: HISTORIC SCOTLAND: APR–SEP DAILY; OCT–MAR REDUCED HOURS

CRAIGSTON

Built in 1604–7 (according to an inscription on a wall), Craigston belonged to John Urquhart who was the grandfather of Sir Thomas Urquhart, translator of François Rabelais' *Gargantua*. Craigston is a massive structure, with two wings at the front linked by an *arc de triomphe* over the entrance. The tower is painted white, as are the later buildings that surround it. Many original features are retained in the tower.

LOCATION: NR TURRIFF, ABERDEENSHIRE
MAP REF: NJ 762550

CRATHES

Crathes is an impressive and much restored tower-house castle known for some interesting painted ceilings, most notably in the Chamber of the Nine Muses.

Begun as an L-plan tower house in 1553, many of the alterations and improvements were by masons from the Bell family. There were also further alterations, including a three-storeyed east wing, another later wing, and some ornamental corbelled turrets. The original tower was equipped with a 'luggie', an iron yett by the door and a re-entrant tower for a staircase. There is a collection of family portraits and furniture displayed inside the house and a fine garden to enjoy.

LOCATION: BANCHORY, ABERDEENSHIRE
MAP REF: NO 735968
OPEN: NATIONAL TRUST FOR SCOTLAND: APR–OCT DAILY; NOV–MAR REDUCED HOURS. GARDEN AND GROUNDS DAILY

CRICHTON

Crichton Castle is a formidable structure dating from several periods. Its buildings are ranged round a square courtyard; from the top of the old tower house it is possible to see Borthwick Castle. The castle is now in ruins and has little more than its walls but it is possible to trace the various building periods. The first structure was a rectangular tower house, probably built by John de Crichton towards the end of the 14th century and originally surrounded by a barmkin. The basement is vaulted, and has a prison cell and a kitchen. In the 15th century the once massive gatehouse-tower at the south-west was built by John de Crichton's son, William, who became Lord Chancellor and who virtually managed Scotland during some of the minority years of James II. Further alterations, including the addition of more buildings, were made in the 15th century.

The castle was besieged and captured in 1559 in the struggle between Protestants and Catholics during the Scottish Reformation. Later in the 16th century, Francis, Earl of Bothwell, a cousin of Mary, Queen of Scots, who had spent time in Spain and Italy, transformed the castle into a Renaissance mansion including a notable diamond-faceted stonework façade on the north range.

LOCATION: NR PATHHEAD, MIDLOTHIAN
MAP REF: NT 380611
OPEN: HISTORIC SCOTLAND: APR–SEP DAILY

CROOKSTON

This was a substantial rectangular tower-house castle whose origins go back to the late 12th century, although the tower house dates from the 15th century. Its plan was a rectangular tower with four rectangular corner towers. The castle is managed by Historic Scotland and is open daily (the key is held at Castle Cottage).

LOCATION: GLASGOW
MAP REF: NS 525627

CUBBIE ROO'S

One of the earliest stone castles built in Scotland, Cubbie Roo's is a slightly rhomboid great tower constructed in the middle of the 12th century. The walls are roughly 1.5m (5ft) thick and its dimensions are about 7.5m (25ft) square. The tower is enclosed in an oval-shaped earthwork with ditching. Cubbie Roo's was probably the castle (*steinkastala*) built c.1145 by the Viking, Kolbein Hruga.

LOCATION: ISLE OF WYRE, ORKNEY ISLANDS
MAP REF: HY 438261

CULCREUCH

Culcreuch is a rubble-built 16th-century tower house probably on the site of an earlier building; it was extended in the 17th century. The castle, a seat of the Clan Galbraith, is now a country house hotel.

LOCATION: FINTRY, STIRLING
MAP REF: NS 620876

DAIRSIE

Once the property of the bishops of St Andrews, the first castle built on this site was a simple rectangular great tower in the 14th century. It was enlarged into a Z-plan tower house in the 16th century and became the home of John Spottiswood, Archbishop of St Andrews and Chancellor of Scotland. Dairsie fell into a ruinous condition with little more than the shell of the tower remaining. It has since been restored and rebuilt and is now private.

LOCATION: NR CUPAR, FIFE
MAP REF: NO 414160

DALCROSS

A 17th-century L-plan tower house that was once the mustering point of government troops before the battle of Culloden in the 18th century. Dalcross was the seat of Clan Fraser and then home of the Mackintosh clan. Private; it is currently let out for holidays.

LOCATION: NR CROY, HIGHLAND
MAP REF: NH 779483

DALHOUSIE

Owned by the Ramsey family for much of its history, Dalhousie is now a country house hotel. It dates from the 13th century but most of the present structure is of the 15th century, with later additions. The great tower house stands in a courtyard enclosed by a curtain wall. A drawbridge over a dry moat protected one of the entrances and the lifting slots are still clearly seen in the walling above. The castle also has a bottle dungeon into which prisoners were lowered on a rope. Dalhousie was occupied by Cromwell during his campaign in Scotland.

LOCATION: BONNYRIGG, MIDLOTHIAN
MAP REF: NT 323636
OPEN: HOTEL

DALKEITH

Dalkeith House is a palatial residence of about 1700. It incorporates part of the much earlier 15th-century L-plan tower house, which was later encircled by a curtain wall. The castle belonged to the Douglases of Dalkeith, notably James Douglas, 4th Earl of Morton, Regent of Scotland, 1572–8. Dalkeith is leased as a study centre.

LOCATION: MIDLOTHIAN
MAP REF: NT 333678

DARNICK

Sir Walter Scott was so attached to Darnick when he was a boy that he was called 'Duke of Darnick'. The castle is basically a T-shaped tower house originally dating from the 15th century and built on an earlier site. The tower is privately owned and not accessible.

LOCATION: DARNICK, MELROSE, BORDERS
MAP REF: NT 532343

DEAN

Until about 1700 Dean was known as Kilmarnock Castle. It comprises a straightforward, 14th-century high, rectangular tower house with lower and more palatial buildings next to it from the 15th century and later: all have been restored. Although part of the present palatial structure, the tower, which was built for defence as well as residential purposes, has no communication with the rest of the complex. The other buildings were designed for comfort more than defence and the entire site was surrounded by a barmkin. The gatehouse was built in the early 20th century following 16th-century style. Beside the stonework is the remnant of a low motte. Dean belonged to the Boyds of Kilmarnock, the parvenu but ambitious family that dominated King James III during some of his minority years in the late 1460s. Set in the midst of a country park, which is always open to the public, the castle has collections of arms and armour, musical instruments and medieval tapestries.

LOCATION: KILMARNOCK, EAST AYRSHIRE
MAP REF: NS 437394
OPEN: EAST AYRSHIRE COUNCIL: APR–OCT DAILY; NOV–MAR SAT–SUN

DELGATIE

Mary, Queen of Scots stayed here briefly and visitors can view her room. Rebuilt c.1570–80 on the site of a much earlier castle dating from c.1100, whose main feature was the rectangular great tower, Delgatie was an L-plan castle with wings added in the 18th century. Some of the rooms still have very fine 16th-century painted ceilings.

LOCATION: TURRIFF, ABERDEENSHIRE
MAP REF: NJ 754505
OPEN: PRIVATE. APR–OCT DAILY

DIRLETON

Dirleton began as an earth-and-timber castle built by the Norman de Vaux family who were encouraged to settle in Scotland by David I in the 12th century. Some time in the early 13th century a cluster of stone towers was built. In the 14th and 15th centuries the castle was coverted into a more elaborate enclosure. In 1298 the castle was besieged and surrendered to the English and the garrison was compelled to surrender; but later it was retaken and then slighted by Robert Bruce. During the 17th century Royalists used the castle as a refuge and in 1650, General Lambert besieged the castle on behalf of Cromwell. Although a ruin, albeit an impressive one, the castle gardens have always been maintained and boast a long herbaceous border.

LOCATION: NORTH BERWICK, EAST LOTHIAN
MAP REF: NT 516839
OPEN: HISTORIC SCOTLAND: DAILY

DOUNE

The name Doune is derived from 'dun', the ancient word for a fortified town and there are traces of prehistoric earthworks around this splendid stone enclosure castle. It was built towards the end of the 14th century for Robert Stewart, Duke of Albany and Regent of Scotland from c.1396–1420. When Albany died in 1420 his son, Murdoch, inherited the castle but he was put to death by James I in 1425 and Doune was taken over by the Crown. It was held for more than a century by royalty and then passed to the Earls of Moray who owned it until it was passed into the care of Historic Scotland in the 1980s. The castle was restored in the first half of the 19th century and then again towards the end of the 20th century. The Lord's Hall, on the first floor above the gateway passage, is laid out much as it would have been and to the west is the vast great hall. The castle was one of the locations for the film *Monty Python and the Holy Grail*.

LOCATION: NR DUNBLANE, STIRLING
MAP REF: NN 728011
OPEN: HISTORIC SCOTLAND: APR–SEP DAILY; OCT–MAR SAT–WED

DOUNE OF INVERNOCHTY

A Norman-style motte castle was raised here with moat and encircling rampart in the late 12th or early 13th century. The summit of the mound, which is nearly 18.5m (61ft) tall, is surrounded by the remains of a low mortared stone wall 2m (6ft) thick, which was originally much taller.

LOCATION: STRATHDON, ABERDEENSHIRE
MAP REF: NJ 351129

DRUM

The castle at Drum is a fine example of a late 13th-century great tower: one of the three oldest in Scotland and the only one to remain intact. It has rounded corners and few window openings, a spiral staircase from the first floor up to the battlemented parapet and wall-walk and adjoins an early 17th-century mansion built by Alexander, the 9th Laird of Drum. The castle was further altered during Victorian times. William Irvine, armour-bearer to Robert Bruce, was given the charter to the Royal Forest of Drum in the 1320s but it is likely that the tower already existed, probably from before the 1280s. Its site, on a ridge above a crossing point of the River Dee, would have afforded important protection for the nearby town of Aberdeen. Irvine descendants held the castle until 1976 when it was passed to the National Trust. Inside there are fine portraits and a collection of Georgian furniture.

LOCATION: BANCHORY, ABERDEENSHIRE
MAP REF: NJ 796005
OPEN: NATIONAL TRUST FOR SCOTLAND: APR–SEP DAILY; GROUNDS: DAILY

DRUMCOLTRAN

Drumcoltran is a rectangular L-plan tower house of the mid-16th century, built by the Maxwells and then occupied by various families until the end of the 19th century. It is three storeys tall, with gabled roof and a staircase wing. There is an overhanging parapet supported on corbels, and a narrow wall-walk behind. The tower stands amid farm buildings but is under the stewardship of Historic Scotland and is accessible all year.

LOCATION: KIRKGUNZEON, NR DALBEATTIE, DUMFRIES & GALLOWAY
MAP REF: NX 869683

DRUMMINOR

Now only a fraction of its original size, this castle was begun between about 1440 and 1456 by the head of the Forbes family. The licence to fortify was granted after the structure was built: the Forbes were continually under attack by their rivals, the Gordons. The castle was sacked in 1571. It was a tower palace connected with buildings round a courtyard and has been restored with great care to retain something of its original shape and atmosphere.

LOCATION: NR RHYNIE, ABERDEENSHIRE
MAP REF: NJ 513264

DRUMMOND

The present mansion at Drummond, seat of the Earls of Ancaster, incorporates the lower part of a late 15th-century tower house in its entrance gate. The original castle, built by Sir John Drummond, was heavily damaged by Cromwell in the 1650s but rebuilt. Later, a Victorian mansion was added. Drummond boasts one of the finest formal gardens in Europe.

LOCATION: NR CRIEFF, PERTH & KINROSS
MAP REF: NN 844180
OPEN: GARDENS: MAY–OCT DAILY PM

DUART

Duart Castle was extensively rebuilt and restored early in the 1900s by Sir Fitzroy Maclean after it had become ruinous during the 17th century. It stands high upon a rocky mound over the entrance to the Sound of Mull and it belongs, as it has from the 13th century, to the Clan Maclean. It began as a late Norman enclosure castle. A rectangular tower, built by Lachlan Lubanach in the 14th century, forms an integral part of the curtain wall.

LOCATION: ISLE OF MULL, ARGYLL & BUTE
MAP REF: NM 748354
OPEN: PRIVATE. APR–MID-OCT DAILY

DUDHOPE

Predominantly an L-plan tower house of the 16th century, Dudhope was owned by the celebrated Graham of Claverhouse, otherwise known as Bonny Dundee. The castle was used as army barracks until nearly the end of the 19th century. Dundee Town Council then bought the castle and the grounds were turned into a public park. The castle is not open.

LOCATION: DUDHOPE PARK, DUNDEE
MAP REF: NO 395307

DUFFUS

Founded by Freskin de Moravia, a Norman-Scottish baron in the reign of David I, Duffus began as a tall motte surrounded by a ditch with a ditch-encircled bailey and was surrounded by marsh ground which has now given way to flat farmland. Scottish patriots burned the wooden castle and c.1300, the motte was given a stone great tower and a stone curtain round the bailey. In the 15th century a range of buildings was added along the north side of the bailey. The castle is now ruinous but remains one of the finest examples of a motte and bailey in Scotland.

LOCATION: ELGIN, MORAY
MAP REF: NJ 175687
OPEN: HISTORIC SCOTLAND. OPEN ACCESS

DUMBARTON

Recorded as a stronghold for longer than any other site in Britain, the castle is built on Dumbarton Rock, a volcanic neck of basalt jutting out into the Clyde. There was certainly a settlement here in 450 when St Patrick wrote a letter to the King of Strathclyde at Alcuith (Clyde Rock). By the early 13th century there is a reference to a 'new castle' on the site but the only surviving structure from this period is the Portcullis Arch. The medieval history of Dumbarton is one of changing ownership; it was besieged several times. During the 17th and 18th centuries most of the medieval buildings (which were ruinous) were replaced with the extant buildings. These provided a base for government troops during the Jacobite risings and to defend the Clyde against France.

LOCATION: WEST DUMBARTONSHIRE.
MAP REF: NS 400745
OPEN: HISTORIC SCOTLAND: APR–SEP DAILY; OCT–MAR SAT–WED

DUNBAR

Once an important stronghold due to its position on the route from England to the Scottish capital, Dunbar is now a jumble of red freestone ruins. An earlier wooden fortification was rebuilt in stone late in the 11th century. The castle was destroyed in 1333 by its owner but rebuilt on the orders of Edward III. Dunbar was the scene of a five-month siege by England in 1338 when it was defended by Black Agnes, Countess of Moray. Regent Moray dismantled the castle in 1568. The ruins can be viewed at any time.

LOCATION: MIDLOTHIAN
MAP REF: NT 678793

DUNDERAVE

Although this castle on the shore of Loch Fyne was built as the seat of Iain, chief of the MacNaughtons c.1590, there are earlier charters relating to Dunderave. MacNaughton's castle was L-plan with a substantial cylindrical tower on one corner, and was restored in the 19th century.

LOCATION: INVERARAY, ARGYLL & BUTE
MAP REF: NN 143097

DUNDONALD

Built for both residential and military purposes by an ancestor of Robert II of Scotland in the early 13th century, this was a stone-curtained enclosure with a twin-towered gatehouse. Robert II inherited the castle in 1371, appreciated its defensive position and converted the original work into a bigger, rectangular tower block. The castle was said to be a favourite lodging of Robert II; he died there in 1390. There were three main phases of building, and substantial ruins of the 14th-century castle include parts of the earlier fortification. Stone heraldic shields carved into the west wall are among the oldest in Scotland.

LOCATION: SOUTH AYRSHIRE
MAP REF: NS 363345
OPEN: APR–OCT DAILY

DUNGLASS

This 15th-century L-plan tower house was, in the early part of the 20th century, associated with artist Margaret Macdonald Mackintosh, wife of Charles Rennie Mackintosh. The house is boarded up and inaccessible.

LOCATION: DUNGLASS, EAST LOTHIAN
MAP REF: NS 435736

DUNOLLIE

The site of a fortress owned by the Lord of Argyll, father of the founder of the MacDougall clan. The principal structure of this 13th-century castle is the ruin of the rectangular 15th-century tower house. The site is freely accessible during daylight hours.

LOCATION: NR OBAN, ARGYLL & BUTE
MAP REF: NM 852315

DUNNOTTAR

Dunnottar Castle sits on a flat-topped promontory surrounded by the North Sea and joined to the mainland by a small low-level isthmus. The site of fortifications for hundreds of years, an earthwork and clay castle from the 12th century was used by William the Lion as an administrative centre. At the end of the 14th century an early L-plan tower house was built on the headland; it was converted in the late 16th and early 17th centuries into one of the most palatial residences in Scotland as the castle had been granted to the Earl Marischals of Scotland in 1531 by James V. Besieged by Montrose in 1645 and again in 1651 by Cromwell's forces, Dunnottar was finally dismantled in the 18th century but the ruins are still impressive.

During Cromwell's time at Edinburgh Castle, the Honours of Scotland, the crown, sceptre and sword of state, were hidden at Dunnottar Castle.

LOCATION: NR STONEHAVEN, ABERDEENSHIRE
MAP REF: NO 881838
OPEN: PRIVATE: EASTER–MID-OCT DAILY; MID-OCT–EASTER FRI–MON

DUNOON

The earliest castle here, a royal residence, was raised on an artificial mound in the 1100s. Later it was enlarged to consist of three cylindrical towers arranged in a triangular plan. The castle was abandoned in the middle of the 17th century and the stone was used for other buildings, including Castle House, which houses a museum. The earthworks remain and are in a public park.

LOCATION: DUNOON, ARGYLL & BUTE
MAP REF: NS 175763
OPEN: FREE ACCESS

DUNROBIN

This magnificent castle palace is largely the creation of the 17th and 19th centuries built on an early 15th-century great tower, which belonged to the Earls of Sutherland (then Morays). The most northerly of Scotland's great houses, in the 17th century the tower was converted to a courtyard-plan castle-mansion. Sir Charles Barry remodelled it in the 19th century. There is much for visitors to see here.

LOCATION: GOLSPIE, HIGHLAND
MAP REF: NC 852 008
OPEN: SUTHERLAND TRUST: APR–MID-OCT DAILY

DUNSKEY

The romantic cliff-top ruin of 15th-century Dunskey is on a promontory jutting into the sea. The tower house is L-plan and outside the tower are the remains of an enclosure wall.

LOCATION: PORT PATRICK, DUMFRIES & GALLOWAY
MAP REF: NX 004534

DUNSTAFFNAGE

Dunstaffnage sits on a rock on the edge of the Firth of Lorn. The castle originally dates from the 13th century and was occupied until the end of the 1800s. Alexander II and Alexander III used the site during their campaigns against the Vikings in the Western Isles. Its importance as a checkpoint to the approach to Glen Mor was also recognized by Edward I. It was captured by Robert Bruce in 1309 from the MacDougalls and passed to the Campbell family via the first Earl of Argyll and then to his cousin, who became Captain of Dunstaffnage. The family retains ownership. Flora Macdonald was held here after she helped Bonnie Prince Charlie.

LOCATION: NR OBAN, ARGYLL & BUTE
MAP REF: NM 883344
OPEN: HISTORIC SCOTLAND: APR–SEP DAILY; OCT–MAR SAT–WED

DUNURE

Dunure was started in the 13th century, a tower was built in the 15th century and buildings added in the 16th. In the 1550s the Earl of Cassilis, who held Dunure, seized the abbot of Crossraguel Abbey and roasted him to get him to sign over the abbey lands: the abbot survived to sue the earl.

LOCATION: SOUTH AYRSHIRE
MAP REF: NS 252158

DUNVEGAN

This romantic fortress is still occupied by the Chiefs of the Macleod clan whose ancestors erected it in the Middle Ages. The present structure is a 19th-century transformation of a castle begun in the 13th century and it is possible to see relics from many of the ten building periods.

Dunvegan stands on a rock projecting into the sea. One early feature of the castle is the remnant of a sea gate which was once the only entrance to the castle. Displayed inside are MacLeod heirlooms including the bull horn, which dates from the 14th century: it is still filled with claret for each male heir to the MacLeod Chiefdom who then has to drain it. The castle gardens were laid out in the 18th century.

LOCATION: ISLE OF SKYE, HIGHLAND
MAP REF: NG 250480
OPEN: PRIVATE: DAILY

EARLSHALL

Built by Sir William Bruce, the original 16th-century castle here was a rectangular tower block with one cylindrical tower, and a square-plan tower. Earlshall was restored in the 19th century by architect and garden designer Sir Robert Lorimer. The fine gardens are open to the public.

LOCATION: LEUCHARS, FIFE
MAP REF: NO 465211

EDINAMPLE

This Z-plan castle of the 16th century was erected by the Campbells of Glenorchy. It can only be viewed from the road.

LOCATION: LOCHEARNHEAD, STIRLING
MAP REF: NN 625235

EDINBURGH

LOCATION: ROYAL MILE, EDINBURGH
MAP REF: NT 252736
OPEN: HISTORIC SCOTLAND: DAILY. TIMES VARY FOR INDEPENDENT MUSEUM
SEE PAGE: 140

Edinburgh

The most famous of all the the Scottish fortresses, Edinburgh Castle sits atop a great volcanic ridge. When the Romans came to Scotland the rock was inhabited by the local Votadini tribe and became known as Din Eidyn. The Angles (English) took the stronghold in 638 and Din Eidyn was renamed Edinburgh

The history of the craggy fortress at Edinburgh, entwined with that of Scotland itself, reaches back for several thousand years and at the end of the 11th century this royal stronghold was known as the Castle of Maidens. During the reign of David I the castle emerged as a major royal fortress; it was here that the first recorded assembly of the forerunner of today's Scottish Parliament took place in 1140 and it was David I who built the tiny St Margaret's chapel (named for his mother), which still exists as the oldest surviving building in the castle precincts.

Most of the buildings were rebuilt in stone during the 13th century before Edward I's campaign in Scotland. Nevertheless Edward captured the castle in 1296 and the great Scottish fortress fell, not for the first time or the last, into English hands. It was Robert Bruce's son, David II who then rebuilt the fortress after it was finally back in Scottish hands and remnants of the 14th century David's Tower still lie beneath the 16th-century Half-Moon Battery.

Much of the medieval castle was destroyed in the 'Lang Siege' of 1571–3 and more still in the 17th century when Oliver Cromwell set up his Scottish headquarters here and the castle's role shifted from palace to garrison. Many of the castle's extant buildings

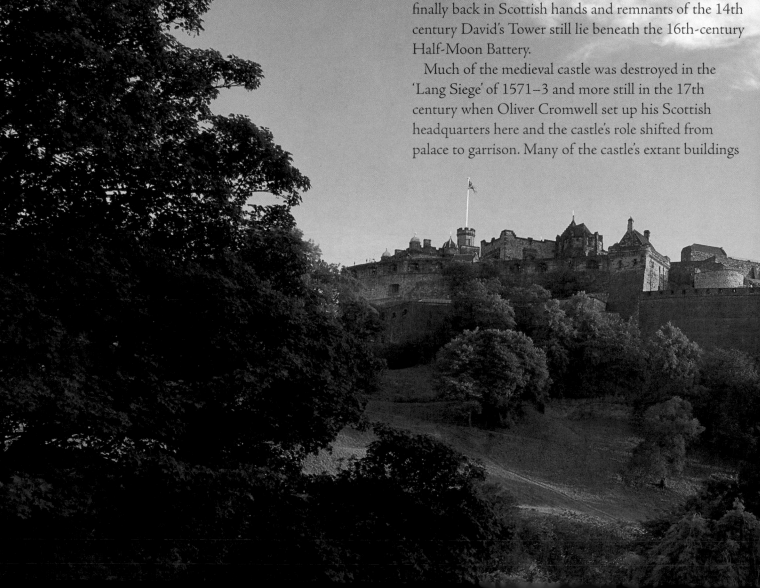

date from this time and later although the main courtyard, Crown Square, was begun during the 15th and 16th centuries. Built over vast stone cellars (used at various times to incarcerate prisoners of war) the square contains the most important castle buildings including the royal palace and great hall. The creation of Edinburgh as the Scottish capital during the reign of James III meant that, like England's Tower of London, the fortress was to serve as the realm's chief arsenal, home to the Honours of Scotland and repository of the state archives.

Edinburgh's Military Tattoo, staged each year in August on the Castle Esplanade, has grown into a world-renowned spectacle. Each tattoo closes with the appearance of a lone piper on the battlements. The castle is home to a military museum, the National War Museum of Scotland, and also the magnificent Scottish National War Memorial.

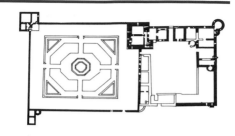

Edzell began as a substantial rectangular L-plan tower house built by the Lindsay family in the early 16th century. Later a quadrangle of buildings was added and connected to the tower by an entrance hall, and in the first years of the 1600s, Sir David Lindsay added a spacious pleasaunce or walled garden to the eastern side of the courtyard. Sir David died before his project was completed. A bath-house tower and a summer house, which is still intact, were added to the corners of the highly decorated walls of the pleasaunce and the garden here is one of the most notable of any British castle. As a fortress, Edzell had a peaceful history and it was the scene of various royal visits, including one by Mary, Queen of Scots when she held a Privy Council meeting in the hall. Although fortified, the castle was never besieged but suffered through the misfortune of the families that owned it. Edzell was finally sold to the York Building Company and when it went into liquidation, the company assets, including Edzell, were stripped. The castle then passed into the hands of the Dalhousie family. Today it is an interesting and attractive ruin with a wonderful, well-maintained garden.

LOCATION: NR BRECHIN, ANGUS
MAP REF: NO 585691
OPEN: HISTORIC SCOTLAND: APR–SEP DAILY; OCT–MAR CLOSED THU AM, SUN PM; OCT– DEC SAT–WED

ELCHO

Elcho is a much restored, massive five-floor tower house of the 16th century and particularly fascinating for its tower attachments. A substantial square-plan tower projects from the south-west corner of the block with three more tower projections along the north wall, one square, one semi-cylindrical and one cylindrical. Elcho's windows are protected by iron grilles and the walls have gun-ports, but the castle was also designed to provide handsome family accommodation. There is evidence that the tower house was enclosed inside a barmkin with a ditch outside. The nearby quarry, now a garden, was flooded and connected to the River Tay, and this would have provided a private dock for the castle. Visitors can view the interior.

LOCATION: NR PERTH, PERTH & KINROSS
MAP REF: NO 164211
OPEN: HISTORIC SCOTLAND: APR–SEP DAILY

ELGIN

Mentioned as early as the 1220s, Elgin Castle was a simple stone enclosure with a great tower. Very little remains of the building which is thought to have been derelict since the 15th century. The enclosure was about 19 x 9.5m (62 x 31ft) with rubble-built walls about 2.5m (8ft) thick. The site has a monument to the 5th Duke of Gordon.

LOCATION: MORAY
MAP REF: NJ 212628

ELPHINSTONE

Elphinstone was built c.1440 to a rectangular plan and once rose five storeys to the parapet, plus an attic storey above. Each level had a substantial main room. The whole tower was short of window space and had no gun-ports or shot-holes and yet was strongly defensive. In the 1950s it was demolished to the lowest storey because of subsidence.

LOCATION: NR EDINBURGH, LOTHIAN
MAP REF: NT 390698

ETHIE

Ethie started as an E-plan tower house built in the 15th century, although there has been a castle on the site from the 1300s. In the 16th century the castle was the home of Cardinal David Beaton, the Abbot of Arbroath who later became the Chancellor of Scotland and also Archbishop of St Andrews. Ethie is also reputedly the inspiration for the Castle of Knockwhinnock in Sir Walter Scott's novel *The Antiquary*. The castle is now a small private hotel.

LOCATION: INVERKEILOR, NR ARBROATH, ANGUS
MAP REF: NO 687468

EVELAW

A partly ruinous, three-floor-16th century tower house, Evelaw is L-plan, with rounded corners, corbelled out to square at the level of the eaves and with wide-mouth splayed gun-ports in the south and east walls.

LOCATION: WESTRUTHER, BORDERS
MAP REF: NT 661526

FAIRBURN TOWER

This is a ruined tower house dating from the 16th century. Fairburn was a Mackenzie stronghold and its demise was foretold by the Brahan Seer, Scotland's answer to Nostradamus.

LOCATION: URRAY, HIGHLAND
MAP REF: NH 469523

FALKLAND

James II began the present magnificent palace at Falkland in about 1500 and James V continued construction work. It was built near the site of an earlier castle whose origins can be dated to the 13th century, and there are still traces of its round towers in the palace grounds.

The Royal Palace of Falkland was the country residence of the Stuart kings and queens, and contains some fine portraits of the Stuart monarchs. In the garden you will find the original royal tennis court, built in 1539.

LOCATION: CUPAR, FIFE
MAP REF: NO 254076
OPEN: NATIONAL TRUST FOR SCOTLAND: MAR–OCT DAILY

FALSIDE

Falside (or Fa'side, Fawside) was built in the 15th century as a rectangular tower, with four floors, the top storey of which was vaulted. This tower was badly damaged by the English during the Battle of Pinkie in 1547. In the 17th century Falside was enlarged by adding an L-plan tower house to the south wall of the original tower, constructed to the same height. It was restored in the 1980s after it had been threatened with demolition.

LOCATION: TRANENT, EAST LOTHIAN
MAP REF: NT 377709

FARNELL

Farnell is a three-storey building with a semi-cylindrical projecting turret containing the entrance door and a staircase. This is a modern restoration of a late 13th-century castle rebuilt in the 16th century and has absorbed features of the 13th-century castle.

LOCATION: ANGUS
MAP REF: NO 624555

FAST

A motte castle dating from the 12th century, sometimes known as Castle Knowe, was erected on a bank of Rule Water close by Bedrule Castle. The natural mound was about 14m (46ft) high, and about 3m (10ft) of extra height was added before the wooden great tower was built on the summit.

LOCATION: NR ST ABBS, BORDERS
MAP REF: NT 595182

FATLIPS

One of two castles of this name in Scotland (few traces remain of the other near Wiston), it stands in a commanding position. The basic structure is 16th century. The original rectangular tower was 8 x 10m (26 x 33ft), and rose to four floors with an additional garret. It was built of local whinstone with freestone dressings. The 16th-century tower was restored in 1857, and renovated in 1897–8 by Sir Robert Lorimer as a shooting box and private museum, although today the tower is again in a state of decay. The site can be viewed from the road.

LOCATION: MINTO, BORDERS
MAP REF: NT 581208

FENTONS TOWER

James VI took refuge at Fentons Tower with the Carmichael family. The tower castle was sacked and ruined by Cromwell in 1650. From that time, this 16th-century, rectangular L-plan tower house with a small wing attached remained a sad ruin until just a few years ago. It was comprehensively restored and converted into a hotel.

LOCATION: NORTH BERWICK, EAST LOTHIAN
MAP REF: NT 543820

FERNIE

Fernie was first recorded in 1353 when it belonged to the Earl of Fife. The present building, a tall, L-plan castle mainly dates from the 16th century but has later additions. It is now run as a luxurious hotel.

LOCATION: LETHAM, NR CUPAR, FIFE
MAP REF: NO 316147

FERNIEHURST

This castle, now owned by the Marquis and Marchioness of Lothian, is largely a 16th-century reconstruction of an earlier building which was seized by forces of Henry III during the 1547 war between Scotland and England. For much of the 20th century the castle was a youth hostel, but is once again a private house and has been restored. There is a small museum and the castle is open to the public at times.

LOCATION: JEDBURGH, BORDERS
MAP REF: NT 632179

FETTERESSO

This rectangular block, dating from the 15th century, received further additions in the 17th century to make two sides of a quadrangle. Montrose burned the eastern block in 1645 but it was rebuilt later in the century.

The Old Pretender, James Edward, was proclaimed King James VIII of Scotland here in 1715.

LOCATION: NR STONEHAVEN, ABERDEENSHIRE
MAP REF: NO 842855

FINAVON

The ruins of a castle begun in the 14th century stand near the present 19th-century mansion that is now known as Finavon Castle (part of which is rented out as holiday accommodation). It was a stronghold of the Earls of Crawford.

LOCATION: NR FORFAR, ANGUS
MAP REF: NO 497565

FINDLATER

Now in ruins, this was a substantial castle on a tiny peninsula jutting out into the North Sea. A ditch on the mainland gave extra protection. The castle appears to have had several towers and some curtain walling. The ruins probably date from the late 14th or early 15th century, and the castle was a Sinclair stronghold. The remains are currently accessible but care should be taken when visiting them.

LOCATION: SANDEND, ABERDEENSHIRE
MAP REF: NJ 542672

FINGASK

The oldest part of the castle dates from the late 16th century although Fingask has been greatly altered. Originally built by Patrick Bruce, for much of its history the castle has been in the hands of the Threipland family. Now it is a private home, used as a venue for events, with holiday cottages in the grounds and a magnificent garden which was laid out in the 17th century.

LOCATION: RAIT, PERTH & KINROSS
MAP REF: NO 228274

FINLARIG

A panel over the entrance dates this Z-plan tower house to about 1609. A former Campbell stronghold, it was raised on a mound, possibly the site of an earlier castle. The tower house has gun-ports. Finlarig is now ruinous.

LOCATION: KILLIN, STIRLING
MAP REF: NN 575338

FORDELL

Fordell was a Z-plan castle of c.1580 on the site of an earlier building The plan is a main rectangular block with two square towered wings containing staircases and cylindrical turrets. Although it is a small structure, its 1.5m (5ft) thick walls indicate that it was a fortified residence. The late Nicholas Fairburn QC, Member of Parliament and Solicitor General for Scotland restored it as a private home.

LOCATION: DALGETY, FIFE
MAP REF: NT 147853

FORDYCE

Built in 1592 by Thomas Menzies of Durn, Fordyce Castle is a typical laird's house: a three-floor tower house of L-plan with a tall semicircular projection corbelled out from the first-floor level upwards to the roof of the main block. The turrets and walls have shot-holes. Part of the castle is rented out as holiday accommodation.

LOCATION: FORDYCE, ABERDEENSHIRE
MAP REF: NJ 555638

FOWLIS

The remains of a 17th-century four-floor tower block enlarged by a later wing stand here. It was once part of a much larger medieval structure.

LOCATION: ANGUS
MAP REF: NO 321333

FRAOCH EILEAN

On an island in Loch Awe, this was a rectangular hall-tower of the 13th century. In the 1600s, the hall-tower, which had been abandoned, was taken over and adapted to contain a house.

LOCATION: LOCH AWE, ARGYLL & BUTE
MAP REF: NN 108252

THE ACT OF UNION

When James VI of Scotland became King of England after the death of Elizabeth I, union between the countries was mooted. However it was not until more than 100 years later in 1707 that the Act was passed by the Scottish Parliament. The delay lay in mutual suspicion born out of centuries of conflict.

One of Scotland's great royal fortress-palaces, visited by both Edward I and Robert the Bruce and owned by five successive families, Fyvie's long, rectangular block has four-storeyed towers with garret and cylindrical corner bartizans on each end. In the centre is a massive gatehouse-like projection of twin semi-cylindrical towers, flanking a recess containing a doorway at ground level. This whole south front has a formidable appearance but is not, in fact, properly fortified. The first mention of stonework at the castle is c.1390. The south-east tower (Preston) was built c.1390–1430; the south-west (Meldrum) tower, some time between c.1433 and c.1590. The gatehouse is from the late 16th century. Additions were made right up to the 1890s. The wheel staircase at Fyvie, with wide sweep steps and a solid newel, is the finest example in Scotland. The castle has an opulent interior and displays collections of portraits and arms and armour. The grounds were landscaped in the 19th century.

LOCATION: TURRIFF, ABERDEENSHIRE
MAP REF: NJ 764323
OPEN: NATIONAL TRUST FOR SCOTLAND: APR–JUN & SEP FRI–TUE; JUL–AUG DAILY. GROUNDS: ALL YEAR DAILY

GARDYNE

Gardyne, built by the family of the same name, has been well maintained and is still occupied. It began in the 15th century as an L-plan tower house with a rounded staircase turret bearing a rectangular cap-house. It was further extended in the 16th and 17th centuries to include a block on the north-west.

LOCATION: KIRKDEN, NR FRIOCKHEIM, ANGUS
MAP REF: NO 574488

GARTH

Garth is a square-plan tower house about 18.5m (61ft) high to the parapet, with walls 2m (6ft) thick and built of rough boulders. The tower dates from the 14th century and was built by Alexander Stewart, Earl of Buchan and known as the 'Wolf of Badenoch'. After a long period of decay it was restored in the 19th century as a hunting lodge.

LOCATION: COSHIEVILLE, PERTH & KINROSS
MAP REF: NW 764503

GIGHT

Built in the third quarter of the 16th century, Gight is a ruined L-plan tower house which stands near the River Ythan. The castle's gun-loops are interesting: a crosslet (arrow slit in the shape of a cross) at the top of a slit and an oillet at the base. Gight was the family home of Lord Byron. It is still associated with the Gordon family.

LOCATION: METHLICK, NR FYVIE, ABERDEENSHIRE
MAP REF: NJ 826392

WEAPONS

WEAPONS WERE ESSENTIAL EQUIPMENT IN MEDIEVAL TIMES. NOTIONS OF CHIVALRY DICTATED THAT SOME WEAPONS WERE MORE 'NOBLE' THAN OTHERS, WITH THE SWORD AT THE APEX, BUT BATTLE AXES, SPEARS AND BOWS AND ARROWS WERE CENTRAL PARTS OF CASTLE ARMOURIES. IN THE HANDS OF AN ANGRY OR FRIGHTENED MAN EVEN THE HUMBLE PITCHFORK COULD BE A DEVASTATING WEAPON.

The nobility had swords that were beautifully made and which were often said to have special powers. The swords of ordinary soldiers were more modest, but even these were excellent examples of medieval technology. Light, flexible and razor-sharp, a sword could pierce metal armour and cut off limbs or heads with one blow.

Longbows were a speciality of England and Wales, and helped to change the nature of warfare in the 14th century. Usually made of yew, a longbow was as tall as the archer, with the arrows about half that length. Longbow archers had to be immensely strong, since pulling the bowstring back was very difficult. An idea of the force of these weapons can be gleaned from stories of them driving 10cm (4in) into solid oak. Archers trained on smaller bows when still boys, and their bodies developed strangely, with their arms and upper chests hugely muscled in comparison to their legs. A skilled longbowman could fire an arrow every 10 seconds if he was aiming carefully, but more than that if accuracy was not needed. In battle, a hail of arrows could devastate the enemy, as happened to the French army at Agincourt.

A late 15th-century siege. The besiegers have brought a wheeled cannon and a larger, static mortar. Both have stone balls for ammunition. Such weapons were very prone to failure, and accidental explosions were not uncommon.

Longbowmen and one crossbowman rain arrows on castle defenders to provide cover for the soldiers who are scaling the walls. Skilled archers fired devastating fusillades that could inflict appalling wounds. There were different kinds of arrowhead, intended to inflict different kinds of injuries.

Crossbows were less accurate but could fire farther. They required much less skill to fire, but could take up to a minute to load, since their bowstrings could not be pulled by hand, but had to be winched into place.

Artillery and gunpowder began to appear late in the 14th century. At first used in much the same way as trebuchets and mangonels (see page 202) and firing stones as they did, early ordnance could strike fear into the hearts of castle defenders. These weapons did not rely on accuracy: they battered away at castle walls to weaken them until they collapsed under their own weight.

Fortifications changed as a direct result of the developing sophistication and power of artillery weapons. Tall castle walls were easy targets, and by the 16th century lower walls, often protected by thick earthen ramparts, were becoming common. By then, traditional castles were much less needed for defence anyway.

The majority of castles were last used in conflict during the Civil War, but some, like Dover, continued in use until 1945, armed with the latest weapons.

GLAMIS

This magnificent mansion of the Earls of Strathmore and Kinghorne, one of the finest in Scotland, conceals a number of earlier structures. In 1372 Robert II granted the site to Sir John Lyon and c. 1400 the second Sir John began to build an L-plan tower house. This had outer defences of barmkin wall and flanking towers and was surrounded by a moat. Remains of the medieval castle are incorporated into the present castle which evolved during the 17th and 18th centuries.

It was the childhood home of the late Lady Elizabeth Bowes Lyon who married the Duke of York in 1923 and was mother to Elizabeth II. Glamis features in Shakespeare's *Macbeth*.

LOCATION: FORFAR, ANGUS
MAP REF: NO 386480
OPEN: PRIVATE: APR–OCT DAILY

GLENGARNOCK

This castle was based on a square great tower integrated in a polygonal stone-curtained courtyard, which had other buildings inside. It was begun in the 15th century and the tower (or keep) was 14 x 11m (46 x 36ft) with vaulted ground and first floors. The castle, which Mary, Queen of Scots visited in 1563, was abandoned by the 18th century; it is now a romantic ruin.

LOCATION: KILBIRNIE, NORTH AYRSHIRE
MAP REF: NS 311574

GRANDTULLY

Principally a late 16th-century Z-plan tower house with rectangular corner turrets. This is thought to have been raised upon the remains of a c.1400 square-plan tower house which itself was enlarged to L-plan in the early 16th century. The gatehouse contains oval gun-loops, and a feature of 17th-century origin is the tall, cylindrical stair turret projecting out of one long side; it is six-floored with an ogee roof. The castle is a private residence but can be viewed from the road.

LOCATION: NR ABERFELDY, PERTH & KINROSS
MAP REF: NN 891515

GLENBUCHAT

This late 16th-century castle was built on the Z-plan, with square towers, and belonged to the powerful Gordon family. One of its owners was John Gordon, a hero of both Jacobite Risings. Known as Old Glenbuchat, John Gordon's devotion to the Pretender's cause was such that George II was haunted by him in his dreams and would wake up screaming 'De gread Glenbogged is goming'. The entrance to the castle building is in the east wall of the south-west tower, and it had an outer door and an inner yet, the door could not be opened until the yet behind had opened. A staircase led up from opposite this entrance to the first floor, where there was access to the spiral staircase in the cylindrical projection: the castle's staircases are supported by squinch-arches and not corbelling. The tower walls were equipped with gun-loops all round. Glenbuchat remained in the hands of the Gordon family until the 18th century; the roof was taken off in the middle of the 19th century. Some restoration work has been undertaken and much of the castle is still standing.

LOCATION: GLENBUCHAT, NR STRATHDON, ABERDEENSHIRE
MAP REF: NJ 398149
OPEN: HISTORIC SCOTLAND. OPEN ACCESS

GREENKNOWE TOWER

An interesting tower house of L-plan, built c.1581 by the Seton of Touch family. It stands on rising ground and was surrounded by marshland. The tower is 11 x 6.5m (36 x 21ft) with a shorter wing containing the spiral staircase. The entrance is in the angle and is still guarded by its iron yett. It was occupied to the mid-19th century.

LOCATION: GORDON, NR DUNS, BORDERS
MAP REF: NT 639428
OPEN: HISTORIC SCOTLAND: OPEN ACCESS

GUTHRIE

James II granted this barony to Sir David Guthrie, his Treasurer, who was licensed to build a castle and yett in 1468. The original square-plan tower was extended, particularly in the 18th century when a house was built close by. It was connected to the tower in the middle of the 19th century. The yett, the original entrance to the castle, now guards the entry to the wild-flower garden. The Guthrie family lived at this story-book castle until the last century, and it remains private.

LOCATION: GUTHRIE, NR FORFAR, ANGUS
MAP REF: NO 562505

HAILES

Hailes Castle is an impressive a ruin on the River Tyne. It is one of the few Scottish castles that has remnants of its 13th-century origins and is thought to contain some of the oldest standing stonework in the country. This is found in the lower part of the tower in the north range of buildings, which has a pit prison and was later converted into a doocot (dovecote). The de Gourlay family put up these early buildings but they supported the English during the Wars of Independence, so in the 14th century the castle was granted to the wild, dangerous Hepburns, later the Earls of Bothwell. The Hepburns added buildings, including a substantial square-plan tower at the west and lofty curtain walls, much of which can be seen though in a dilapidated state. The 4th Earl of Bothwell was involved in the murder of Lord Darnley. He then married Mary, Queen of Scots, a union that led to Mary's forced abdication. The castle saw its share of action but was dismantled by Cromwell in 1650.

LOCATION: NR EAST LINTON, EAST LOTHIAN
MAP REF: NT 575758
OPEN: HISTORIC SCOTLAND: OPEN ACCESS

HALLFOREST

A ruined rectangular tower, Hallforest was built in the late 13th to early 14th centuries. It had six floors, including an attic, though little remains of it now. It is said to have been built at the encouragement of Robert Bruce, and was granted in 1309 to Sir Robert Keith, Great Marischal of Scotland, who commanded a major wing at Bannockburn in 1314.

LOCATION: KINTORE, ABERDEENSHIRE
MAP REF: NJ 777154

HARTHILL

Harthill is now a roofless ruin of a Z-plan tower house built by the Keiths c.1600. The plan was a rectangular tower with one square tower built diagonally opposite a cylindrical tower. There are a limited number of gun-ports and none in the barmkin. Harthill has had some restoration.

LOCATION: OYNE, ABERDEENSHIRE
MAP REF: NJ 686252

HATTON

Lord Oliphant built a three-storeyed Z-plan tower house with gable top here in the 1570s. The main tower is rectangular and has square towers on the north-east and south-west angles. The building was equipped with gun-ports all round at ground-floor level, providing defensive fire over every direction of assault. Hatton became ruinous but was restored in the 1980s.

LOCATION: NEWTYLE, ANGUS
MAP REF: NO 302411

HAWICK

Hawick motte is an artificial mound dating from the 12th century, now measuring about 7.5m (25ft). A coin from Henry II's time was found in the earth round the motte. A flight of stone steps to the top of the mound re-creates the appearance it doubtless had 800 years ago, except the steps would have been timber. The mound is set in a public park.

LOCATION: BORDERS
MAP REF: NT 499140

HAWTHORNDEN

Sited on a triangular promontory at the end of a ravine above the River Esk and not far from Edinburgh, Hawthornden Castle has a ruined 15th-century tower adjoining the 17th-century L-plan house. Its owner was the poet William Drummond who helped to organize the celebrations of the coronation of Charles I. Notable men of letters Dr Samuel Johnson and James Boswell, and playwright Ben Jonson were visitors here and appropriately, this pretty castle is now used as a retreat for writers.

LOCATION: NR ROSLIN, MIDLOTHIAN
MAP REF: NT 286636

HERMITAGE

This brutal-looking tower-house castle, set against a backdrop of bleak moorland, was built over several centuries. Its position meant that it figured in many episodes of Scottish history and it changed hands several times, particularly during the Wars of Independence in the 13th century. For a time Hermitage was held by the wild and dangerous James Hepburn, Earl of Bothwell, whose liaison with Mary, Queen of Scots was the scandal of 16th-century Scotland.

The castle's beginnings were in the early 13th century when Sir Nicholas de Soules put up a wooden fortress on the site, which was captured, in 1338, by the Knight of Liddesdale, Sir William Douglas. Later the 1st Earl of Douglas inherited Hermitage and he built the original stone structure, a small rectangular enclosure, in the late 13th to early 14th century. Four great stone towers were added at the end of the 14th century: these are close together on the east and west sides and linked at the top by a continuous storey, giving the appearance of a huge stone wall with a great central pointed arch, reaching to the top storey from the ground. There were subsequent alterations, notably the provision of wide-mouth gun-ports in the 1540s. The castle fell into disuse in the 1600s but its reputation as a forbidding ruin endured. Sir Walter Scott was painted with Hermitage in the background in the 19th century.

LOCATION: NR NEWCASTLETON, BORDERS
MAP REF: NY 497961
OPEN: HISTORIC SCOTLAND: APR–SEP DAILY

HODDOM

One of the last great towers built in the Borders, Hoddom is an interesting variant on the L-plan. It was built in the 16th century, incorporating stonework of an earlier building and its use was more probably intended as a barracks rather than a residence. Among other features added in the 17th century were the distinctive pinnacle rooftops; then in the 19th century the building was incorporated into a baronial mansion. These Victorian additions were demolished after World War II. The tower remains uninhabited and forms the central feature of a caravan site.

LOCATION: NR LOCKERBIE, DUMFRIES & GALLOWAY
MAP REF: NY 156729

HOLLOWS TOWER

Hollows Tower is also known as Gilknockie. This was a 16th-century rectangular tower house which rose to four storeys plus an attic, with a bold parapet and equipped with gun-ports on all sides. The tower still has a beacon grate perched on the roof: it served as part of a signalling system to warn of impending attack. Hollows Tower belonged to the wild, aggressive and lawless Armstrongs who terrorized much of the Border district in the 16th century. The tower has been restored and can be viewed by private tour arranged through the Armstrong Museum at Langholm.

LOCATION: NR CANONBIE, DUMFRIES & GALLOWAY
MAP REF: NY 382786

HUNTERSTON

The first structure at Hunterston was a rectangular tower four storeys high. The small square stair turret was added in the 17th century at the same time as an extension to the tower, which contained the banqueting hall. Sir Robert Lorimer undertook some restoration work at Hunterston early in the 19th century.

LOCATION: WEST KILBRIDE, NORTH AYRSHIRE
MAP REF: NS 193515

HUNTINGTOWER

This tower house is made up from two separate rectangular tower blocks dating from the 15th century, joined by adding walling up to three storeys in the 17th century to form one building. Huntingtower, which was originally known as the House of Ruthven, is perhaps most famous as the scene of the Ruthven Raid of 1582 when William Ruthven, the Earl of Gowrie, and the Earl of Mar, kidnapped the boy-king James VI to get him away from the political and religious influence of their rivals, the Duke of Lennox and the Earl of Arran. For this treasonous act, William Ruthven was later executed. The House of Ruthven was abolished after two later Ruthvens were disgraced. Its arms were deleted from the Book of Arms, hence the name change to Huntingtower.

The castle then passed to the Earls of Tuillibardine and the Earls of Atholl, who lived at Huntingtower until early in the 19th century. The castle has exceptional 16th-century painted ceilings, uncovered during restoration work early in the 20th century.

LOCATION: PERTH, PERTH & KINROSS
MAP REF: NO 0842252
OPEN: HISTORIC SCOTLAND: APR–OCT DAILY; OCT–DEC FRI–WED; JAN–MAR REDUCED HOURS

Described as one of the noblest baronial ruins in Scotland this remarkable structure, a mixture of building periods, was the fortified residence of one of the most powerful and wealthiest families in Scotland, the Earls (and later Marquises) of Huntly. There are the remains of three castles on the site at Huntly, the first was a motte castle built in the 12th century: the mound and some ditching are still there. Then a substantial L-plan tower was built in the bailey about the end of the 14th century, but only the foundations of this remain. The Gordon family owned Huntly Castle, and by the middle of the 15th century they were created the Earls of Huntly. The first earl, to reflect the family's new importance, built another, more palatial castle south of the L-plan, which was then much modified and altered and repaired during subsequent centuries, but the whole block is fascinating. The basement is all that remains from the 15th century; the top floor has oriel windows which were put in very early in the 17th century. The façade above and below the oriel window line has an inscription bearing the name of the 5th Earl of Huntly, who by then had become the 1st Marquis of Huntly, and his wife. This earl had joined a revolt against James VI, had his home blown up and then, reconciled with the king, rebuilt it in an even grander style. By the time Huntly was held by government troops against the Jacobites in 1746 it had been abandoned and was falling into decay. The ruins of this castle, which until c.1506 was known as the Peel of Strathbogie, remain an impressive testament to its former grandeur.

LOCATION: ABERDEENSHIRE
MAP REF: NJ 532407
OPEN: HISTORIC SCOTLAND: APR–SEP DAILY; OCT–MAR SAT–WED

INCHDREWER

Inchdrewer Castle was built in the 16th century as an L-plan tower house. It was destroyed by fire in 1713 following the murder of its owner, Lord Banff, an unpopular laird. During 18th-century restoration, the L-plan was enlarged. This dramatic castle was restored more magnificently in the 20th century: it is now owned by Count Robin de la Lanne Mirrlees.

LOCATION: NR BANFF, ABERDEENSHIRE
MAP REF: NJ 656607

INCHMURRIN

This is an early tower-house castle built round a courtyard and was possibly used as a hunting lodge. The tower was probably raised in the 14th century. Little remains of the castle but its setting, on the largest inland island in Britain, in the Loch Lomond National Park, inspired poets, writers and artists in the 18th and 19th centuries.

LOCATION: INCHMURRIN ISLAND, LOCH LOMOND
MAP REF: NS 373863

INNERPEFFRAY

The remains of an L-plan towered castle dating from the early 17th century, built by James Drummond, 1st Lord Madderty, stand here. The castle is privately owned and is now ruinous and can only be viewed externally. The town of Innerpeffray is better known for its 18th-century public library, the oldest surviving such library in Scotland and still in use.

LOCATION: CRIEFF, PERTH & KINROSS
MAP REF: NN 905179

INNISCHONNEL

Also spelled Inchconnell, this began as a rectangular stone enclosure of the early 13th century; the castle was greatly altered in the 15th century. Additions included a range of buildings joining a tower on the south-east. Innischonnel, once a chief stronghold of the Campbells; it has a splendid mountain backdrop.

LOCATION: LOCH AWE, ARGYLL & BUTE
MAP REF: NM 977119

INVERGARRY

The remains of this L-plan tower house, built during the 17th century and slighted in the 18th century after the Jacobite Rising, stand on the shore of Loch Oich. The castle ruins are set in the grounds of the MacDonnell mansion, built for the family after their castle was destroyed, and which is now the Glengarry Castle Hotel.

LOCATION: NR FORT AUGUSTUS, HIGHLAND
MAP REF: NM 315006

INVERLOCHY

The contemporary Inverlochy Castle, built in the 19th century, is now a luxurious hotel but the original Inverlochy, built around 1270–80, stands on a site south of this. A fairly complete and striking ruin, it was one of Scotland's earliest stone castles. It was built by the Comyn family as a quadrilateral stone enclosure, with four corner cylindrical towers, with the north-west tower as a donjon. A moat round three sides of the enclosure and the River Lochy provided further defences.

LOCATION: FORT WILLIAM, HIGHLAND
MAP REF: NN 121755
OPEN: HISTORIC SCOTLAND: OPEN ACCESS

INVERMARK

Invermark dates from the 14th century but the tower house is primarily of two later building periods. The lower floors were built in the 16th century, and then early in the 17th century the upper parts were completed to create an extremely tall tower. The gun loops on the ground floor were added at this time. The entrance to the castle is at first-floor level and is still guarded by an iron yett. Invermark belonged to the Lindsays from Edzell Castle and was used by the family until the 18th century. Materials from the castle and surrounding buildings were used to build the church at Lochlee early in the 19th century.

LOCATION: LOCHLEE, GLEN ESK, BRECHIN, ANGUS
MAP REF: NO 442804
OPEN: EXTERNAL ACCESS ONLY AT ALL TIMES

INVERNESS

Only part of the curtain wall, a restored well and some earthworks remain of the first stone castle built here in the 12th century. It guarded the routes to the Highlands. The castle was captured by the Lord of the Isles in 1491 but was retaken by James IV. It was severely damaged in Mary, Queen of Scots' reign, damaged again during the Civil War, and all but destroyed by the Young Pretender, Bonnie Prince Charlie, in 1746. A vast 19th-century neo-Norman castle, built on the site, is used as a court house. An exhibition about the castle's history is on display in one of the towers.

LOCATION: HIGHLAND
MAP REF: NH 666451
OPEN: SUMMER DAILY

INVERQUHARITY

Inverquharity was built by the Ogilvy family in the 1440s. A smaller tower house, it rises four floors to the parapet, behind which is a wall-walk and an attic level. Inverquharity remained in the hands of the Ogilvies until late in the 18th century. The castle was restored in the 20th century and remains a private home.

LOCATION: NR KIRRIEMUIR, ANGUS
MAP REF: NO 411579

KELBURN

This interesting castle, home to the Boyle family for many centuries, is really in two parts. One is a four-storeyed, late 16th-century, rectangular Z-plan tower house with cylindrical flanking towers on the south-west and north-east corners. Early in the 18th century this was enclosed in more palatial buildings as the Boyle family became more influential. David Boyle (1666–1733), a distinguished Scottish statesman, created the 1st Earl of Glasgow in 1703, built the grand mansion house which joins the earlier castle. A Victorian wing, enclosing one of the 16th-century towers, was added; its dining room is decorated with William Morris wallpaper. Although still used as a home by the present Earl of Glasgow and his family, the grounds and gardens have been opened as a country centre, and there are occasional tours of the castle.

LOCATION: NR LARGS, NORTH AYRSHIRE
MAP REF: NS 217567
OPEN: CASTLE TOURS: JUL–AUG. GROUNDS/RIDING SCHOOL: DAILY ALL YEAR. COUNTRY CENTRE: EASTER–OCT DAILY

KELLIE

Owned by the Oliphants and later the Lorimer family, Kellie is huge. Three towers are joined to a main block, the plan roughly in the shape of a 'T'. The north tower was built in the 15th to 16th centuries, the east tower was added in the 16th and a few years later a substantial main block, ending in another tower at the south, joined the two. The Lorimer family came to the castle towards the end of the 19th century. It was the architect and designer Sir Robert Lorimer who carried out much of the restoration work, and he and his descendants lived at the castle until 1970. Kellie has some magnificent plaster ceilings and painted panelling, and houses a permanent exhibition of the work of Sir Robert's son, the noted sculptor Hew Lorimer (1907–93).

LOCATION: PITTENWEEM, FIFE
MAP REF: NO 520052
OPEN: NATIONAL TRUST FOR SCOTLAND: EASTER, JUN–SEP DAILY. GROUNDS: ALL YEAR DAILY

Sited on a peninsula in Loch Awe, Kilchurn Castle stands as a splendid ruin among reeds and marshes. It began as a five-floor, square tower at the east, built in the middle of the 15th century by Colin Campbell of Glenorchy, 1st Earl of Breadalbane. Additions were made during the 16th century, and by the end of the 1600s there were numerous buildings grouped round a courtyard. Kilchurn was abandoned in the middle of the 18th century and is now a gaunt shadow of its obvious former splendour. Access by ferry or on foot.

LOCATION: LOCH AWE, ARGYLL & BUTE
MAP REF: NN 133276

KILCONQUHAR

Kilconquhar dates back to the 13th century and was the ancestral home of Adam of Kilconquhar, Earl of Carrick and father of Robert Bruce. The castle today is a much altered L-plan tower house built during the 16th century, and forms part of a 19th-century mansion which is now used as a holiday resort, timeshare complex and venue for events.

LOCATION: FIFE
MAP REF: NO 493027

KILCOY

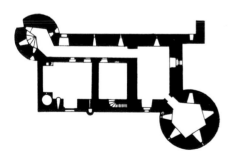

Kilcoy is an interesting 17th-century Z-plan castle which has been restored. The castle belonged to the Mackenzies of Kintail: by the middle of the 19th century it had fallen into ruin, but it was later restored by architect Alexander Ross. It is a private home but the gardens are occasionally open.

LOCATION: KILLEARNAN, HIGHLAND
MAP REF: NH 576512

KILDRUMMY

A remarkable early 13th-century, red sandstone castle, Kildrummy was built by the Earl of Mar. A substantial D-shaped enclosure castle with a range of buildings was erected along the inner face of the north-west curtain surrounded by banks and ditches. Early in the 16th century the estate was handed to the Elphinstone family who added a tower house, known as the Elphinstone Tower.

Kildrummy is now an impressive ruin but there is a model of how it looked in its heyday in the visitor centre.

LOCATION: NR ALFORD, ABERDEENSHIRE
MAP REF: NJ 455164
OPEN: HISTORIC SCOTLAND: APR–SEP DAILY

KILHENZIE

This rectangular tower house of the 16th century was thoroughly restored and is part of a much larger mansion.

LOCATION: NR MAYBOLE, SOUTH AYRSHIRE
MAP REF: NS 308082

KILLOCHAN

Said to be one of the finest fortified houses in southern Scotland and today in very good repair, Killochan is a late 16th-century, roughly L-plan tower house, whose main block is five floors tall. The castle, a former Cathcart stronghold, is privately owned.

LOCATION: SOUTH AYRSHIRE
MAP REF: NS 227003

KILRAVOCK

A small rectangular great tower was built c.1460. In the 17th century it received a square-plan stair tower on the south-west corner, and a rectangular structure extended from that to make half a quadrangle. The castle is now a small hotel.

LOCATION: CROY, HIGHLAND
MAP REF: NM 814494

KINCARDINE

Kincardine is a very early Scottish castle of 13th-century origin. It was a simple enclosure castle of curtain wall on a natural hill which was surrounded by marshland. There were rectangular gate-towers on the south wall. Kincardine was a royal castle for a time. John Balliol (1292–6) is thought to have drafted his abdication document there. Only fragments remain.

LOCATION: NR FETTERCAIRN, ABERDEENSHIRE
MAP REF: NO 671751

KINCLAVEN

This ruined rectangular enclosure of stone, with projecting square corner towers, dates from the 13th century. It had a curtain that overlooked the junction of the Tay and Isla rivers. Only fragments remain of this once royal castle.

LOCATION: PERTH & KINROSS
MAP REF: NO 158377

KINDROCHIT

Kindrochit began as a royal hunting lodge in the reign of Robert II. The king then granted the site to his friend, Malcolm Drummond, who in the 1390s erected a substantial horizontal hall-tower, among the largest of this type of tower built in Scotland. The rather forlorn remains belie the castle's former grandeur.

LOCATION: BRAEMAR, ABERDEENSHIRE
MAP REF: NO 151913

KINNAIRD HEAD

Built by Sir Alexander Fraser of Philort, this is an interesting 16th-century rectangular tower house. In the 1780s the castle was converted into the first lighthouse in Scotland. Another tower was built nearby and further buildings were added to the complex in 1820. Today it houses a lighthouse exhibition.

LOCATION: FRASERBURGH, ABERDEENSHIRE
MAP REF: NJ 999675
OPEN: KINNAIRD HEAD TRUST: DAILY

KINNAIRD (ANGUS)

A 15th-century castle, rebuilt after a fire, with a substantial rectangular tower at its core. Improvements and extensions were made in the 16th and 17th centuries, and more changes later still incorporated some walling of the earlier building. Much of Kinnaird was destroyed by fire in the 19th century and it had to be rebuilt. The castle has been the seat of the Carnegie family since the 15th century and houses a famous art collection. It is not open but has occasional tours.

LOCATION: BRECHIN, ANGUS
MAP REF: NO 624571

KINNAIRD (PERTHSHIRE)

Kinnaird is a late 15th-century rectangular tower house within a curtain wall. First held by the Kinnairds, it passed through the Colville and Threipland families. Derelict by the mid-19th century, it was restored and is a fine private home.

LOCATION: INCHTURE, PERTH & KINROSS
MAP REF: NO 241289

KINNAIRDY

Kinnairdy began as a 12th-century motte castle. A stone tower was raised on the motte stonework and a curtain wall added, with a tall arched entrance at the north-west. Later, possibly in the 15th century, a six-storey tower with a crenellated parapet was built which was further altered in the 18th century.

LOCATION: MARNOCK, ABERDEENSHIRE
MAP REF: NJ 609498
OPEN: DAILY: ACCESSIBLE BY FERRY ONLY SUBJECT TO WEATHER

KISIMUL

Kisimul or Kiessimul is an enclosure castle dating from the late 12th or early 13th century and stands on a small island. This, the westernmost castle in Scotland and stronghold of the MacNeils, has been painstakingly restored by architect and 45th Clan Chief, Robert MacNeil. It is a family home.

LOCATION: CASTLEBAY, WESTERN ISLES
MAP REF: NL 665979
OPEN: HISTORIC SCOTLAND: APR–SEP DAILY

LAURISTON

Lauriston is a 19th-century mansion grafted round a late 16th-century tower house built for Sir Archibald Napier. Overlooking the Firth of Forth, the original tower house was rectangular. A central projecting tower on the north side contained the staircase. The mansion was left to the nation in the 1920s by Mr and Mrs WR Reid, and displays Edwardian interiors together with an eclectic mix of objets d'art collected by the Reids.

LOCATION: DAVISON'S MAINS, EDINBURGH
MAP REF: NT 203760
OPEN: EDINBURGH CITY COUNCIL: GUIDED TOURS ONLY APR–OCT SAT–THU; NOV–MAR SAT–SUN

LENNOXLOVE

This used to be known as Lethington Castle because it belonged to the Maitlands of Lethington (William Maitland was 'Mr Secretary' Maitland, the Protestant statesman in the time of Mary, Queen of Scots). It began as an L-plan tower in the early 15th century. The parapet was altered in the 16th century, with more alterations in the 17th century and later; the architect Robert Lorimer carried out some of the work. The tower is in good condition, and among the original features are dungeons and two iron yetts. The Duke of Hamilton bought the castle in the 1940s and the family still lives there. A collection of memorabilia, which includes Mary, Queen of Scots' death mask, is on display at the castle.

LOCATION: HADDINGTON, EAST LOTHIAN
MAP REF: NT 515720
OPEN: EASTER–OCT WED, THU, SUN

LESLIE

Built in 1661, Leslie Castle was owned by the Forbes family. It was a stepped L-plan tower house with a square stair tower in the angle. The castle has been restored and is now run as a hotel.

LOCATION: INSCH, ABERDEENSHIRE
MAP REF: NJ 599248

LETHENDY

Lethendy Tower is thought to be one of the last tower houses built in Scotland in around 1678. It was a three-floor L-plan with attic and has been much altered. The tower can be rented as a holiday retreat.

LOCATION: NR BLAIRGOWRIE, PERTH & KINROSS
MAP REF: NO 14041

LIBERTON TOWER

The rectangular tower house of Liberton 10.5 x 8m (34 x 26ft), with four floors beneath its parapet and a garret in the roof, was built in the 15th century. There are few windows or loops in the tower walls. The tower is rented out as holiday accommodation.

LOCATION: EDINBURGH
MAP REF: NT 265696

Sited on a mound overlooking Linlithgow Loch, this is a ruin of a great palace castle. It is roofless but has most of its walling, still showing its impressive size and architecture. The fabric is of several building periods, from the 1400s to the 1600s. Linlithgow may have begun as a royal manor house for Scottish kings, first of all for David I. The site fell into English hands in c.1300, and in 1302–3 an enclosure with turrets made of 'great logs not split too small' was erected on the mound by the order of Edward I and under the supervision of Master James of St George. The castle was besieged in 1303 but was not taken. After the Battle of Bannockburn, just over a decade later, the castle was returned to the Scots and continued as a royal residence. In 1425, after a damaging fire, James I decided to build

a fortified palace on the site and during the next decade more than £4,500 was spent. The structure that eventually emerged under the aegis of several kings was a fine mix of the best contemporary residential apartments and up-to-date fortifications. The eastern side of the palace contains, on the first floor, the 15th-century Lyon Chamber. The northern side of Linlithgow was reconstructed in the 1620s and the resulting Renaissance-style range is known as the New Wark. After the Union of the Crowns the court moved to London. The palace, the birthplace of Mary, Queen of Scots, was badly damaged by fire in the 18th century and never restored.

LOCATION: KIRKGATE, LINLITHGOW, WEST LOTHIAN
MAP REF: NT 003744
OPEN: HISTORIC SCOTLAND: DAILY

LITTLE CUMBRAE

There was a fortress on this island dating from the 14th century, which was probably owned by Robert II. It was considerably enlarged by the 16th century to include a rectangular great tower and gun-ports in the front façade. The castle was destroyed by Cromwell's soldiers in the 17th century and only ruins remain.

LOCATION: BUTE, NORTH AYRSHIRE
MAP REF: NS 152513

LOCH DOON

This late 13th-century enclosure castle was originally sited on an island in Loch Doon, stronghold of the Earls of Carrick. The stonework was moved piece by piece to the west shore of the loch in 1934–5 because the water level in the loch was to be raised to service a hydroelectric scheme.

LOCATION: DALMELLINGTON, EAST AYRSHIRE
MAP REF: NX 484950
OPEN: HISTORIC SCOTLAND: DAILY

LOCHINDORB

An interesting early 13th-century quadrilateral enclosure castle was raised by the Comyns family on Lochindorb island. The plan resembles Inverlochy and there are substantial remains. By end of the 14th century the castle was in the hands of the Wolf of Badenoch, Robert II's notorious son.

LOCATION: NR GRANTOWN ON SPEY, HIGHLAND
MAP REF: NH 974353
OPEN: PRIVATE: ACCESSIBLE BY BOAT

LOCH LEVEN

One of the earliest tower houses in Scotland, Loch Leven stands inside an enclosure on an island and was begun in the 14th century. The simple building has its principal entrance at the second floor on the east wall, leading into the great hall. Today, the entrance to the castle is in the basement. Mary, Queen of Scots was imprisoned here from June 1567 until May 1568, when she escaped.

LOCATION: CASTLE ISLAND, LOCH LEVEN, PERTH & KINROSS
MAP REF: NO 137017
OPEN: HISTORIC SCOTLAND: APR–SEP DAILY. ONLY ACCESSIBLE BY FERRY FROM KINROSS

LOCHMABEN

There have been two Lochmaben castles. The first was built by the Bruce family as a motte castle and given stonework in the 13th century. Edward I built a new castle very late in the 13th century in a more strategic position, although it is now ruinous. This was a substantial castle in its time.

LOCATION: DUMFRIES & GALLOWAY
MAP REF: NY 088811
OPEN: HISTORIC SCOTLAND: OPEN ACCESS

LOCHRANZA

The substantial remains of this castle stand on the edge of a promontory jutting into Loch Ranza. These are of two periods: the later 16th-century work was a reconstruction of the earlier 13th-century castle. Lochranza had a two-storeyed rectangular hall tower, much of which remains, with a small square-plan tower projecting from one corner. The castle is locked but the key is held at the local store.

LOCATION: ISLE OF ARRAN, NORTH AYRSHIRE
MAP REF: NR 933507

LUFFNESS

The roughly T-plan, three-storey house at Luffness which overlooks Aberlady Bay was built in the late 16th century by a cousin of Lord Bothwell, Sir Patrick Hepburn. The new building incorporated what remained of a much earlier structure after a slighting by the English. It was positioned inside a strong arrangement of fortifications built by the French in 1549 and was demilitarized in 1560.

LOCATION: ABERLADY, EAST LOTHIAN
MAP REF: NT 475804

MACDUFF'S

Macduff's was originally a late 14th-century rectangular tower house with a range of buildings built on to the south wall in the 16th century. At the end of this range was another rectangular tower with a rounded projecting turret containing the staircase. Some of the outer walling was looped for guns. The castle belonged to the Wemyss family and was abandoned in the 17th century in favour of another castle erected a few miles away. There are scant remains.

LOCATION: EAST WEMYSS, FIFE
MAP REF: NT 346961

MACLELLAN'S

MacLellan's Castle is another 'borderline' castle. Basically L-plan, built in 1582, it has an extra, small square tower at one corner. It was built by Sir Thomas MacLellan, from the stones of an old convent of the Greyfriars that stood on the site and which had become derelict after the Reformation. MacLellan's was a mix of defendable castle (minimum window space in the lower storeys, no direct access between the basement and the hall, and a spy-hole, which doubtless could be used as a shot-hole) and a spacious, comfortable residence. The castle was stripped of its roof and contents in the 18th century and remains an empty shell.

LOCATION: KIRKCUDBRIGHT, DUMFRIES & GALLOWAY
MAP REF: NX 682510
OPEN: HISTORIC SCOTLAND: MAR–SEP DAILY

MAINS

Mains Castle, originally held by the Comyn family, is a 15th-century tower house surrounded by ditching and restored to its medieval splendour late in the 20th century.

LOCATION: JAMES HAMILTON HERITAGE PARK, EAST KILBRIDE, SOUTH LANARKSHIRE
MAP REF: NS 627560

MAUCHLINE

Mauchline is the castle of the village that was home to Robert Burns. This 15th-century tower house, also known as Abbot Hunters Tower, was a monastic residence for Melrose Abbey.

LOCATION: EAST AYRSHIRE
MAP REF: NS 498273

MAYBOLE

Maybole Castle, built in the 16th century, was the town house of the notorious Cassilis family. Originally an L-plan tower house of four floors plus garret, it was given corbelled circular turrets on the angles. The castle was restored in the 19th century and is the oldest inhabited house in the town of Maybole.

LOCATION: SOUTH AYRSHIRE
MAP REF: NS 301100

MEARNS

Herbert, Lord Maxwell, built Mearns Tower in the middle of the 15th century. In 1449 he was granted a licence to 'surround and fortify it with wall and ditches, to strengthen by iron gates and to erect on the top of it all warlike apparatus necessary for its defence'. The restored tower has been converted into a church hall.

LOCATION: NEWTON MEARNS, NR GLASGOW, EAST RENFREWSHIRE
MAP REF: NS 552553

MEGGERNIE

A simple 16th-century square tower with rectangular corner turrets was attached to a later rather grand hunting lodge here. James Menzies, who introduced the larch tree into Scotland, owned Meggernie in the 18th century.

LOCATION: GLEN LYON, PERTH & KINROSS
MAP REF: NN 554460

MEGGINCH

This late 15th-century L-plan tower house with gun-ports, built by the Hay family, became part of a larger and less fortified structure in the 18th century. The castle was used as a location for the 1990s film *Rob Roy*. The gardens are open in the summer.

LOCATION: NR ERROL, PERTH & KINROSS
MAP REF: NO 242246

MELGUND

Although its style is more typical of the great Scottish 15th-century tower houses, Melgund dates from the middle of the 16th century and was reputedly built by Cardinal Beaton. The tower is four-storeyed plus attic, with gun-ports at lower-storey levels. Melgund is privately owned.

LOCATION: NR ABERLEMNO, ANGUS
MAP REF: NO 546563

MENSTRIE

The birthplace of Sir William Alexander, founder of Nova Scotia, Menstrie Castle is a late 16th-century L-plan tower house, which was enlarged. The castle deteriorated and by the 1950s it was a subject for demolition, but after public protest the local authority and the National Trust for Scotland stepped in to save it. Menstrie has now been converted into residential accommodation but the building displays an exhibition to commemorate the castle and the life of Sir William.

LOCATION: CLACKMANNANSHIRE
MAP REF: NS 849967
OPEN: EXHIBITION: EASTER SUNDAY, MAY–SEP, WED, SUN PM

MIDMAR

Midmar is one of the Z-plan castles that was given diagonally opposite smaller towers of different shapes: the north-west tower is square-plan, the south-east is cylindrical.

The castle, built by the Bell family of masons who also worked at Crathes, dates from the 1570s.

LOCATION: ABERDEENSHIRE
MAP REF: NJ 704052

MENZIES

Also called Castle Menzies, this tower house dates from the 1570s with a Victorian addition. The diagonally opposite corner towers are massive constructions, described by SH Cruden as 'no less commodious than many an isolated tower house of the same period'. The castle is a substantial fortified residence of formidable appearance described on the Clan Menzies website as 'a splendid example of the transition between earlier rugged fortress and later mansion house'. It is now the headquarters of the Clan Menzies Society.

LOCATION: ABERFELDY, WEEM, PERTH & KINROSS
MAP REF: NN 828503
OPEN: MENZIES CHARITABLE TRUST: APR (OR EASTER)–MID-OCT DAILY

MERCHISTON

Merchiston tower house was built in the 15th century and then remodelled in the 17th century, when sash windows were added, but still retains its entrance on the second floor. It was the family home of the Napiers, and birthplace of the inventor of logarithms, John Napier, Lord of Merchiston (1550–1617). The castle is now a part of Napier University.

LOCATION: EDINBURGH.
MAP REF: NT 242718

METHVEN

Margaret Tudor, daughter of Henry VII and sister of Henry VIII, lived at the earlier Methven Castle for nearly three decades after she married Henry Stewart following the death of her husband, James IV. The Duke of Lennox built the present castle, an imposing and attractive tower house, in the middle of the 17th century. The castle was restored during the 1980s. It is now a private residence with bed-and-breakfast accommodation.

LOCATION: PERTH & KINROSS
MAP REF: NO 042260

MEY

Built to a Z-plan in the late 16th century by the 4th Earl of Caithness, the Castle of Mey (later renamed Barrogill Castle) was falling into disrepair when the late Queen Mother bought it. The castle and its gardens, with much input from Her Majesty, were completely restored and renovated. Her grandson, HRH Prince Charles, Duke of Rothesay, is now President of The Queen Elizabeth Castle of Mey Trust.

LOCATION: NR JOHN O'GROATS, HIGHLAND
MAP REF: ND 290739
OPEN: CASTLE OF MEY TRUST: MAY–JUL; 10 AUG–29 SEP SAT–THU. PLEASE CHECK OPENING TIMES

MIGVIE

The 13th-century enclosure castle at Migvie was probably destroyed in the time of King Robert Bruce in the 14th century. It was a stronghold of the Fraser family but there are only scant remains.

LOCATION: ABERDEENSHIRE
MAP REF: NJ 436066

MINGARY

Begun in the 13th century, Mingary was the seat of the MacIans of Ardnamurchan. It was an irregular hexagonal enclosure castle with rounded angles. It received later additions and alterations, including a barrack block, and was garrisoned by government troops in the 18th century.

LOCATION: NR KILCHOAN, HIGHLAND
MAP REF: NM 503631

FOOD AND DRINK

In medieval castles, food and drink were at the heart of social life, most meals taking place in the great hall. Here, everyone gathered to eat and, on special occasions, to be entertained.

At feasts, a great variety of dishes and courses would be served, with the cooks trying their best to make the food taste good as well as making it look interesting. Swans might be served up re-clothed in their feathers and stuffed with dozens of smaller birds. Sweet dishes made of sugar paste might be presented as elaborate sculptures depicting well-known stories and myths.

Meat was the central part of most meals, including breakfast. Animals of many kinds, both domestic and wild, were eaten, with venison from deer being considered an especially luxurious food, only served at the lord's table.

Fish was eaten in large quantities. This was because meat was forbidden on Tuesdays, Fridays and Saturdays, as well as on numerous holy days and other special days. Fish did not count as meat, so could be eaten on those days. Fish of all sorts were eaten, and moats were well stocked. Fish were also kept and bred in special pools.

Everyone – including children – drank alcohol all the time. It was safer than water as the ingredients would have been boiled as part of the brewing process. It also provided energy, and a good deal of the 'food' of medieval people was alcohol. Wine was drunk by everyone who could afford it, and it was not considered to be a luxury. Cheap, sour wine was disguised by sweetening it or by adding spices. Beer was the everyday drink of poorer people. It came in two sorts – 'single' ale or small beer, which was weak, and 'double' ale which was strong. And it really was strong; as strong as today's

Richard II entertaining nobles and bishops. This picture shows essential ingredients of a formal meal in a great hall: elaborate clothes, servants bringing food, an entertainer on the right and musicians in the gallery.

strongest ales. All were consumed in large quantities – soldiers were given three litres (more than five pints) of wine a day, for example.

Bread was a staple food for all people. The richest would have eaten good quality bread made with wheat flour that had been carefully sifted, while the poorest ate bread that was made with a mixture of barley flour, peas and beans. Castles usually had numerous bread ovens, as it was consumed in such high quantities. Large numbers of people were entitled to eat at the monarch's expense, with bread being the food most commonly provided as part of their wages.

This applied to servants of all sorts, up to and including senior government officials. For example, in King Stephen's reign, the Chancellor received each day one loaf of bread of the best quality, and two of ordinary quality, as well as one measure of good wine and one of ordinary wine. This was in addition to the meals he ate each day at the king's table.

Some special dishes were highly spiced. This was not because the meat was bad and its taste needed disguising, but rather it was to show how wealthy the lord was, since he could afford to let his cooks use costly and rare herbs and spices. Salt was valuable, and could mark your social status. The salt was kept in a large container on the table in the hall. All those 'below the salt' were of lower social status.

Left: a feasting scene from the Bayeux Tapestry. Alcohol was consumed in large quantities by nearly everyone in society, from monarch to children.

Salt was an essential part of food preservation in medieval times, and was the main way to keep meat fresh. Meat was also preserved by smoking in chimneys. Other foods were kept by immersion in honey or by drying.

MONIACK

Moniack is an L-plan tower house dating from the 16th century. The castle has been modernized but is still home to the Fraser family who run a winery and also produce sauces and condiments: tours of the winery and kitchens daily except Sunday.

LOCATION: NR INVERNESS, HIGHLAND
MAP REF: NH 552436

MORTON

In a beautiful location on a high promontory overlooking Morton Loch, the ruins of this rectangular hall-tower castle date from the 14th century. It was built by the Earls of March on the site of an earlier castle and was lived in until the early 18th century.

LOCATION: NR CARRONBRIDGE, DUMFRIES & GALLOWAY
MAP REF: NX 891992
OPEN: HISTORIC SCOTLAND: OPEN ACCESS

MOTE OF ANNAN

This motte castle of the early 12th century on the east side of the River Annan was built by the Brus (Bruce) family and mentioned in a document of 1124. The motte was raised to about 15m (49ft) tall, and a ditch was cut to separate it from its bailey.

LOCATION: DUMFRIES & GALLOWAY
MAP REF: NY 192668

MOTE OF URR

A motte castle of the mid-12th century, this is the most extensive motte and bailey castle in Scotland. It was excavated in the 20th century.

LOCATION: DUMFRIES & GALLOWAY
MAP REF: NX 815649

MOY

This is a ruined tower house of the 15th century, probably built by the brother of Lachlan MacLean. The castle was garrisoned during the Jacobite rebellion but abandoned in the 18th century.

LOCATION: NR CRAIGNUIRE, ISLE OF MULL, ARGYLL & BUTE
MAP REF: NM 617247

MUCHALLS

Built here in the 1620s around a courtyard, two of the sides and part of the third are a tall range of apartments.

LOCATION: NR STONEHAVEN, ABERDEENSHIRE
MAP REF: NO 892918

MURTHLY

Murthly was built in the 14th century as a royal hunting lodge. The earliest building was the tall, slim square tower, which was incorporated in the late 16th century into a later courtyard and range. The castle is private, lived in by the same family since the 1600s.

LOCATION: NR STANLEY, PERTH & KINROSS
MAP REF: NO 072399

MUGDOCK

The remnants of the courtyard-plan castle (the oldest parts are from the 14th century) are now in a country park. Mugdock was sacked twice in the 17th century and some of the rubble was used to build a new house, later replaced by a Victorian mansion.

LOCATION: WEST DUNBARTONSHIRE
MAP REF: NS 550772

MUNESS

Muness, the most northerly castle in Britain, is a ruinous 16th-century Z-plan tower house with cylindrical corner towers. It had shot-holes of dumb-bell and quatrefoil design.

LOCATION: ISLE OF UNST, SHETLAND ISLANDS
MAP REF : HP 629013
OPEN: HISTORIC SCOTLAND: ACCESS AT REASONABLE TIMES (KEYHOLDER)

MYRES

Myres started as a small, 16th-century three-floor Z-plan tower house with two cylindrical towers projecting from opposing corners. One of the round towers has an interesting corbelled-out square-plan turret at the top: built of grey ashlar, finely carved and with a parapet, it contrasts with the ochre of the rest of the castle, a much grander edifice today, the result of subsequent modification and addition.

LOCATION: AUCHTERMUCHTY, FIFE
MAP REF: NO 242109

NEIDPATH

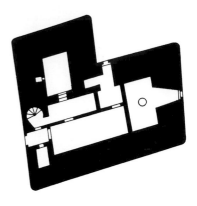

Neidpath Castle is a formidable L-plan tower house built in the late 14th century by the de Hay family. Set on a rocky slope leading to the River Tweed, the tower house, with its rounded corners, has other buildings (chiefly 16th-century) including an interesting gateway with a round-headed arch.

LOCATION: NR PEEBLES, BORDERS
MAP REF: NT 236404
OPEN: PRIVATE: JUL–MID-SEP DAILY. ALSO EASTER WEEKEND AND MAY BANK HOLIDAYS

NEWARK (BORDERS)

Newark tower house was a Douglas-held, rectangular tower-house castle built on a mound c.1423–4. After the Battle of Philiphaugh in 1645, at which Montrose was defeated by the Covenanters but escaped, many of his followers were put to death in the courtyard here. It was eventually destroyed by Cromwell's forces in the 17th century and is a substantial ruin.

LOCATION: BOWHILL, NR SELKIRK, BORDERS
MAP REF: NT 421293

NEWARK

These days Newark Castle has an unusual location in the shipyards of Port Glasgow. When it was first built, in the 15th century, it would have been set in a greater acreage and surrounded by a barmkin of which the dovecot was one of its original corner towers. In the 16th century a mansion was added to the tower and gatehouse.

LOCATION: PORT GLASGOW, INVERCLYDE
MAP REF: NS 338741
OPEN: HISTORIC SCOTLAND: APR–SEP DAILY

NIDDRY

Niddry is a tall, massive tower of L-plan shape built in the early 16th century by the 4th Lord Seton. Mary, Queen of Scots was brought to Niddry on the evening of her escape from Loch Leven in 1568. The castle was a ruin but was restored as a private residence late in the 20th century and its parkland turned into a golf course.

LOCATION: EDINBURGH, WEST LOTHIAN
MAP REF: NT 095743

NOLTLAND

Founded in the 1560s by Gilbert Balfour (party to the murder of Cardinal Beaton in 1546), Noltland is one of the earliest of the Z-plan castles. The tower house was well fortified, and both the main block and corner towers are fitted with tiers of gun-ports to give covering fire in all directions. In almost every respect, the castle's military features overwhelmed the domestic: even the great hall on the first floor had windows on only one side. Gilbert Balfour was also involved in the murder of the Earl of Darnley, husband of Mary, Queen of Scots.

LOCATION: ISLE OF WESTRAY, ORKNEY ISLANDS
MAP REF: HY 429488
OPEN: HISTORIC SCOTLAND: JUN–SEP DAILY

OLD DUNDAS/DUNDAS CASTLE

Old Dundas has the distinction of being the earliest Scottish castle for which a proper licence to crenellate was issued, in 1416: 'to build a tower … of Dundas in the manner of a castle with the kernels, etc., usual in a fortalice of this sort according to the manner of the Kingdom of Scotland …' The old keep is now part of the stately 19th-century Dundas Castle, which is available for private events.

LOCATION: SOUTH QUEENSFERRY, EDINBURGH
MAP REF: NT 117767

OLD WICK

The ruins of Old Wick stand on a promontory of rock with three of its four sides protected by cliffs. The castle was built in the early 13th century and is thought to have been of Viking origin. It is in the care of Historic Scotland and can be visited at any time.

LOCATION: WICK, HIGHLAND
MAP REF: ND 369488

ORCHARDTON

The only freestanding cylindrical tower house in Scotland, built in the 15th century. The internal arrangements are much the same as those of a rectangular tower house: the entrance to the tower is at first-floor level accessed by an external stairway, and the very narrow spiral staircase inside is in the wall thickness. The top of the tower had a gabled cap-house resting on a corbelled parapet. There are remains of courtyard buildings.

LOCATION: NR DALBEATTIE, DUMFRIES & GALLOWAY
MAP REF: NX 817551
OPEN: HISTORIC SCOTLAND: DAILY

PITCAPLE

Pitcaple is a good example of a Z-plan castle of c.1570. It was renovated by William Burn in the 1830s. The castle's main building is four storeys tall with two round towers on diagonally opposite corners.

LOCATION: ABERDEENSHIRE
MAP REF: NJ 727260

PITCULLO

Pitcullo is a small, 16th-century L-plan tower house with a cylindrical staircase tower that is centrally placed along the northern long wall. There is a surviving undercroft at the east end, vaulted, and now used as a dining room.

LOCATION: LEUCHARS, FIFE
MAP REF: NO 413193

PITSLIGO

Pitsligo Castle, a former home of the Forbes family, is largely in ruins. There is an outer shell of a tower of the early 15th century. The tower was absorbed into a quadrangular-plan mansion in the 16th. The tower appears to have had one large room on each floor, the normal arrangement found in many earlier English and Welsh keeps.

LOCATION: NR ROSEHEARTY, ABERDEENSHIRE
MAP REF: NJ 937670

PITTEADIE

This ruinous castle began as a rectangular tower house of the late 15th century, with four storeys and a cap-house on top of one corner. There are signs of later alterations.

LOCATION: NR KINGHORN, FIFE
MAP REF: NT 257891

PLANE TOWER

Plane (Plean) is a rectangular tower house built in the 15th century by Thomas Somervell, with a courtyard partly bounded by a range of buildings including a manor house built in the 16th century, also by a Somervell. It was restored in the 1990s and is now let out as holiday accommodation.

LOCATION: ST NINIANS, STIRLING
MAP REF: NS 849869

PORTENCROSS

This decaying but majestic castle on the coast of the Clyde began as a rectangular tower of three storeys and a garret. Most of the massively built walls remain today and there is a fundraising project to preserve it. Begun in the 14th century, Portencross was given by Robert Bruce to the Boyd family of Kilmarnock. It guarded a crossing to Bute.

LOCATION: NORTH AYRSHIRE
MAP REF: NS 175489

RAIT

Rait Castle is a rectangular hall-tower dating from the 13th century and unusually, its horizontal dimension was greater than its height. Built by the de Rait family, the castle was held by both the Comyns and Mackintoshes. The walls of the hall and the cylinder tower are about 2m (6ft) thick.

LOCATION: NAIRN, HIGHLAND
MAP REF: NM 894525

Ravenscraig was the first castle in Britain specifically planned for defence with guns. James II of Scotland, who initiated the work in 1460, intended it to be a coastal fortress to guard against any attack from the Firth of Forth. The castle is positioned on a prominent rocky site jutting into Kirkcaldy Bay. A wide, natural gully divides the site from the mainland, and this was artificially extended. There were two huge D-plan towers with 3–4.5m (10–15ft) thick walls: the western tower, whose outer wall stands sheer on a slope down to the beach, is in reality a great tower, fortified and residential with mural chambers on each floor, as well as main centre rooms with garderobes. Both towers were given keyhole gun-ports, some of them designed for falconets (small cannons) and the whole front of the castle presented a formidable array of gun-ports through which the garrison could have discharged the most murderous fire. Ravenscraig was never finished; however, James II's widow lived in the castle for a time after her husband's death, and the Sinclairs held it until the middle of the 17th century.

LOCATION: KIRKCALDY, FIFE
MAP REF: NT 290924
OPEN: HISTORIC SCOTLAND: OPEN ACCESS

REPENTANCE

John Maxwell, Lord Herries, built Repentance Tower in the 16th century. Sited a short distance from Hoddom Castle, it was on a square plan with three main storeys to the parapet and equipped with more gun-ports and shot-holes than windows. It has been restored and is in good condition.

LOCATION: ANNANDALE, DUMFRIES & GALLOWAY
MAP REF: NY 155722

ROSSEND

An ecclesiastical castle at first, built by the abbots of Dunfermline in the 13th century, Rossend was converted in the 16th century to a T-plan tower house incorporated with some of the original stonework. Threatened with demolition, the castle was saved and restored during the 1970s.

LOCATION: BURNTISLAND, FIFE
MAP REF: NT 220850

ROSSLYN

Rosslyn Castle stands on a strong position on a peninsula created by the River Esk. Owned by the St Clair family, Princes (and later Earls) of Orkney, the second earl erected a tower house on the site in the 1390s. It was later extended. The property is now rented out.

LOCATION: LASSWADE, MIDLOTHIAN
MAP REF: NT 275627

ROSYTH

Rosyth Castle lies in the Royal Naval Dockyard at Rosyth. It consists of a rectangular enclosure of the 16th to 17th centuries with a 15th-century tower house. The tower house was free-standing and built with ashlar facing. The ground and first floors were vaulted.

LOCATION: NR DUNFERMLINE, FIFE
MAP REF: NT 108821

ROTHESAY

The 12th-century low-level motte at Rothesay was crowned with a huge and tall circular stone curtain during the 13th century. Built of sandstone, it was one of the few shell enclosures in Scotland. Four stout cylindrical towers, placed equidistantly round the circumference, were added to the outside of the shell and, between the west and east towers, a simple but tall square-plan gateway was inserted; this was enlarged by James IV. Vikings besieged Rothesay in 1230 and broke through the soft stone and mortar of the wall by hacking away at it with axes. In 1263, the castle fell again to the Vikings, led by their king, Haakon of Norway. Shortly after this, Haakon and his forces were decisively defeated by Alexander III at the Battle of Largs. When the Stewarts became Kings of Scotland in the 14th century, Rothesay passed into royal hands.

The castle was burned late in the 17th century but was partly restored by the Marquises of Bute during the 19th and 20th centuries.

LOCATION: ISLE OF BUTE, ARGYLL & BUTE
MAP REF: NS 088645
OPEN: HISTORIC SCOTLAND: APR–SEP DAILY; OCT–MAR SAT–WED

ROXBURGH

Once a major Border fortress, Roxburgh began as a motte castle built on the north side of the River Teviot early in the 12th century; it is mentioned in a charter of c.1128. The original owner is not known.

The castle was held by Henry II of England from 1175 to 1189. Edward III rebuilt the castle in the 1330s, including a small wooden pele tower with some prefabricated parts that were brought by sea from Newcastle to Berwick and then by river (or land) to Roxburgh. During Richard II's reign a gatehouse and great wall with towers were built and the existing towers heightened: the works cost about £2,000. Roxburgh changed hands, and was destroyed but then rebuilt many times in its history; but only fragments of this once strong fortress remain.

LOCATION: NR KELSO, BORDERS
MAP REF: NT 713337
OPEN: SITE FREELY ACCESSIBLE

ST ANDREWS

This interesting fortress stands on a rock promontory to the north-east of the ancient city of St Andrews. The first stonework was erected late in the 12th century. Towards the end of the 14th century a major building programme began, and this included, erecting a substantial curtain round the whole enclosure with two new towers, and rebuilding the earlier fore-tower.

St Andrews later became a favourite residence of royalty; James III was probably born there in 1451. The next phase of building was in the first half of the 16th century. The castle was besieged in 1546–7 when Cardinal Beaton, Archbishop of St Andrews, was murdered there by Protestant infiltrators. The Protestants captured the castle and held out for a year against the Catholic forces under Mary of Guise although extensive damage was inflicted on the castle. It finally fell into ruins after the Reformation.

LOCATION: FIFE
MAP REF: NO 513169
OPEN: HISTORIC SCOTLAND: DAILY

RUSKO (RUSCO)

This 16th-century rectangular tower house still has three floors plus attic, with a two-floor wing, added in the 17th century. Rusko, which was built by the Gordon family, was ruinous but restored at the end of the last century.

LOCATION: NR GATEHOUSE OF FLEET, DUMFRIES & GALLOWAY
MAP REF: NX 584604

SADDELL

An interesting tower house was built here between 1508 and 1512 with four floors plus garret, a battlemented parapet with open angle-turrets and a cap-house on one side. The entrance is on the ground floor. The tower house was enclosed by a barmkin. For a time it belonged to the Bishops of Argyll and later became a Campbell possession. After years of neglect, it has been restored, and is owned by the Landmark Trust.

LOCATION: MULL OF KINTYRE, ARGYLL & BUTE
MAP REF: NR 785315

Mines at St Andrews

During the 1546–7 siege of St Andrews the attackers sank a mine through the rock under the castle, tunnelling towards the fore tower. The defenders heard of the attempt, calculated the direction the tunnel was taking, and sank a counter-mine, hoping to join up with the besiegers' tunnel and fight them off. The former is about 2m (6ft) high and about 1.5m (5ft) wide and slants down to pass under the ditch. The counter-mine is much the same size and it reached the head of the besiegers' mine nearly 12m (39ft) out from the fore-tower where it was begun.
The mine and the counter-mine have survived to this day and visitors can walk (or crawl) through the tunnels.

SANQUHAR

Begun by the Crichton family in the 14th century, Sanquhar is now in ruins: it was a rectangular courtyard castle with a substantial front mass (like Doune), and with a tall tower at the south corner. The quadrangle had a range of buildings on each inner side, of varying periods, beginning in the 15th century. There are also remnants of associated buildings in front of the rectangular enclosure, dating mainly from the 1800s.

The 3rd Marquis of Bute started restoring the castle at the end of the 19th century, but when he died the work stopped and the ruins are a mixture of this later restoration and original stonework. The castle is accessible at any reasonable time.

LOCATION: DUMFRIES & GALLOWAY
MAP REF: NS 785092

SAUCHIE TOWER

A square-plan tower built c.1425, probably by James Schaw, is the principal feature of this courtyard castle. The tower was built of ashlar and parts are still in good condition.

The arched entrance is at ground floor level in the centre of the west wall.

LOCATION: NR ALVA, CLACKMANNANSHIRE
MAP REF: NS 896597

SCALLOWAY

Scalloway is a four-storeyed, rectangular-plan tower house dating from the end of the 16th century. Patrick Stewart, Earl of Orkney, a man of violent and cruel disposition, said to have mixed the blood of his victims with the mortar for his castle at Scalloway. After his death, Scalloway was used as an administrative centre for Shetland and was also a barracks for Cromwell's troops in the 17th century. Today the castle is a substantial and partially restored ruin.

LOCATION: NR LERWICK, SHETLAND ISLANDS
MAP REF: HU 405393
OPEN: HISTORIC SCOTLAND. KEY IS AVAILABLE FROM THE SHETLAND WOOLLEN COMPANY SHOP OR AT WEEKENDS FROM THE SCALLOWAY HOTEL

SCOTSTARVIT TOWER

Scotstarvit is a fine, well-preserved tower house of L-plan design built between 1550 and 1579. At one time it was the home of antiquarian Sir John Scott who wrote a book called *Scott of Scotstarvit's Staggering State of Scots Statesmen* (later described by Carlyle as a 'homily on life's nothingness enforced by examples'). With few windows, the tower is six-storeyed. A very small wing containing the spiral stair that runs all the way up and is topped with a stone-cap house.

LOCATION: NR CUPAR, FIFE
MAP REF: NO 370113
OPEN: HISTORIC SCOTLAND: EASTER, MAY–SEP DAILY; OCT SAT–SUN. KEY AT NTS HILL OF TARVIT

SINCLAIR GIRNIGOE

The seat of the Earldom of Caithness used to be known as Castle Girnigoe but early in the 17th century George Sinclair, the fourth earl applied to Parliament to change the name to Castle Sinclair. Only the new buildings (the castle was being remodelled at the time) became known as Castle Sinclair. The castle is now known as Castle Sinclair Girnigoe. There were at least three major phases of development here dating from the 14th or early 15th centuries with subsequent periods of development in the 16th and 17th centuries. The castle was held for a time by the Campbells of Glenorchy: the Sinclairs' attempt, in 1679, to recover their ancient seat and title resulted in a bloody battle with the loss of many Sinclair lives. The earldom did eventually revert to the Sinclair family in 1681 but the castle was left to become a ruin. It is still listed as the official seat of the Earls of Caithness and is maintained by the Clan Sinclair Trust which is working to preserve this impressive ruin.

LOCATION: NOSS HEAD, WICK, HIGHLAND
MAP REF: ND 379 549
OPEN: CLAN SINCLAIR TRUST: ACCESS AT ANY REASONABLE TIME

SKELMORLIE

Skelmorlie, a rectangular tower house, was erected here c.1500 with additions made in the 1630s including a smaller tower in the barmkin. The castle was renovated in the 19th century and converted into a mansion, and a part of it is now rented out as holiday accommodation. Skelmorlie is the ancient seat of the chiefs of the Clan Montgomery.

LOCATION: NORTH AYRSHIRE
MAP REF: NS 195658

SKIPNESS

Skipness was an enclosure castle built in the 13th century. Today it is an impressive ruin with good quality stonework that dates from the earliest building period. The castle developed into a stone quadrangle with a tower house of L-plan in one corner. The first structure was a rectangular hall-house, enclosed by a timber palisade upon an encircling rampart. Skipness Castle was abandoned in the 17th century.

LOCATION: NR TARBERT, ARGYLL & BUTE
MAP REF: NR 907577

SORBIE TOWER

Sorbie is a 16th-century L-plan tower house built for the Hannah family and now owned by the Clan Hannah Society; it was abandoned in the middle of the 18th century after the Second Jacobite Rising. Its main block is 12 x 7.5m (39 x 25ft) and probably rose to four storeys. It is possible that the site was occupied by earlier fortifications. The castle is a ruin but is undergoing preservation work.

LOCATION: SORBIE, DUMFRIES & GALLOWAY
MAP REF: NX 451470

SORN

This 16th-century great tower and curtain-wall castle of rectangular plan, was later restored and modified. Sorn was built by the Hamilton family. It is still privately owned and occasionally open to the public.

LOCATION: NR MAUCHLINE, EAST AYRSHIRE
MAP REF: NS 548269

SMAILHOLM

A favourite castle of Sir Walter Scott, Smailholm Tower is a four-floor rectangular tower house standing on a rocky spur surrounded on three sides by cliffs and enclosed by a ditch and stone walling. The tower walls are almost 3m (10ft) thick and the tower reaches nearly 18.5m (60ft). The castle, which was built by the Pringle family in the 15th century, is now decayed and a fairly substantial ruin.

LOCATION: SANDYKNOWE, BORDERS
MAP REF: NT 637346
OPEN: HISTORIC SCOTLAND: APR–SEP DAILY; OCT–MAR, SAT–SUN

SPEDLINS TOWER

This is an interesting ruin of a once-splendid rectangular tower house. The tower was considerably altered in the 17th century by adding two storeys to the original three. Spedlin's had an unusual roof although this no longer exists: it was double with two gables in between which ran a horizontal stretch, and this roofed a central corridor in the storey below, which had rooms off both sides.

LOCATION: LOCHMABEN, DUMFRIES & GALLOWAY
MAP REF: NT 097875

STAPLETON TOWER

This is a rectangular tower, measuring about 13 x 8m (43 x 26ft) and over 12m (39ft) from the ground to the parapet. It was built in the 16th century and is now joined to a more modern house.

LOCATION: DORNOCK, DUMFRIES & GALLOWAY
MAP REF: NY 235689

STIRLING

LOCATION: STIRLING, ABERDEENSHIRE
MAP REF: NS 790941
OPEN: DAILY
SEE PAGE: 166

STRANRAER

Restored Stranraer Castle now houses a museum. In the middle of the town, it was used as the gaol from the 17th to the 19th century. It was built in the 16th century as an L-plan tower house and heightened in the 17th century.

LOCATION: DUMFRIES & GALLOWAY
MAP REF: NX 061608

Stirling

The landscape looks very different today but in medieval times marshes, hills and two rivers rendered Stirling Castle's towering rocky site highly defensible and with central Scotland's major route into the Highlands passing by this craggy site, control of Stirling Castle meant control of much of Scotland. Its strategic position led to its status as one of the most important fortresses in the kingdom and Stirling represented Scotland's resistance to English aggression in the Middle Ages.

By the time Alexander I died at the castle in 1124 Stirling was an important royal stronghold and later in the same century the fortress was one of the five castles surrendered to Henry II of England under the 1174 Treaty of Falaise, which made Scotland a feudal possession of England.

The treaty was overturned by Richard I in 1189.

During the Scottish War of Independence Stirling Castle was often under attack, its buildings destroyed and then rebuilt. In 1296, it was seized by Edward I during his Scottish campaign: a year later, William Wallace recovered the castle after the Battle of Stirling Bridge but lost it again in 1298 when the Scottish were defeated at Falkirk. In 1299, the Scots took the fortress again and held it until 1304, the year of the great siege by Edward I. By this time Stirling was the only noteworthy stronghold still under Scottish control and Edward planned his siege with care. For three months the garrison resisted everything Edward threw at it but eventually it surrendered. The English then held the castle for the next ten years, but in 1314 it was yielded to the Scots after their victory nearby at Bannockburn, and then dismantled.

The structure that endured so much battering had begun as a timber- and earthwork castle. Nothing remains of Stirling's 12th- and 13th-century buildings; the complex that graces the huge rock stems from the 15th century and later. The great hall, the largest in Scotland and restored to all its medieval glory at the end of the 20th century, was one of the first and certainly the finest of the 15th-century Renaissance buildings erected anywhere in the British Isles.

Stirling was at the centre of the sumptuous court surrounding James IV and then his son, James V (who was crowned at Stirling aged just 17 months in 1513 after his father's death at the Battle of Flodden).

Queen Margaret's Defiance of the Scottish Parliament, at Stirling Castle, by John Faed (1820–1902). Margaret was a Tudor: her father was Henry VII and Henry VIII was her brother. She acted as Regent for her infant son but the Scottish nobles came to Stirling Castle to demand that she hand over her son to their keeping. Margaret refused and told the earls to return to Edinburgh.

James V was responsible for the most outstanding building in the castle precincts, the magnificently facaded palace building, erected for James's second wife, Mary of Guise.

James and Mary's daughter was crowned Mary, Queen of Scots in the Chapel Royal at Stirling in September 1543 and her son, Prince James was baptized at the castle in December 1566. Eight months later the castle saw the coronation of the 13-month-old infant after the forced abdication of his mother. James VI largely grew up at Stirling but when he succeeded to the English throne in 1603 he returned once more, in 1617.

The fortress was strengthened between 1708 and 1714 during the Jacobite Rebellions. These new defences were tested in 1746 when Bonnie Prince Charlie besieged the castle: this was Stirling's last experience of warfare although its military connections remained until 1964 as it became the base for the Argyll and Sutherland Highlanders whose regimental museum remains open to visitors.

Other attractions here are exhibitions and re-creations of the kitchens. Audiovisial tours help explain the history and development of the castle.

STRATHAVEN

The ruins of this rectangular tower with a four-storeyed round tower extension are set on a rocky outcrop in the centre of the town. There is little left of this fortress, once held by the Douglas family. It is also known as Avondale Castle after James II gave the castle to his relative, Lord Avondale.

LOCATION: SOUTH LANARKSHIRE
MAP REF: NS 702444

STRATHENDRY

Now incorporated in a modern mansion, the military part of the castle was a 16th-century tower house.

LOCATION: LESLIE, FIFE
MAP REF: NO 225019

STROME

The ruins of 15th-century Strome, a rectangular hall-tower with a cross-wall, are romantically situated on a promontory overlooking Loch Carron. Much of the tower has crumbled. Strome was a fortress of the Lords of the Isles built during the 15th century. It was blown up in 1602.

LOCATION: LOCHCARRON, HIGHLAND
MAP REF: NG 862354
OPEN: NATIONAL TRUST FOR SCOTLAND: DAILY

STRUTHERS

This 16th-century L-plan tower house incorporates work from the 14th century; alterations were made in the 17th century. Struthers was abandoned at the beginning of the 1900s and only fragments of wall remain.

LOCATION: NR CERES, FIFE
MAP REF: NO 377097

SUNDRUM

The original part of this attractive castle is an early rectangular tower dating from the 14th century. It came into the hands of the Cathcart family and was their seat until the mid-18th century. The Hamiltons then bought it and made alterations in the 1700s. It is now rented for holidays.

LOCATION: COLYTON, NR AYR, SOUTH AYRSHIRE
MAP REF: NS 411212

SWEEN

Castle Sween, an interesting and well-preserved ruin, stands on the rocky coast of Knapdale. It was a quadrilateral stone enclosure castle; the remains of the south wall has a small entrance with a rounded arch and on the west wall is a sea gate. The castle probably dates from the late 11th or early 12th century suggesting a structure begun at least under Norman influence, a theory supported by the Norman-type wall pilaster buttresses. Originally built by the McSwine family (the name possibly coming from the Viking 'Sweyn') who were the owners until the middle of the 13th century, the castle was, for a time, owned by the Stewart Earls of Menteith who remodelled some of the structure and built additions outside. Towards the end of the 14th century it was held for the Lords of the Isles when more works were carried out, including a number of buildings inside along the east wall.

LOCATION: KNAPDALE, NR TARBERT, ARGYLL & BUTE
MAP REF: NR 713789
OPEN: HISTORIC SCOTLAND: OPEN ACCESS

TANTALLON

This is a fascinating and powerful castle on a coastal site. It sits on a promontory with three of its sides jutting into the Firth and below high, sheer rock cliffs falling straight down to the sea. On the fourth side, a ditch about 6m (20ft) wide is cut into the rock. Inside the ditch is a massive, 15m (49ft) tall and 3.5m (11ft) thick battlemented curtain wall of dressed red freestone: in the curtain is a central mid-tower containing the entrance and remains of end towers at the north west and south-east, and the ruins of all three towers rise to nearly 24.5m (80ft). The gatehouse tower had four floors of residential accommodation above the room that contained the portcullis mechanism and consisted at the front of a pair of square-plan wings up to the second floor. This structure, together with a two-hall block at the north, dates from the 14th century when the castle was in the hands of William, 1st Earl of Douglas of the 'Black Douglas' family. Tantallon was attacked and bombarded by Cromwell's troops in 1651, and then it was abandoned.

LOCATION: NORTH BERWICK, EAST LOTHIAN
MAP REF: NT 596850
OPEN: HISTORIC SCOTLAND: APR–SEP DAILY; OCT–MAR SAT–WED

TARBERT

Tarbert is an interesting agglomeration of ruins. It appears to have been begun in the 13th century with a plain rectangular tower. Another tower was raised in the 15th century.

LOCATION: KILCALMONELL, TARBERT, ARGYLL & BUTE
MAP REF: NR 868690

TARINGZEAN

A much restored and altered tower house, begun in the 15th century, beside a 13th-century hall-house.

LOCATION: CUMNOCK, EAST AYRSHIRE
MAP REF: NS 556205

TERPERSIE

One of the earliest Z-plan castles in Scotland. It was raised in 1561 and was smaller than most that followed. Terpersie was a rectangular tower block, with small cylindrical towers.

LOCATION: ALFORD, ABERDEENSHIRE
MAP REF: NJ 546202

THIRLESTANE

This splendid building began as a 13th-century structure, and was extended by the Maitland family in the 16th century. However, the major work was carried out by architect William Bruce for John Maitland, Duke of Lauderdale in the 17th century. Bruce embellished the original shell of the tower house and crowned the whole building with a tower bearing an ogee roof: parapets, cap-houses, conical turrets and fine windows made it more sumptuous.

LOCATION: LAUDER, BORDERS
MAP REF: NT 533479
OPEN: CHARITABLE TRUST: MAY–SEP SUN–FRI

TIBBERS

This was built by the English at the end of the 13th century, during Edward I's campaign in Scotland. It was a simple, quadrangular curtain enclosure of stone with a cylindrical tower on each corner. Almost nothing remains here now.

LOCATION: NR CARRONBRIDGE, DUMFRIES & GALLOWAY
MAP REF: NX 863982

THREAVE

Threave stands on an islet in the River Dee and even as a ruin it is a mighty and forbidding structure. The massive great tower was partly enclosed by a powerful 'artillery' wall which had three cylindrical corner turrets. Built by Archibald 'the Grim', 3rd Earl of Douglas, Lord of Galloway, in about 1370, Threave was a defensive structure as well as a building intended to impress. During the reign of James II the Earls of Douglas were locked in a deadly quarrel with the king who was determined to break their power. In c.1454, defences were reinforced with the addition of the earliest 'artillery' wall in Britain along the sides of the castle that faced the mainland. The wall was 5.5m (18ft) tall and it was provided with vertical loops with embrasures for hand-guns and for cross bows: its towers were equipped with two types of gun-port, inverted keyholes and dumb-bells. Threave was besieged in 1455 by James II using the latest cannons and bombards, including the famous Mons Meg, and was eventually taken. It was slighted in the 17th century.

LOCATION: NR CASTLE DOUGLAS, DUMFRIES & GALLOWAY
MAP REF: NV 739623
OPEN: HISTORIC SCOTLAND: APR–SEP DAILY

TILLYCAIRN

This mid-16th-century L-plan castle has interesting gun-ports; crosslet top and oillet bottom loops, wide-mouth ports all round and pistol shot-holes in the roundels. Built in 1540 by Mathew Lumsden, Tillycairn was restored in the 20th century by David Lumsden a member of the same family.

LOCATION: ABERDEENSHIRE
MAP REF: NJ 665114

TIMPENDEAN TOWER

The remains of this rectangular four-storey tower house of the late 16th century consist of walls, two opposites reaching to gable height. The tower was equipped with wide-mouth gun-ports. The ruins are visible from the road.

LOCATION: TIMPENDEAN, BORDERS
MAP REF: NT 635226

TIORAM

Tioram stands impressively high up on a rock on an island in Loch Moidart. It is a stone enclosure, approximately five-sided, with rounded angles. The curtain dates from the 13th century but other buildings, including a great tower, were erected inside the enclosure during the 14th to 16th centuries. The castle, now just a shell, was a seat of the MacDonalds of Clan Ranald.

LOCATION: MOIDART, HIGHLAND
MAP REF: NM 662724

TORTHORWALD

Torthorwald is now just the shell of a tower house which was once part of a stone curtain enclosure. The castle, which had two vaulted storeys, dates from the middle of the 14th century but was raised on the site of an earlier earthwork castle. The site has the remains of considerable ramparts and ditches.

LOCATION: DUMFRIES & GALLOWAY
MAP REF: NY 033782

TOWIE BARCLAY

The renovated Towie Barclay is a late 16th-century L-plan tower house, which has the unusual feature of a rib-vaulted great hall reached by a spiral staircase within the tower wall thickness. Above the entrance to the hall is a small oratory reached by another mural staircase that rises over the doorway. In the late 18th century, Towie Barclay was altered, the most substantial change being the removal of two storeys of the tower. The castle is privately owned.

LOCATION: TURRIFF, ABERDEENSHIRE
MAP REF: NJ 744439

TOLQUHON

A Preston and then a Forbes family castle, the substantial ruins of stunning Tolquhon derive from two main building periods, the late 15th century and between 1584–9. The first period saw the construction of the 'auld tour' (old tower) by the Prestons, but only the vaulted basement and parts of the first floor of this remain. In 1584, William Forbes enlarged the castle by building, round the old tower, a substantial irregular quadrangular enclosure with ranges of buildings along the inside of three of its walls and adding two further towers, both equipped with gun-ports. The parapet of the 'auld tour' was machicolated. The castle was abandoned at the end of the 19th century.

LOCATION: TARVES, ABERDEENSHIRE
MAP REF: NJ 874286
OPEN: HISTORIC SCOTLAND: APR–SEP DAILY; OCT–MAR SAT–SUN

TROCHRIE

This was an early 14th-century hall-house with a remarkable undercroft, rib-vaulted from central piers, built on a natural rock outcrop. A strong curtain wall was built round most of the central structure. The castle, now a ruin, was the seat of the Gowrie family but passed to the Stewarts of Banchrie at the beginning of the 17th century.

LOCATION: TROCHRIE, PERTHSHIRE
MAP REF: NN 978402

TULLIBOLE

Finely restored after World War II, Tullibole was built in the early 17th century on the site of an earlier building mentioned in 14th-century documents. The newer castle was fortified with turrets and gun-ports. Two interesting features are a 'luggie', a 17th-century form of room 'bugging', and a shot-hole positioned beside the main entrance door. Tullibole has been home to the Moncrieff family since the 18th century. It now offers bed-and-breakfast accommodation.

LOCATION: BY CROOK OF DEVON, PERTH & KINROSS
MAP REF: NO 053005

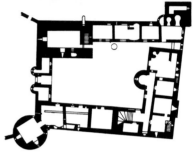

TURNBERRY

There are very few remnants of Turnberry, which was raised to the south of Maiden's Bay. It began as a cylindrical great tower castle in the 13th century and is thought to have been the childhood home of Robert Bruce, as the castle was his mother's home. Bruce besieged the castle in 1307 after it had fallen into English hands.

LOCATION: SOUTH AYRSHIRE
MAP REF: NS 196072

UDNY

This five-storeyed rectangular tower has rounded corners like Drum Castle and was built in the 15th and 16th centuries. Originally the tower rose only to three storeys the extra two floors were added in the 16th century. Two of the earlier storeys have vaulted ceilings. In the 1800s a mansion was built on to the tower: this has been demolished, leaving the older tower much as it was, with restoration at the end of the 20th century. The castle is privately owned.

LOCATION: UDNY GREEN, ABERDEENSHIRE
MAP REF: NJ 882268

Urquhart was a substantial enclosure castle built on the site of an earlier motte castle. It was once one of Scotland's largest castles with a roughly figure-of-eight plan. On a sandstone promontory overlooking Urquhart Bay, the enclosure was defended from the landward side by a wide, deep ditch, crossed by a bridge with high walls on either side and broken in the middle by a drawbridge. The bridge led out from a massive twin-cylindrical-towered gatehouse in the length of the high stone curtain: the curtain, which followed the line of the rocky outcrops on which the castle sits, survives in part, At the north-east end of the enclosure is the ruined shell of the great tower whose basement dates from the 14th century: the next storeys are 16th century

(probably rebuilding of older work) and the top is 17th century. Gun-ports were inserted in the 16th century. South of the great tower is a range of now ruined buildings which once contained the great chamber, hall and kitchen and at the end of this range, an inlet for the loch water, a landing place and a sea gate. A Scottish-built castle, by 1297 Edward I of England had Urquhart under his control. It was retaken by the Scots in 1303, changed hands twice more, and in 1313 became the property of Randolph, Earl of Moray, one of Bruce's greatest friends and counsellors.

LOCATION: DRUMNADROCHIT, LOCH NESS, HIGHLAND
MAP REF: NH 531286
OPEN: HISTORIC SCOTLAND: DAILY

WALLACE'S

There are fragments of walling on Ha'Hill in Glen Minnonie that date from the 13th century and are thought to be the remnants of a simple tower or enclosure, possibly used by William Wallace during his war against Edward I, c.1297–1305. Wallace was helped by Anthony de Moravia who was operating in and around Morayshire.

LOCATION: MINNONIE, ABERDEENSHIRE
MAP REF: NJ 773605

WEMYSS

A 15th-century tower house built on the E-plan. This has been considerably altered, enlarged, altered again and reduced in size during its history. The Wemyss family also owned the nearby MacDuff's Castle. After renovations in the 20th century Wemyss is now a palatial and stately home. The garden is open on summer afternoons.

LOCATION: WEST WEMYSS, FIFE
MAP REF: NT 329951

YESTER

These remains in the grounds of the privately owned Yester estate are of one of the oldest fortresses in Scotland. Built by the alleged wizard Hugo de Gifford some time in the 13th century, Yester was redesigned as a courtyard castle. It passed to the Hay family who, in the mid-16th century, abandoned it in favour of a grander residence nearby.

LOCATION: GIFFORD, EAST LOTHIAN
MAP REF: NT 556667

Wales

For the Normans, Wales was a land of two parts: the gentle lowlands and hills of the south, and the wild, untamable mountain lands of the north. They came to the south early, and claimed much of it, building castles as they went. The Welsh retreated to the hills and mountains and fought on until Edward I built his 'iron ring' of castles in the north at the end of the 13th century.

Widespread open revolt against English rule began again under the 15th-century campaign of Owain Glyndwr. Castles were a central focus of this rebellion, but Owain's own castle headquarters at Sycarth is now a forgotten, inaccessible tree-covered mound.

The legacy of castles in Wales is tremendously rich, with many evocative ruins in outstanding landscape settings.

ABER

The motte remains of this castle, built by the Earl of Chester in the last decade of the 11th century, stand here. It is also known as Pen-y-Mwd. The site can be seen from the road.

LOCATION: BANGOR, GWYNEDD
MAP REF: SH 656727

ABER AFAN

There was a motte castle here which was attacked in 1153 at the end of the Anarchy in England. The attack was possibly carried out by the Welsh. The site is now under housing.

LOCATION: WEST GLAMORGAN
MAP REF: SS 762901

ABERCOWYN

Alternative names are Castell Aber Taf or Castell Aber Cafwy. This was a motte castle and oval bailey with the 7.5m/25ft motte sitting astride the bailey. It was probably destroyed by the Welsh c.1116. Much of the motte has been ploughed up.

LOCATION: NR ST CLEARS, CARMARTHENSHIRE
MAP REF: SN 279136

ABEREDW

There are two castles here: a motte castle, and the stone castle at SO 076474. The earthen motte may have been built in the 1090s by the Normans. The stone castle was built in about 1284; a century later it was a forgotten ruin. Aberedw was an enclosure castle with small towers. The site was damaged by railway construction during the 19th century, but the ruined curtain wall remains. Both castles are overgrown ruins, and both are on private ground.

LOCATION: NR BUILTH WELLS, POWYS
MAP REF: SO 076474

ABEREINION

Confusingly, this castle is also known as Aberdyfi, and is marked on maps as Domen Las. It was a fortified mound enclosed by a ditch of the mid-12th century. The site is private..

LOCATION: NR MACHYNLLETH, CEREDIGION
MAP REF: SN 687968

ABERGAVENNY

Abergavenny Castle stands on a spur overlooking the confluence of the Usk and Gwenny. Begun in 1087, it was a motte castle with later stone additions. A square great tower was let into the mound on one side and traces survive, together with the remains of a curtain wall and two towers. The gatehouse and barbican are from the 13th century.

In 1175 the castle was the scene of one of Wales' most notorious multiple murders when the famously cruel William de Braose killed a group of Welsh nobles here. The castle was slighted during the Civil War.

LOCATION: MONMOUTHSHIRE
MAP REF: SO 299139
OPEN: MUSEUM: MAR–OCT DAILY; NOV–FEB MON–SAT

ABERLLEINIOG

Hugh d'Avranches built this motte castle. It was burned by the Welsh. The stone keep dates from the 17th century.

LOCATION: NR LLANGOED, ISLE OF ANGLESEY
MAP REF: SH 617793

ABERLLYNFI

This castle, documented in 1180, was destroyed during an uprising in 1233. Although little remains today, it was a strong, important fortress.

LOCATION: NR ABERLLYNFI, POWYS
MAP REF: SO 171380

ABERRHEIDOL

This is an earthwork enclosure, where there is evidence of a motte which was subsequently encased in stone.

The castle was raised by Gilbert de Clare, c.1110. It was attacked by the Welsh in 1116, and again in 1136 when it was burned down. The site was reoccupied, and ownership changed often; it was finally destroyed in the 13th century and has been a ruin ever since.

LOCATION: NR ABERYSTWYTH, CEREDIGION
MAP REF: SN 585790

ABERYSTWYTH

Edward I ordered this substantial lozenge-plan concentric castle. It consists of walls within walls, each on raised ground and each with flanking round towers on the angles and twin-towered gatehouses. It was rebuilt after being destroyed in 1282 by Welsh patriots. Aberystwyth was taken by Owain Glyndwr in 1403 and recaptured in 1409 by Henry of Monmouth. It was battered by the sea and gradually decayed. The Parliamentarians took it in the Civil War and in 1649 slighted it. Aberystwyth's remains are substantial and fascinating.

LOCATION: CEREDIGION
MAP REF: SN 579815
OPEN: LOCAL AUTHORITY: OPEN ACCESS

AMROTH

This motte castle was built by the Norman invaders early in the 12th century. A stone enclosure with an interesting gateway was erected a few hundred metres away towards the sea, probably in the 14th century. The 18th-century mansion next to the castle was built to replace it.

LOCATION: EARWERE, PEMBROKESHIRE
MAP REF: SN 170073
OPEN: PRIVATE; HOLIDAY HOMES

BALA

Known as Tomen y Bala, this large motte was probably superseded by nearby Carndochan as early as 1202. There are excellent views of the town's medieval layout from the top. The mound was famous in the 19th century as a place at which the town's women gathered to knit socks – a notable Bala export at the time!

LOCATION: GWYNEDD
MAP REF: SH 928361
OPEN: OPEN ACCESS

BASINGWERK

Basingwerk Castle was built by the Normans inside the earthworks of a Saxon burgh. It is very close to the holy well of St Winefride. Henry II came here to visit the well – then a place of pilgrimage – in 1157, and had the castle rebuilt. Nearby Basingwerk Abbey is closely linked with the story of the castle, and the monks were given the Well Church in 1240. The castle fell into disuse when Flint Castle was built towards the end of the 13th century. It may have been replaced by a fortified manor house. Of the castle, only overgrown earthworks now remain; these can be viewed from the path to the abbey.

LOCATION: NR HOLYWELL, FLINTSHIRE
MAP REF: SJ 220734

BEAUMARIS

LOCATION: ISLE OF ANGLESEY
MAP REF: SH 607763
OPEN: CADW: DAILY
SEE PAGE: 176

BENTON

A small enclosure castle, with a cylindrical tower and another, smaller, cylindrical turret on one side, was built here in the 13th century. It has been merged into later buildings. The tower is still standing and the restored building is residential and private.

LOCATION: BENTON, PEMBROKESHIRE
MAP REF: SN 005069

BLAENLLYNFI

A stone castle probably dating from the 12th century was built here on a knoll below Llangorse Mountain, surrounded by a ditch fed by local streams. The remains are fragmentary but indicate a curtain-walled enclosure with towers and with a gateway in the east. The castle was taken in the 1230s by Llywelyn the Great, and by the 14th century was in a ruined state. The site has been excavated.

The castle changed hands many times between its foundation and eventual abandonment. It was badly damaged on several occasions: in 1233 Llywelyn ap Iorweth sacked it and a generation later in 1262 Llywelyn ap Gruffydd captured it. Eventually it became a Crown property, but it never recovered from Llywelyn's last attack.

LOCATION: CATHEDINE, POWYS
MAP REF: SO 145229

Beaumaris

The ultimate in concentric castles, Beaumaris is the last of the fortresses built by Edward I during and after his conquest of Wales. Started in 1295, it cost nearly £15,000 and took over 35 years to build, but it was never completed. At the peak of construction more than 3,500 people were working on the castle.

Edward I commissioned Master James of St George to build the fortress here shortly after an uprising by Madog Ap Llewellyn, and his final work in Wales is considered by many to be the finest of all his castles, and one of the most technically perfect in all Britain. James of St George was brought from Europe by Edward I; the military architect and master mason had worked on some of the great European fortresses. At Beaumaris he built two perfectly symmetrical wings of walling with flanking towers and gatehouses surrounded by a broad wet moat fed by waters from the Menai Strait. A sea gate in the outer ring enabled supply vessels to moor close to the castle which at the time was connected to tidal waters.

Beaumaris' defences were designed to be impregnable, but were never put to the test. Protected by a wide moat, the low curtain wall of the outer ward with 16 towers and two gates was the second line of defence. To breach this and get through to the castle's vast inner ward there would have been more than a dozen obstacles to overcome.

The outer ring of walls (about half as thick as the walls of the inner ward) were built to an octagonal plan with cylindrical flanking turrets. Inside these, the 5m- (16ft-) thick walls of the inner ward were built to a square plan with six towers and two vast gatehouses. The keep-like gatehouses both had residential accommodation and were the strongest parts of the castle. None of the towers or gatehouses was completed to their full height.

Despite grand intentions for Beaumaris, the initial flurry of construction lasted only about three years until 1298 when funds dried up. Small-scale building resumed again early in the 14th century but within 20 years Beaumaris was deteriorating.

Edward's plans for Beaumaris were never fulfilled but his legacy here is powerful enough to have earned World Heritage inscribed status.

Beaumaris was built on the flat marshy lands on the south edge of the Isle of Anglesey. It was given the Norman French name of Beau Mareys, meaning fair marsh, and the level site allowed James of St George the scope to build his perfectly symmetrical castle. The town of Llanfaes used to exist on the site, but Edward moved the native population to a new settlement called Newborough so that he could build his castle here.

XIII

Edward I was determined to subdue the rebellions of the Welsh against English rule. Henry III, his father, had established a network of castles in Wales that Edward either maintained, or replaced. He then built four major castles, concentrating them in the north of Wales where resistance was fiercest. Rebellions had been led by Llywelyn ap Gryffydd ('the Last') in 1277 and 1282. Edward's great castles were Beaumaris on Anglesey, and Caernarfon, Conwy and Harlech.

They were built between 1283 and 1295. The architect was Master James of St George. The total cost of the four castles was about £60,000; today's equivalent is £15.5 million. Each castle was integrated into a town which was populated with English settlers. The Welsh were allowed to enter the towns but not to carry weapons.

In 1284 the conquest was complete and Wales became a principality of England. Edward's son, born at Caernarfon Castle in 1284, became the first English Prince of Wales. But the Welsh fought on sporadically until Owain Glyndwr disappeared some time after 1405.

BLAENPORTH

Also called Castell Gwythian, this was a motte castle and has good traces of a stone shell enclosure. The motte may have been raised by the de Clares c.1110 and it was destroyed c.1158.

LOCATION: ABERPORTH, DYFED
MAP REF: SN 266488

BLEDDFA

This is a motte castle with fragments of a square tower. Excavations have uncovered a 12th-century mural staircase. The castle was destroyed in the 13th century.

LOCATION: POWYS
MAP REF: SO 209682

BOUGHROOD

At this motte castle site, excavation found masonry in the mound of earth; this was possibly a collapsed stone tower. The castle was documented in 1206. The site is private.

LOCATION: POWYS
MAP REF: SO 132391

BRECON

The remains of Brecon Castle stand in the grounds of a hotel. It began as a Norman motte castle erected at the end of the 11th century. A polygonal shell enclosure was built in the 12th century, and later more buildings including a hall and towers were added. In c.1380 it became the property of Henry of Bolingbroke through marriage. Decline began in the late 15th century.

LOCATION: POWYS
MAP REF: SO 043288

BRONLLYS

A 12th-century motte castle with two baileys and a cylindrical three-level tower of the 13th century can be seen here. The motte was encircled and domestic buildings added in the 14th century. Bronllys changed hands several times but by 1521 was 'beyond repair'.

LOCATION: NR TALGARTH, POWYS
MAP REF: SO 149346
OPEN: CADW: OPEN ACCESS

BUILTH

The Welsh destroyed an 11th-century motte castle here in 1260. Edward I built a new castle between 1277–82 as part of his programme of conquest, spending around £1,666. By 1280 the great tower, a stone curtain with flanking turrets, and gatetower were in place. Llywelyn the Last was ambushed and killed near here. Builth was damaged by Owain Glyndwr in the 15th century. Only earthworks remain.

LOCATION: BUILTH WELLS, POWYS
MAP REF: SO 044510
OPEN: FREE ACCESS

BWLCH Y DINAS

A small enclosure castle with rectangular turrets was raised here in the 12th century inside the remains of a possible Iron Age hill fort. All that can be seen today are a few tumbled walls and grass-covered heaps of rubble, but the setting is superb.

LOCATION: POWYS
MAP REF: SO 179301

CAERGWRLE

The ruins of this castle stand inside earthworks, probably from the Iron Age. The enclosure had flanking towers and excavation has revealed free-standing buildings inside. One report says the enclosure had the feel of a builder's yard; this may be because it was never completed. Anyway, Caergwrle's existence was short, from initial construction in the later 13th century to abandonment in the 1330s. The remains consist of little more than broken walls but the view from the site is excellent.

LOCATION: NR MOLD, FLINTSHIRE
MAP REF: SJ 307572

CAERLEON

This steep motte castle was built c.1086 close to the site of a Roman fortress. The remains of a tower foundation were found in the excavations: the tower may date to 1158–73. A twin-towered barbican at the motte base leads to the bailey, and the bailey wall had flanking towers, one of which has survived. The castle was attacked several times by the Welsh. The stone building on the motte was robbed and used for local buildings. Today the mound is almost completely hidden by trees.

LOCATION: NEWPORT
MAP REF: ST 342905

CAERNARFON

LOCATION: GWYNEDD
MAP REF: SH 477626
OPEN: CADW: DAILY
SEE PAGE: 180

CAERPHILLY

Caerphilly was the first concentric castle to be built from scratch in Britain. Its combination of land and water defences represented a very high level of military architectural sophistication. Despite several sieges and long periods of neglect the great bulk of the castle has survived and it is now a spectacular concentric military ruin. Henry III ordered Gilbert de Clare to construct a stone castle against the activites of Llywelyn, Prince of Wales and, despite Llywelyn's attempt in 1270 to halt the building, de Clare pressed on with construction and the castle was completed in a remarkably short period of time. In 1316 Caerphilly was attacked by the Welsh but the fortress was defended with little damage inflicted. The castle was threatened again in the winter of 1326 when Isabella, the estranged wife of Edward II, laid siege to the fortress where Edward had taken refuge. At the time, Caerphilly was still in the hands of the hugely powerful Despenser family: Hugh Despenser built the great hall in 1322. The castle began to fall into disrepair later in the 14th century, but was restored in the early 1900s by the Marquess of Bute. Today, Caerphilly stands as one of the most outstanding 13th-century castles anywhere.

LOCATION: CAERPHILLY
MAP REF: ST 155870
OPEN: CADW: DAILY

Caernarfon

Edward's principal symbol of power in Wales had to be novel, vast, majestic, and appears to have been derived from Imperial Rome: the design of Caernarfon strongly resembles the great wall around Constantinople which Edward would have seen when he was on the Crusades. Using the town as part of his defensive system it, too, was enclosed within a fortified wall with towers all round. In 1987 both town and castle became a World Heritage Site.

THE INVESTITURE

On 1 July 1969 the investiture of Charles as Prince of Wales took place at Caernarfon Castle. Prince Charles became the 21st Prince of Wales when he was just nine years old but he was 20 when he received the Insignia of the Principality and Earldom of Chester, a sword, coronet, mantle, gold ring and gold rod, from his mother Queen Elizabeth II. The Constable of the Castle, Lord Snowdon, directed the ceremony while many other members of the royal family looked on. Afterwards the Queen presented the newly invested Prince of Wales to the crowds in castle square from the castle's Queen Eleanor's Gate.

Caernarfon, part of Edward I's defensive ring of castles, was intended more as a powerful symbol of the conquest of Wales. The castle was never finished but it was the grandest of Edward's Welsh structures. Edward's son, the first English Prince of Wales, was born there in 1284.

The position of Caernarfon, on the banks of the River Seiont where it flows into the Menai Strait, was strategically important. First the site of a Roman fort, a motte and bailey were erected by Hugh D'Avranches c.1090. Building began in 1283, overseen by Master James of St George: this included the huge polygonal Eagle Tower. The castle was taken in 1294 by Madog ap Llewellyn but regained by the English in 1295 when work resumed to incorporate the mighty twin-towered King's Gate. Edward's attention eventually turned to Scotland and the castle was never completed. Caernarfon lost its defensive and administrative importance after the Act of Union in the 16th century. The castle is packed with interest and there is much to explore, including the Museum of the Royal Welsh Fusiliers.

A illustrated manuscript recording the marriage in 1307 of Edward II, who was born at Caernarfon Castle, to Isabella of France.

Caldicot began as a motte castle with two baileys, built beside a stream, probably in the 11th century. The present castle, erected by the Earl of Hereford, developed from the early 13th century into a stirrup-shaped stone enclosure with high walls, flanking towers, an unusual gatehouse and a cylindrical great tower erected on the motte. More building took place during the next century and includes the 14th-century gatehouse which is rectangular with square turrets at each end and handsome accommodation, as it was built as a residential structure. The castle was bought and restored in the middle of the 19th century. The restoration made it even more picturesque and today the castle is the excellent focal point of a 25ha (55-acre) country park.

LOCATION: MONMOUTHSHIRE
MAP REF: ST 487885
OPEN: LOCAL AUTHORITY: MAR–OCT DAILY

CAMLAIS

Also known as Cwm Camlais, this motte castle was built on a rocky mound more than 305m (1,000ft) above sea level on the wild and windswept edge of Mynyth Illtyd. The motte had a cylindrical tower, of which some ruins remain. The property is privately owned.

LOCATION: POWYS
MAP REF: SN 956260

CAMMAIS

Alternatively called Nevern or Nanhyfer, Cammais was a motte castle. It took advantage of its position, but with the addition of a rock-cut ditch, as well as the actual castle walls and mound. A stone square tower, among other buildings, was added in the late 12th century. Earthworks remain.

LOCATION: NEVERN, PEMBROKESHIRE
MAP REF: SN 082401

CANDLESTON

This fortified manor house dates from the 14th century. It had a polygonal courtyard enclosing a square tower, and more domestic buildings were added later. The manor was built by the Cantelupes, a powerful Norman family. The house was occupied until the 19th century. Extensive ruins remain.

LOCATION: NR BRIDGEND, MID-GLAMORGAN
MAP REF: SS 871772

CARDIFF

Cardiff began as a motte castle, raised by about 1080 on the site of a Roman fort by the Norman Lord of Gloucester. The motte is over 12m (40ft) tall and in the 12th century a 12-sided shell enclosure was erected on the motte with a tower-like projection on one side. Henry I imprisoned his eldest brother Robert, Duke of Normandy, at Cardiff (c.1110–34). Among the medieval additions were the Black Tower built in the 1200s below the motte and connected to the motte by a wing wall, an octagonal tower, c.1420s, on the south side of the shell enclosure and a substantial gatehouse linked to the Black Tower by a massive wall across the bailey. Later, apartments were raised in the bailey including a range against the western wall, substantially remodelled in the 18th and 19th centuries. Cardiff is a very good example of how an earth-and-timber motte castle was converted to a stone fortress. It has passed through the hands of some of the most powerful families in the land, including the de Clares and, in the 14th century, the Despensers. The castle was attacked and held by the Royalists for

A detail of the ornate ceiling of the Arab Room at Cardiff Castle, decorated with 22-carat gold leaf. Architect William Burges' decorative hand is evident throughout the castle.

most of the Civil War. Then in the 19th century, the fabulously wealthy 3rd Marquess of Bute lavished money on his castle at Cardiff, employing architect William Burges to remodel it in the Gothic Revival style.

This is a superbly satisfying castle to visit, with features from every part of its development, culminating in the glorious 19th-century decoration and furnishings.

LOCATION: CARDIFF
MAP REF: ST 180767
OPEN: CARDIFF COUNTY COUNCIL: DAILY

CARDIGAN

There were two castles with this name: a Norman enclosure of c.1093 (at SN 164464) was converted to stone by the Welsh who sold it to King John in 1199. In 1231 Llywelyn the Great took and destroyed it. Cardigan town was recovered by the English c.1240 and a castle built near the older structure. This may have included the curtain wall and flanking towers, and the cylindrical great tower. Private site.

LOCATION: CEREDIGION
MAP REFS: SN 177459 AND SN 164464

CAREW

Carew stands on a rock above the shore overlooking a rare tidal mill where the River Carew enters the sea. It began as an earthwork castle early in the 12th century. Later that century the original gatehouse was altered to make a tower, and later still, a square-plan curtain wall was built round the tower. The curtain had four large flanking towers of various shapes, two of which were cylindrical on spur bases. It was in the late 13th century when an outer ward with its own gatehouse into the main enclosure was added. A great hall and imposing porch was added when the enclosure was altered in the 14th and 15th centuries, converting the castle into a grand mansion with more alterations in the 16th century. Carew was badly damaged in the Civil War, and by 1685 it had been abandoned.

The setting, and nearby tidal mill and beautiful Carew Cross, make this an excellent place to visit.

LOCATION: PEMBROKESHIRE
MAP REF: SN 045037
OPEN: PEMBROKESHIRE COAST NATIONAL PARK AUTHORITY: APR–OCT DAILY

CARMARTHEN

Carmarthen began as a 12th-century Norman motte castle. It was attacked several times by the Welsh and was necessarily strengthened in 1181–3. In 1215 Llywelyn the Great destroyed it, but it was rebuilt with stonework. Carmarthen was an administrative centre and the castle was maintained. Then, Owain Glyndwr captured it c.1403 and held it for six years. The gatehouse is one of the features that can be seen today. The site is in the centre of Carmarthen.

LOCATION: CAMARTHENSHIRE
MAP REF: SN 413420

CARREG CENNEN

This powerful courtyard castle stands on a 91.5m (300ft) high limestone crag overlooking the Towy valley. The stonework was begun in the late 13th century with the inner enclosure and a long range along the east wall and including a hall, the gatehouse and the cylindrical tower on the north-west corner. A covered gallery along the cliffside leads to a 'secret' cave that may have contained a source of fresh water. Carreg Cennen is very much a ruin, but its layout and sophisticated defences are clear. It was severely damaged by Owain Glyndwr, who destroyed most of the defences early in the 15th century. It was a refuge for a number of Lancastrians during the Wars of the Roses and finally rendered useless as a castle by the Yorkists after their victory at Mortimer's Cross in 1461. This is one of the most beautifully set of all Welsh castles, with truly breathtaking views across the valley from the parapets.

LOCATION: NR LLANDEILO, CARMARTHENSHIRE
MAP REF: SN 668191
OPEN: CADW: DAILY ALL YEAR

CASTELL CARNDOCHAN

This small Welsh-built castle of the mid-13th century is set on a crag above the Afon Lliw valley. There is a tower at the south-west end.

LOCATION: NR DOLGELLAU, GWYNEDD
MAP REF: SH 846306

CASTELL COCH

A fairy-tale reconstruction of an earlier medieval castle was undertaken here in the 19th century for the 3rd Marquis of Bute. A unique experience.

LOCATION: CARDIFF
MAP REF: ST 131826
OPEN: CADW: DAILY

Owain Glyndwr

The name of Glyndwr resonates through Welsh history. A dispute with an English neighbour who had annexed common land led Glyndwr to take up arms. The Welsh rallied to fight the English and they attacked town after town. By 1403 Glyndwr was in control of much of Wales. He convened a Welsh Parliament and for four years ruled Wales. Glyndwr's fate is unknown but his name lives on.

CARREGHOFA

An earthwork enclosure of c.1100; ownership changed often between Welsh and English. Traces of earthworks can be seen today.

LOCATION: POWYS
MAP REF: SJ 255222

CASTELL-Y-BERE

This Welsh-built castle was raised on a spur below Cadair Idris. It resembles the medieval German hill castles such as Staufen. It was begun probably in 1221 by Llywelyn the Great (c.1196–1240), and comprised an irregular curtained enclosure with flanking towers. Instead of a drawbridge over the moat there was a fixed timber pontoon. It was formidable because of its position. In 1283, Bere was seized by Edward I's men and a stretch of tall curtain wall was erected round the outside of the original castle. The castle was abandoned after c.1295. The remains are very ruinous but most impressive.

LOCATION: ABERGYNOLWYN, GWYNEDD
MAP REF: SH 667086
OPEN: CADW: OPEN ACCESS

CEFNLLYS

A large castle once stood here, inside an Iron Age hill fort. The tumbled remains of two mounds give excellent views of the surrounding countryside.

LOCATION: LLANDRINDOD WELLS, POWYS
MAP REF: SO 089614

CHEPSTOW

Begun in 1067 as one of the very first stone castles in Britain, Chepstow stands on a natural limestone ridge on a steep vertical cliff falling into the River Wye. It was started by William FitzOsbern, Earl of Hertford, who also built the first stone great tower in Britain here. This was a substantial quadrilateral two-floor building, about 30.5 x 12m (100 x 40ft), standing on a splayed plinth. A thick curtain wall was built by William Marshal, Earl of Pembroke, c.1190–1220 on the east side of the ridge, with cylindrical towers and a gate to divide the central bailey from the lower bailey. Soon after, c.1225–50, the great tower was heightened, the upper bailey was constructed and next to it the barbican with cylindrical towers. The lower bailey was given a curtain and a twin cylindrical-towered gatehouse (with a prison in the northern tower). Also during the 13th century, a huge D-end tower (19m/63ft) was built in the lower bailey (later called Marten's Tower after Henry Marten, a signatory to the death warrant of Charles I, was imprisoned there after the Restoration of Charles II). Chepstow overlooked a harbour on the Wye which meant the castle could be provisioned by ships coming from Bristol. Never attacked in the Middle Ages, the castle was besieged twice in the Civil War as a Royalist stronghold. Much renovation was undertaken in the 17th century to equip the castle for guns and musketry. The ruins stretch magnificently along the Wye, and parts of the original stonework from 1067 can still be seen.

LOCATION: MONMOUTHSHIRE
MAP REF: ST 533941
OPEN: CADW: DAILY

CHIRK

In the 1280s the Mortimer family began a lordship castle here with a view across Cheshire towards the Pennines. The fortress became a quadrangle with squat but substantial cylindrical corner towers and half-round towers, which remain in the present mansion. It is thought that the work went on into the 1320s when Roger Mortimer was disgraced and put to death. In 1595 the castle was sold to Thomas Myddleton who remodelled it; his descendants still live here. Chirk was besieged in the Civil War but was surrendered to prevent destruction. The castle, gardens and parkland are open in summer. The castle's interior is magnificent, with sumptuous furnishings and decoration.

LOCATION: CLWYD
MAP REF: SJ 268380
OPEN: NATIONAL TRUST: MAR–OCT WED–SUN

CILGERRAN

Built on a rocky promontory of great natural strength overlooking the Teifi Gorge, with rock-cut ditches at the south end, Cilgerran began as a Norman enclosure castle with an outer bailey early in the 12th century. About a century later, a powerful stone castle was built making the Norman enclosure an inner enclosure and raising another curtain round the old outer bailey. Cylindrical towers were built into the inner curtain c.1233 and a strong gate inserted. By the 1320s the castle was ruinous. To counter a threatened invasion from the French, repairs were ordered by Edward III in 1377, one of the king's last acts. Owain Glyndwr attacked Cilgerran early in the 1400s, but enough work must have been carried out as the garrison here held out and repelled the attackers.

LOCATION: NR CARDIGAN, CEREDIGION
MAP REF: SN 195431
OPEN: CADW: DAILY

CLYRO

Only fragments remain of this castle on a hillock that was surrounded by good ditching. It is not clear when the castle was first raised.

LOCATION: NR HAY-ON-WYE, POWYS
MAP REF SO 214436

COITY

'Marry my daughter and you can have the castle of Coity without having to fight for it.' This, according to legend, was the offer of Welsh Lord Morgan to the Norman knight, Payn de Turbeville in the 11th century. Then, Coity was simply a circular earthwork enclosure with good banks and ditches. Stonework was later added, including a curtain round the greater part of the inner bailey (partly surrounded by a moat) and a rectangular great tower. The ribbed vaults and other internal features date from the 14th century when the great hall was built. Further additions came in the 16th century but by the 17th century the castle was falling into ruins. Modern buildings now partly encircle this evocative and interesting ruin.

LOCATION: BRIDGEND
MAP REF: SS 923816

COLWYN

There have been two castles on this site, which was originally a Roman fort. A motte castle was built here in 1093. That was destroyed in 1196 and replaced by a stone castle, of which no traces remain. The castle changed hands several times during the 12th and 13th centuries, but by the 15th century it was already a ruin. The motte and earthwork are on private farmland.

LOCATION: LLANSANTFFRAID, POWYS
MAP REF: SO 108540

CONWY

One of Edward I's second tranche of castles in Wales, Conwy was designed by architectural genius and innovator Master James of St George and completed very quickly in 1283–7. The bill came to nearly £20,000, the biggest sum spent on any castle in Wales between 1277 and 1304. At the end of it, Edward I was presented with an almost perfect structure, the most compact agglomerate of turretry in the British Isles. Tailored to fit the rock site chosen for guarding the entrance to the River Conwy, the castle was a vast enclosure divided into an inner and an outer ward, separated by a thick wall with, at each end, one of the eight flanking towers. The towers themselves are massive, over 21.5m (70ft), well over 9m (30ft) in diameter with walls up to 4.5m (15ft) thick, and like great towers or keeps they have several storeys equipped with rooms and staircases. The castle was part of an impressive walled town with its circuit of walls guarded by 22 towers, and this massive construction represented all that Edward I stood for – strength, terror, dominion, permanence. The castle was hated by the Welsh, yet it was not besieged until the Civil War. Conwy was used sporadically during the 14th century and then gradually began to decay over the years. In 1609 it was described in an official report as 'utterly decayed' and after its Civil War slighting it was left as an impressive, but nevertheless empty, shell. This extraordinary building is a World Heritage Site and is one of Britain's most impressive castle ruins.

LOCATION: CONWY, GWYNEDD
MAP REF: SH 781777
OPEN: CADW: DAILY

CRICCIETH

Raised by the Welsh during the reign of Llywelyn the Great, Criccieth began as a curtain enclosure of grey stone on a high peninsula. Nearly half the perimeter was protected by a steep cliff above the sea shore. Ditches and banks were cut and raised on the remaining sides. The enclosure was covered by a rectangular great tower at the south-west corner, let into the curtain, and by a second rectangular tower at the north corner, also let into the curtain. Most of the work was completed before 1250. More buildings were added during the reigns of Edwards I and II. It was captured by Owain Glyndwr in 1404, and appears to have been burned. A splendid seaside setting makes it well worth a visit.

LOCATION: GWYNEDD
MAP REF: SH 500377
OPEN: CADW: DAILY

CRICKHOWELL

This Norman motte castle was probably added to in the early 13th century, when it was given a stone shell enclosure on the summit. It possibly had a gate at bailey level. A pair of towers (cylindrical and rectangular) in fragmentary state are close to the motte. The castle was attacked by Owain Glyndwr and probably allowed to deteriorate after that.

LOCATION: POWYS
MAP REF: SO 217182

DEGANNWY

Twin hillocks here were made into a double motte castle c.1090 and linked by ramparts and ditching. This was taken by the Welsh in the 12th century and was in the hands of Llywelyn the Great c.1200. It was taken again by the English c.1210, refortified with timber, but retaken by Llywelyn c.1213. It was attacked in 1241 by Henry III and destroyed by Llywelyn's sons before its capture. Henry rebuilt it, but finally, in 1257, Llywelyn the Last recaptured and destroyed it. As with so many Welsh castles, the setting alone makes a visit here worthwhile.

LOCATION: GWYNEDD
MAP REF: SH 781794
OPEN: LOCAL AUTHORITY: OPEN ACCESS

DENBIGH

There was a Welsh motte castle here of unknown date but it was taken by Edward I's army. Henry de Lacy was granted the right to build Denbigh Castle, which arose during 1282–1311 in two stages. De Lacy died in 1311 before its completion. The south and west curtain walls were erected first and then the enclosure was completed from 1286 on. Domestic apartments were raised in the enclosure, including a great hall with a dais, and a barbican was added to the south postern tower. Access was through an entrance in the curtain wall. The great gatehouse, the most imposing feature of the whole castle, dominates the ruins today although much of it has disappeared. The castle was besieged during the Civil War, in an assault lasting nearly six months in 1646. The Royalist garrison surrendered and the castle was used as a prison for captured Royalists.

LOCATION: DENBIGHSHIRE
MAP REF: SJ 051657
OPEN: CADW: DAILY

DINAS BRAN (CASTELL)

An early castle of Welsh construction, probably 13th century, Dinas Bran was a stone-walled enclosure, roughly rectangular, containing a square great tower. The curtain wall was flanked by a large D-ended tower, inserted in the 13th century. There was also a twin-towered gatehouse, likewise probably dating from the 13th century. The castle was taken from the Welsh before 1282. Its setting is outstanding.

LOCATION: LLANGOLLEN, DENBIGHSHIRE
MAP REF: SJ 223430
OPEN: LOCAL AUTHORITY: OPEN ACCESS

DINAS EMRYS (CASTELL)

Connected with some of the earliest Welsh legends concerning Merlin, this evocative ruin is fragile and difficult to reach. It stands on the site of an Iron Age fort and preserves traces of both native Welsh and Norman construction.

LOCATION: NR BEDDGELERT, GWYNEDD
MAP REF: SH 606492

DINAS POWYS CASTLE

Two structures are at this site: an earthwork enclosure at ST 148722 is surrounded by a rubble-reinforced bank on which a wooden palisade was set, with a ditch cut in rock. The second castle (ST 152716) had a square late 12th-century tower beside a later rectangular enclosure of stone. Very little remains.

LOCATION: ST ANDREWS MAJOR,
VALE OF GLAMORGAN
MAP REF: ST 152716

ROYAL CASTLES

THE STORY OF THE CASTLES OF BRITAIN AND IRELAND IS INEXTRICABLY LINKED WITH THE CHANGING FORTUNES OF KINGS AND QUEENS. AS MONARCHS CAME AND WENT, SO CASTLES WERE BUILT, DESTROYED AND REBUILT, ACCORDING TO THE CIRCUMSTANCES OF THE TIME.

William the Conqueror depended on his barons, and on the castles they built, to impose Norman rule and to keep rebellion firmly under control. They did this very successfully for the most part, although Wales, Scotland and Ireland were often barely under control, and hostilities were close to the surface. Open rebellion was quashed with appalling ruthlessness.

As the centuries wound on, and society became more settled, castles were often used by monarchs as temporary headquarters when they toured the country. Their retinues often ran into hundreds of people – servants, advisers, soldiers, secretaries, tax collectors and the like. All needed housing and feeding, so castles were not only bustling at such times, they were also at the heart of local economies. Foodstuffs were required in huge quantities for both men and horses, but also needed was bedding material, clothing, and all of the other paraphernalia required by what amounted to a small travelling town.

The kitchen at Windsor Castle in 1819. Today, the modern Windsor kitchen still caters for the royal family and for banquets hosted by Queen Elizabeth II.

A bird's-eye view of Windsor Castle in 1660 by Wenceslaus Hollar showing its layout and listing all the major rooms and chapels. The great mound, or motte, is clearly seen, as are the two baileys, with St George's Chapel on the left.

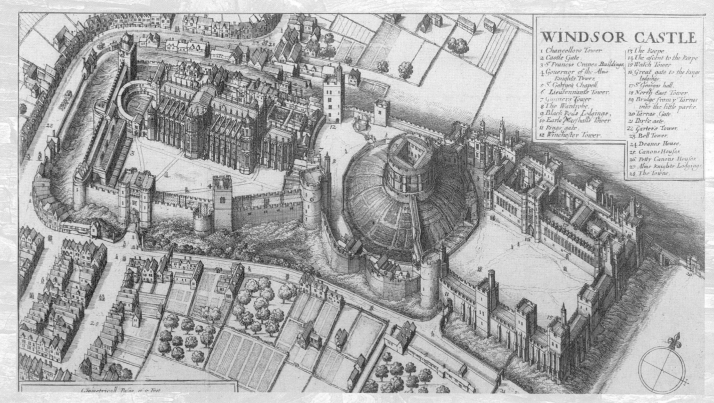

The most famous royal castle is the Tower of London. Begun by William the Conqueror, it was added to and changed by successive monarchs. It was a royal residence for 500 years, and has served the monarchy in many ways – as storehouse, armoury, mint, treasure vault and prison. The Crown Jewels are still kept there, as are such items as the armour of Henry VIII.

Today's primary royal castle is Windsor. It is the oldest surviving continuously occupied castle in the world. William the Conqueror built it to guard the western approaches to London.

Much remains unchanged at Windsor: the outer walls follow the same lines as those erected by William, and his great motte stands at the core of the castle. Many monarchs have changed Windsor, however. St George's Chapel is one of its primary buildings. This was begun by Edward IV and completed by Henry VIII. No fewer than ten British monarchs are buried here.

George IV made many changes, both inside and out, transforming its exterior into a vision of Gothic perfection with the addition of towers and turrets. Queen Victoria and Prince Albert spent much time at Windsor, and it was they who opened parts of it to the public for the first time.

The great fire at Windsor Castle in 1992 damaged or destroyed a fifth of this great complex, but restoration was completed by 1997, allowing this most special of castles a new life in an age where the future of monarchy itself is in more doubt than the future of castles.

The Highland Home: *sheet music cover picturing Balmoral Castle in Scotland, then the favourite residence of Queen Victoria (1819–1901). The castle is a 19th-century re-creation of the romance sought after by medieval lords. It remains a much loved retreat for the royal family.*

DINEFWR

A polygonal inner stone enclosure was raised on the top of a cliff here in the late 12th century or early 13th century. Inside the enclosure, a cylindrical keep was built at the east, between 1150 and 1250. The north side had a defensive moat cut out of the solid rock. There was also an outer enclosure. Domestic buildings were added in later periods, after the conquest of Wales by King Edward I. Dinefwr was besieged c.1402 by Owain Glyndwr but not taken. Today, the remains stand in Dinefwr (Dynevor) Park. The summer house on the great tower is a folly added in the late 17th or early 18th century. Some of the buildings and the wall walk have been restored.

LOCATION: LLANDEILO, CARMARTHENSHIRE
MAP REF: SN 611217
OPEN: CADW: DAILY (NATIONAL TRUST FEE MAY BE PAYABLE FOR PARK ENTRY)

DOLBADARN

From its boomerang-shaped platform between the Peris and Padarn lakes, Dolbadarn Castle commanded the entrance to the Llanberis Pass. The east side of the platform slopes down to the Padarn and the west is protected by a sheer rock cliff. The cylindrical great tower, forming part of the curtain round the site, is of slate and grit rubble. Its walls are 2–2.5m (7–8ft) thick and contain a spiral staircase. The height once reached nearly 15m (50ft). Dolbadarn was probably erected over several years by Llywelyn the Great in the early 13th century. It was abandoned after Llywelyn the Last's death at the end of 1282.

LOCATION: NR LLANBERIS
MAP REF: SH 586598
OPEN: CADW: OPEN ACCESS

DOLFORWYN

A Welsh-built mid- to late 13th-century castle on a ridge, with a stone curtain enclosure of rectangular plan. It was probably built by Llywelyn the Last. Excavations revealed details of a square great tower and a round tower.

DOLWYDDELAN

Built upon a rock ridge on the slopes of Moel Siabod, Dolwyddelan was built by Llywelyn ap Iorwerth in the 13th century. Surrounded by rock-cut ditches, the castle is protected on all sides by its fine position. The first building was a rectangular great tower, Welsh-built on Norman lines, with its entrance at the first floor. The approach was covered by a forebuilding which had a drawbridge over a pit to deflect direct assault on the tower door. At first the tower had two floors; its third floor, battlements and new roofline are of a later date. The castle rock was skirted by a stone curtain whose two arms projected from either end of the great tower (north-east and south-west) along to two ends of a second rectangular tower. This was from c.1270 and also had two floors and used part of the north and west curtain as two of its four walls.

The ruins are substantial and the restored keep houses an exhibition. As with so many Welsh castles, the views from here are magnificent.

LOCATION: CONWY, GWYNEDD
MAP REF: SH 722523
OPEN: CADW: DAILY

The castle was taken by Edward I in 1278. Today, the walls are visible but many are reduced to stumps.

LOCATION: BETTWS CEDEWAIN, POWYS
MAP REF: SO 152950
OPEN: CADW: OPEN ACCESS

DRYSLWYN

Dryslwyn was a Welsh-built castle of 12th-century origin on the possible site of an early Celtic hill fort. It was a large earthwork enclosure holding three stonework enclosures in line. The inner ward held a large rectangular building, discovered in 1980, with a cellar. This was a great hall, begun in the 12th century and which was altered over the next two centuries.

The castle figured in an interesting siege in 1287. Its holder, Rhys ap Maredudd, rose against the English and Edward I besieged the castle. A detachment led by Lord Stafford dug a tunnel to come up under one of the towers, but the earth collapsed. Most of the men, including Lord Stafford, were asphyxiated. Some of those behind, however, dug through the fallen earth and entered the chapel.

This dramatic hill-top ruin is accessible today by a public footpath. The view from the top is wonderful and well worth the effort.

LOCATION: LLANDEILO, CARMARTHENSHIRE
MAP REF: SN 554203
OPEN: CADW: OPEN ACCESS

DYSERTH

A castle was built by the English c.1241–2 near the present house (not in this gazetteer). It had two baileys, the outer one with masonry for part of its circumference, the inner one enclosed in stone, a twin-towered gatehouse and two more polygonal towers. The site commanded an approach to the Vale of Clwyd. Dyserth was captured in 1263 by Llywelyn the Last, who demolished it. The ruins have been used as a quarry, and practically nothing remains. The site was excavated in the last century.

LOCATION: DENBIGHSHIRE
MAP REF: SJ 060799

EWLOE

A stone castle was built here in the early 1200s by Llywelyn ap Gruffudd. The first building was probably a substantial two-storey great tower, which had a forebuilding along its south wall. The inner bailey was partly enclosed by a stone curtain. The outer (lower) bailey, polygonal in plan with a stone curtain, had a cylindrical two-storey west tower. The outer work was probably by Llywelyn the Last, in the late 1250s. Today, Ewloe is surrounded by trees; its ruins are substantial enough to discern the layout.

LOCATION: NR HAWARDEN, FLINTSHIRE
MAP REF: SJ 288675
OPEN: CADW: OPEN ACCESS

FLINT

Flint was the first of the Edwardian castles to be built in Wales during the king's campaign of 1277. It was planned, like Rhuddlan, to be associated with a fortified town nearby

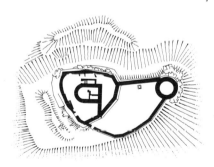

and, also like Rhuddlan, was given direct access to tidal waters. The roughly rectangular stone enclosure has three substantial cylindrical corner towers and, on the fourth corner, separated by its own moat, was a huge great tower protected by the River Dee. The cylindrical great tower was the dominating feature: the mural chambers included a chapel, kitchen, garderobes and residential rooms. Construction was spread mainly over the years 1277–86 and cost a little over £6,000. Henry Bolingbroke (soon to be Henry IV) captured Richard II at Flint before forcing him to return to London and abdicate. In the Civil War the castle changed hands several times, surrendering finally to Parliament in 1646. It was slighted so thoroughly that an eye-witness stated six years afterwards, it was 'almost buried in its own ruins'. However, there is enough left to see the general plan of the castle and the cylindrical great tower.

LOCATION: FLINTSHIRE
MAP REF: SJ 247733
OPEN: CADW: DAILY

FONMON

Founded c.1200, this was a stonework structure with two round towers and one square tower which was absorbed into a 17th-century mansion that was further modified in the 18th century. The mansion is still a home; the property has only changed hands once in its 800-year history. Today, visitors can enjoy the wonderful gardens and view some of the rooms.

LOCATION: PENMARK, VALE OF GLAMORGAN
MAP REF: ST 047681
OPEN: PRIVATE: APR–SEPT TUES–WED PM

GARN FADRYN

A small fort inside an Iron Age fort, probably built c.1190. There are scant remains today.

LOCATION: NR GARNFADRYN, GWYNEDD
MAP REF: SH 278352

GROSMONT

Grosmont is an interestingly planned castle built on a large mound on the main border route between Wales and England. It is a compact enclosure of stone surrounded by a moat which contained a rectangular hall tower, a gatehouse building at the south-east corner and a rectangular building with a D-ended tower at its west end. A stone curtain with two semi-cylindrical flanking towers completed the enclosure. The earliest structure was the hall tower, built c.1210, on the site of an earlier earthwork castle. Together with the gatehouse and the four-storeyed cylindrical towers of c.1220–40, these were all partly the work of Hubert de Burgh who held the 'Three Castles' of Grosmont, Skenfrith and White Castle at Llantrilio. The northern building between the hall tower and the D-ended tower was built in the 14th century when the castle was in the hands of the Lancasters. Grosmont was attacked by Owain Glyndwr in 1404–5 but the Welsh attackers were eventually defeated as reinforcements were sent from Hereford. The castle was falling into ruin by the 16th century.

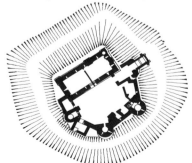

LOCATION: NR ABERGAVENNY, MONMOUTHSHIRE
MAP REF: SO 405244
OPEN: CADW: OPEN ACCESS

HARLECH

The second phase of Edward I's fortress-construction programme in Wales in the 1280s embraced four of the biggest castles in Britain – Beaumaris, Caernarfon, Conwy and Harlech. One of the two concentric castles, Harlech, designed by Master James of St George, was completed between 1283–90. It was one of the architect's most splendid creations and from 1290–93 he was its constable, a job that gave him status as well as the time to oversee the other castles being built to his plans. Harlech's design was simple yet immensely formidable: the dominant structure is the gatehouse, a massive, oblong structure like a great tower with three storeys and flanking twin cylindrical towers out front and inwards, towards the inner bailey, and two more cylindrical towers, both containing fine residential apartments. Harlech's impregnability was tested in 1294, when it was attacked by Welsh patriots led by Prince Madog ap Llywelyn – just 37 men beat off the assault. However, Owain Glyndwr had more success when he besieged the castle in 1404. Harlech was the last Royalist stronghold to fall during the Civil War and when it fell the Royalist cause was lost and the Parliamentary forces slighted it. This World Heritage Site is well worth a visit for its superb architecture and setting.

LOCATION: GWYNEDD
MAP REF: SH 581312
OPEN: CADW: DAILY

HAVERFORDWEST

Strategically placed upon a ridge above the River Cleddau, this castle has two enclosures. The inner enclosure contains two towers, one of which is a great tower of unusual plan. The stonework is local gritstone. The castle may have begun as a stone structure in c.1100; its curtain wall is very thick. The castle was attacked by Owain Glyndwr, whose army was assisted by a force of some 3,000 Frenchmen, but the garrison held out. The town museum is now on the site.

LOCATION: PEMBROKESHIRE
MAP REF: SM 953157

HAWARDEN

This was one of the four lordship castles in north Wales built or fortified by Edward I in the years before the conquest of the region (c.1277–82). It began as a motte castle and received stonework in the 13th century. A small round tower was added as part of the Edwardian improvement, and a complex barbican in the 14th century. Hawarden was slighted by Cromwell in 1647–8. The ruins stand in the grounds of a private estate.

LOCATION: FLINTSHIRE
MAP REF: SJ 319653
OPEN: PRIVATE

HAY-ON-WYE

Two earthwork sites stand close to one another at Hay. One was a motte castle and the other an enclosure castle. The motte, at SO 226422, was built in the early 1100s and was destroyed in 1216 by King John. The other site, SO 229423, has stonework remains that are incorporated into an Elizabethan period mansion, and was an enclosure of timber and earth converted to stone in the 12th and 13th centuries, with a curtain wall and a square gate-tower. The remains house part of the famous assemblage of secondhand bookshops.

LOCATION: POWYS
MAP REF: SO 229423
OPEN: PRIVATE

HEN DOMEN

Also called Old Montgomery Castle, Hen Domen has undergone a lot of excavation. First it was a motte castle of c.1071, built by Roger de Montgomeri, one of the Conqueror's principal generals. It is a motte astride the line of the oval bailey. There was a timber palisade round the base of the motte as well as a ditch. The whole castle had a double ditch, and access from the bailey to the motte top was by a timber bridge. A number of wooden buildings from varying periods have been revealed, including a chapel and a hall, as well as towers along the wooden palisade. It declined after about 1223. The site is private, but the grass-covered motte can be seen from the road.

LOCATION: NR MONTGOMERY, POWYS
MAP REF: SO 214980

HOLT

There is little to see of this lordship castle built on the bank of the River Dee soon after 1282 by John de Warenne, Earl of Surrey, on land granted by Edward I. It was a single enclosure castle with flanking round towers. It was demolished in the late 17th century, and the stonework was used for Eaton Hall in Cheshire.

LOCATION: WREXHAM
MAP REF: SJ 411537
OPEN: WREXHAM COUNTY BOROUGH MUSEUM: OPEN ACCESS

HOLYWELL

A small motte castle was raised here in the early 13th century. It is known more locally as Castle Hill.

LOCATION: CLWYD
MAP REF: SJ 186762

HUMPHREY

A motte castle of c.1110 founded by a follower (called Humphrey) of Gilbert de Clare. It was raised on a spur of land in the Teifi Valley, then destroyed by the Welsh c.1137 and rebuilt in 1151. It is possible to view the site from a footpath.

LOCATION: NR LLANDYSUL, CEREDIGION
MAP REF: SN 440477

KIDWELLY

The striking ruins of Kidwelly Castle stand on a bluff beside the estuary of the River Gwendraeth. The castle began as a large Norman earthwork of c.1106 consisting of a banked, roughly oblong site surrounded by ditching with an oval site in the centre. The first major stonework dates from the 1270s when the de Chaworth family held the castle. A square curtain with cylindrical towers on the four corners was built, and the enclosure was later surrounded on three sides by a second, lower stone enclosure curtain with flanking half-cylindrical towers; this second curtain, dating from the 14th century, made the castle concentric on three sides. A chapel tower, supported on a spur base

KENFIG

This castle was built by the Normans, probably in the late 12th century. The great tower stood on a splayed plinth under an earth mound and was surrounded by a narrow curtain wall. Kenfig and its surrounding town were attacked and burned by the Welsh on several occasions. The scant ruins of the castle are all that remain of the medieval settlement of Kenfig. The town is now buried under the sands of Kenfig Burrows which overwhelmed it in the 15th century. The site is within a nature reserve.

LOCATION: NEATH PORT TALBOT
MAP REF: SS 801827

and built into the slope of the bluff, was added, along with domestic buildings. The substantial south-west gatehouse was begun at the end of the 14th century and not completed until 1422. It had three storeys and spacious accommodation, probably for the castle's constable. By then Kidwelly was an important administrative centre for the Duchy of Lancaster. The castle withstood an attack in 1403 by Owain Glyndwr. Today, there is a site exhibition and audio tours guide visitors around this splendid castle.

LOCATION: CARMARTHENSHIRE
MAP REF: 409070
OPEN: CADW: DAILY

KNIGHTON

There are two early motte castle sites at Knighton, one in town near the church, and the other a few hundred yards away near the river (SO 290722). The first-named is thought to have lasted until the 1260s when it was destroyed, probably by the Welsh.

LOCATION: POWYS
MAP REF: SO 284722
OPEN: PRIVATE

LAUGHARNE

A castle was built here in the 12th century, but it is difficult to ascertain its shape. Later, probably in the 13th century, rebuilding added a cylindrical great tower, another tower and a gatehouse, although the latter might be a 14th-century addition. The inner bailey was converted to a mansion in the 16th century by Sir John Perrott, owner of Carew Castle. The existing medieval gatehouse has four floors and a Perpendicular-style arch. In the Civil War Laugharne was held by the Royalists but fell to Parliament and was left to decay. The ruins, in a beautiful setting by the River Taf estuary, have recently been restored.

LOCATION: CARMARTHENSHIRE
MAP REF: SN302107
OPEN: CADW: APR–SEP DAILY

KNUCKLAS

A castle on a hill site that was possibly an Iron Age hill fort; the prime remains are a small square stone block with what appears to be round corner turrets, dating from around the 13th century. It was besieged in 1262 and the garrison immediately capitulated.

LOCATION: BEGUILDY, POWYS
MAP REF: SO 250745

LAMPETER

Otherwise known as Llan Ystyffan, a Norman motte castle was raised here; it was destroyed in 1136. The location of the bailey is unknown.

The remains – consisting of a green mound – are in the grounds of St David's College, Lampeter.

LOCATION: CEREDIGION
MAP REF: SN579483

LLANBLETHIAN

Otherwise called St Quintin's Castle, this was a late 13th- or early 14th-century stone enclosure with flanking towers, one square, two cylindrical and a twin-towered gatehouse (now the main remains). A great tower from the early 12th century appears to have been incorporated into the enclosure.

LOCATION: VALE OF GLAMORGAN
MAP REF: SS 989742

LLANDAFF

Llandaff was a bishopric castle and is believed to have been destroyed by Owain Glyndwr c.1402. Two of its three towers (one square, the other cylindrical) remain.

LOCATION: CARDIFF
MAP REF: ST 156780

LLANDEILO TALYBONT

A motte castle was raised here in the 12th century; only earthworks remain.

LOCATION: SWANSEA
MAP REF: SN 587027

LLANDOVERY

This castle was founded by the Norman lord, Richard FitzPons in the early 12th century. Today's visitors can freely access the mound and ruins.

LOCATION: CARMARTHENSHIRE
MAP REF: SN767342

LLANELLI

Also known as Carnwillion Castle, this motte castle has been almost wholly submerged in the reservoir at Llanelli.

LOCATION: CARMARTHENSHIRE
MAP REF: SN501004

LLANFAIR DISCOED

Llanfair Discoed was a small, square-plan enclosure with curtain, cylindrical turrets and part of a square-plan gatehouse of the mid-13th century. Later additions obscured the original work, but the remains are overgrown.

LOCATION: CAERWENT, MONMOUTHSHIRE
MAP REF: ST 445924

LLANGADOG

A motte castle with a narrow ditch was raised on this site in the 12th century. The bailey is horseshoe-shaped and was at one time bordered on one side by the River Sawdde. The castle was taken by the Welsh c.1209. A modern house has been built in the bailey.

LOCATION: CARMARTHENSHIRE
MAP REF: SN 709276

LLANGIBBY

Also known as Tregrug Castle, 14th-century Llangibby stands on a high site and was one single huge enclosure with a large gatehouse and a rectangular great tower. There were also four turrets on the walls and a second (smaller) gateway .

LOCATION: LLANGYBI FAWR, MONMOUTHSHIRE
MAP REF: ST 356974

LLANGYNWYDD

A small castle, probably of the 13th century, which may have been Welsh-built. Traces of a twin-towered gatehouse remain. The poet Wil Hopcyn was born here in the 18th century; his tragic love for a local girl is recorded in *The Maid of Cefn Ydfa*.

LOCATION: BRIDGEND
MAP REF: SS 853887

LLANQUIAN

There was a stone-revetted mound here. Its history is unknown but it is thought to have been a 12th-century earthwork castle, rebuilt in stone in the 13th century. The remains are on private land.

LOCATION: NR COWBRIDGE, BRIDGEND
MAP REF: ST 019744

LLANSTEFFAN

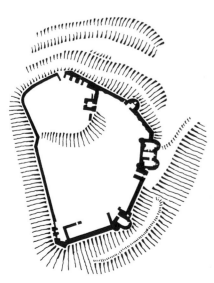

Llansteffan was an imposing double enclosure castle and its ruins make a dramatic gesture standing high above the golden sandy beaches of the coast below. The inner enclosure was the first structure, dating chiefly from the 12th century with early and mid-13th century completion. It was a simple irregular polygon of stone with a gate-tower standing on a ridge with all but one of its sides protected by natural scarping. The remaining side was given a ditch for protection. The outer enclosure was protected by a double ditch and was fortified in the 13th century with a stone curtain, flanking towers and a bastion at the eastern corner. Late in the 13th century the great gatehouse was erected in the southern side of the enclosure wall and much of it stands today. It was turned into a grand residence in the last years of the 15th century. The castle was frequently attacked and sometimes held by the Welsh, but for much of the Middle Ages it was in the hands of the de Camvilles. Owain Glyndwr captured it briefly in the 15th century. In later years it became a farmyard.

LOCATION: CARMARTHENSHIRE
MAP REF: SN 352102
OPEN: CADW: OPEN ACCESS

LLANTRISANT

The origins of this castle appear to go back to the early 13th century, when it was constructed with two baileys, the inner one smaller than the outer. The inner bailey contains fragments of wall and of a large cylindrical great tower thought to originate from the mid-13th century.

LOCATION: RHONDDA CYNON TAF
MAP REF: ST 047834
OPEN: LOCAL AUTHORITY: OPEN ACCESS

LLAWHADEN

A fortified palace was built by the Bishops of St Davids on the site of an earthwork enclosure of the 12th century. The palace was destroyed c.1192. Soon after, stonework was raised, including a small cylindrical tower and a curtained wall of irregular shape but following the line of the earlier earthwork. In the 1280s, Bishop Thomas Bek converted the castle into a palace, obliterating much of the earlier work, although there are still remains of the cylindrical tower and traces of the curtain. The new work produced a courtyard surrounded by buildings with two polygonal towers on two angles. A gatehouse was erected during the late 14th century, and its façade still stands to full height.

LOCATION: NR NARBERTH, PEMBROKESHIRE
MAP REF: SN 073174
OPEN: CADW: OPEN ACCESS

LOUGHOR

Today, this castle consists of a tower projecting from a curtain wall on a natural mound. The stonework is from the 13th to 14th centuries, raised on the 12th-century motte castle site originated by the Normans and then demolished c.1150 by the Welsh. The castle was repaired but demolished again in 1215. It is sited over the remains of a Roman fort.

LOCATION: SWANSEA
MAP REF: SS 564980
OPEN: CADW: OPEN ACCESS

MACHEN (CASTELL)

Also known as Castell Meredydd, this Welsh castle was built in the 13th century on a rocky ridge. Little remains. It had a cylindrical tower. The site is in the neighbourhood of a complex of ancient lead mines used by the Romans.

LOCATION: CAERPHILLY
MAP REF: ST 226887
OPEN: PRIVATE: VIEW FROM THE ROAD ONLY

MANORBIER

This was the birthplace in 1146 of Giraldus Cambrensis (Gerald of Wales), the celebrated Welsh scholar and chronicler who served Henry II, Richard I and John. The castle began as an earthwork of the late 11th century, and in the 12th century it received a square three-storeyed great tower. Other stone buildings were added, including a hall block, and by the 13th century it consisted of two high stone curtain enclosures in line, with flanking towers (cylindrical in the case of the outer enclosure) and with a strong square gatehouse. Giraldus described the castle as 'excellently well defended by turrets and bulwarks'. Manorbier's residential features were manifest, notably the state apartments in the inner enclosure, the fish-pond and the park. The castle is superbly sited on the beautiful Pembrokeshire coast, and thanks to a relatively peaceful history and the attentions of a 19th-century tenant, is in a good state of repair.

LOCATION: NR TENBY, PEMBROKESHIRE
MAP REF: SS 064978
OPEN: PRIVATE: EASTER–SEP DAILY

MEURIG

Also known as Castell Ystrad-Meurig, this is one of the few Cardigan castles to have been refortified with stone buildings and defences. It had a substantial great tower possibly 18.5m (60ft) square. Only fragments remain.

LOCATION: GWNNWS ISSA, CEREDIGION
MAP REF: SN 702675

MOLD

A late motte castle that retained its earthwork and timber structures right into the 13th century. The mound is in the town centre and accessible.

LOCATION: FLINTSHIRE
MAP REF: SJ 235644

MONMOUTH

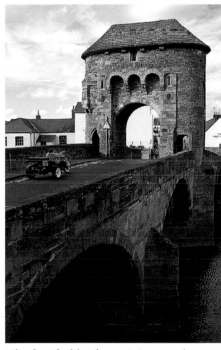

The fortified bridge at Monmouth

An earthwork enclosure castle was built here between 1067–71, above the Wye and Monnow rivers. In 1120–30, a rectangular two-storey hall tower was raised on the motte. In 1399 its owner, Henry Bolingbroke, became Henry IV; his son was born here. Monmouth was slighted in the Civil War. The ruined great tower and hall – the only remains – house a military museum.

LOCATION: MONMOUTHSHIRE
MAP REF: SO 507129
OPEN: REGIMENTAL MUSEUM: APR–OCT DAILY; NOV–MAR SAT–SUN)

MONTGOMERY

This was a stone double enclosure castle begun in the 1220s. It superseded Old Montgomery Castle (Hen Domen, q.v). It has been extensively excavated: Montgomery was built upon a promontory of greenstone running roughly north to south, the northern end protected by sheer rock cliffs. There were five wards, and buildings were added throughout the following centuries. The curtain walls were thick and were flanked by rounded turrets. Outside the south gatehouse was a rock-cut ditch crossed by a timber causeway.

LOCATION: POWYS
MAP REF: SO 221968
OPEN: CADW: OPEN ACCESS

MORGRAIG

Morgraig was never completed and was probably allowed to decay as early as the mid-13th century. It was a Welsh-built castle.

LOCATION: CARDIFF
MAP REF: ST 160843

MORLAIS

This 13th-century castle was raised probably after Edward I's final conquest of Wales (1282–3). It appears to have been the cause of friction between two lords because it lay on a common boundary between their lands. Morlais contained a cylindrical great tower, a curtain enclosure with probably four flanking turrets, and extensive ditching.

LOCATION: MERTHYR TYDFIL, MID-GLAMORGAN
MAP REF: SO 049097

NANTCRIBBA

Traces of a stone curtain and towers, surrounded by a moat, stand here. Quarrying has changed the look of this area, but enough remains to make out the remnants of walls and towers. Nantcribba is on the line of Offa's Dyke, and there may be a historical connection between the two.

LOCATION: POWYS
MAP REF: SJ 237014

NARBERTH

This was a stone enclosure on a ridge at the south end of the town. It contained a cylindrical great tower, and the ruins of four out of five original round flanking towers can still be seen. It was built during the 13th century, near the site of a Norman motte castle built c.1100, which was destroyed by the Welsh in 1116.

LOCATION: PEMBROKESHIRE
MAP REF: SN 110144

NEATH

In the 1180s, a motte castle was raised here, on the site of an earlier castle, in a bend of the river that supplied the ditch with water to isolate the motte. In the 13th century the motte was revetted with stonework and two towers were erected on the north side, towards the river. The existing wall round the town was brought within the castle grounds by enclosing it with a curtain. Neath was attacked in 1231 and 1258, and captured in 1321 when the buildings were levelled. The whole castle was remodelled and received new buildings. The original round towers were modified to D-end towers.

LOCATION: NEATH PORT TALBOT
MAP REF: SS 753977
OPEN: LOCAL AUTHORITY: EXTERIOR ONLY

NEWCASTLE

A stone enclosure of the mid- to late 12th century was raised here against a steep spur overlooking the River Ogmore, probably upon the site of an earthwork castle of c.1106. The plan is polygonal with nine unequal sides and two almost square-plan towers in the curtain, one at the west angle, one at the south. The second tower was residential (with fireplaces, windows, staircases) and rose to three storeys. Further buildings in the enclosure were residential. The entrance to the enclosure was adjacent to the south tower, through an elaborately decorated round-headed arch.

LOCATION: BRIDGEND
MAP REF: SS 902801
OPEN: CADW: OPEN ACCESS

NEWCASTLE EMLYN

On a fine site overlooking the Teifi river, Newcastle Emlyn was raised as a quadrangle in the 1240s by the Welsh. The twin polygonal-towered gatehouse ruin is Welsh, but the second polygonal tower is probably English-built. The castle changed hands several times in the 1281–83 war between England and Wales. Later it was taken for Charles I in the Civil War and withstood a seige, but was finally captured and blown up.

LOCATION: CARMARTHENSHIRE
MAP REF: SN 311407

NEWPORT

Part of the castle remains today, consisting of a long curtain wall facing the Usk, with three towers. The centre tower is a square gate-tower with an arched entrance. The water-gate allowed the river to come into the ground floor of the tower at high tide and boats could draw up alongside a quay at the rear of the tower. Flanking this gateway are two polygonal towers in the curtain. There was a hall in the range between the gateway and the north polygonal tower. There are remains of other parts, including some walling of the remainder of the quadrangle. Most of the building work dates from the 15th century.

LOCATION: NEWPORT
MAP REF: ST 312884
OPEN: CADW: OPEN ACCESS

NEWPORT (PEMBROKESHIRE)

Built in the early 13th century, on a natural mound surrounded by a moat, Newport now has only ruins. It was originally built by Robert Martin, the first Norman lord to capture land in this part of Wales. A few traces of the curtain and the remains of three towers and a twin-towered gatehouse (of later date) may be seen. The present mansion, of 19th-century origin, absorbed the medieval remains in a romantic and successful way.

LOCATION: PEMBROKESHIRE
MAP REF: SN 057389
OPEN: PRIVATE: VISIBLE FROM THE ROAD

OGMORE

This is a stone-walled enclosure on an earlier earthwork site. It is surrounded by a moat except for the north side which is bounded by the River Ewenny and it guards an important ford where stepping stones lead from the outer bailey across the river. The earliest stone building was the rectangular great tower of the late 12th century. In the 13th century, the earthwork rampart line was followed by the erection of a stone curtain to form a polygonal enclosure. It was once used as a prison.

LOCATION: BRIDGEND
MAP REF: SS 882769
OPEN: CADW: OPEN ACCESS

OLD BEAUPRE

This castle is an Elizabethan quadrangular mansion (with an extension at the south-east), which incorporates stonework remains of an earlier structure of the late 13th to early 14th centuries. The principal medieval remains include a gatehouse, incorporated in the south wing of the quadrangle and which may have led to other buildings now vanished, other segments of the same wing, which are now part of the Elizabethan structure, and a block adjacent to and projecting north along the east wing. The differences in the periods of masonry can best be seen in the medieval gatehouse and the inner porch beside it to the west which is c.1600, where the porch joins the north wall of the south wing.

LOCATION: NR COWBRIDGE, BRIDGEND
MAP REF: ST 009721
OPEN: CADW: OPEN ACCESS

OYSTERMOUTH

A castle of c.1099 on a natural rock hill site with bailey beside, overlooking Swansea Bay, was abandoned for a masonry enclosure of later date. The enclosure contained a rectangular tower of the late 13th century, and a twin-towered gatehouse at the other end. Today the tower remains with decorated windows, added in the 14th century, adjoining a second rectangular building and an attached gateway, which are in ruins.

LOCATION: SWANSEA
MAP REF: SS 613883

PAINSCASTLE

This was a substantial motte castle, raised in the 1130s by Sir Payn FitzJohn. Fragments of walling on the motte suggest a cylindrical tower, and there are the remains of another stone tower in the bailey, work of the rebuilding c.1230–1. It is recorded as having been captured in 1215.

LOCATION: POWYS
MAP REF: SO 167461
OPEN: PRIVATE

Pembroke began as an oval earthwork enclosure built by Roger de Montgomery on a rocky promontory by the river in the 1090s. It grew into one of the grandest of the earlier castles built in Wales with stonework added during the 12th and 13th centuries by William Marshal, one of King John's staunchest allies. Pembroke's dominating feature was, and still is, its cylindrical great tower built c.1200–10 by Marshal. It is a massive, four-storey structure rising from a splayed plinth to almost 24.5m (80ft) with thick walls and capped by a remarkable stone dome. The castle's enclosure was divided into two, an inner smaller bailey of triangular plan, two sides of which were cliffs overlooking the River Pembroke and the third side a substantial curtain wall with flanking towers (a trapezoid-shaped stone hall was built in this bailey in the 12th century) and the larger outer bailey.

This was enclosed with a stone curtain and several cylindrical corner towers on the angles, a twin rectangular-towered gatehouse and a powerful postern tower: part of the southern curtain wall along the outer bailey was of double thickness for extra defence. Pembroke escaped attack by Owain Glwyndyr in the 15th century, but the castle was severely slighted after the Civil War and then the local population plundered it for stone. For centuries it languished as an ivy-covered ruin, and it wasn't until the 19th century that the restoration of this great castle began. Henry Tudor, later to become King Henry VII, was born here in 1457. In summer the castle stages historical re-enactments.

LOCATION: PEMBROKESHIRE
MAP REF: SM 982016
OPEN: PEMBROKE CASTLE TRUST: DAILY

PENCADER

A grass-covered mound is all that remains of this 12th-century motte which was originally 7.5m (25ft) high. It was built by the Normans, but was captured by the Welsh shortly afterwards when they regained the area. Henry II came here in 1162 as part of a peace-seeking initiative.

LOCATION: LLANFIHANGEL-AR-ARTH, DYFED
MAP REF: SN 445362

PENCELLI

Little remains of the motte castle here, following the raising of modern farm buildings. The motte was surrounded by a ditch. There are fragments of a tower. In the 13th century it was given a twin-towered gatehouse. It was captured in 1215 and 1234.

LOCATION: POWYS
MAP REF: SO 095249

PENCOED

The remains of a 13th-century tower and curtain are situated beside a 16th-century fortified mansion here. Plans for a theme park were rejected in 1999. The site is private but it can be viewed from a distance. It is a wonderfully evocative ruin.

LOCATION: NEWPORT
MAP REF: SO 095249

PENHOW

This is a small enclosure castle of irregular polygonal plan, with buildings round a tiny courtyard. The principal feature is a rectangular-plan tower, battlemented and three storeys high. The entrance used to be at first-floor level, but a doorway was inserted later to the ground floor. The tower has a mural staircase and two garderobes, one of which was later altered to lead into the great hall. The castle was probably begun in the early 13th century by Sir William St Maur, an ancestor of Edward Seymour, brother-in-law of Henry VIII and Protector during the reign of Edward VI. Alterations took place in the 15th and 16th centuries.

LOCATION: NEWPORT
MAP REF: ST 423908
OPEN: PRIVATE

PENLLINE

Also spelled Penllyn. So little of the 12th- and 13th-century buildings remain that it is difficult to determine its original shape, which is also obscured by a later mansion.

LOCATION: SOUTH GLAMORGAN
MAP REF: SS 979761
OPEN: PRIVATE

PENMAEN

Known also as Penmaen Burrows Motte, this was an earthwork enclosure. Traces of a timber gateway have been found. This was burned down and later replaced by an entrance formed by drystone walls. There was also a timber watch-tower, again replaced by a larger drystone structure.

LOCATION: SWANSEA
MAP REF: SS 534880

PENMARK

Penmark is a 13th-century stone enclosure with cylindrical turrets and an outer bailey. The ruins are very overgrown, but a tower can be seen.

LOCATION: NR FONMON, VALE OF GLAMORGAN
MAP REF: ST 059689

PENNARD

An enclosure of earth and timber on rock was erected here, probably in the early 12th century. Later in that century a stone rectangular hall was raised. The castle was further expanded into an enclosure with towers and gatehouse (probably of the late 13th century); the buildings were mainly of light construction. It is thought that the stone hall replaced an earlier wooden one.

LOCATION: SWANSEA
MAP REF: SS 544885

PENRICE

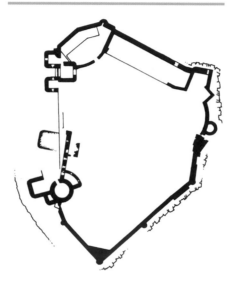

The first castle here was built in about 1100. The remains of some wooden structures were found during excavations at SS 492879. This is sometimes called Old Penrice Castle. A stone castle was raised nearby in the mid-13th century at SS 497885, and there are remains of a hall block and enclosure walls with small solid turrets, and a gatehouse. Later, a residential complex was built beside an earlier tower, and stood as a separate fortified structure within the enclosure. Near the ruins is a mansion built in the 18th century. Both stand in beautifully landscaped grounds. Remarkably, the estate has belonged to the same family since Norman times.

LOCATION: SWANSEA
MAP REF: SS 497885
OPEN: PRIVATE

PENTREFOELAS

A motte, with some traces of stone walls stands here.

LOCATION: CONWY
MAP REF: SH 870522

PEN-YR-ALLT (CASTELL)

A small earthwork enclosure, with ditching and some stone fragments.

LOCATION: CILGERRAN, PEMBROKESHIRE
MAP REF: SN 158420

PETERSTON

Some traces of a square-plan tower survive here.

LOCATION: MONMOUTHSHIRE
MAP REF: ST 084764

PICTON

A motte castle was built here c. 1087–1100 at the top of rising ground. About 150 years later a second castle was raised near the original site. The new castle was a quadrangular enclosure with strong corner towers and mid-wall towers. The castle is still a home; with its last major remodelling in the 1750s. Guided tours include the woodland garden as well as the castle.

LOCATION: DYFED
MAP REF: SN 011135
OPEN: PRIVATE. APR–SEP TUE–FRI & SUN PM TOURS ONLY)

The Marcher Lords

Norman lords who held land and castles on the border of Wales became known as the Marcher Lords. Their territories often included land deep inside Wales. The Marches were outside the law of England and the lords were free to rule as they wished. Unlike the English lords they were able to build castles without a licence from the king, to wage wars and build towns. They were a concern to the king but many were killed in the Wars of the Roses, when their lands reverted to the Crown.

Powys Castle is a graceful residence of towers and battlements, mullioned windows and turrets incorporated into the site of a 13th-century castle. The original castle on this site was destroyed by Llywelyn the Last in the 1270s because its Welsh owner sided with the English. It had two baileys, with a twin-towered gatehouse. In the 16th century Powys came into the hands of Sir Edward Herbert, in whose family it remained until late in the 20th century. During the 16th century and again after the Civil War the buildings underwent extensive restoration and remodelling. Further work was carried out in all of the following centuries and Powys today houses an extensive collection of treasures from India, fine painting and furniture; it also has a world-famous garden.

LOCATION: NR WELSHPOOL, POWYS
MAP REF: SJ 216064

PRESTATYN

A low-level motte castle with a half-moon bailey inside a larger rectangular enclosure, Prestatyn was destroyed in 1167. All that remains on the outskirts of the town is a low mound marked by a stone pillar.

LOCATION: CLWYD
MAP REF: SJ 073833
OPEN: LOCAL AUTHORITY: OPEN ACCESS

PRYSOR

Based on a natural hillock, Prysor was a simple motte castle. Today there is very little to see, but the setting is wild and rugged. It was a Welsh fortress, later captured and visited by Edward I.

LOCATION: TRAWSFYNYDD, GWYNEDD
MAP REF: SH 758369
OPEN: LOCAL AUTHORITY: OPEN ACCESS

RADNOR

There appear to have been three castles of some kind at various times in this area. The reference SI 212610 is of New Radnor, of which some evidence exists of strong earthworks of the late 12th century. Today the tall earthworks give a magnificent view over the town.

LOCATION: POWYS
MAP REF: SO 211610

SIEGES

CASTLES WERE PLACES OF REFUGE, AND THEY WERE BUILT TO WITHSTAND ATTACK, BUT NEARLY ALL CASTLE DEFENDERS WERE AFRAID OF SIEGES, WHICH COULD MEAN DEATH BY ATTACK OR STARVATION.

Capturing castles was an essential part of any war or campaign, as they controlled the surrounding lands. Dover, for example, the strongest fortress in Britain, was called 'the key of England'.

Sieges could last for weeks or even months, and this was the worst outcome for both defenders and attackers, as either side could become victim to bad weather, illness or starvation. So sieges were often avoided by negotiation at the outset, intended to reduce suffering on both sides.

If the siege was in earnest, the attackers might use siege engines to bombard the castle. The most powerful was the trebuchet, a giant catapult capable of firing stones as heavy as 136kg (300lb). Its range was not much more than 300m (238yd.), but in skilled hands it could be formidably accurate, firing missiles right over the castle walls. The mangonel was less powerful. It could fire at, but not over, walls. Its advantage was its longer range.

Ladders and belfries were employed to scale the walls of a castle under siege. The climbing gear was hooked at the top to get a purchase on the top of the wall. The attackers risked attack from within the castle by arrows, rocks, fire and scaldingly hot sand, which could penetrate chinks in armour and cause unendurable pain.

Ships besiege a fortified sea port in 1445. The attackers are using ladders to climb to the defenders who are massed ready to fight for themselves and their port.

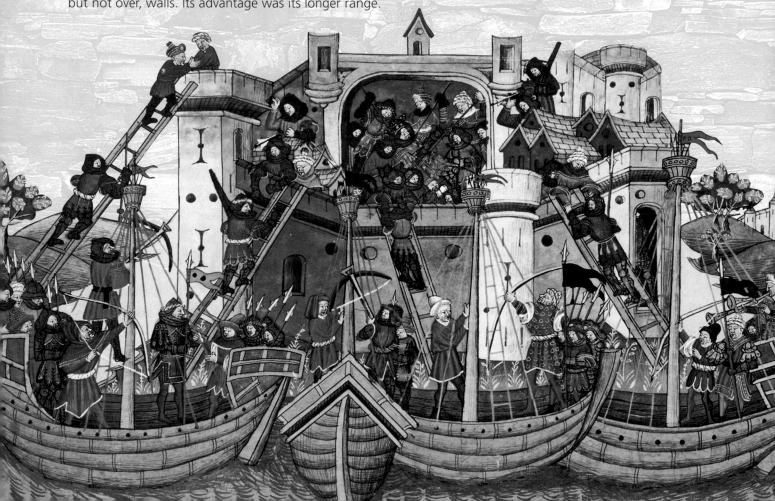

These engines could also fire other things: rotting animal corpses in the hope that they would spread disease (this is probably how the Black Death spread into Europe: plague victims were fired into a besieged town in the Crimea in 1346); the heads of captured defenders to demoralize the survivors.

Undermining walls was a threat to any castle not surrounded by water or built entirely on solid rock. Dover was attacked in this way in 1216, when the 'sappers' successfully brought down a gatehouse tower. But the defenders drove back the attackers and blocked the breach with rocks and tree trunks. The tunnel through the chalk used by the sappers can still be seen.

Other machines used during sieges were the cat, a battering ram housed inside a wheeled building for protection, and the belfry, a wheeled tower as high as the castle walls so that the attackers could jump directly into the castle.

Good, strong walls were usually the best defence the besieged could hope for, and walls could be as much as 10m (33ft) thick. Multiple defences helped, too, and castles became increasingly complex, culminating in the concentric castles with rings of outer 'curtain' walls overlooked by towers from which the defenders could fire arrows and throw stones. If one stretch of wall or even a tower was captured, the defenders could withdraw to other parts of the castle.

Soldiers clamber up ladders in a dangerous attempt to get into the castle. Special armour was developed for such attackers, including helmets with very wide brims to protect head, neck and shoulders while they climbed. Other soldiers with axes batter at the wooden doors.

Raglan Castle stands on the site of a Norman motte castle of c.1070. The earlier castle survived in some form up to the early 1400s and included a lord's hall. In 1432, it became the property of Sir William ap Thomas, a Welsh knight who had fought at Agincourt, and he started to build the structure whose magnificent ruins still dominate the local landscape. His first building was an unusual hexagonal-plan great tower, whose foundations and lowest courses of walling encase the old Norman motte. Known as the Yellow Tower of Gwent, it was built c.1430–45: around the outside of the basement is the remnant of a low curtain wall, added in c.1450–60. This tower stood surrounded by its own wide and deep ditch. When the castle was enlarged in c.1450–69, a great gate was built and a new approach from the great tower into the newer parts was constructed in the form of a three-storey forebuilding. Ranging round two courtyards, the lavish principal buildings were of polygonal plan. The gatehouse and its adjoining huge Closet Tower were equipped with gun-ports and with machicolation at parapet level. Raglan Castle was held by the Somerset family who, in the 16th century, were Earls of Worcester. The fifth earl sided with Charles I in the Civil War and Parliament beseiged Raglan in June 1646. It sustained a devastating bombardment for several weeks before surrendering. The Somersets used Raglan as a quarry for their new home at Badminton. Interpretive displays help explain the castle to visitors.

LOCATION: NR USK, MONMOUTHSHIRE
MAP REF: SO 415083
OPEN: CADW: DAILY

The Great Tower at Raglan Castle was mostly destroyed during the Civil War. Arrow slits and gun-ports defended the lower levels of the five-storey structure.

RHAYADER

A motte castle, built by the Welsh, known as Tower Mount, which confirms the motte-and-bailey character. It dates from the late 12th century and was probably destroyed soon afterwards. Rhayader is a quiet, charming mid-Wales town.

LOCATION: POWYS
MAP REF: SN 968680

RHUDDLAN

A motte castle was raised here c.1070: the mound can still be seen south of the second of Edward I's great fortifications built by Master James of St George in 1277–82. This later concentric castle has a lozenge-shaped inner stone enclosure with towers at the north and south corners and substantial gatehouses at the east and west corners. Most of the polygonal outer curtain, which had flanking rectilinear turrets on every angle and occasionally mid-wall, was surrounded by a wide moat, the rest by the River Clwyd. Four kinds of stone were used in the construction of Rhuddlan Castle: purple sandstone from a quarry near St Asaph, a red stone from Cheshire, yellow sandstone from the neighbourhood of Flint and a local grey limestone. The river was diverted to create a deep-water channel running for 3km (2 miles) and this 'canal' meant that building materials could be brought from many sources by ship.

Rhuddlan's building was interrupted when the castle was attacked by Llywelyn the Last, but otherwise the castle survived throughout the Middle Ages and served as a centre for civil administration in North Wales. In the Civil War, it was held for the king but surrendered to Parliament in 1646 and two years later it was slighted. The riverside ruins are of great interest.

LOCATION: DENBIGHSHIRE
MAP REF:: SJ 024779
OPEN: CADW: APR–SEP DAILY

RHYMNEY

Also known as Rumney Castle, this timber and earth enclosure castle was first mentioned in records in 1184 but was probably founded at the end of the 11th century. More timber buildings were added over the first half of the 12th century, and it then received a stone donjon and gate-tower later in the century. After about 1270, it was converted into a manor house. The site has been excavated.

LOCATION: CAERPHILLY
MAP REF: ST 210789

ROCH

Built on a rocky outcrop and consisting of a D-end tower with lengthened sides of the late 13th century, also earthworks and a double ditch, Roch has been considerably altered in later centuries. The castle's moments of glory were during the Civil War, when it changed hands several times. After renovation last century, the property is now a hotel.

LOCATION: NR HAVERFORDWEST, PEMBROKESHIRE
MAP REF: SM 880212

RUTHIN

Now part of the Castle Hotel, Ruthin was one of the new lordship castles ordered by Edward I and work began in the summer of 1277. This castle was formidable: its basic plan appears to have been two stone enclosures, each with a twin-towered gatehouse and flanking cylindrical towers. The 19th-century reconstruction work is considered tasteful but it is unhelpful in assessing the original form.

LOCATION: DENBIGHSHIRE
MAP REF: SJ 124579
OPEN: HOTEL

ST CLEARS

A motte castle near the river, possibly built in the mid-12th century. It changed hands between the Welsh and English on at least three occasions until 1215, when it was destroyed. Visitors can explore the mound.

LOCATION: CARMARTHENSHIRE
MAP REF: SN 280154
OPEN: LOCAL AUTHORITY. OPEN ACCESS

ST DONATS

St Donats was an imposing double-enclosure castle of the late 13th century on a striking foreland site. The inner enclosure was flanked with towers, but the outer polygonal curtained enclosure was unflanked. Considerable alterations have been made over the centuries, and it is now an international school.

LOCATION: NR LLANTWIT, VALE OF GLAMORGAN
MAP REF: SS 934681
OPEN: PRIVATE. TOURS MID–LATE AUG MON–FRI PM

ST FAGANS

A small castle of two enclosures. Little remains of the original works, as they have been obscured by the 16th-century mansion built on the site. The superb Museum of Welsh Life includes over 40 buildings from across Wales, re-erected here. There are many activities and events.

LOCATION: CARDIFF
MAP REF: ST 120771
OPEN: MUSEUM OF WELSH LIFE: DAILY

SKENFRITH

Technically, Skenfrith is a compact quadrilateral enclosure with corner cylindrical towers, surrounding a great tower with a semi-cylindrical buttress on its western side. The tower, of 13th-century construction, stands on an earlier low-level motte of the late 11th century. The tower certainly had three floors. The ground and first floors were connected by trap-door. The entrance to the first floor was by timber staircase, and access to the second storey was by spiral stair in the buttress.

LOCATION: MONMOUTHSHIRE
MAP REF: SO 457202
OPEN: CADW: OPEN ACCESS

SWANSEA

The motte castle here was attacked and burned in 1115–6. Later, an enclosure castle with towers was built near the site. This also declined and parts of it are incorporated in a third structure raised there by William de Braose in the late 13th century. The castle itself was severely damaged during Owain Glyndwr's struggle for independence. The ruins are freely accessible.

LOCATION: SWANSEA
MAP REF: SS 657931

SYCHARTH

Today Sycharth is a forgotten mound. But it is hugely important in Welsh history, having been Owain Glyndwr's base between 1400 and 1403. For a brief period, Glyndwr ruled an independent Wales. The castle was razed to the ground by Prince Henry in 1403. Excavations revealed stone fragments and traces of burned timber.

LOCATION: NR LLANGEDWYN, POWYS
MAP REF: SJ 205259

TENBY

Now in ruins, this interesting castle is sited on a headland overlooking Tenby harbour. It began as a late Norman tower-gate complex, a square tower with D-ended barbican. Later buildings were added, but in time the town was much better defended than the structures on the headland.

LOCATION: DYFED
MAP REF: SN 138005

TINBOETH (CASTELL)

Some stone foundations and a remnant of a tower are all that remain of an enclosure that dates possibly from the 12th century.

LOCATION: NR LLANDIDROD WELLS, POWYS
MAP REF: SO 090755

TOMEN-Y-MUR

This motte castle was built inside the remains of a Roman earthwork fort. Remnants of masonry, including ashlar blocks, have been found on the site.

LOCATION: MAENTWROG, GWYNEDD
MAP REF: SH 705386

TRETOWER

This Norman motte castle of c.1100 was converted to stonework in the 12th century, with additional work in the 13th century. Some time in the 12th century the motte summit was surrounded by a thick stone curtain with buildings ranged round the walls inside, in the manner of a shell enclosure. A strong square-plan gate-tower was inserted in the wall at the east. Then, probably in 1220–30, the buildings were replaced by a cylindrical great tower.

LOCATION NR CRICKHOWELL, POWYS
MAP REF SO 184212
OPEN: CADW: OPEN MAR–OCT DAILY

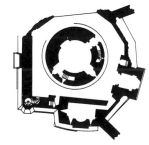

UPTON

Once a 13th-century small enclosure castle, with hall, towers and gate, Upton has been absorbed by later works. The site is private.

LOCATION: NR COSHETON, DYFED
MAP REF SN 020047

USK

Usk is an earthwork castle of c.1138 built by de Clare, with a second structure of stone raised in the bailey during the reign of Henry II. A small square tower of rubble and ashlar quoins projects from a curtain of later date. Improvements were made in the 13th and 14th centuries, but it was severely damaged by Owain Glyndwr c.1403–4. Repaired, it was held for Charles I in the Civil War but slighted by Parliament. The well-preserved three-floor gatehouse is incorporated in Castle House at Usk.

LOCATION: MONMOUTHSHIRE
MAP REF: SO 377010
OPEN: PRIVATE. OPEN ACCESS (DONATION)

WELSHPOOL

The motte castle here was captured some time in the 12th century. It was superseded by Powys Castle. The mound can be viewed from the road. Parts of the bailey are a bowling green.

LOCATION: POWYS
MAP REF: SJ 230074

WEOBLEY

A compact enclosure castle comprising an irregular square of buildings joined together, principally of 13th- to 14th-century construction. It is more in the manner of a fortified manor house. A rectangular tower in the south-west corner had a splayed plinth and was entered at first floor. At the same time an interesting hall and kitchen block were added. The square consists of a variety of tower-like buildings, which after 15th- and 16th-century rebuilding are in good condition. The attractive ruins are in a lovely setting. There is an on-site exhibition.

LOCATION: SWANSEA
MAP REF: SS 478927
OPEN: CADW: DAILY

WHITCHURCH

Also known as Treoda, a motte castle was built here probably in the 12th century. No stonework has been found.

LOCATION: CARDIFF
MAP REF: ST 156804

WHITE CASTLE

Originally called Llantilio Castle and then named White Castle because of its masonry coating of white plaster (traces of which remain), this was predominantly a defensive structure with little attempt to make it very generous as a residence. This castle, together with Skenfrith and Grosmont, was built to protect one of the main routes between England and South Wales. While the others were rebuilt when they came under the control of Hubert de Burgh, White Castle, the first of the three to be rebuilt in stone, was left unchanged, an impressive military stronghold. The central pear-shaped enclosure is flanked on the north-west and south-east by two outer enclosures, and all three are moated. The north enclosure has a 13th-century curtain wall with flanking cylindrical towers and an outer gateway; impressively, the outer bailey defences are largely still intact. The central enclosure also has a stone curtain with flanking towers and a towered gatehouse which date from late in the 13th century, but the curtain is earlier, c.1184–6, and at about the same time a square great tower was built, the foundations of which still exist. Later, various buildings were erected, including a hall, a solar and a kitchen and oven block. The castle's importance declined after the end of the Glyndwr campaign, and by the end of the 16th century it was becoming a ruin.

LOCATION: LLANTILIO, MONMOUTHSHIRE
MAP REF: SI 380168
OPEN: CADW: DAILY. OPEN SITE APR–SEP MON AND TUE; OPEN SITE NOV– MAR DAILY

WISTON

A motte castle with a polygonal shell enclosure with sloping plinth that was erected here in the early 12th century by a Flemish settler. The mound was surrounded by a 3m (10ft) deep ditch, and the bailey attached was rectangular. Remains of a doorway into the shell enclosure can be seen. It was captured by Llywelyn the Great during his campaign for independence. Visitors can reach the ruins by climbing steep steps.

LOCATION: NR HAVERFORDWEST, PEMBROKESHIRE
MAP REF: SN 022181
OPEN: CADW: OPEN ACCESS

WREXHAM

This motte castle on raised ground by the Clywedog river was mentioned in the Pipe Rolls in 1161. Remains of masonry were reported in 1912 in the grounds of Erddig House.

LOCATION: WREXHAM
MAP REF: SJ 327487

YSTRADFELLTE

The date for this overgrown and neglected castle is uncertain, and only traces of stone fragments survive.

LOCATION: POWYS
MAP REF: SN 936145

Ireland

THE MAJORITY OF IRELAND'S CASTLES WERE IMPOSED ON THE COUNTRY BY INVADERS AND SETTLERS.
THEY WERE PHYSICAL MANIFESTATIONS OF IMPERIALIST DOMINATION AND AS SUCH WERE DEEPLY
RESENTED, AND UNTIL RECENTLY THEY WERE STILL SEEN AS SYMBOLS OF HATED FOREIGN RULE.

IN TOTAL, THERE ARE MORE THAN 3,000 CASTLES IN IRELAND. MOST ARE OVERGROWN RUINS, BUT AN
INCREASING NUMBER HAVE BEEN RESTORED IN RECENT YEARS.

MANY CASTLE ENTHUSIASTS WILL SEEK OUT THE REMOTE AND FORGOTTEN RUINS, AS OFTEN AS NOT FOR
THEIR WONDERFUL RURAL SETTINGS AS FOR THEIR HISTORY. BUT 'SET PIECE' CASTLES SUCH AS CAHIR,
ENNISKILLEN, PARKE'S AND TRIM ARE REMARKABLY PRESERVED AND LOVINGLY RESTORED AND ARE
LIKELY TO BE ON ANY LIST OF 'MUST-SEES'.

The castle at Adare, set beside the River Maigue, was among the biggest in Ireland. It began as an earthwork enclosure with gateways, beyond which was a ditch with additional banking. The Anglo-Normans added a timber palisade to the enclosure and, soon after, the first stone buildings. One was a rectangular two-storeyed hall on the edge of the river, outside the enclosure. The upper storey was the first great hall. This building has loops at ground level and, above that, remains of fine Romanesque round-headed windows in pairs. Inside the enclosure a rectangular-plan great tower with three storeys was raised, about 13 x 12m (43 x 40ft); today it is largely demolished, although one wall still stands to its original full height.

In the mid-13th century the palisade wall was replaced by a stone curtain wall with a gateway on the south side, which housed a drawbridge. Later, a second, larger hall building was erected, about 22.5 x 11m (74 x 35ft), also with its south wall along the river edge. A major reconstruction in the 15th century added battlements, and the great hall took on its present form. More repairs were completed by Lord Dunraven in the late 19th century. New structural consolidation, conservation and repair mean that by 2007 the castle and grounds should be fully accessible.

LOCATION: CO. LIMERICK
MAP REF: R 4746
OPEN: OFFICE OF PUBLIC WORKS: GUIDED TOUR ONLY JUL, AUG AND POSSIBLY SEP. TOURS BOOKED AT ADARE HERITAGE CENTRE

ARDEE

There are two tower houses in the same street in Ardee; the larger is now used as a court house. It began as an early 13th-century square tower with two projecting turrets at the front. Its present appearance is of a much later date. The tower is four-storeyed and has trefoil-point windows; some of the battlements are stepped. Nearby are remains of a late 12th-century motte. The other tower house is known as Hatch's (a private residence); it is also four-storeyed but is less tall than the first tower.

LOCATION: CO. LOUTH
MAP REF: N 9690

ARDFINNAN

This is an example of the successful building of a stone great tower upon a motte summit. Here, a 13th-century cylindrical donjon of three storeys (including a vaulted basement) was raised by King John on a motte of the 1180s. The donjon's staircase was located in a smaller cylindrical turret built into the donjon wall and bulging as a semicircle outwards. Other surviving buildings are of later and different dates. A siege took place here during the Cromwellian wars. Ardfinnan is now a private residence.

LOCATION: CO. TIPPERARY
MAP REF: S 0818

ARDGLASS

Five separate fortified structures in Ardglass can be classified as castles, and they were all tower houses. The largest, Jordan's, has been restored and now accommodates a museum. It is rectangular, with two projections along the north wall, one of which had a spiral stair up to the roof, serving the four storeys. It has an extra small chamber on top of the stair turret. The windows are narrow loops externally. The castle was built in the mid-16th century and is probably the oldest of the five fortified buildings.

LOCATION: CO. DOWN
MAP REF: J 5637

ASKEATON

This is an oval enclosure of stone inside a larger enclosure that skirts a rock islet in the River Deel and contains two rectangular buildings. One was begun as a large hall in the early 13th century by William de Burgo and was altered in the 15th century to produce a tower house. A small tower at the west contains chambers and garderobes. The castle was slighted in the Civil War. Beyond the inner enclosure are the remains of a 15th-century banqueting hall, one of the finest medieval secular buildings in Ireland.

LOCATION: CO. LIMERICK
MAP REF: R 3450
OPEN: OPEN ACCESS

ATHLONE

Athlone was one of the main fording points of the Shannon, recognized by Toirrdelbach Ua Conchobair, King of Connacht and for a time *ard ri* (High King of Ireland). In c.1129 he raised a ring fort here beside a new bridge he had built across the river. The fort was one of the seven pre-Norman 'castles' of the 1120s to 1160s. At the end of the 12th century, the Anglo-Norman Geoffrey de Costentin built a motte castle on the site, which was later burned. In 1210, King John ordered a stone castle here, and replaced the wooden bridge with a stone one. The old motte was encased in stonework, but it collapsed and a new ten-sided tower was built on the ruins. This structure, albeit altered and modified, can be seen today.

Modifications and additions have been made, especially in the last 200 years, but some of the medieval curtain and relics of D-plan towers remain. The castle was besieged several times: the Confederate War of the 1640s, the fighting between William III and ex-King James II in 1689–91, and even during Wolfe Tone's rebellion in 1798–9. A visitor centre expands on the history of the castle and the town.

LOCATION: CO. WESTMEATH
MAP REF: N 0341
OPEN: MAY–SEP DAILY

ATHENRY

In c.1235, Meiler de Bermingham founded a castle at Athenry on the River Clareen surrounded by a roughly D-plan stone enclosure with round towers on the corners. Within a generation, Meiler's son, Piers, had raised the height of the first floor, lifting its ceiling and walls, and embellishing its entrance with the fine arched door at the south-east end. This was reached from outside by a staircase from the ground, probably of timber (a reproduction stair exists there today), and it was protected by a forebuilding. At the same time he raised a banqueting hall. Among the decorations Piers inserted were unusual narrow windows with trefoil heads. In the 15th century, the tower was raised yet again to provide two more floors and the top of the tower was equipped with battlements. At this time, the basement received an entrance (previously it had been accessed by ladder) which was cut into the splayed plinth.

Athenry was linked to the town that expanded beside it during the Middle Ages, itself enclosed by a complex system of walls, towers and gates, much of which remains today.

LOCATION: CO. LIMERICK
MAP REF: M 5028
OPEN: OFFICE OF PUBLIC WORKS: APR–OCT TUE–SUN

ATHLUMNEY

A double structure overlooking the Boyne, consisting of a 15th-century tower house, also known as Dowdall Castle, and a late 16th-century, semi-fortified three-storey stronghouse with gabled roofing and mullioned windows. The tower house has four storeys with gabling that has partly survived. The whole edifice was burned in 1649 by the owners, determined not to let Cromwell take the castle.

LOCATION: NR NAVAN, CO. MEATH
MAP REF: N 8966

ATHY

Known as White's Castle, this formidable-looking rectangular tower house, with battlements, rises to nearly 18.5m (60ft) and sits on the River Barrow in the town. Some of the present windows are replacements. There are also arrow loops, notably in the rectangular corner turrets. The entrance on the east side is through a narrow, Gothic, arched door. The castle is privately owned.

LOCATION: CO. KILDARE
MAP REF: S 6894

AUDLEY'S

Inside a five-sided enclosure in the north corner is a 15th-century three-storeyed tower house with projecting turrets on two corners, bridged at the top by arched machicolation. The entrance is in the south turret at ground level. The tower was raised in the 15th century by the Audley family, and in the 17th century it was sold to the Ward family of Castle Ward.

LOCATION: NR STRANGFORD, CO. DOWN
MAP REF: J 5851

AUGHER

A restored square plantation tower house of three storeys, with four faces that have a central triangular projection from ground to parapet, containing windows, and doors. The entrance is through a simple arched doorway covered by a box machicolation on the parapet above. The tower stood in a bawn of which only traces remain, including a small turret. A later, small mansion was built on to the west side.

LOCATION: CO. TYRONE
MAP REF: H 5654

AUGHNANURE

Sited on the edge of Lough Corrib, this is a substantial early 16th-century tower house, which today stands six storeys high. The tower house was built upon the remains of a much earlier castle of which little is known.

The structure has square corner box machicolations, or bartizans, on the external corners at third-storey level. The tower stands on a sloping plinth, rises to stepped battlements, and inside there are various gun-ports, shot-holes and fireplaces. Two of the storeys display fine vaulting. At first-floor level there is a fireplace with a flue going right to the top of the tower. Some of the ornamentation in the tower features, such as the windows and doors, is elaborate. The remains of a banqueting hall can be seen in one of the outer courtyards.

The tower house has been carefully restored by the Office of Public Works.

LOCATION: OUGHTERARD, CO. GALWAY
MAP REF: M 1544
OPEN: OFFICE OF PUBLIC WORKS: LATE SPRING TO EARLY AUTUMN DAILY

BALLINAFAD

'The Castle of the Curlews' was raised c.1590. It has four cylindrical turrets with a square interior plan clasping a rectangular tower house. Its plan is much like the 13th-century great towers at Carlow and Terryglass. The castle was built by Sir Richard Bingham as an English stronghold but was successfully besieged by the Healys and McDermotts. It was the site of several fierce battles as the families struggled against English attacks.

LOCATION: CO. SLIGO
MAP REF: G 7808

BALLINALACKAN

A late 16th-century six-storey tower house in good condition (but roofless) stands in its bawn, which has a round-headed entrance near the tower. The original fortress is thought to date back to the 10th century when the O'Connor clan ruled the area. The castle declined during the Cromwellian era. It is private and next to a hotel.

LOCATION: NR FANORE, THE BURREN, CO. CLARE
MAP REF: M 1001

BALLINTOBER

An early 14th-century stone enclosure, roughly square, with polygonal corner turrets, and a twin drum-towered gatehouse on the east, this castle was attacked many times. It was probably built by the Ua Conchobair family (which had once provided kings of Connacht).

LOCATION: CO. ROSCOMMON
MAP REF: M 7274

BALLINTOTTY

This building, not far from Nenagh, is an impressive ruin of a large, rectangular, four-storey tower house, with rounded corners and arrow-loops in the angles as well as elsewhere, and 18 windows. It is believed to have been built by the O'Kennedy clan around 1480 and was the home of the Ormond O'Kennedys up until Cromwellian times. The Kennedys are one of the great Irish clans, able to trace their ancestry back to Brian Boru.

LOCATION: CO. TIPPERARY
MAP REF: R 9178

BALLINTRA

A motte here was found to contain a square stone tower with walling, which may have been the core of a small tower house.

LOCATION: CO. DONEGAL
MAP REF: G 9068

BALLYCARBURY

A substantial 15th-century rectangular tower house inside a rectangular enclosure, most of which is missing. It is 23 x 13m (75 x 43ft), with walls nearly 2.5m (9ft) thick, rising three storeys plus attic level, although the top of the tower is very badly damaged. Large parts of this tower house have collapsed, and now the remains are neglected. It belonged to the MacCarthaigh family. To reach the remains visitors need to take the car ferry (10 minutes) from the mainland near Cahirciveen.

LOCATION: VALENCIA ISLAND, RING OF KERRY, CO. KERRY
MAP REF: V 4580
OPEN: DAILY

BALLYCOWAN

The ruins of a substantial L-plan tower house measuring 18.5m (60ft) in length and 10.5m (35ft) in width. It was built in the early 17th century by the Herbert family and consists of three storeys plus roof in height, with the shorter arm of the 'L' slightly indented along the longer part. The ground floor has a cross-wall dividing the area into cellars and kitchen. The ruins include ranks of chimneys, but much of the south-west side of the building has collapsed.

LOCATION: NR RAHAN, CO. OFFALY
MAP REF: N 2925

BALLYGALLY

A Scottish-style L-plan tower house of about 1625, with conical topped bartizans on cone corbels and walls some 1.5m/5ft thick. It was built by James Shaw of Greenock and reflects the interplay between Scotland and Ireland in this period. Renovations in the 1760s changed some of the original appearance, but the castle, now a hotel, retains some fine early 17th-century internal features, including narrow staircases and huge fireplaces. Before becoming a hotel, it served as a coastguard station and as a private residence.

LOCATION: CO. ANTRIM
MAP REF: D 3708

BALLYHACK

Sited in a commanding position on a steep slope overlooking the Waterford estuary, this is a mid-15th century tower house of five storeys, with box machicolations and gabled roof. The ground and second floors are vaulted, and there are interesting recesses on the third floor, including a chapel. It is believed to have been built around 1450 by the Knights Hospitallers of St John, the famous military order founded in the 12th century.

LOCATION: CO. WEXFORD
MAP REF: S 7111
OPEN: OFFICE OF PUBLIC WORKS: JUN–SEP DAILY

BALLYLOUGHAN

The great gatehouse of twin drum towers, three storeys tall, is the main remnant here of a once-substantial enclosure castle with corner towers. The two-storey south-west tower was almost square, with one wall nearly 3m (10ft) thick to allow the addition of flights of stairs. The castle is of late 13th-century origin and was probably abandoned by the 15th century. In late medieval times it was occupied by the Kavanagh family. The castle is on private land.

LOCATION: BAGENALSTOWN, CO. CARLOW
MAP REF: S 7158

BALLYMALIS

On the banks of the River Laune, this is an interesting example of a 16th-century, four-storey tower house, having corner bartizans among its defences. There are two that clasp opposite corners of the tower at second-floor level. The dimensions of the castle are 15 x 9.5m (49 x 30ft). The east wall is twice as thick as the others, and it contains a staircase and also chambers. Various defensive features can still be made out including gun ports for musket fire, and holes to drop things on besiegers. From here there are good views of Carrantuohill, Ireland's highest mountain.

LOCATION: NR KILLORGIN, CO. KERRY
MAP REF: V 8494

BALLYMOON

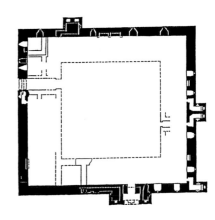

One of the major castles of the 13th to early 14th centuries, Ballymoon is an almost square enclosure. Surprisingly, it has no corner towers, but there are the remains of rectangular projections on the east, south and north walls, all of which have garderobes. The enclosure wall is of granite, about 2.5m (8ft) thick, and for much of its length about 6m (20ft) tall.

The history of the castle is barely known, and tradition maintains that it has never been inhabited. It may have been built by the Bigods, an East Anglian family of considerable power.

LOCATION: CO. CARLOW
MAP REF: S 7362
OPEN: OFFICE OF PUBLIC WORKS: ACCESS DIRECT FROM THE ROAD VIA SMALL TIMBER FOOTBRIDGE

Norman invasion

The first Normans arrived in Ireland by invitation. Dermot Mac Murrough, King of Leinster, was forced to recognize Rory O'Connor as High King of Ireland. To reclaim lost lands and authority, Dermot turned to the Norman lords. Strongbow became his son-in-law and heir. He regained Leinster and on Dermot's death was King of Leinster. Henry II, concerned that an independent power was forming close to his kingdom, forced Strongbow to pass Leinster to the English Crown.

An enclosure castle of the later 13th or very early 14th century, almost square in plan with massive round towers on the corners, a D-plan flanking tower along east and west walls, and a sally-port or postern tower on the south wall. But its main structure is a huge gatehouse of two half-round towers of four storeys flanking the entrance on the north wall. Ballymote's enclosing walls are – where they survive intact – over 3m (10ft). At some stage, the gatehouse towers were strengthened by the addition of a protective skin of outer walling.

Ballymote was raised by the de Burgo family, but was besieged and taken by the Ua Conchobair and MacDiarmaid families in the 14th century. Thereafter, the castle has a long history of further siege, capture, recapture and sale or lease. It also appears to have been left unoccupied for long periods, although it has been restored.

LOCATION: CO. SLIGO
MAP REF: G 6615
OPEN: OFFICE OF PUBLIC WORKS: DAILY

BALLYNACARRIGA

This 16th-century four-storey tower house, with a stone staircase still intact, stands on a rock base overlooking Lough Ballynacarriga. A date of 1585 is carved in a window on the top floor, but it is thought the tower may well be older. This top floor was for a time used as a chapel and there are some interesting stone carvings with a religious theme to be seen here.

LOCATION: OFF THE ROAD BETWEEN BALLINEEN AND DUNMANWAY, CO. CORK
MAP REF: W 2951

BALLYNAHOW

One of only a few cylindrical great towers and tower houses in Ireland, this 17.5m (57ft) structure is of late 16th-century origin. It has five storeys, two of which are vaulted double storeys. The ground and first floor are cylindrical internally, but higher up, the apartment area forms a quadrilateral plan. Outside, the wall-walk and parapet are well preserved, and have four equidistant box machicolations.

The tower has some 28 gun-ports as well as several pairs of narrow arched windows, some rounded, some of ogee shape, and a murder hole covering the area inside the door. This is a national monument administered by the Office of Public Works.

LOCATION: THURLES, CO. TIPPERARY
MAP REF: S 0860

BARRY'S COURT

A substantial castle of medieval origin, which was rebuilt during the last quarter of the 16th century.

LOCATION: CO. CORK
MAP REF: W 8273

BENBURB

Site of a great victory by Owen Roe O'Neill who commanded the Confederate army in 1646, Benburb had once been a seat of the O'Neills, leaders of opposition to English rule in Ulster. In about 1611, Sir Richard Wingfield built the plantation castle there, on a high cliff some 61m (200ft) above the River Blackwater, which consisted of a triangular enclosure with walls about 5m (16ft) tall. One of its sides is the cliff face, a sheer drop down to the river. On the north side are two three-storeyed rectangular towers, one at each end. At the south end of the north–south wall is a smaller round turret near the cliff edge that has a staircase. Nearby is a house of a much later period.

The castle is today in the grounds of a Servite monastery.

LOCATION: CO. TYRONE
MAP REF: H 8152
OPEN: SERVITE MONASTERY: 1ST SUN IN JUNE

BIRR

The 19th-century 'reproduction' castle here started out as a simple motte castle of c.1186, which was destroyed in about 1207 and rebuilt five years later. Its history and development thereafter are almost unknown until in the 1620s an imposing castellar-like house was erected on the site. This was substantially modified in the early 19th century. It has been the seat of the Earls of Rosse for 14 generations and is now the home of Ireland's Historic Science Centre. It also has magnificent grounds. The castle is owned by the Earl of Rosse and is open daily.

LOCATION: CO. OFFALY
MAP REF: N 0504

BLARNEY

LOCATION: CO. CORK
MAP REF: W 6174
OPEN: PRIVATE: DAILY
SEE PAGE: 216

BOURCHIER'S

A castle of unknown size and shape, but noted as having been built during the 13th century, lies under the later 15th-century tower house known as Bourchier's. The latter is five-storeyed, about 17 x 11m (55 x 36ft), with, among other features, a gun-port beside its entrance. Excavations in the castle area revealed traces of two medieval houses that were part of a village that grew up around the original castle. It had been built by the Earls of Desmond.

LOCATION: LOUGH GUR, 6.5KM (4 MILES) SOUTH OF BALLNEETY, CO. LIMERICK
MAP REF: R 6542

BUNCRANA

The building started out as an almost square-plan tower house of the early 14th century, and had its entrance at first-floor level. There were many passages, straight staircases and chambers in the wall thicknesses. The top of the tower is of much later construction, part of repairs that were instigated by the O'Dochertys in c.1600. It was burned by the English in 1602 but repaired again later in the century. Revolutionary leader Wolfe Tone was imprisoned here in 1798.

LOCATION: INISHOWEN, CO. DONEGAL
MAP REF: C 3531

Blarney

Underground tunnels lead from Blarney Castle. Cromwellians besieging the castle found that the garrison had escaped by means of these tunnels, which are known as Badger's Caves.

Blarney's tremendous rectangular great tower – one of the biggest in Ireland – has an interesting building history. It was erected in two stages. Firstly, in the early 15th century a small 6m (20ft) square turret, rising to four storeys and containing small rooms, was built as part of some other construction that has since been superseded. This original turret, not then machicolated, remained where it was, until about 40 years later, the castle owner, Cormac MacCarthaigh, decided to restructure by imposing a huge rectangular great tower, 18.5 x 12m (60 x 39ft), with five storeys, on the earlier building. He also incorporated the small square turret at its north-west corner, making the whole an L-plan tower. The new rectangle has walls around 3.5m (12ft) thick at the lower levels. The second floor of the rectangle is vaulted, and the tower has its own staircase in the north wall.

The most striking feature of the newer tower is the massive parapet with its machicolation all round the top of the fifth storey. On the top of the parapet are stepped battlements. In the 18th century the then owner added a Gothic-style extension at the south end; however, this was severely damaged by a fire in the 19th century. The castle is famous for the Blarney Stone, a stone set in the machicolation. By means of inverting yourself head downwards between two machicolations you can kiss the stone, an act that will, it is claimed, 'confer eloquence'.

KISSING THE BLARNEY STONE

Kissing the Blarney Stone is supposed to bless a person with eloquence. The origin of the term 'blarney' meaning to talk persuasively but without malice is believed to date from the 16th century. Cormac MacCarthaigh, the holder of the castle, was ordered to give his castle up to the Crown. Rather than refuse outright, he delayed the event by inventing a series of excuses. Queen Elizabeth is reputed to have referred to this as 'blarney'.

An aerial view of Blarney's towers and the surrounding woods. Rock Close in the castle grounds and the woods are associated with druids, witches and magic.

Instigated by the Macconmaras and once the seat of the Thomond O'Briens, this is a vast great tower of mid-15th-century construction. It has a rectangular central core with four massive square corner towers. Originally, it stood inside an extensive enclosure with various buildings, but these have almost disappeared. The rectangular core of the great tower is 19 x 12.5m (62 x 41ft) with walls over 2m (7ft) thick. These walls contain a number of mural stairs, straight and spiral. The northern wall, 3m (10ft) thick, contains the entrance, which leads straight into a great hall that is vaulted, as is the storage floor underneath. Above the great hall is a second hall that was magnificently decorated with fine plasterwork in the 17th century and has now been restored. The core contains the only large rooms. The four huge corner towers, each five storeys high and over 7m (23ft) square, contain the many bedrooms, garderobes, a chapel, and a plethora of passages and stairways.

Opened to the public in 1960, it is Ireland's most complete and authentically restored castle. There is a folk park in the grounds.

LOCATION: CO. CLARE
MAP REF: R 4561
OPEN: THE SHANNON DEVELOPMENT COMPANY: DAILY

BURNCHURCH

Burnchurch is one of the 15th-century rectangular tower houses that have the special feature where the two narrower sides continue upwards for an extra storey above the wall-walk, in the manner of additional wide turrets. In these turrets there are passages or rooms, with their own wall-walk on the roof above. All sides had battlemented parapets.

LOCATION: NR. CALLAN, CO. KILKENNY
MAP REF: S 4847

BURNCOURT

Burncourt is a many-windowed and gabled tower house of 1641. This rectangular building with four huge square turrets on its corners was partly defensible. It is still in the ruinous condition in which it was left after its owners set fire to it to prevent it being taken by Cromwell's forces in 1650. Parts of Burncourt's surrounding bawn have survived.

LOCATION: SOUTH OF CAHIR, CO. TIPPERARY
MAP REF: R 9518

BURT

A late 16th-century, Z-plan tower house, with two opposing cylindrical corner towers, much like Scottish tower houses, Burt stands on a hill with fine views. It is mostly ruinous, but the staircase-tower on the south-west corner is of interest. The tower stands to its full height of three storeys plus attic, and there are traces of machicolation. It is on private land.

LOCATION: CO. DONEGAL
MAP REF: C 3119

CAHIR

Cahir Castle, built on a rocky island in the River Suir, and among the biggest castles in Ireland, is preserved in remarkably good condition. Work started in the 13th century, with major additions in the 15th century and lesser works in the 16th and 17th centuries. Today, after some restoration work in the 1840s which included renovating the great hall and the rectangular western tower, it still retains an almost unrivalled grandeur. From c.1375 the castle was for centuries the seat of the Ormonde Butlers, one of whom initiated the mid-19th-century renovations.

Cahir was captured after a ten-day siege by the Earl of Essex, Elizabeth I's favourite, during his Irish campaign in 1598–1600. The castle was taken, without a fight, by Cromwell in 1650.

LOCATION: CO. TIPPERARY
MAP REF: S 0525
OPEN: OFFICE OF PUBLIC WORKS: DAILY

CARBURY

A late 16th-century, irregularly shaped tower house with later additions was raised on the site of a much earlier motte castle that had two baileys. The tower house appears to have begun as a large rectangular building with an off-centre cross-wall. On the west side a smaller turret probably contained the staircase.

LOCATION: CO. KILDARE
MAP REF: N 6935

CARLINGFORD (KING JOHN'S)

One of the principal early castles of the Anglo-Normans, King John's at Carlingford stands on a rock mound beside Lough Carlingford, overlooking the harbour. Possibly there was an earth-and-timber structure at the site put up during Prince John's lordship of Ireland in the 1180s. The stonework castle of basically D-plan was started towards the end of the 12th century.

In the 1260s the gap between the ends of the north and south walls was re-sealed with a large hall structure, a block of at least two storeys, and roofed, over a basement with cellars. This block contained a hall, smaller apartments and other chambers. In the 15th century, more apartments were added on to the southern end of the 1260s work.

LOCATION: CO. LOUTH
MAP REF: J 1812
OPEN: OFFICE OF PUBLIC WORKS: SEP (OPEN ON 2 SUNDAYS IN HERITAGE WEEK)

CARLOW

This once huge castle's central tower was a substantial rectangular block of three storeys on a sloping plinth, some 20.5 x 14m (67 x 46ft). Situated by the River Barrow, it was built by William the Marshal between 1207 and 1213. A century later it was granted to the Earl of Norfolk, and remained a Crown castle until 1537. The building was largely demolished in the early 19th century to make way for housing.

LOCATION: CO. CARLOW
MAP REF: S 7376
OPEN: OFFICE OF PUBLIC WORKS: ACCESSIBLE

CARRICK KILDAVNET

A striking, narrow tower house of four storeys plus attic, with box machicolations on each of the four parapets, Carrick Kildavnet, erected in the 14th century, stands on an islet of the sea and was once enclosed by a bawn. It is also known as Grace O'Malley's Castle after the woman who was effectively the chief of the O'Malley clan in the 16th century (see the box on this page). The building rises to three storeys and is 12m (39ft) high. The building is roofless and the interior is in poor condition.

LOCATION: NR. CLOUGHMORE, ACHILL ISLAND, CO. MAYO
MAP REF: L 7294

CARRICKFERGUS

LOCATION: CO. ANTRIM
MAP REF: J 4187
OPEN: ENVIRONMENT AND HERITAGE SERVICE: MON–SAT DAILY, SUN PM
SEE PAGE: 220

CARRICK ON SUIR (ORMONDE CASTLE)

An Elizabethan undefended house and courtyard built by the Earls of Ormonde, attached to a double-towered stone enclosure castle of the mid-15th century. The towers, of slightly differing dimensions but nearly parallel, were both five-storeyed, and one wall of each continued southwards and parallel to a joining wall at right angles, forming a courtyard. This latter wall was removed in the 16th century. The Elizabethan house at the northern end is lower than the earlier towers and is two-storeyed with a steep, gabled attic storey and impressive porch.

LOCATION: CO. TIPPERARY
MAP REF: S 4021
OPEN: OFFICE OF PUBLIC WORKS: MID-JUN TO MID-SEP DAILY

CARRIGAFOYLE

A rectangular tower house of the 15th century, standing centrally inside a high-walled bawn on the Shannon estuary. The enclosure reaches the water and a dock for ships was built by the base of the tower, which is five-storeyed, with vaulted ceilings on the second and fourth floors. At one level it has an arched recess between the spiral staircase inside and the main room, the door of which opened inwards. The tower is badly damaged. Access is across a raised path of stones that might be submerged at high tide.

LOCATION: BALLYLONGFORD, CO. KERRY
MAP REF: Q 9947

CARRIGAHOLT

This is a much-restored 16th-century tower house. Tall, slender, with five storeys, it stands in the corner of a bawn. Its walls have gun-ports, the fourth floor is vaulted, and a fireplace on the fifth floor bears the date 1603. The castle was taken by Cromwell's forces in 1651 but it was restored to the O'Briens (its owners) by Charles II after the Restoration of 1660. William III granted it to one of his army commanders in 1691. Carrigaholt is a national monument administered by the Office of Public Works. Access is through a field.

LOCATION: CO. CLARE
MAP REF: Q 8552

Grace O'Malley

Also known as Granuaile, Grace, born about 1530, had an adventurer's life. The daughter of the head of the O'Malley clan, she joined her father on his sea voyages. Later, Grace took to the sea herself, earning a reputation as a pirate. When her lands were annexed by the Governor she petitioned Queen Elizabeth for their return. The women met and Grace was granted her lands although they were never actually returned to her.

Carrickfergus

This is a large three-ward castle, the wards of differing dates, situated on the northern shore of Lough Belfast. The first of its three-phase building was carried out between 1178 and 1195 and begun by John de Courcy, the Anglo-Norman lord who conquered much of Ulster. This early phase included the polygonal enclosure (still remaining) and is called the inner ward, together with a great hall along its east wall, now only in fragmentary condition. The other work of this phase was the nearly square great tower that still dominates the castle and the adjoining town today.

The castle is in remarkable condition. It was passed to the government for renovation and preservation in the 1920s.

The castle was taken over by King John in 1210 and he made it an administrative centre for the English government, which it remained for more than seven centuries. The second phase of building in 1216 included finishing the great tower and adding a middle ward by erecting a wall west to east ending in a square tower on the edge of the lough, and a further stretch of wall north to south feeding into the inner ward's walling to the south. The third phase, c.1226–42, consisted of an outer ward on the north that was given a twin cylindrical-towered gatehouse to the north, the towers being about 12m (40ft) in diameter and flanking a passage protected by a portcullis. On the first floor of the eastern of the two towers is a chapel.

During its turbulent life Carrickfergus has served as a prison, armoury and air-raid shelter.

A plan of the fortifications at Carrickfergus. The plan was drawn up in 1612 by John Dunstall, who has named the place Cragfergus.

CARRIGAPHOOCA

A 16th-century rectangular tower house of four storeys, the third storey double-vaulted; it stands on a rock base. Carrigaphooca has two turrets remaining on opposite corners at the top. One wall contains straight staircases all the way up. The tower has no windows, only loops, nor does it have fireplaces or chimneys. There is only one room to each floor, with some mural recesses. It was built by the MacCarthaigh family, and it was sacked in 1601–2.

LOCATION: KINSALE, CO. CORK
MAP REF: W 2974

CARRIGOGUNNEL

This was an O'Brien possession built on top of a rock over the Shannon. It is now ruinous, and the principal remains include a severely damaged tower house, a fragmentary enclosing wall and a chapel. Work started in the early 13th century when the rock top was converted into a motte. The main works were of the 14th and 15th centuries and included the hall block immediately south of the round tower, and an enclosing wall. There was additional work in the 16th century.

LOCATION: CLARINA, NR. LIMERICK, CO. LIMERICK
MAP REF: R 5050

CASHEL

Approaching Cashel from Urlingford you can see, miles before reaching the town, the High Rock of Cashel, 30.5m (100ft) above the plain. This was where Cormac, a fourth-century king in Munster, built his capital.

In the next century St Patrick visited the stronghold and it became an important Christian centre. Several of the kings of Munster became bishops. Brian Boru, later to become *ard rí* (High King of Ireland), and the greatest figure in Irish history, was crowned there in the 970s as Munster's king. A century after his death in 1014 at Clontarf, his descendants gave the land to the Church and in 1127 Cormac MacCarthaigh started to build the small Romanesque church known later as Cormac's chapel. In 1169, a cathedral was started next door, where in 1172 the assembled Irish clergy paid homage to Henry II.

By the 1260s the cathedral had gone, but it was replaced by another, the ruins of which remain. At the end of the nave of this later building, a tower house was built in the early 15th century, 12.5 x 9m (41 x 28ft) and some 22m (73ft) tall, with thick walls and lots of passages; this is also now a ruin. It is, however, possible to visit the restored 15th-century Hall of the Vicars, complete with its minstrels' gallery. This is one of Ireland's most popular attractions.

LOCATION: CO. TIPPERARY
MAP REF: S 0741
OPEN: OFFICE OF PUBLIC WORKS: DAILY

CASTLE ARCHDALE

Overlooking Lower Lough Erne on its eastern side, this plantation castle was built c.1615. It consisted of a T-plan stronghouse standing in a square bawn. The castle was ravaged by the Maguires during the Confederate War and was attacked again in the war between William III and the exiled James II, 1689–91. A house built on the site in 1773 was left derelict in 1959.

LOCATION: IRVINESTOWN, CO. FERMANAGH
MAP REF: H 1859
OPEN: DEPARTMENT OF ENVIRONMENT AND HERITAGE SERVICE NORTHERN IRELAND: DAILY

CASTLE BALFOUR

An eccentrically shaped plantation castle was erected here at Lisnaskea in the early 17th century (c.1615–20) by the Balfours. It was a long, rectangular building of three storeys, on a north–south axis, having a square wing to the west, a later rectangular block put up on the northern end and, later still, more works at the south. Open access in daylight hours.

LOCATION: LINASKEA, CO. FERMANAGH
MAP REF: H 3634
OPEN: DAILY

CASTLECARRA

Located near Lough Carra, this is a 13th-century rectangular great tower of three storeys, about 15 x 10.5m (50 x 35ft), with an east wall about 2m (6ft) thick, the others slightly less, and with its entrance in the south. The earliest part of the castle was built at the end of the 13th century by the Anglo-Norman Baron de Staunton. The tower was altered over the centuries and at one time given a cross-wall in the ground storey. An entrance tower was set on the south wall in the 14th century. The biggest development was the 15th-century five-sided enclosure about 2m (6ft) wide around the great tower, which had a small circular flanking tower at the north-east angle, although the overall structure retained fragments of the earlier building.

LOCATION: MAYO, CO. MAYO
MAP REF: G 1775
OPEN: PRIVATE

CASTLE CAULFIELD

A plantation castle of c.1611–19 erected by Sir Toby Caulfield and burned down during the Confederate War in 1641. It had been built upon the site of an earlier native Irish enclosure, of which part of the twin-towered gateway remains to two-storey height. What emerged was a U-plan stronghouse, three storeys tall, with mullion windows. One of the wings is no longer standing. The castle is sited on the outskirts of the small town, and is now surrounded by a modern housing estate. There is open access.

LOCATION: NR DUNGANNON, CO. TYRONE
MAP REF: H 7563
OPEN: DAILY

CASTLE CONNELL

Beside the village street at Castleconnell is a huge rock mass on which in the early 13th century a castle of unknown shape was raised. This was attacked and destroyed by the Irish in about 1260, and the site was taken over by the de Clares who built an enclosure with cylindrical corner towers of which there are some remains. The castle was blown up by the forces of William III in the war against the exiled James II.

LOCATION: CO. LIMERICK
MAP REF: R 6563

CASTLEGRACE

A 13th-century stonework enclosure of rectangular plan, with two round corner towers, and traces of rectangular towers on the other corners.

LOCATION: CO. TIPPERARY
MAP REF: S 0415

CASTLE KIRK

On an island in Lough Corrib are the remains of a substantial rectangular enclosure with square corner turrets, built in the early 13th century. A rectangular tower was raised against the south side of the enclosure during or soon after the initial work. Built by the O'Flaherty clan, its position on the island made it virtually impregnable.

LOCATION: MAAM, LOUGH CORRIB, CO. GALWAY
MAP REF: L 9980

CASTLEKNOCK

This 12th-century castle of earth-and-timber origins today lies alongside St Vincent's College in north-west Dublin. It began as a motte castle of c.1180 located on a natural hillock, creating a very tall mound. Within a few years, the mound top was encased in stonework and then heightened in order to create a polygonal great tower of three storeys.

Today there is still some of the stonework of the tower and there are traces of other buildings. The mound top is now a cemetery.

LOCATION: CASTLEKNOCK, DUBLIN, CO. DUBLIN
MAP REF: O 0836

CASTLEMARTYR

An earth and timber castle was raised here, probably by the Anglo-Normans in the late 1170s. Nearly three centuries later, a quadrangular enclosure castle was built on the same site. This had a large square tower on the north corner, of which two storeys survive today, and positioned at the east, a five-storey tower house. The castle's location, between Cork and Youghal, was strategically important.

LOCATION: CO. CORK
MAP REF: W 9674

CASTLEROCHE

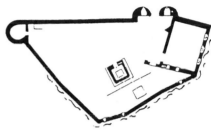

Castleroche, close to the Ulster border, stands on a rocky cliff overlooking a pass in the Armagh hills. Although now dilapidated through both age and assault, it is complete enough to see the arrangement of buildings in what was a major 13th-century castle. Triangular in plan, the enclosure's north wall has at its east end the remains of a huge four-storeyed twin-cylindrical-towered gatehouse with loops, and at the other end the lower levels of a cylindrical tower. Immediately next to the gatehouse is the shell of a substantial hall building, which points south.

LOCATION: NR DUNDALK, CO. LOUTH
MAP REF: H 9913

CASTLETOWN DELVIN

The original motte castle, built by Hugh de Lacy in the 12th century, is still visible today. Nearby, on the other side of the street, a century or so later, a long, rectangular stone tower house with rounded corner turrets was built by the Nugent family. Only two of the original four turrets remain.

LOCATION: CO. WESTMEATH
MAP REF: N 6062

CASTLETOWN GEOGHEGAN

A fine, prominent motte castle close to the road, it has most of its ditch surviving, and the lines of the bailey are clear. The motte is over 12m (40ft) tall.

LOCATION: CO. WESTMEATH
MAP REF: N 3444

CASTLE WARD

An early 17th-century tower house in good external condition stands in the grounds of the 18th-century mansion which is now in the care of the National Trust. The tower is 8.5 x 8m (28 x 26ft) and rises 15m (49ft) to the stepped battlements. The estate stretches to 750 acres, with fabulous views of Strangford Lough.

LOCATION: STRANGFORD, DOWNPATRICK, CO. DOWN
MAP REF: J 5750
OPEN: NATIONAL TRUST: DAILY

CLARA

The five-storeyed (plus attic) 15th-century tower house surrounded by its 17th-century bawn would be almost insignificant but for the relatively good condition of its outside and, more importantly, the survival of many of the original oak beams of the floor inside. Today you can look upwards from the ground through several horizontal 'trellises', to the vaulted fourth-storey ceiling. The storeys can still be reached by flights of winding stone stairs, lit by loops. A secret chamber on the third floor was accessible only by a lift-up seat in the floor above.

LOCATION: KILKENNY, CO. KILKENNY
MAP REF: N 5747
OPEN: OFFICE OF PUBLIC WORKS: ACCESS ONLY BY GUIDED GROUP

CLAREGALWAY

A 15th-century four-storey tower house in good condition located on the River Clare and built by the Burke family. It is nearly 18.5m (60ft) tall, and has many original features such as gun-ports, angle-loops and even a meurtrière (murder hole) in the ceiling of the entry passage in the east wall.

LOCATION: CO. GALWAY
MAP REF: M 3833

CLONMACNOIS

Outside the famous monastic 'city' of St Ciaran, near the Shannon, is what is left of Clonmacnois Castle. This was originally a motte castle and the mound and bailey are still clearly visible. In the 13th century, a substantial stone great tower was built on the motte, with encircling walls and a gatehouse in the bailey. The great tower was blown up in 1650 on English orders, and today huge chunks of mortared stone blocks straddling the mound top are all that remain.

LOCATION: SHANNONBRIDGE, CO. OFFALY
MAP REF: N 0130

CLONMINES

Clonmines, which became rich in the Middle Ages from the lead and silver mines nearby, has several buildings that appear to have been fortified in these times. There was the town hall and the church with its strong tower (both 15th century), and the Augustinian church of the late 14th century, which may be associated with the wall fortifications nearby. Close by is a ruined 15th-century tower house of four storeys, which has straight stairways. It is privately owned.

LOCATION: WELLINGTON BRIDGE, CO. WEXFORD
MAP REF: S 8413

CLONMORE

Now largely in ruins, this castle was a late 13th- to early 14th-century quadrilateral enclosure of stone with flanking towers along the walls and on the corners. Traces of buildings against the east wall inside remain, and in these there are interesting trefoil-pointed windows and elsewhere some cross-loops.

LOCATION: CO. CARLOW
MAP REF: S 9676

CLONONY

Clonony is a 16th-century tower house with an outer bawn, neglected until recently, which caused the deterioration of some structures. The house dates from the early 16th century and is approached via an imposing round-headed gateway, lower down the slightly rising ground on which the tower house stands. The four-storey tower has narrow loops. There are also the remains of much later additional buildings in poor condition.

The current owner has undertaken a major plan of renovation to conserve the castle.

LOCATION: NR CLOGHAN, CO. OFFALY
MAP REF: N 0521
OPEN: PRIVATE: OPEN

CLOUGH

A motte castle of the late 12th or early 13th century has been excavated here. Post-holes were found suggesting timber buildings, and artefacts such as axe heads, bowls, arrow heads, buckles and coins of King John's reign (1199–1216) were also found. Later, in the mid-13th century a hall was built in stone to the north-east of the motte summit and, towards the end of the 13th century, a small rectangular tower was raised towards the south-west edge, to which an extension in a north-east alignment was added in the 15th century. Of these, the tower's walls survive to two storeys, and there are also the remains of some of the 15th-century works. The castle has commanding views towards the Mourne Mountains.

LOCATION: CO. DOWN
MAP REF: J 4140
OPEN: OPEN ACCESS

CLOUGHOUGHTER

On an islet in Lough Oughter, a cylindrical great tower with a cross-wall, at least three storeys tall, was built in two stages in the 13th century. The first two storeys were followed after a long interval by one, possibly two, more. The original entrance was at first-floor level. There is another, 16th-century entrance on the ground floor. Part of the tower has fallen away. A national monument administered by the Office of Public Works, it has open access.

LOCATION: ISLET IN LOUGH OUGHTER, NR KILLESHANDRA, CO. CAVAN
MAP REF: H 3405

COOLHULL

Only the ruins of a late 16th-century, long, rectangular tower house remain; these consist of three storeys, rising to a fourth storey in a rectangular turret at one end for stairs, garderobes and the entrance. The tower top has stepped battlements all round, with a square bartizan on one corner. Inside the tower are interesting fireplaces, and the upper windows are round-headed.

LOCATION: BANNOW, CO. WEXFORD
MAP REF: S 8810

COPPINGER'S COURT

A substantial tower house – perhaps more accurately a tower block – of the early 17th century, this castle has an interesting plan. A long, rectangular main core on an east–west axis has two square projections, one at each end on the north side, while on the south there is a third central projection that has the staircases. It was built by Sir Walter Coppinger in the years 1620–40. The Coppinger family is believed to date back to Viking times.

LOCATION: ROSS CARBERY, CO. CORK
MAP REF: W 2636
OPEN: DAILY

CRATLOE

A large rectangular tower house of the end of the 15th century, Cratloe is 17 x 10m (55 x 33ft), with thick walling on all sides, mostly over 2m (7ft) thick. It has four storeys, the second and third vaulted, and has small rooms in one end wall. The staircases are straight, and they are set in the wall thicknesses. The castle was built by the MacNamara family in 1610 who also owned nearby Bunratty Castle.

LOCATION: CO. CLARE
MAP REF: R 5259

BUILDING CASTLES

CASTLES SUCH AS THOSE SHOWN ON THE BAYEUX TAPESTRY COULD BE BUILT IN A FEW DAYS. SOME OF EDWARD I'S EXTRAORDINARY 13TH-CENTURY CASTLES IN WALES REMAINED UNFINISHED YEARS AFTER THEY WERE BEGUN, AND BEAUMARIS WAS NEVER COMPLETED. BUILDING CASTLES BECAME EVER MORE COMPLEX AS THE REQUIREMENTS OF THEIR OWNERS CHANGED OVER TIME.

When the Normans first arrived their priority was to dominate and to make sure rebellion was kept down as much as possible. Motte and bailey castles were a perfect solution in many ways: quick to build, they could be thrown up using materials found on the spot.

As stone replaced wood and earth, castle building became more expensive and time-consuming, especially when prestigious castles were involved. Here, the owners wanted to show not only that they had power and strength, but that they had both the taste and the wealth to buy the best.

For example, Caen stone from Normandy was considered to be not only the right quality for castles, but it was also lovely to look at, so it was imported at great expense. As castles became ever more sophisticated, so they required greater and wider building skills and increasingly more workers.

Harlech, one of Edward I's great strongholds in Wales, had a workforce of 546 labourers, 227 masons, and 115 quarrymen, not to mention smiths, carpenters and

Highly skilled masons and carpenters would have found almost continual employment in the Middle Ages as castles were built, destroyed and rebuilt. Armies of labourers were also needed to build castles quickly – a half-built castle was a target for a lord's enemies.

other highly skilled workers. Even so, this stage of the work took seven years, and at an enormous cost. While Edward's great work of building a ring of castles around North Wales went on, the country must have looked and felt like a gigantic building site. Records show that most of the workers came from England. But with some coming from as far away as the south-west the local economies must have been deeply affected as the demand for foodstuffs and raw materials grew.

Medieval castle builders had limited technologies to call on, but they used scaffolding in exactly the same way that we do today, except that their scaffolding poles were made of wood. Their skills are not in doubt, since so many castles survive today, albeit in ruined condition. Such ruins are often not the fault of weathering or natural causes but of deliberate destruction, or slighting, at some point. Castles frequently changed hands, and if this happened after a siege, it was often the case that the besiegers would attempt to make the castle incapable of being defended again.

Since castle walls could be several metres/feet thick at their base, destroying the work of the original masons

Architects of castles were often highly regarded. Master James of St George built castles in Europe and attracted the attention of Edward I. He designed strong, imposing castles and was rewarded with good pay and a pension.

could be very time-consuming, as the would-be demolishers of such castles as Corfe found to their cost. It took them weeks.

The Victorians, influenced in part by work undertaken at Balmoral Castle by Queen Victoria and Prince Albert, repaired many medieval castles, often to make them look like romantic ruins. Some went further: the Marquis of Bute employed architect William Burges to re-create a dreamlike medieval castle at Cardiff, complete with shimmering gold-inlaid interior decorations. The pair went even further at Castel Coch, a few miles away, where they rebuilt a medieval castle almost from scratch. To see the conical towers of this fairytale creation peeping above the trees is like seeing a medieval illustration come to magical life.

Building a tower. Two labourers are using a hand-wound winch to raise materials. Building castles required great skills, and large numbers of workers, often engaged on the same project for a number of years.

CROM

On the shores of Upper Lough Erne the remains of a plantation castle of c.1611, gutted by fire in the 18th century, lie next to a 19th-century mansion. Still surviving are parts of the outer enclosing walls and two small flanking turrets. The castle is owned by the National Trust for Northern Ireland, and is part of the Crom estate; it can be viewed from the grounds.

LOCATION: CO. FERMANAGH
MAP REF: H 3624

DERRIHIVENNY

A four-storeyed tower house with an enclosing L-plan bawn with round towers on two opposite corners, and along one wall a hall-style building, make up this interesting castle. It can be dated to 1643 from an inscription in the north-east angle machicolation. It was built by Donal O'Madden and became the family's principal seat. Its parapet and wall-walk partly overhang the walls at the top. Overall the building is in a fair condition. It was one of the last true tower houses to be built in Ireland.

LOCATION: NR PORTUMNA, CO. GALWAY
MAP REF: M 8708

DESMOND

Built as a custom house by the Earl of Desmond c.1500, this three-storeyed tower house was also known as the French Prison. From time to time it housed foreign prisoners of war, including Spaniards, Dutch and even Americans. It has interesting windows and a fine doorway. It now houses the International Museum of Wine (Office of Public Works: Tue–Sun).

LOCATION: KINSALE, CO. CORK
MAP REF: W 6451

DOE

This is a much altered and improved castle (the seat of the McSweeney family) centred on an original four-storeyed tower house of the early 16th century. Much of the castle to be seen now is the result of improvement work of the early 19th century, undertaken after the original castle had been left derelict for over a century.

LOCATION: SHEEPHAVEN BAY, NR CREESLOUGH, CO. DONEGAL
MAP REF: C 0832
OPEN: NOT GENERALLY OPEN TO PUBLIC, KEY HELD BY THE CARETAKER

DONEGAL

A great tower castle was begun here in the late-15th century by the O'Donnell family, lords of Tyrconnel. The first building was the great tower itself, rectangular, 17 x 10.5m (55 x 35ft), with walls nearly 2.5m (8ft) thick. Its five storeys began with a vaulted ground floor. It has been greatly altered, disguising its original form although not concealing its obvious defensiveness. The tower was set on fire by the family in about 1600 to prevent it being captured by the Earl of Essex's successor, Mountjoy. A few years later it came into the possession of the Brookes, a prominent Protestant family, who carried out several major reconstructions, adding a substantial residential three-storey rectangular wing on the great tower's west side. The tower itself was restored, windows were enlarged, and a huge bay window was inserted just above the original entrance on the east side.

LOCATION: CO. DONEGAL
MAP REF: G 9377
OPEN: OFFICE OF PUBLIC WORKS: MON–FRI, SAT–SUN PM (CLOSED DURING STATE BUSINESS)

DONORE

This is a good example of the small tower-house type of castle known as the £10 castle, an incentive that was paid by the government in 1429 to build fortifications as protection against Gaelic rebels. It has three storeys that are reached via a spiral staircase in a small round turret projecting on one corner. The corners of the tower are rounded. The ground storey is vaulted.

LOCATION: CO. MEATH
MAP REF: N 7149

DOWNPATRICK

A motte castle of the early Anglo-Norman settlement, about 1177, occupied the whole summit of one of the low hills here. Its bailey rampart was probably part of a pre-Norman ring fort.

LOCATION: CO. DOWN
MAP REF: J 4844

DROGHEDA

The Anglo-Normans recognized the strategic position of Drogheda on the River Boyne, and raised a large motte castle on a prehistoric mound, now known as Mill Mount. Only parts survive of a later stone bailey wall. On the opposite riverbank are the remains of a substantial four-storey twin drum-towered gateway with a round-headed entrance, known as St Laurence's Gate (you can drive through the gate, but not access the interior). It dates from the 13th century and is probably part of the castle barbican that protected the castle gatehouse. The tower's battlements survive, and it has long, narrow loops and windows at higher levels, some of them round-headed.

LOCATION: CO. LOUTH
MAP REF: N 0976

DUBLIN

Possibly the castle least liked by the Irish because it was the headquarters of English government for so many centuries. Dublin Castle has been through numerous changes, so that it is not possible today to get any real idea of what it looked like in the late Middle Ages. The first works were at the start of the 13th century (there is a Royal Writ for them dated 1205) and they were positioned on or near fortifications in Dublin which were almost certainly of mid-10th-century Viking origin. A drawing of the late 17th century shows the castle as a five-sided enclosure, with no great tower, but with huge round corner towers on the angles. Parts of some of these have survived, incorporated in various later works. These include the base of the Bermingham Tower on the south-west end of the enclosure; parts of what is now the Record Tower on the south-east end, 17m (56ft) in diameter, whose parapet and machicolation are of the 19th century; and stretches of the southern curtain. What was known as the Storehouse Tower, on the north-east corner, may have been used as a residential tower in place of a great tower, but it was demolished in the 18th century. On the north-west corner was the Corke tower, a round tower, rebuilt in the 17th century.

There have been several excavations: one revealed part of the causeway from the city across a moat into the castle.

LOCATION: DAME STREET, DUBLIN, CO. DUBLIN
MAP REF: O 1534
OPEN: OFFICE OF PUBLIC WORKS: MID-MAR–NOV DAILY

The interior of Dublin Castle has been remodelled extensively. Its magnifence reflects its use for state occasions.

DUNAMASE

Among the most impressive sites in Ireland, Dunamase was erected upon an early Christian site on the towering rock overlooking Portlaoise. For a time it was also the site of a fortress that belonged to the kings of Leinster, and in the reign of King John was granted to William Marshal. Only a part of the great tower remains and this is badly damaged. The enclosure had walling over 2m (6ft) thick on the east side, with flanking rectangular turrets, while the west wall was thinner. The great tower was rectangular, some 20.5 x 35m (67 x 116ft), with two cross-walls. In the 17th century this was adapted to make the northern section into a separate tower house. To the east of the great tower, sited in the east wall, are the remains of a twin round-ended towered gateway leading into a triangular outer ward, which is very much smaller than the enclosure on the rock top. The castle, although impressive and having covered a lot of the rock, is in a very ruinous condition.

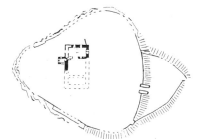

LOCATION: STRADBALLY, CO. LAOIS
MAP REF: S 5298
OPEN: OPEN ACCESS

DUNBOY

Here stand the remains of a 15th-century tower-house castle, with three main storeys over the ground floor. The bawn wall had two turrets. Later a square wing was added on one corner of the tower house. In about 1602, a second bawn wall was added, after which the castle was taken and then slighted. In the mid-17th century, the castle was replaced with a star-plan fort. The site is privately owned.

LOCATION: NR CASTLETOWNBERE, CO. CORK
MAP REF: V 6644

DUNDRUM

Dundrum Castle was built on the site of an Irish ring-fort. It is one of the finest Norman castles in Northern Ireland, with excellent views. It was built by John de Courcy in c.1177. By 1211 it had four storeys, its walls over 2m (7ft) thick. The topmost storey contained a range of mural chambers and passages all the way round.

In the 1260s, the enclosure was given a square-plan twin-towered gatehouse on the south side, built on the remains of an earlier cylindrical wall-tower.

Two centuries later, a second enclosure of stone was erected as an outer (lower) ward on the south west.

By the mid-1330s it was apparently ruinous and was taken over by the Magenis family who retained it for two centuries. Large and dominating as it is, its life as a feudal castle seems to have been short.

LOCATION: CO. DOWN
MAP REF: J 4036
OPEN: ENVIRONMENT AND HERITAGE SERVICE NORTHERN IRELAND: SAT, SUN (OPENED ON REQUEST OTHER TIMES)

DUNGUAIRE

This 16th-century castle is raised on an old Irish ring-fort that stands on a rocky promontory in a commanding position on the shores of Galway Bay. It rises to four storeys and an attic, and the lower part of one of its walls makes up part of the wall of a six-sided surrounding bawn. It has a central machicolation box at parapet level on each of its four walls. The castle takes its name from the nearby ancient fort of Guaire, King of Connaught who died in 662 CE. During the early 20th century it became a venue for the great Irish literary figures of the day, including George Bernard Shaw, WB Yeats and Oliver St John Gogarty, the surgeon and literary man who was responsible for much of the renovation. The castle has been restored with a great deal of care and attention to

historical detail, and medieval banquets are hosted during the summer in the tower house, complete with 'King Guaire' and plenty of music.

LOCATION: KINVARA, CO. GALWAY
MAP REF: M 3811
OPEN: SHANNON HERITAGE: MAY–OCT DAILY

One of the most dramatically sited castles in Ireland, Dunluce stands on a rock surrounded by the sea, attached to the mainland by a wooden bridge, formerly joined by a drawbridge. The castle was originally a four-sided enclosure, approximately rectangular, with corner towers. Of this oldest work only the south wall facing the land and the remains of two eastern towers survive. It had been erected upon the site of a prehistoric souterrain, later a Christian 'underground' harbour for ships. The Norman castle buildings were begun by Richard de Burgo, Earl of Ulster. The main part of the castle, however, is of much later date, and includes a late 13th-century gatehouse capped on its outer angles by corbelled round turrets. The Great Hall was erected against a somewhat earlier and rather unusual arcaded gallery, or loggia, and some of these pillars remain. Other works here included domestic buildings put up in two baileys.

LOCATION: PORTRUSH, CO. ANTRIM
MAP REF: C 9041
OPEN: ENVIRONMENT AND HERITAGE SERVICE NORTHERN IRELAND: MON–SAT DAILY, SUN PM

DUNMAHON

Dunmahon is a small, late 15th-century tower house with turrets in a ruinous condition. It is four-storeyed, has a square-plan staircase turret and a second turret that has garderobes. Its height, however, is only about 12m (40ft) to the wall-walk.

LOCATION: NR BLACKROCK, CO. LOUTH
MAP REF: J 0605

DUNMOE

This large 14th- to 15th-century great tower overlooking the Boyne is now in a very ruined condition. The tower originally had four turrets clasping the central rectangular core, and they are half round, half polygonal. One is fragmentary.

LOCATION: NR ATHBOY, CO. MEATH
MAP REF: N 9070

DUNMORE

This 14th-century rectangular great tower, which was later given an extra one or two storeys and a gabled attic on top, shows signs of repair work and modifications of several periods. The castle measures 17 x 12m (56 x 39ft) on a sloping plinth. It was raised on the site of a 13th-century castle of the de Bermingham family.

LOCATION: CO. GALWAY
MAP REF: M 5064

DUNSEVERICK

Sited on a rock promontory on the north coast, which was partly skirted by a bawn, this castle has a 16th-century tower-like building, now very ruinous, which may have been a gatehouse leading into the bawn. It was destroyed by the Scots in 1642. It is accessible from the North Antrim coastal path.

LOCATION: CO. ANTRIM
MAP REF: C 9844

DUNSOGHLY

The very tall great tower of Dunsoghly stands in a farmyard north of Dublin. It is remarkable in having its original timber roofing from the 15th century, a valuable and authentic illustration of how such roofs were constructed. The great tower was erected by Sir Thomas Plunkett, a Chief Justice of the King's Bench, in the mid-15th century.

LOCATION: NR FINGLAS, DUBLIN, CO. DUBLIN
MAP REF: O 1143
OPEN: OFFICE OF PUBLIC WORKS: RESTRICTED ACCESS

DURROW

Near the monastery of St Columcille (Columba), where the *Book of Durrow* was compiled, are the remains of a motte castle. This was raised in the 1170s, probably by de Lacy, who is said to have demolished a stone chapel nearby using the stone for a building on the motte, which he had raised within the chapel enclosure. This act was probably the reason for his murder in 1186 on or near the site.

LOCATION: CO. OFFALY
MAP REF: N 3131

ENNISCORTHY

A major Norman castle overlooked the Slaney River in Enniscorthy in the 13th century, but it has largely disappeared under a complete rebuild of the late 16th century and later modifications. The plan may have been the same as at present, a rectangular, four-storeyed tower (in this case with a cross-wall) with four cylindrical towers clamped on the corners. The two corner towers on the west wall act as protector towers for the main tower entrance. In the 16th century the castle was given to the poet Edmund Spenser by Queen Elizabeth I in recognition of his poem *The Faerie Queen*, dedicated to her. The castle currently functions as a museum, the County Wexford Historical and Folk Museum, and it also houses the Tourist Information Office in the summer months.

LOCATION: CO. WEXFORD
MAP REF: S 9739
OPEN: DAILY

ENNISKILLEN

ENNISKILLEN SIEGE

Enniskillen Castle was at the centre of Irish rebellion against English rule in the 16th century.

Sir Hugh Maguire didn't oppose settlers, and was content under English rule. However, when Scottish settlers from neighbouring counties began to invade Fermanagh, Hugh turned to the English for help. No assistance was forthcoming and Hugh fought back, so starting the Nine Years War. Enniskillen was besieged from the sea and the land in February 1594, and withstood a terrific onslaught for eight days. The planters took the castle and the Maguires spent years trying to take it back until it was finally brought to ruin in 1602.

Attractively located on the banks of Lough Erne, this stronghold began as a 15th-century rectangular four-storey tower house with prominent parapet and battlements round the top gabled attic storey, erected by the Maguires. A drawing of it was made in 1594 (see box, left). The tower house stood inside a bawn. It was destroyed in 1602, and a few years later a new Protestant English owner rebuilt it as a plantation castle. The history of the castle and the regiment can be seen in the Heritage Centre and the Museum of the Royal Inniskilling Fusiliers, located inside.

LOCATION: CO. FERMANAGH
MAP REF: H 2144
OPEN: FERMANAGH DISTRICT COUNCIL: MON–SAT PM, TUE–FRI DAILY. CLOSED WINTER WEEKENDS

FEARTAGAR

This is a well-preserved tower house, known as Jennings Castle, dating from the late 16th or early 17th century. It is believed it got its name from a corruption of the Irish name Eion, one-time owners, which was later anglicized to John or Jenning. It is four-storeyed and has staircases in the wall thicknesses. It was abandoned after its last occupant had been removed during the Cromwellian campaign in Ireland, 1649–51.

LOCATION: NORTH OF TUAM, CO. GALWAY
MAP REF: M 3856

FERNS

One of the main early to mid-13th-century, large Anglo-Norman great tower castles (similar to Carlow, Terryglass and Lea), which consist of a central rectangular (or square) core with round towers clasping the corners; substantial parts remain, but in poor condition. There were some buildings in the early 13th century when it was in the possession of William Marshal (d.1219), but the great tower is of a later date, probably 1230–50. By the 14th century Ferns was run down.

LOCATION: CO. WEXFORD
MAP REF: T 0050
OPEN: OFFICE OF PUBLIC WORKS: GUIDED TOURS JUN–AUG DAILY

FIDDAUN

A tall, rectangular five-storeyed tower house with attic. Fiddaun was built in the 16th century. It has box machicolations on the outside walls at third-storey level and stands centrally inside a rectangular bawn whose gateway is on the north side, and on the west side of which is a sharp triangular projection like part of a star fortification. Fiddaun was held by the O'Shaughnessys up to the early 18th century; the last of the family to occupy the castle was Lady Helena O'Shaughnessy who died there in 1729. The bawn is one of the best preserved in Ireland.

LOCATION: GORT, CO. GALWAY
MAP REF: R 4196

GARRAUNBOY

This is a 15th-century tower house of five storeys whose dimensions are 14 x 9m (46 x 30ft), with three walls about 2m (7ft) wide and the fourth originally nearly double that thickness, with space for a spiral staircase. Part of this fourth wall has crumbled away. The tower stands surrounded on all sides by a rectangular enclosing wall, now fragmentary, which had cylindrical turrets, which are also fragmentary. The tower house belonged to the Faltagh family at one time.

LOCATION: ADARE, CO. LIMERICK
MAP REF: R 4345

GLANWORTH

In an attractive setting, this started as a mid- to late-13th-century castle. Its first buildings included a rectangular great tower, now only two storeys high, inside a trapezoid curtain with round turrets of later date, of which parts remain. Some of the curtain is original. To the west of it are remnants of a gatehouse built at much the same time as the great tower. The entrance through the gatehouse was blocked off in the 15th century to create a tower house of five storeys with a garderobe turret that still stands. In the 15th century, a new curtain was built west of the first enclosure, in which a round tower was erected at the north-west and a square tower at the south-west. The castle is in a poor state of repair.

LOCATION: GLANVILLE, CO. CORK
MAP REF: R 7504
OPEN: ACCESSIBLE FROM BEHIND GLANVILLE MILL

GLENINAGH

An L-plan tower house of the 16th century, based largely on Scottish models of the same period, Gleninagh is four storeys tall above a basement, and it has an attic at roof level. The third storey is vaulted. Some window openings were later blocked up to allow for inserting fireplaces. The staircase is in the short arm of the 'L', where the tower is entered at ground floor and a box machicolation at top level covers the entrance. The three other corners of the tower house have round bartizans at parapet level. The walls and the corners have defensive arrow slits. The castle, overlooking Ballyvaughan Bay, was occupied well into the 19th century by the O'Loughlin family. A holy well is sited close by.

LOCATION: NR BALLYVAUGHAN, CO. CLARE
MAP REF: M 1910
OPEN: OFFICE OF PUBLIC WORKS: ACCESS DOWN LANE AND ACROSS A FIELD

GLENOGRA

The early 15th-century castle here was an enclosure of six unequal sides. The north side was an 8.5m (28ft) or so stretch of wall about 3m (10ft) deep, at each end of which was an octagonal tower with equally thick walls. One tower has survived, the other is residual. The survivor is about 12m (40ft) across and still has its staircase. The ruins are very fragmented and stand alone in a field.

LOCATION: BETWEEN BRUFF AND CROOM, CO. LIMERICK
MAP REF: R 5942

GLINSK

An imposing stronghouse with box machicolations on the outer front corners of its two projecting towers, this rectangular building is of the 1620s. The tower is three storeys with tall chimneys and once had a gabled attic storey above, of which not much remains. It was one of the last castles to be built in Ireland and shows the transition from castle to house. The interior of the tower is without its floors due to a serious fire early in its history. The exterior is well preserved. This National Monument is administered by the Office of Public Works.

LOCATION: BETWEEN BALLYMOE AND CREGGS, CO. GALWAY
MAP REF: M 7266

GRANAGH

Granagh is known colloquially as Granny Castle. Standing high on the bank above the River Suire, it was originally a rectangular- (almost square-) plan late 13th-century stone enclosure with, in the northern corner, a residential tower house of the late 14th to early 15th century, with a 16th-century hall block addition. Its south-east and south-west corners had cylindrical flanking turrets. Granagh Castle was held by the Le Poer and Ormond families. The tower house is badly damaged but stands to its full height in parts.

LOCATION: NR WATERFORD, CO. KILKENNY
MAP REF: S 5815

GRANARD

A motte castle was raised on a natural mound, heightening the castle to make it one of the tallest in Ireland. It has a clearly defined bailey, with ditching and an outer bank. It was built at the very end of the 12th century. The foundations of a stone shell wall round the motte summit have been found, and also the remains of a cylindrical tower within. The stonework was probably early 13th century.

LOCATION: CO. LONGFORD
MAP REF: N 3382

GREENCASTLE (DONEGAL)

Greencastle, Inishowen, was built by Richard de Burgo, who became Earl of Chester in 1305. The castle was captured by Edward Bruce in 1316 but was taken by the O'Dohertys in 1333. The ruins of this once substantial enclosure castle dominate the sea at the mouth of Lough Foyle. The castle belonged for a time to Lionel, Duke of Clarence, Edward III's second son. It was attacked and taken by the Irish in the late 14th century and was finally demolished in the 1550s, leaving the ruins that remain today.

LOCATION: INISHOWEN, GREENCASTLE, CO. DONEGAL
MAP REF: M 6540
OPEN: RUINS BY THE SEA

GREENCASTLE (DOWN)

A royal castle of the mid-13th century, strategically located at the entrance to Carlingford Lough. Probably the first work was a stone enclosure, very little of which remains today. In about the 1230s, a substantial rectangular great tower of hall type, only two storeys tall and with a steep roof, was erected inside the curtain. The castle was sacked soon after the great tower was built, and it was besieged again by Edward Bruce in 1316. Major work was carried out in the 15th century when the walls were heightened to form a third storey. In the 16th century

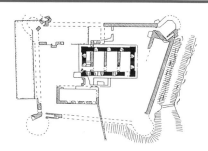

further work was carried out, but by the 17th century Greencastle had been abandoned.

LOCATION: KILKEEL, CO. DOWN
MAP REF: J 2411
OPEN: ENVIRONMENT AND HERITAGE SERVICE, NORTHERN IRELAND: JUL–AUG TUE, FRI–SUN PM, WED–THU AM

HARRY AVERY'S TOWER

Named after Henry Aimbreidh O'Neill, who died in 1392 and who possibly built the castle, this building consisted of a stone enclosure built upon a hillock, commanding a fine view of the valley of the River Derg close to Newtonstewart. What is visible today is the remnant of a rectangular tower having two half-circular projections of two storeys' height each, which were three-storeyed before the assault by Viceroy Chichester in the first years of the 17th century. The tower features in the local 'The Journey in Time' archaeological tour.

LOCATION: NEWTONSTEWART, CO. TYRONE
MAP REF: H 3985
OPEN: ENVIRONMENT AND HERITAGE SERVICE NORTHERN IRELAND: OPEN ACCESS

HOWTH

The present Howth Castle is largely an 18th-century modification of what remained of the original structure. The main original building of the 15th century is the slightly L-plan gate-tower with round-headed archway at left of the front face, leading through to the rear. Howth's tower has domestic-style windows. The castle is closed to the public but can be viewed from the grounds.

LOCATION: CO. DUBLIN
MAP REF: O 2839

IGHTERMURRAGH

This interesting tower house of the early 17th century is of cruciform plan, with a long, rectangular block 22 x 9.5m (73 x 32ft), with walls nearly 2m (6ft) thick. Centrally across this block is a pair of square towers projecting from the block, with somewhat narrower walls. All four arms of the 'cross' rise to four storeys plus the attic storey (18.5m/60ft to the top) behind a bold parapet with tall chimneys. Inside are several fireplaces, one of which has an inscription dated 1641.

LOCATION: CASTLEMARTYR, CO. CORK
MAP REF: W 9973

INCH

The remains of a three-storey rectangular tower house inside an enclosure of the 15th century can be seen on the small peninsula of Inch Island in Lough Swilly. It belonged for a time to the powerful Gaelic family of the O'Domhuaills who were, among other things, Lords of Tyrconnel and held sway in much of Donegal in the 15th and 16th centuries. Access is possible but requires a long walk across farmland.

LOCATION: CO. DONEGAL
MAP REF: C 3222

INCHIQUIN

A substantial cylindrical great tower on a sloping plinth, beside the river. Inchiquin rises to two full storeys in its present ruined state, but was clearly three if not four storeys originally.

LOCATION: NR KILLEAGH, CO.CORK
MAP REF: X 0176

CROMWELL IN IRELAND

By 1649, when Cromwell arrived to subdue rebellion in Ireland, the country was being torn apart by fighting between Anglo-Normans, Scottish settlers, native Irish, Royalists and Parliamentarians. Cromwell's response to opposition was completely ruthless and he oversaw the slaughter of thousands of Irish Catholics. Cromwell's legacy echoes through the years to the present day.

Oliver Cromwell besieges Drogheda in 1649–50

KANTURK

An early 17th-century castle having a four-storeyed rectangular core, on the four corners of which are sizable five-storey square towers. The windows are mullioned and take up much of the walls, unusual for a stronghouse originally intended to be defensible. It is said that the owner stopped work on the castle because neighbouring lords complained to the English Privy Council about the size and fortifications. It is owned by the National Trust for Ireland.

LOCATION: CO. CORK
MAP REF: W 3801
OPEN: NATIONAL TRUST FOR IRELAND: FREE ACCESS

KELLS

This is one of two castles of the same name. It began as a motte castle of the late 12th century, which had a later walled bailey. Nearby, the famous ruined Augustinian priory, which was first fortified at the end of the 12th century, was provided with several square towers.

LOCATION: CO. KILKENNY
MAP REF: S 4943

KILBOLANE

The design of this building is very much on the lines of late 13th-century strongholds but is most likely to be of the 15th or 16th century. It survives with its two outer walls with a pair of circular turrets. The walls are defended by a water-filled moat on the south-west side.

LOCATION: MILFORD, NR CHARLEVILLE, CO. CORK
MAP REF: R 4221

KILCLIEF

A 15th-century tower house, c.1412–40, this has two turrets on its east wall, one for the entrance and staircase, one for garderobes. The turrets are linked higher up by arching, behind which are machicolations. Smaller turrets also project above the four-storey height. It is an early example of a gatehouse design, used as a model for later strongholds.

LOCATION: NR STRANGFORD, CO. DOWN
MAP REF: J 6046

KILKENNY

At first a motte castle of c.1171, built by Strongbow and destroyed, presumably by the native Irish, in 1174, the castle in this important early Norman town was begun again by William Marshal during his years in Ireland (1207–12). The castle came into the possession of the Butlers, Earls (and later, Dukes) of Ormonde in the 15th century, and over the centuries, they carried out extensive remodelling of the original works. Today, Kilkenny is a national monument and houses the Butler Art Gallery in the former servants' quarters.

LOCATION: THE PARADE, KILKENNY, CO. KILKENNY
MAP REF: S 5155
OPEN: OFFICE OF PUBLIC WORKS: DAILY

KILLARNEY (ROSS CASTLE)

An impressive and well-preserved tower house of the late 15th century, Killarney has later additions and a bawn with flanking round turrets. It stands on a wooded isthmus extending into Lough Leane. The tower is five storeys to the parapet, has box machicolations on two opposing corners and is rectangular in plan.

LOCATION: CO. KERRY
MAP REF: V 9589
OPEN: OFFICE OF PUBLIC WORKS: APR–OCT DAILY

KILKEA

Hugh de Lacy originally built a castle here around 1180. The motte is now covered by trees. An L-plan tower house was built in the 15th or 16th century and was completely restored in the 19th century in medieval style. This is one of the oldest continuously inhabited castles in Ireland. Nowadays it is a hotel and golf course with extensive grounds.

LOCATION: CASTLEDERMOT, CO. KILDARE
MAP REF: S 7497

KILLENURE

A late 16th-century modified tower house that had four cylindrical corner turrets, mostly now in a ruinous state. The ground floor had no living quarters and the windows were much smaller than those of the upper floors. It was presumably made to be defensible. It has been described as a tower house that became more house than tower.

LOCATION: NR DUNDRUM, CO. TIPPERARY
MAP REF: S 0044

KILLYLEAGH

Close to Strangford Lough's western shore, this is a greatly modified castle. Begun in the 13th century, the only original work now is part of the large south-west cylindrical tower clasping the central rectangular core. In the 17th century it was converted to a stronghouse by an ancestor of the present owner, and again altered in the 19th century to give it its present French château look. Part of the castle is now luxury apartments.

LOCATION: STRANGFORD LOUGH, CO. DOWN
MAP REF: J 5253

KILTARTAN

A large imposing 13th-century castle, now in ruins, Kiltartan had a three-storey tower with very thick walls and a gateway flanked by powerful round towers set in an enclosing curtain. It was built by the de Burgo family.

LOCATION: NR. GORT, CO. GALWAY
MAP REF: M 4605

KILTEEL

A five-storey tower house built in the late 15th century, Kilteel adjoins a gate-tower of the same period. This may have been part of a range of residential buildings belonging to the Knights Hospitallers (there are fragmentary remains a few hundred metres/yards away from the tower). The tower house has a cylindrical turret projecting on one corner, which has loops at each level. Part of the parapet and battlements remain.

LOCATION: NR. NAAS, CO. KILDARE
MAP REF: N 9821

KINNITTY

This is a low motte and bailey of c.1213 erected on rising ground and located about 1.5km (1 mile) from the village. The ditching has become obscured, probably through prolonged farming. Beside the motte is the fragment of the head of a High Cross, possibly from the monastery founded by St Barrind in the 6th century.

LOCATION: CO. OFFALY
MAP REF: N 1508

KINSALE

South of this important and historic port town are the remains of a 15th-century fortified area of headland known as the Old Head of Kinsale owned for a time by the de Courcys. Here, a long stone wall with flanking turrets was the front defence. Behind a gateway in the wall is the shell of a tall tower house, which rises to about 15m (50ft), with five storeys now very badly damaged and incomplete. Two of the storeys were vaulted.

LOCATION: OLD HEAD OF KINSALE, CO. CORK
MAP REF: W 6415

KNAPPOGUE CO. CLARE

This mid-15th-century rectangular tower house has five storeys and attic, with corner box machicolation, long, narrow loops, battlements, and two raised corner turrets with projecting machicolation. These have been restored and supplemented with newer buildings at the lower levels. The castle was built by Sean MacNamara and is a fine example of a medieval tower house. In the mid-16th century it became the seat of the MacNamara clan and remained in the family's hands until 1650 when it was captured by Cromwell's troops. In 1670 the castle was returned to its MacNamara owners, to be sold in 1800 when much of the restoration and extension work took place. By the 1920s it had fallen into disrepair, but it was then purchased by an American architect who restored the castle in association with Shannon Development.

LOCATION: QUIN, CO. CLARE
MAP REF: R 4472
OPEN: SHANNON DEVELOPMENT: APR-OCT DAILY

KNOCKGRAFFON

This is one of the most famous motte castles in Ireland – it is certainly widely photographed. It was raised in about 1192. The site has commanding views over the Suir valley, and when the motte was first raised with its wooden tower, it would have demonstrated great strategic power. The motte rises to around 17m (55ft) and is about 20m (65ft) across its summit. It was built upon an earlier Irish hill site that may have been a seat for the kings of Munster before they moved to the site at Cashel, not far away. Below the mound is a churchyard with the ruins of a church and several rows of graves and tombstones. Beyond that, situated about 1km (0.5 mile) from the mound, there is a 16th-century rectangular tower house, built by the Cahir Butlers, which is 11.5 x 9m (38 x 29ft) and which has round bartizans on two corners.

LOCATION: CAHIR, CO. TIPPERARY
MAP REF: S 0241
OPEN: NATIONAL MONUMENT

ENTERTAINMENT AND SPORT

LIFE IN MEDIEVAL CASTLES WAS NOT UNREMITTINGLY GRIM. THERE WAS SINGING AND LAUGHTER, AND THERE WERE GAMES. JOUSTING AND HUNTING WERE FOR THE NOBILITY, BUT ORDINARY PEOPLE COULD WATCH THE JOUSTS, AND SOMETIMES FEASTS FOR ALL WERE HELD TO MARK SPECIAL OCCASIONS.

The lord may have had a resident jester, and part of his job was to entertain during the long evenings, primarily by making people laugh. Travelling troubadours, or minstrels, provided songs and music, often accompanied by harps, trumpets or fiddles. Storytelling was hugely important, and epic stories would be told around the fire. Especially loved were tales about chivalry and the brave deeds of knights. Stories about King Arthur and the Knights of the Round Table were favourites, and they often extolled the virtues that the listeners aspired to themselves.

Outside, an early form of soccer called camp-ball was played. Using a pig's bladder stuffed with dried peas, the idea was to score goals – as today – but there were virtually no rules: the pitch could be of any size and any number of players could join in. It was chaotic and dangerous. Hunting was very popular with nobles; many different kinds of animal were hunted, but deer were the most prized. Large areas of countryside were set aside for hunting purposes, the most well-known being the New Forest in Hampshire. Some smaller castles, such as Odiham, were used primarily as places from which to undertake hunts. Hares were considered to be good sport, partly because they were difficult to catch, and wild boars were also hunted, although these formidable animals were very dangerous, especially when cornered.

Dogs were an essential part of the hunt, and nobles made a great fuss of their dogs, sometimes treating them better then they did their servants. Favoured hunting dogs slept by the fire in the hall.

Falconry was very popular, and all manner of birds were caught by the falcons. They were also trained to catch rabbits and hares. Keeping falcons was expensive as they required a good deal of care and training, and they were fed good meat. A lord might employ several falconers.

The wonderful 14th-century Luttrell Psalter shows many aspects of ordinary life, including games and entertainment. These men are engaged in piggy-back wrestling.

Golf in the early 16th century. The player on the right is concentrating hard on his final putt.

Tournaments were among the most popular events. Here, knights would joust for rich prizes. Knights rode against each other in lists, which kept the horses from running into one another. They were watched by large numbers of onlookers, including noblewomen, who might very well have 'favourites' to whom they might offer gifts or even romance.

Before the jousts were confined to lists, the knights fought pretty much where they chose, destroying crops and terrifying people in the process. Jousting could be fatal, even though the lances were specially made to splinter on impact. In order to minimize the danger, knights wore heavier armour when jousting then they did in actual warfare. They wore helmets with narrow eye slits, but even this could be dangerous, so at the last moment before impact the knight would raise his head. This made the slits safe from splinters, but also ensured that for the last few seconds the knight could not see where he was going. He had to rely on the momentum and steadiness of his horse. Some knights earned their living by travelling from tournament to tournament.

Hunting was considered a noble pursuit and dogs were specially trained to chase game. Servants would attend to the dogs and assist the lords to blow horns to flush out the prey. Such retainers were well paid for their work. In the 13th century hornblowers might be paid three pence a day. Archers were paid five pence a day.

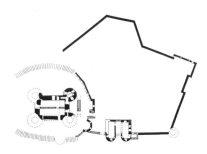

This great structure must, in its heyday, have been one of the most imposing castles in all Ireland. It also had a stirring history, changing hands several times. It was used as a mint until it was finally slighted by the forces of Cromwell in 1650. Three and a half centuries afterwards, it is still a dramatic and impressive aggregation of ruins.

It began as an oval motte with two baileys, constructed at the beginning of the 13th century by William de Vesey. Half a century later it was owned by one of the Fitzgeralds, probably Maurice, 2nd Lord of Offaly, and it was then that the motte was used as a base for a major great tower, rectangular

with four corner towers, like Carlow, Ferns and Terryglass. It was four-storeyed including the basement, with a main staircase in straight flights in the core wall.

Outside the great tower's bailey, a second stone enclosure was raised,

more or less on the site of the palisade of the second original bailey, extending north to the edge of the River Barrow. Most of this work was done at much the same time as the great tower.

LOCATION: NR PORTARLINGTON, CO. LAOIS
MAP REF: N 5712
OPEN: OPEN ACCESS

LEAMANEH

This tower house castle belonged to the O'Brien family. It began as a tall, narrow, five-storey rectangular tower house of about 1480, with loops and not windows. Three sides stand on a slightly sloping plinth. Inside, the main rooms are rectangular and take up about half of the tower, the other half containing the staircase. About 160 years later, a long rectangular stronghouse of four storeys was added on the west, the walls of which were much the same width as the original tower; the castle became L-plan. In the newer work, the windows are large and mullioned. The front entrance is a round-headed doorway. This evocative and melancholy ruin can be seen from the road but is on private land.

LOCATION: THE BURREN (NEAREST TOWN KILFENORA), CO. CLARE
MAP REF: R 2494
OPEN: PRIVATE

Overlooking the River Shannon, the first building here was started in about 1200 on the site of an Anglo-Norman earthwork enclosure of six sides, which were rapidly converted to stonework. The early work may have included a large round tower at each end of the west wall, and a twin round-towered gatehouse in the northern wall, and slightly to the north-east another large flanking tower. The gatehouse was for a time the residence of the castle's constable. In Edward I's reign (1272–1307) more building was carried out, including the start of work on a substantial great hall along the Shannon.

Limerick Castle (also known as King John's Castle) was intended as an administrative centre to control not only the activities of the Irish north-west of the Shannon but also to check the expansionism of Norman lords. It has been altered over the centuries because of its key role. It was captured by Edward Bruce in 1316, and was briefly in the hands of the O'Briens in the mid-14th century; it subsequently declined in importance to be re-occupied in the 17th century. A British army barracks was built in the courtyard in c.1750.

Major excavations began at the castle in the early 1990s. The most interesting result has been the exposure of significant remains of the 13th-century great hall, built in two stages.

The remains of a medieval garrison and soldiers' quarters were more recently discovered, and the castle now includes exhibitions and archaeological excavations which are open to the public.

LOCATION: NICHOLAS STREET, KING'S ISLAND, LIMERICK, CO. LIMERICK
MAP REF: R 5857
OPEN: SHANNON DEVELOPMENT: DAILY

LISCARROLL

A large 13th-century castle, Liscarroll consists of a huge rectangular stonewall enclosure with a substantial gatehouse on the south wall with portcullis grooves, and on the opposite (north) wall a rectangular flanking tower. Later, in the 15th to early 16th centuries, the gatehouse was altered to make a tower house. Much of the castle walls and towers remain, even though badly damaged in places.

LOCATION: NR KANTURK, CO. CORK
MAP REF: R 4512

LISCARTAN

This site has a pair of rectilinear tower houses (probably of the 15th century) on the same axis, joined now only by a short wall. Their shapes are unequal: one is roughly T-plan with a small square corner turret at the bottom of the down-stroke of the 'T'; it is only two storeys high. The other is a nearly square tower house with two projecting square turrets on one wall, one of them housing the staircase.

LOCATION: NR NAVAN, CO. MEATH
MAP REF: N 8609

LISMORE (WATERFORD)

Superbly located above the River Blackwater, this building began as a motte castle erected c.1185, according to Giraldus. The castle passed into the hands of Sir Walter Raleigh in 1598 and was sold to the Earl of Cork in 1602, who was responsible for creating a superb estate park. The castle was subject to 19th-century remodelling by the Duke of Devonshire. Lismore is now a private hotel.

LOCATION: CO. WATERFORD
MAP REF: X 0498

LISTOWEL

Visitors today can see the impressive ruins of the great Listowel Tower that was built in the 15th century by the Fitzmaurices, Lords of Kerry, based on a Norman castle. Only parts still stand, chiefly a pair of square corner towers with a connecting wall, and fragments of other walling. Restoration has been undertaken by the Office of Public Works, and guided tours are available.

LOCATION: CO. KERRY
MAP REF: Q 9934

LOHORT

A 15th-century tower house, Lohort was badly damaged by Cromwell's forces in 1650, but was restored in the 18th century and completely renovated in the 1870s. It had six storeys with rounded corners and a machicolated parapet most of the way round at the top. It has recently been allowed to decay and is now ruinous. It can be viewed from a distance.

LOCATION: NR KANTURK, CO. CORK
MAP REF: R 4602

LOUGH MASK

Lough Mask is a four-storey tower house, 18.5 x 12m (60 x 40ft), built in the early 17th century. It is joined to part of the surviving bawn of an earlier castle building on the site, about which little is known. This later tower has substantial walls, in particular the east one which is nearly 6m (20ft) thick, containing chambers and staircases.

LOCATION: NR CONG, CO. MAYO
MAP REF: M 1560

LOUGHMOE

This is a huge ruin of more than one period of construction. The first work was the 15th-century rectangular tower house on the south end of the castle. It has four storeys, two of them vaulted, with rounded external corners and box machicolations at high level. It is about 17.5m (57ft) high to the wall walk. The two narrower walls extend a further storey upwards and contain mural passages and chambers About two centuries later, a much less defensible long house was added on the north wall of the earlier tower, 26m (86ft) long and only 10.5m (34ft) wide, the rear wall continuing in the same line as the older tower's rear wall. The property was once owned by the Purcell family who were connected with this area at least as early as the 14th century.

LOCATION: NR TEMPLEMORE, CO. TIPPERARY
MAP REF: S 1266
OPEN: PRIVATE: ACCESS BY PERMISSION OF THE LANDOWNER

LOUTH

Now known locally as Fairy Mount, Louth has ditching all the way round and some counterscarp. It was attacked and burned in 1196 but re-occupied in 1204. There are no signs of a bailey. The motte, raised on natural rising ground, is about 9m (30ft) high.

LOCATION: CO. LOUTH
MAP REF: N 9800

MALAHIDE

Although this much-modernized castle was the home of the Norman family of Talbot for several centuries, the remains of the original castle have been almost completely obscured. Nonetheless the present structure is handsome, and may even be described as formidable-looking; it gives a good account of the Talbot family who lived in the castle from 1185 until 1973, save for a brief occupation by a follower of Cromwell lasting about 11 years. Henry II granted the lands of the last Viking ruler of Dublin to Robert Talbot, one of his Norman knights who had come over to Ireland with him in the 1170s.

There are some remains at ground and cellar levels, and the cylindrical tower on the eastern side is probably part of the first major rebuilding of the 16th century.

LOCATION: MALAHIDE, CO. DUBLIN
MAP REF: O 2446
OPEN: DUBLIN TOURISM IN CONJUNCTION WITH FINGAL COUNTY COUNCIL: DAILY

MALLOW

This great tower house was built at the end of the 16th century. The front of its long, now badly damaged, rectangular core of three storeys and attic floor (whose gables have gone), is flanked by two hexagonal towers at the ends of the north wall and a pentagonal entrance tower in the centre of that wall. On the south wall of the core, in the middle, is another pentagonal tower that contained staircases and garderobes. The castle was raised upon the remnants of a much earlier structure, probably dating from the 13th century.

LOCATION: CO. CORK
MAP REF: W 5698
OPEN: PRIVATE: RUINS IN HOTEL GROUNDS

MANORHAMILTON

This is a much-damaged stronghouse of the 1630s, which centred on a rectangular core 25 x 9.5m (82 x 32ft) with two projecting wings, one at each end of the longer core wall at the north. The wings and the southern longer core wall had spur-shaped towers. The history of the castle is extremely brief since it was destroyed in the aftermath of the Confederate War, barely 15 years after its construction by Sir Frederick Hamilton. There is a heritage centre in the grounds of the castle.

LOCATION: CO. LEITRIM
MAP REF: G 8839

MATRIX

A tall, 18.5m (60ft) high rectangular tower house, of seven storeys in the thick end wall and four storeys in the rest of the tower (as for the Scottish castle at Amisfield, see page 121); it was built in the mid-15th century and has been renovated. Originally a Desmond castle, Matrix was a home for Edmund Spenser, the poet, during the 1580s. The castle has undergone renovation and now houses a bed-and-breakfast establishment. It is open to the public between June and September.

LOCATION: CO. LIMERICK
MAP REF: R 3040

MAYNOOTH

Maynooth has a substantial great tower, one of the largest of its kind in Ireland, inside an enclosure that is roughly rectangular. Very close to the great tower's south-east corner is a large, three-storeyed gatehouse, and to the east of this is another rectangular tower, also three-storeyed. The great tower is an impressive ruin and rises over 21.5m (70ft).

There is evidence of at least three stages of building of the great tower, from the first work of c.1200 up to the 15th century. It was probably begun by the Offaly Fitzgeralds. In the 1530s it belonged to 'Silken Thomas', Lord Offaly, son of Gearoid Og, Earl of Kildare, Lord Deputy, but in Thomas' rising of 1534–5 the castle was taken by the new Lord Deputy, William Skeffington. It was returned to the Fitzgeralds in 1552, and was finally abandoned halfway through the 17th century. It was acquired by the state in 1991 and restoration began in 2000 and is ongoing. There is an exhibition on the history of the castle and the family, and there are guided tours of the keep.

LOCATION: CO. KILDARE
MAP REF: N 9337
OPEN: OFFICE OF PUBLIC WORKS: JUN–SEP DAILY MON–FRI, SAT–SUN PM

MINARD

A large tower house probably of the 15th century; Minard had four storeys, but is now ruinous. The ground floor has thick walls, between 2.5 and 3m (8 and 10ft). The first floor, equipped with chambers at one end, was reached presumably by step-ladder as there are no signs of staircasing. There are stairs up to the second floor above, which is vaulted. There was a top storey that is only a fragment now.

LOCATION: NR LISPOLE, CO. KERRY
MAP REF: V 5598

MONEA

Monea is an impressive ruin of an early 17th-century plantation castle, built by Malcolm Hamilton, who incorporated Scottish castle features (such as the rectangular gabled tops of the circular towers flanking the entrance). It was a rectangular enclosure of stone with round towers on the north corners (now fragmentary), and an undetermined rectangular building at foundation level in the south-west corner. The castle was badly damaged during the Confederate War, and was abandoned in the 18th century.

LOCATION: CO. FERMANAGH
MAP REF: H 1649
OPEN: ENVIRONMENT AND HERITAGE SERVICE, NORTHERN IRELAND: OPEN ACCESS

MONKSTOWN (CORK)

A 17th-century rectangular tower house, of five storeys with gabled roofing, Monkstown or Mahon Castle as it is also known, is an interesting structure. It has two large projecting towers in front of its central core, and two similar towers projecting at the rear. The front towers have a corner box machicolation at parapet level on the outer side. This castle must have been formidable. It has fallen into serious decay and is on the National Trust's 'Buildings at Risk' register.

LOCATION: CO. CORK
MAP REF: W 7666

MONKSTOWN (DUBLIN)

This is a late 15th-century rectangular tower of four storeys that was extended in later times. The main part of the tower has corner turrets that are now badly damaged.

LOCATION: CO. DUBLIN
MAP REF: O 2428

MOYGARA

A rectangular great tower, probably of the 13th century, was the first building here, and only fragments remain above ground. In the 16th century the tower was enclosed within a large square-plan enclosure, using the north wall of the old tower for part of its north side. At each corner of the enclosure is a square tower, well equipped with loops. The castle was built by the O'Gara family as their principal fortress and home, and has excellent views of the surrounding countryside from its farmland setting.

LOCATION: NR GURTEEN, CO. SLIGO
MAP REF: G 6903

MOYNE

This late 15th-century rectangular tower house, about 14 x 10m (46 x 33ft) with walls over 2m (7ft) thick, had an east end-wall that was more than 3m (10ft) thick for chambers and stairs. The square tower has a spiral stair that connects to a covered passage extending around the walls. The castle is located by the River Black and near an ancient oval church site that is enclosed by a cashel.

LOCATION: NR HEADFORD, CO. MAYO
MAP REF: M 2549

NARROW WATER

Sited at the northern edge of Carlingford Lough, this three-storey plus attic tower house of the mid-16th century is 11.5 x 10m (37.5 x 33ft) and has 2m (7ft) thick walling. It is protected by a quadrilateral enclosure, with a gateway on the north side and a corner turret on the lough edge.

NAAS

A motte castle (behind the post office) was raised here in the early years of the Anglo-Normans, and is mentioned by Giraldus Cambrensis c.1180. It is almost certainly the oldest man-made structure in the town. It is about 10.5m (35ft) tall, having been raised on rising ground, and is the highest point in Naas, with extensive views to the north and west. The motte is some 100m (328ft) at the base.

LOCATION: CO. KILDARE
MAP REF: N 8919

The tower house has most of its battlements, and has been restored inside and out. The tower house is on the Narrow Water Castle estate and was given to the state in 1960s.

LOCATION: WARREN POINT, CO. DOWN
MAP REF: J 1319
OPEN: ENVIRONMENT AND HERITAGE SERVICE NORTHERN IRELAND: OPEN ACCESS

NENAGH

Nenagh Castle has as its main feature one of the finest cylindrical great towers in Ireland, and also one of the oldest; it was founded by Theobald Walter, an ancestor of the Ormonde Butlers, in the early 13th century. It is unusual in that, although round, it is placed in the perimeter of the whole castle, with the castle curtains coming out of it on opposite sides as they continue on to form the roughly horseshoe-shaped enclosure.

The tower is unusual in Britain and Ireland in that it had a forebuilding, which has now disappeared. It was formed between the east part of the curtain and a small projection. Apart from the tower, there are few remains.

LOCATION: CO. TIPPERARY
MAP REF: R 8679
OPEN: OPEN ACCESS

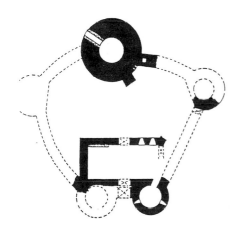

NEWCASTLE LYONS

This interesting settlement originally supported six castles. The only survivors are the following:

◆ A low-level motte on flat ground, about 7.5m (25ft) tall in a field next to the main street.

◆ A small, L-plan tower house on the side of the road about 0.5 km (0.25 mile) from the motte; it is two-storeyed now, but may have been higher. It is about 4m (13ft) square and has a projection which has loops.

LOCATION: NEWCASTLE, CO. DUBLIN
MAP REF: O 0234

NEWTOWN

Not far from Ballyvaughan Bay in the north of Co. Clare is the restored round tower house at Newtown. This belonged first to the O'Briens and then to the O'Loghlens, who for a time referred to themselves as Kings of the Burren.

The tower house was begun in the 15th century. It is a cylindrical tower standing on a four-spur base. Approach to the tower is covered by pairs of gun-loops all round at the first floor, and just above each spur is a loop with double gun-ports. The tower is over 15m (50ft) tall, has four storeys below the roof level, and measures about 9m (30ft) in diameter. The first three floors show various defensive features such as narrow slit windows, gun-loops and meurtrières. The restoration begun in the early 1990s was undertaken with much thought for the tower's history and the original building skills employed. The main floor presents a visual record of the castle's restoration and the second floor houses what is known as the Scriptorium.

LOCATION: BALLYVAUGHAN, CO. CLARE
MAP REF: M 2206
OPEN: EASTER–OCT DAILY

PALLAS

Pallas is an impressive and well preserved tower house of the 16th century. Inside is an equally well preserved bawn with a two-storey gatehouse and corner towers; the tower is five-storeyed, rectangular in plan, with one wall more than twice the thickness of the other three, to take in staircases, garderobes and chambers. The exterior has a number of narrow loops, but few windows. The castle is now a private hotel.

LOCATION: TYNAGH, NR PORTUMNA, CO. GALWAY
MAP REF: M 7608

This is a lovingly restored early 17th-century plantation castle, in the form of a tower house with extensions and of formidable appearance. Parke's started as a 16th-century rectangular tower house, with both east and west walls much thicker than the other two. Around it was a five-sided bawn with round flanking towers on two corners (north and north-east) of differing sizes. Part of the bawn, which seems to be of later date than the original tower house, skirts the edge of Lough Gill. There are traces of other buildings along the inside walls.

After the defeat of the Spanish Armada in 1588, the tower house was destroyed by the English, allegedly because its owner had given sanctuary to a Spanish sea captain, Francisco de Cuellar, who described his stay. Stone from the tower was used in the 1620s by Robert Parke to build a plantation castle inside the bawn, using the east bawn wall as one of the sides and rebuilding the round flanking tower as part of his new tower house. The remains of the old tower were levelled, and the whole area was covered over with a cobbled yard. Today there are guided tours and exhibitions.

LOCATION: FIVEMILE BOURNE, LOUGH GILL, CO. LEITRIM
MAP REF: G 7835
OPEN: OFFICE OF PUBLIC WORKS: APR–OCT DAILY

PORTAFERRY

This early 16th-century L-plan tower house of three storeys, with the shorter arm being a staircase wing on the south side, was raised to command the narrow passage between Strangford Lough and the sea. The wing carries the stair to the first floor. Access to the higher levels is by stairways in the wall thickness of the tower's west wall.

LOCATION: PORTAFERRY, CO. DOWN
MAP REF: J 5950

PORTUMNA

This is a substantial stronghouse-type mansion of c.1610–18 built by Richard Burke (de Burgos), 4th Earl of Clanricarde, Lord President of Connacht, who is believed not to have seen his palace completed. Above the door there is box machicolation at parapet level. The four corner towers clamped on to the central rectangular core represented a formidable all-round defence by means of battlements and more gun-ports. Most rooms were of massive proportions, and some surviving fireplaces are huge. The castle was gutted by fire in the 1820s.

The fortress-residence stands in its own bawn with strong round turrets at the east and west ends of the northern wall, with gun-ports along the east and west bawn walls. Restoration began in the 1970s and conservation is ongoing. The grounds, too, have been subject to extensive renovation, including restoration of the 17th-century walled kitchen garden.

LOCATION: PORTUMNA, CO. GALWAY
MAP REF: M 8502
OPEN: OFFICE OF PUBLIC WORKS: APR–OCT DAILY

QUIN

An enclosure castle of stone and symmetrical plan built by the de Clares in 1278–80. It was destroyed by the MacNamara family before the 14th century. In the 15th century, descendants of the family used the ruins as a framework for a Franciscan friary. Open occasionally in summer; the caretaker has a key.

LOCATION: CO. CLARE
MAP REF: R 4274

QUOILE

Part of this 16th-century tower house has been repaired and is incorporated into the Quoile Countryside Centre beside the Downpatrick-to-Belfast road. The lowest storey has a cross-wall dividing it into two vaulted rooms that are equipped with several gun-ports.

LOCATION: NR DOWNPATRICK, CO. DOWN
MAP REF: J 4947

RAPHOE

A 17th-century rectangular three-storeyed stronghouse, reinforced with four-storeyed corner towers. All the walls have large window openings, many from the 18th century. Raphoe Palace, as it is also known, was built in the 1630s by Bishop Leslie. It was besieged in 1641 in the Confederate War and captured by Cromwellian forces in 1650. The structure is today considered dangerous.

LOCATION: CO. DONEGAL
MAP REF: C 2603

RATHFARNHAM

This building is in good condition, due largely to renovations carried out in the 18th century by the then owners, the Loftus family; it is now a national monument. Rathfarnham began as a substantial rectangular stronghouse built in the 1580s for Adam Loftus, Archbishop of Armagh intended as a comfortable, defensive residence. It had four corner towers affixed to a central core, whose outer angles are pointed, like those at Raphoe. The 18th-century interiors are by Sir William Chambers and James Athenian Stuart.

LOCATION: DUBLIN 14, CO. DUBLIN
MAP REF: O 1529
OPEN: OFFICE OF PUBLIC WORKS: MAY–OCT DAILY

RATHMACKNEE

Rathmacknee is a smallish, five-storey, nearly square tower house, about 13m (42ft) tall, whose walls have very little illumination. It stands in the corner of an irregular pentagonal enclosure of thick walling, which is 5.5m (18ft) tall. It was built in the late 15th century and early 16th centuries, possibly by John Rossiter, and is in good condition today. It has a rounded box machicolation on one corner of the bawn.

Now a national monument, Rathmacknee is a good example of a 15th-century tower house with connecting bawn.

LOCATION: NR MURNTOWN, CO. WEXFORD
MAP REF: T 0414

RINNDOUN

The original castle located here, on a small peninsula on the west side of Lough Ree, was built in about 1227 by the Justiciar Geoffrey de Marisco. It was besieged by the Irish soon afterwards, and then rebuilt in the 1270s. The great tower still has its north wall up to about 10.5m (35ft) high, but not much else remains.

LOCATION: CO. ROSCOMMON
MAP REF: N 0054

ROCKFLEET

This small, 16th-century tower house stands on the shore by Clew Bay. It belonged for a time to Grace O'Malley during the reign of Elizabeth I.

LOCATION: NR. NEWPORT, CO. MAYO
MAP REF: L 9395

ROODSTOWN

Roodstown is a rectangular tower house built in the 15th century and in good external condition, with two polygonal turrets at the top on the summit of two diagonally opposite projecting square turrets emerging from the tower, in the form of a prolongation of the wall. It is four-storeyed, five if you take the turrets as an extra level, but no battlements remain. Round the top is a crude form of machicolation that may be little more than a series of holes to drain off the water from the gabled roofing. One of the turrets has a staircase all the way to the top, the other has chambers, two of which were garderobes.

There are good views over the surrounding flat countryside from north to east, and towards hills to the south.

LOCATION: ARDEE, CO. LOUTH
MAP REF: N 9993

ROSCOMMON

This is one of a number of castles in Ireland raised in the second half of the 13th century, more or less according to the same basic plan. This is a rectangular or square enclosure of strong, high walls clasped at the corners by massive towers, taller than the walls, with a powerful gatehouse located in the curtain wall on one side of the enclosure.

Roscommon was begun by Robert de Ufford, Lord Justice of Ireland, but the building was destroyed soon after. A new castle, similar to Harlech, but built before it, was raised c.1280. Ownership changed often.

LOCATION: CO. ROSCOMMON
MAP REF: M 8764
OPEN: MANAGED BY ROSCOMMON TRUST: DAILY

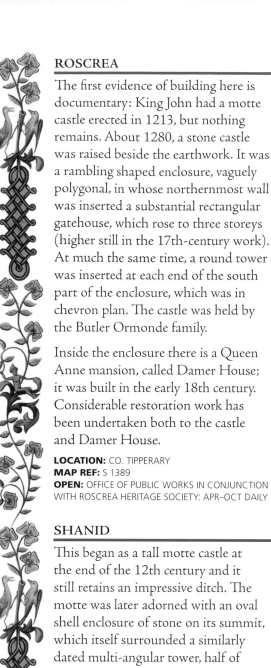

ROSCREA

The first evidence of building here is documentary: King John had a motte castle erected in 1213, but nothing remains. About 1280, a stone castle was raised beside the earthwork. It was a rambling shaped enclosure, vaguely polygonal, in whose northernmost wall was inserted a substantial rectangular gatehouse, which rose to three storeys (higher still in the 17th-century work). At much the same time, a round tower was inserted at each end of the south part of the enclosure, which was in chevron plan. The castle was held by the Butler Ormonde family.

Inside the enclosure there is a Queen Anne mansion, called Damer House; it was built in the early 18th century. Considerable restoration work has been undertaken both to the castle and Damer House.

LOCATION: CO. TIPPERARY
MAP REF: S 1389
OPEN: OFFICE OF PUBLIC WORKS IN CONJUNCTION WITH ROSCREA HERITAGE SOCIETY: APR–OCT DAILY

SHANID

This began as a tall motte castle at the end of the 12th century and it still retains an impressive ditch. The motte was later adorned with an oval shell enclosure of stone on its summit, which itself surrounded a similarly dated multi-angular tower, half of which has disappeared. Below the tower and its motte, the bailey is oval in shape and has its own ditch.

LOCATION: NR SHANAGOLDEN, CO. LIMERICK
MAP REF: R 2445

SHRULE

Located on the Black River, Shrule is a 16th-century tower house consisting of four storeys, with polygonal-plan corner machicolations at the top. The tower's four walls splay outwards sharply from the top of the first storey downwards. Inside there are interesting carved stone mantelpieces and an intact spiral staircase. The castle is adjacent to a modern farmhouse.

LOCATION: SHRULE, CO. MAYO
MAP REF: M 2753

SLADE

This is a 15th-century L-plan tower house, built by the Laffan family. It was constructed in different phases but retains most of its early battlementing. The tower still stands to 17m (56ft). The entrance to the first tower is protected by a machicolation box at the top level. A national monument administered by the Office of Public Works, there is open access here.

LOCATION: NR CHURCHTOWN, CO. WEXFORD
MAP REF: X 7597

STRANGFORD

Built in the late 16th century, this tower house, only about 7.5m (25ft) square, guarded the entrance to Strangford Lough. It is three-storeyed and has some of its battlements. There are no signs of staircasing, and access will have been by ladder, as was the case of a number of Border castles. The original door was most likely at first-floor level.

LOCATION: CO. DOWN
MAP REF: J 5950

SWORDS

Swords Castle was a bishop's castle and was started in about 1200. The five-sided enclosure of stone remains standing and is in reasonably good condition. On the north side is a three-storey rectangular tower house. Inside the enclosure, not quite central, is a large earth mound motte, erected in the early 13th century.

LOCATION: SWORDS, CO. DUBLIN
MAP REF: O 1847
OPEN: OFFICE OF PUBLIC WORKS: OPEN ACCESS

TERRYGLASS

A number of castles based on this plan were built in Ireland in the 13th century, although each was quite individual in many of its features. Here, a rectangular great tower with four cylindrical towers on the corners was built near Lough Derg. At present the building is only two storeys high. Its corner towers, of different diameters, are lower than the core now.

LOCATION: CO. TIPPERARY
MAP REF: M 8600

TIMAHOE

Just outside the present village is a motte of c.1182, listed by Giraldus Cambrensis. In the village, close to a tall (29m/95ft) monastic round tower of uncertain period is a one-time 15th-century chapel of stone on to which was grafted a stone tower house. This process destroyed most of the chapel.

LOCATION: CO. LAOIS
MAP REF: S 5390

THOOR BALLYLEE

This is a 16th-century four-storey tower house overlooking the Cloon River at Ballylee, near Gort, built for the de Burgo family. Each floor contained one room, reached by a stone spiral staircase built into the thick outer wall. The stairs lead to the flat roof and battlements. The castle was purchased in 1916 and converted into a home for the poet, WB Yeats. He spent his summers in the castle for 12 years and wrote most of his important work here. After he left in 1929 it fell into disrepair, but it has been restored as a national monument to Yeats. The interpretative centre contains a collection of first editions of his work, items of furniture and an audiovisual exhibition devoted to the poet.

LOCATION: BALLYLEE, NR. GORT, CO. GALWAY
MAP REF: M 4403
OPEN: WB YEATS MUSEUM. MAY–SEP DAILY

TRIM

LOCATION: CASTLE STREET, TRIM, CO. MEATH
MAP REF: N 8056
OPEN: OFFICE OF PUBLIC WORKS: MON–SAT, SUN PM
SEE PAGE 250

TULLY

A plantation castle of about 1610, beside Lower Lough Erne, Tully is a T-plan tower house inside a roughly square enclosure. On the south side is an entrance turret with splayed gun-ports on three sides. The enclosure had rectangular and square turrets on the four corners, and remains can still be seen. The castle was attacked by the Maguires in 1641 in the Confederate War and burned down, and it was apparently never occupied again. The castle is administered by the Office of Public Works and is open in July and August.

LOCATION: LOUGH ERNE, CO. FERMANAGH
MAP REF: H 1357

WATERFORD

This important town on the Suir river was, in Norman times, surrounded by a fortification of walls and tall towers. The walls were linked to earlier Viking walls, built by the Viking ruler Reginald in about 1000. The existing Reginald's Tower is Anglo-Norman and was probably erected on the site of an earlier Viking structure. It is still about 15m (50ft) tall and 13m (43ft) in diameter. The four-storey circular tower has few windows, and an unbattlemented parapet; it would have presented a formidable defence for the town.

In its life the tower has been a mint, a prison, and it now houses a museum.

LOCATION: THE QUAY, WATERFORD, CO. WATERFORD
MAP REF: S 6012
OPEN: DAILY

WICKLOW

A castle with stonework was noted by Giraldus Cambrensis at Wicklow as early as 1173. Better known as the Black Castle, this picturesque ruin stands on a rocky headland overlooking the sea at the eastern end of the town. The castle was originally started by Maurice Fitzgerald at the end of the 12th century on land given to him by Strongbow. For centuries the castle was exposed to the frequent raids of the O'Tooles and the O'Byrnes until their conquest by Lord Deputy Mountjoy in 1601. The castle fell into decay after the Cromwellian wars, and is ruinous. The exposed site of the Black Castle has caused damage to the mortar of the remaining sea-facing walls.

LOCATION: WICKLOW HEAD, WICKLOW, CO. WICKLOW
MAP REF: T 3194

URLANMORE

There is a small three-storey tower at one end of this building and an adjoining extension, with remains of a fine large first-storey hall. On the walls of a small upper room in the tower there are paintings of animals. The castle has been partly destroyed.

LOCATION: NEWMARKET ON FERGUS, CO. CLARE
MAP REF: R 3766

Trim

Trim is among the greatest of the Norman castles in Ireland. Built by Hugh de Lacy in 1173 beside the River Boyne, it occupies just over 1ha (3 acres) and has hardly been altered since the 13th century. The site is dominated by a massive stone keep 23m (76ft) tall. The core walls are 3.5m (11ft) or more thick, although the turrets are about half this. The turret on the north wall is missing today although fragments remain of where it was keyed into the core. It is believed the tower was erected in two stages, the first, from c.1200–10, which took it up to two full storeys, and the second, c.1220s. There are signs of the first roof, and the windows of the first stage are rounded, whilst those of the later stage are squared. The lower half had its entrance at first-floor level, using a staircase in the east turret that acted as a forebuilding with a chapel over the entrance into the core. The first floor of the early work was divided in two by a cross-wall, providing a great hall and a lord's bedroom or chamber. When the core was heightened, the extra storey contained a variety of rooms.

When Trim was excavated in the 1970s, remnants of additional buildings were uncovered. A ditch around the keep yielded finds from the 13th century, including pottery and arrowheads. Work to prepare for visitor facilities in the 1990s has exposed the remains of medieval buildings.

The castle was neglected in the second half of the 14th century until, in 1399, Richard II of England, on his famous visit to Ireland, arranged for two of his Crown wards to live there. They were Henry of Monmouth (later Henry V) and his brother, both sons of Henry Bolingbroke. Little is known of the great structure in the 15th and 16th centuries. It was finally yielded to the Cromwellians in 1650. Scenes from the 1995 epic film *Braveheart* were shot here.

HUGH DE LACY

Trim Castle was built by Hugh de Lacy, descendant of Walter de Lacy who was one of the Norman invaders with William the Conqueror. Hugh was trusted by Henry II and was appointed Viceroy of Ireland. He married the daughter of Rory O'Conor, the last native King of Ireland, and he built many other castles in his extensive territories.

GLOSSARY

adulterine unlicensed castle

apse circular or polygonal end of a tower or chapel

arcading rows of arches supported on columns

arrow-loop or slit long, narrow (usually vertical) opening in wall or battlements. Round or triangular ends were for cross-bows, as were horizontal cross-slits which gave greater range

ashlar blocks of smooth, squared stone of any kind

bailey or ward courtyard within the castle walls

barbican outward defensive continuation of a gateway or entrance

barmkin, bawn yard surrounded by outer defensive walling

barrel vault semicircular roof (stone or timber)

bartizan small turret projecting from the corner or flank of a tower or wall, usually at the top

bastion tower or turret projecting from a wall or at the junction of two walls

battlements or crenellation the parapet of a tower or wall with indentations or openings (**embrasures** or **crenelles**) alternating with solid projections (**merlons**)

belfry tall moveable tower on wheels used in sieges

buttress projecting pillar added to strengthen a wall

corbel stone bracket projecting from a wall or corner

cross-wall internal dividing wall in a great tower

curtain general word for walling enclosing a courtyard. Sited between towers, or tower and gatehouse, and appearing to hang between them

donjon alternative name for a great tower

drawbridge wooden bridge (which could be raised and lowered) across a ditch or moat

dressing carved or smooth stonework around openings and along edges

forebuilding structure on the outside wall of a great tower protecting the entrance and all or part of the approaching stairs. Some forebuildings contained chambers and chapels over the stairs

gallery long narrow passage or room

garderobe latrine

gatehouse room over the castle entrance

great tower or keep the main tower of a castle

gun-loop or gun-port opening in a wall for a gun

hoarding defensive covered wooden gallery placed above a tower or curtain. Floor was slatted to allow defenders to drop missiles or liquids onto besiegers

jamb straight side of a doorway, archway or window

light window pane or window division

lintel horizontal beam of wood or stone positioned across the top of an opening

machiolation projecting part of a stone or brick parapet with holes in the floor, as in hoarding

mangonel stone-throwing machine

meurtrière or murder hole opening in the roof or a gateway or part of gatehouse over an entrance. Popularly believed to be used in the same way as hoardings, but might have enabled defenders to channel water to wooden areas set on fire by attackers

motte a mound on which a castle was built (man-made or natural)

oriel window projecting curved or polygonal window

oubliette dungeon or pit reached by trap-door used for holding prisoners (in Scotland a pit prison)

palisade a defensive fence

pele tower small tower house

pilaster buttress buttress with a projection, positioned in corner or mid-wall

pipe rolls accounts prepared annually by sheriffs for the king

plantation castle castles built in Ireland on land given to those who would support the Crown

portcullis wood and iron grille-pattern gate, raised and lowered in grooves at an entrance

postern small gateway, usually at the side or rear of a castle

quatrefoil four-lobed, six-foil six-lobed; trefoil three-lobed

quoin dressed corner stone at an angle of a building

relieving arch arch built in a wall to relieve the thrust on another opening

revet face with a layer of stone for more strength. Some earth mottes were revetted with stone

rib vaulting arched roof with ribs of raised moulding at the groins (junction of two curved surfaces)

rubble uncut or only roughly shaped stone, for walling

scarp inner wall or slope of a ditch or moat (counterscarp: outer wall or slope)

slight to damage or destroy a castle to render it unfit for use

solar lord's parlour or private quarters

stepped recessed in a series of ledges

stronghouse a mansion capable of being defended

turret small tower

wall-walk path along the top of a wall protected by a parapet

wing wall wall descending the slope of a motte

yett iron gates protecting an entrance

USEFUL ADDRESSES

ENGLAND
English Heritage
Customer Services,
PO Box 569, Swindon SN2 2YP

Customer services
tel 0870 333 1181
Membership enquiries
tel 0870 333 1182

www.english-heritage.org.uk/
Details of the regional offices are given on the website

The National Trust
36 Queen Anne's Gate,
London SW1H 9AS

tel 0870 609 5380

www.nationaltrust.org.uk
Details of the regional offices are given on the website

SCOTLAND
Historic Scotland
Longmore House, Salisbury Place,
Edinburgh EH9 1SH

tel 0131 668 8600
www.historic-scotland.gov.uk

The National Trust Office for Scotland
Wemyss House, 28 Charlotte Square,
Edinburgh EH2 4ET

tel 0131 243 9300

www.nts.org.uk/

WALES
The National Trust Office for Wales
Trinity Square, Llandudno LL30 2DE

tel 01492 860123

Cadw
Plas Carew, Unit 5/7 Cefn Coed,
Parc Nantgarw, Cardiff CF15 7QQ

tel 01443 336000

www.cadw.wales.gov.uk/

IRELAND
The National Trust Office for Northern Ireland
Rowallane House, Saintfield
Ballynahinch, Co. Down BT24 7LH

tel 028 9751 0721

Environment and Heritage Service Northern Ireland
Historic Monuments Enquiries,
Waterman House, 5-33 Hill Street,
Belfast, Co. Antrim BT1 2LA

tel 028 9054 3037

www.ehsni.gov.uk

Office of Public Works (Ireland)
51 St. Stephen's Green,
Dublin 2, Ireland

tel 00-353-1-6476000
LoCall 00353 1890 213414

www.opw.ie

ACKNOWLEDGEMENTS
The publishers would like to thank the following people for their involment in the making of this book. David Lyons for his numerous pictures, Bea Ray for her picture research, Neil Bromley for his illustrations (www.calligraphyandheraldry.com), Amberley Castle (www.amberleycastle.co.uk) and Alnwick Gardens (www.alnwickgarden.com) for the use of their images and June Wilkins for the index. Also, a special thank you to Pip Leahy and Hilary Weston for their research, and Marilynne Lanng for her editorial work.

PICTURE CREDITS

Front cover: Bodiam Castle, Corbis. Back cover: The Long Walk, Windsor Castle, Corbis.

All photographs by David Lyons except: 11tl Art Archive/Musee de la Tapisserie Bayeux, 12t Corbis, 13tr Bridgeman Art Library, 16t Alamy, 17t Heritage Image Partnership/British Library, 19t Skyscan/FlightImages, 19b Alamy/Arcaid, 23 British Library, 25inset Corbis/Historical Picture Archive, 27 British Library, 28 Corbis, 33l Corbis, 33r Bridgeman Art Library/Cecil Higgins Art Gallery/Myles Birkett Foster, 34 Getty, 36 Amberley Castle, 38 British Library, 39 inset Corbis, 41 Art Archive/Musee de la Tapisserie Bayeux, 42-43 Alamy/National Trust, 43 Corbis, 45 Getty, 48 Heritage Image Partnership/British Library, 49t Art Archive/Musee de la Tapisserie Bayeux, 49b British Library, 53t Britain on View, 53b Corbis, 54-55 Corbis, 55 Art Archive/Musee du Chateau de Versailles, 60 Alamy/Les Polders, 62 inset British Library, 63 inset Bridgeman Art Library/Museum of Fine Arts Boston/JMW Turner, 68 inset Mary Evans Picture Library, 69 inset Corbis, 75, 76 & 77 English Heritage, 78 Art Archive/Burnley Art Gallery/Ernest Croft, 79t Art Archive/Private Collection/Jan Wyck, 79b Art Archive, 80 English Heritage, 85 Alamy, 86 inset Corbis, 87 inset Alamy, 92 inset Skyscan, 93 Britain on View, 96 inset Corbis, 97 inset Mary Evans Picture Library, 97b Alnwick Gardens, 98 inset Skyscan, 99 inset Bridgeman Art Library, 106t British Library, 106b Bridgeman Art library/Bibliotheque Nationale de Paris, 111t Alamy, 112b Scottish Viewpoint, 128t British Library, 128b British Library, 129 Bridgeman Art Library/Hermitage St Petersburg, 140 British Library, 141 inset Corbis, 144 Bridgeman Art Library/Private Collection, 146 & 147 British Library, 158 Art Archive, 159 Heritage Image Partnership, 167 inset Bridgeman Art Library/National Gallery of Scotland, 174 Picture Library of Wales, 175 The Heritage Trail, 176 inset Britain on View, 177 inset Corbis, 178 Art Archive, 180 inset Corbis, 181 inset British Library, 183t Alamy, 188t Corbis, 188 Royal Collection, 189 Art Archive/Private Collection, 202t Mary Evans picture Library, 202b Heritage Image Partnership/British Library, 203 British Library, 217b Corbis, 217tr Mary Evans Picture Library, 220 inset Lonely Planet Images, 221 inset British Library, 226t Corbis, 226b Heritage Image Partnership/British Library, 227 Corbis, 229b Lonely Planet Images, 232b Heritage Image Partnership/British Library, 235b Bridgeman Art Library, 236c Lonely Planet Images, 238 t&b British Library, 239 Heritage Image Partnership.

INDEX

Castles are listed alphabetically by region in the Gazeteer.

Page references with suffix 'i' refer to illustrations.